VOICES
OF THE
AMERICAN
PAST

VOICES OF THE AMERICAN PAST

Readings in American History

Edited by **MORTON BORDEN**
University of California
Santa Barbara

D. C. HEATH AND COMPANY
Lexington, Massachusetts Toronto London

PREFACE

Survey courses in American history present extraordinary challenges to both teacher and student: How to cover a vast terrain in a short time period? How to reveal the significance of the past without producing confusion? How to excite interest in further reading and investigation instead of squeezing dry the joy of history? I have long felt that original documents are the best supplement to lectures and text in teaching introductory classes. There are many voices speaking in the 150 selections contained in this volume, taken from letters and diaries, newspapers, books and speeches, laws, court records, poems, advertisements, and other sources. Any collection, of course, is incomplete and inadequate. This one is meant as a historical sampler, to awake, to provoke, to stimulate, to enlighten.

My mother, Mrs. Fanny Borden, has always viewed the United States as a country of unparalleled ambiguities and contradictions, but her memories of the European past serve to confirm her optimism in the American future. To her, with deep gratitude, I dedicate this book.

Published simultaneously in Canada.

Printed in the United States of America.

International Standard Book Number: 0-669-60087-3

Library of Congress Catalog Card Number: 70-163565

CONTENTS

1. Colonial Foundations

2. Empire and Revolution

3. Problems of a New Nation

4. Jacksonian Enterprise

5. Freedom and Slavery

8. Prosperity and Disillusionment

9. The Era of Franklin D. Roosevelt

10. America Searches for Peace

1
Colonial Foundations

A letter of Christopher Columbus reporting on his first voyage, February 15, 1493

"Let us rejoice," Christopher Columbus proclaimed after his initial voyage, "as well on account of the exaltation of our faith, as on account of the increase of our temporal prosperity." The words were really a boast to mask his failure. Instead of treasure and spices Columbus had found only frightened Indians and lush vegetation. The excitement Columbus conveys in the following letter is real; but his exaggeration of the vast wealth is meant primarily to impress the rulers of Spain.

Sir—Believing that you will take pleasure in hearing of the great success which our Lord has granted me in my voyage, I write you this letter, whereby you will learn how in thirty-three days time I reached the Indies with the fleet which the most illustrious King and Queen, our Sovereigns, gave to me, where I found very many islands thickly peopled, of all which I took possession without resistance, for their Highnesses by proclamation made and with the royal standard unfurled. To the first island that I found I gave the name of *San Salvador*, in remembrance of His High Majesty, who hath marvellously brought all these things to pass; the Indians call it *Guanaham.* To the second island I gave the name of *Santa Maria de Concepción;* the third I called *Fernandina;* the fourth, *Isabella;* the fifth, *Juana* [Cuba]; and so to each one I gave a new name. When I reached *Juana,* I followed its coast to the westward, and found it so large that I thought it must be the mainland—the province of Cathay; and, as I found neither towns nor villages on the sea-coast, but only a few hamlets, with the inhabitants of which I could not hold conversation, because they all immediately fled, I kept on the same route, thinking that I could not fail to light upon some large cities and towns. At length . . . I saw another island to the eastward at a distance of eighteen leagues from the former, to which I gave the name of *La Española* [Hispaniola or San Domingo]. Thither I went and followed its northern coast. . . .

Española is a wonder. Its mountains and plains, and meadows and fields, are beautiful and rich for planting and sowing, and rearing cattle of all kinds, and for building towns and villages. The harbors on the coast, and the number and size and wholesomeness of the rivers, most of them bearing gold, surpass anything that would be believed by one who had not seen them. . . . In this island there are many spices and extensive mines of gold and other metals. The inhabitants of this and of all the other islands I have found or gained intelligence of, both men and women, go as naked as they were born, with the exception that some of the women cover one part only with a single leaf of grass or with a piece of cotton, made for that purpose. They have neither iron, nor steel, nor arms, nor are they competent

From R. H. Major, *Select Letters of Christopher Columbus* (London, 1870), pp. 1–17.

to use them, not that they are not well-informed and of handsome stature, but because they are timid to a surprising degree. Their only arms are reeds ... to which they fashion small sharpened sticks, and even these they dare not use; for on several occasions it has happened that I have sent ashore two or three men to some village to hold a parley, and the people have come out in countless numbers, but, as soon as they saw our men approach, would flee with such precipitation that a father would not even stop to protect his son; and this not because any harm had been done to any of them, for, from the first, wherever I went and got speech with them, I gave them of all that I had, such as cloth and many other things, without receiving anything in return, but they are, as I have described, incurably timid. It is true that when they are reassured and have thrown off their fear, they are guileless, and so liberal of all they have that no one would believe it who had not seen it. They never refuse anything that they possess when it is asked of them; on the contrary, they offer it themselves, and they exhibit so much loving kindness that they would even give their hearts; and, whether it be something of value or of little worth that is offered to them, they are satisfied. ... I gave away a thousand good and pretty articles which I had brought with me in order to win their affection; and that they might be led to become Christians, and be well inclined to love and serve their Highnesses and the whole Spanish nation, and that they might aid us by giving us things of which we stand in need, but which they possess in abundance.

They are not acquainted with any kind of worship, and are not idolators; but believe that all power and, indeed, all good things are in heaven, and with this belief received me at every place at which I touched, after they had overcome their apprehension. And this does not spring from ignorance, for they are very intelligent, and navigate all these seas, and relate everything to us, so that it is astonishing what a good account they are able to give of everything; but they have never seen men with clothes on, nor vessels like ours. On my reaching the Indies, I took by force, in the first island that I discovered, some of these natives, that they might learn our language and give me information in regard to what existed in these parts; and it so happened that they soon understood us and we them, either by words or signs, and they have been very serviceable to us. They are still with me, and, from repeated conversations that I have had with them, I find that they still believe that I come from heaven. And they were the first to say this wherever I went, and the others ran from house to house and to the neighboring villages, crying with a loud voice: "Come, come, and see the people from heaven!" And thus they all, men as well as women, after their minds were at rest about us, came, both large and small, and brought us something to eat and drink, which they gave us with extraordinary kindness. ...

Although I have taken possession of all these islands in the name of their Highnesses, and they are all more abundant in wealth than I am able to express; and although I hold them all for their Highnesses, so that they can dispose of them quite as absolutely as they can of the kingdoms of Castile, yet there was one large town in *Española* of which especially I took possession, situated in a locality well adapted for the working of the gold mines, and for all kinds of commerce, either with the main land on this side, or with that beyond which is the land of the great Khan, with which there will be vast commerce and great profit. To that city I gave the name of *Villa de Navidad,* and fortified it with a fortress, which by this time will be quite completed, and I have left in it a sufficient number of men with arms, artillery, and provisions for more than a year, a barge, and a sailing master skilful in the arts necessary for building others. . . .

Finally, and speaking only of what has taken place in this voyage, which has been so hasty, their Highnesses may see that I shall give them all the gold they require, if they will give me but a very little assistance; spices also, and cotton, as much as their Highnesses shall command to be shipped; and mastic, hitherto found only in Greece. . . . I think also I have found rhubarb and cinnamon, and I shall find a thousand other valuable things by means of the men that I have left behind me. . . . Much more I would have done if my vessels had been in as good a condition as by rights they ought to have been. . . .

Our Redeemer hath granted this victory to our illustrious King and Queen and their kingdoms, which have acquired great fame by an event of such high importance, in which all Christendom ought to rejoice, and which it ought to celebrate with great festivals and the offering of solemn thanks to the Holy Trinity with many solemn prayers, both for the great exaltation which may accrue to them in turning so many nations to our holy faith, and also for the temporal benefits which will bring great refreshment and gain, not only to Spain, but to all Christians. This, thus briefly, in accordance with the events.

Done on board the caravel, off the Canary Islands, on the fifteenth of February, fourteen hundred and ninety-three.

THE ADMIRAL

Sir Humphrey Gilbert on the advantages of a northwest passage to the Orient, 1548

English explorers expected to locate a water route through the North American continent to the Pacific, and thus to the Orient. As early as 1548 Sir Humphrey Gilbert spoke of its assured existence and of its economic benefits to England. Despite repeated failures and mounting geographic evidence to the contrary, the belief long persisted and the fruitless search continued.

First, it is the only way for our princes to possess the wealth of all the East parts (as they term them) of the world, which is infinite—as appears by the experience of Alexander the great, in the time of his conquest of India and other Eastern parts of the world—which would be a great advancement to our country, a wonderful enriching to our prince, and an unspeakable commodity to all the inhabitants of Europe.

For through the shortness of the voyage, we should be able to sell all manner of merchandise, brought from thence, far better and cheaper than either the Portuguese or Spaniard doth or may do. And further, we should share with the Portuguese in the East, and the Spaniard in the West, by trading to any part of America where they can no manner of way offend us.

Also we might sail to diverse very rich countries, both civil and others, out of both their jurisdictions, trade and traffic, where there is to be found great abundance of gold, silver, precious stones, cloth of gold, silks, all manner of spices, grocery wares, and other kinds of merchandise of an inestimable price, which both the Spaniard and Portuguese, through the length of their journeys, cannot well attain unto.

Also we might inhabit some part of those countries, and settle there such needy people of our country, which now trouble the commonwealth, and through want here at home are enforced to commit outrageous offenses, whereby they are daily consumed with the gallows.

Moreover, we might from all the aforesaid places have a yearly return, inhabiting for our staple some convenient place of America, about Sierra Nevada, or some other part, wherever it shall seem best for the shortening of the voyage. . . .

Also, we shall increase both our ships and mariners, without burdening of the state.

And also have occasion to set poor men's children to learn handicrafts, and thereby to make trifles and such like, which the Indians and those people do much esteem; by reason whereof, there should be no occasion to

From "A discourse written by Sir Humphrey Gilbert, Knight, to prove a passage by the Northwest to Cathay and the East Indies," in Richard Hakluyt, *The Principal Navigations, Voyages, Traffics and Discoveries of the English Nation* (London and New York, n.d.), Vol. V, Everyman's Library edition, pp. 115–17.

6

have our country encumbered with loiterers, vagabonds, and such like idle persons.

All these commodities would grow by following this our discovery, without injury done to any Christian prince, by crossing them in any of their used trades, whereby they might take any just occasion of offense.

Thus have I briefly showed you some part of the grounds of my opinion, trusting that you will no longer judge me fantastic in this matter; seeing I have conceived no vain hope of this voyage, but am persuaded thereunto by the best Cosmographers of our age, the same being confirmed both by reason and certain experiences.

Starving time in Virginia, 1609–10

Indian attacks, malaria, and their own incompetence, reduced the first colonists in Jamestown to a condition of starvation. So desperate were the settlers that one man, as the following account reveals, killed and ate his wife.

As for corn, provision and contribution from the savages, we had nothing but mortal wounds, with clubs and arrows. As for our hogs, hens, goats, sheep, horse, or what lived, our commanders, officers and savages daily consumed them. Some small proportions sometimes we wasted, till all was devoured. Then swords, arms, pieces, or anything, we traded with the savages, whose cruel fingers were so often embrewed in our blood, that what by their cruelty, our governors indiscretion, and the loss of our ships, of five hundred [settlers] . . . there remained not past sixty men, women and children, most miserable and poor creatures. And those were preserved for the most part, by roots, herbs, acorns, walnuts, berries, now and then a little fish. They that had starch in these extremities made no small use of it; yea, even the very skins of our horses.

Nay, so great was our famine, that a savage we slew and buried, the poorer sort took him up again and ate him; and so did diverse one another boiled and stewed with roots and herbs. And one amongst the rest did kill his wife, powdered [salted] her, and had eaten part of her before it was known; for which he was executed, as he well deserved. Now whether she was better roasted, boiled or carbonadoed [grilled], I know not; but of such a dish as powdered wife I never heard of.

This was that time, which still to this day we called the starving time. It were too vile to say, and scarce to be believed, what we endured. But the occasion was our own, for want of providence, industry and government,

From William Simmons, "The Proceedings and Accidents of the English *Colony* in *Virginia*," in Edward Arber (ed.), *Captain John Smith, . . . Works* (Birmingham, England, 1884), pp. 498–99.

and not the barrenness and defect of the country, as is generally supposed. . . . We had never from England provisions for six months, though it seemed by the bills of lading sufficient was sent us. Such a glutton is the sea, and such good fellows the mariners, we as little tasted of the great proportion sent us, as they of our want and miseries.

Excerpts from a poem on the lottery of the Virginia Company, 1612

When private investments failed to generate enough capital to support the fledgling colony at Jamestown, the Virginia Company turned to lotteries as a source of additional revenue. Members of Parliament complained, however, that the lotteries "do beggar" the mother-land, and they were discontinued by King James I.

LONDON'S LOTTERY

> *With an encouragement to the furtherance thereof, for the good of Virginia and the benefit of this our native country; wishing good fortune to all that venture in the same.*

> *To the tune of Lusty Gallant*

The merchants of Virginia now
    hath nobly took in hand,
The bravest golden lottery
    that ere was in this land.

Well may this famous lottery
    have good success and speed,
When as the states of England thus
    do such good liking breed.
Come gallants, come; come noble minds
    come venture now for gold,
For smiling hope here bids you all
    take courage and be bold.

Here prizes are of great account
    not simple, plain and poor;
But unto thousands do surmount
    whereof there be some store.

From Robert C. Johnson, "Lotteries of the Virginia Company, 1612–1621," *Virginia Magazine of History and Biography* (July 1966), Vol. 74, No. 3, pp. 259–92. Reprinted by permission.

And happily some men there be
    in gaining of the same,
May spend their days like Gentlemen
    in credit and good name.

Full many a man that lives full bare
    and knows no joys of gold,
For one small crown may get a share
    of twice two thousand fold.
Then what is he that fears to try
    his fortune in this kind,
When luck and chance may make a man
    and thus great riches find.

You maids that have but portions small
    to gain your marriage friend,
Cast in your lots with willing hand
    God may good fortune send.
You widows, and you wedded wives
    one little substance try;
You may advance both you and yours
    with wealth that comes thereby.

You farmers and you country men
    whom God hath blessed with store,
To this good work set helping hand
    and God will send you more.
What comes in love will prosper well
    and be redoubled back;
And they that thus for country both
    can never live in lack.

For good intent all this is done
    and no man wronged therein;
Then happy fortune be his dole
    the greatest prize can win.
And happy fortune be their guides
    that nobly thus maintains,
The planting of this new-found land
    with cares, with cost, and pains.

Let no man think that he shall lose
    though he no prize possess;
His substance to Virginia goes
    which God, no doubt will bless.
And in short time send from that land
    much rich commodity,

So shall we think all well bestowed
    upon this lottery.

Who knows not England was once like
    a wilderness and savage place,
Till government and use of men
    that mildness did deface;
And so Virginia may in time
    be made like England now,
Where long-loved peace and plenty both
    sits smiling on her brow.

Our King, the Lord full long preserve
    the cause of all this pleasure;
The Queen, the Prince, and all his seed
    with days of longest measure.
And that Virginia well may prove
    a land of rich increase,
And England's government thereof
    good God let never cease.

The Pilgrims in Holland debate leaving for America: from William Bradford's *History of Plymouth Plantation*, 1619

Statistically the number of Pilgrims was insignificant, and Plymouth was never a major colony. Yet they loom large in American history because of their indomitable spirit and remarkable accomplishment. Few modern readers can fail to be impressed by the courage the Pilgrims displayed in weighing the dangers the new world presented and in deciding to make the journey.

The place they thought on was some of those vast and unpeopled countries of America, which are fruitful and fit for habitation, being devoid of all civil inhabitants, where there are only savage and brutish men, which range up and down, little otherwise than the wild beasts of the same. This proposition being made public and coming to the scanning of all, it raised many variable opinions amongst men, and caused many fears and doubts amongst themselves. Some . . . labored to stir up and encourage the rest to undertake the same; others . . . out of their fears, objected against it, and sought to divert from it, alleging many things, and those neither unreasonable nor improbable; as that it was a great design, and subject to many inconceivable perils and dangers; as, besides the casualties of the seas (which none can be freed from) the length of the voyage was such, as the

From William T. Davis (ed.), *Bradford's History of Plymouth Plantation* (New York, 1908), pp. 46–48.

weak bodies of women and other persons worn out with age and travail (as many of them were) could never be able to endure. And yet if they should, the miseries of the land which they should be exposed unto, would be too hard to be borne; and likely, some or all of them together, to consume and utterly to ruinate them. For there they should be liable to famine, and nakedness, and the want, in a manner, of all things. The change of air, diet, and drinking of water, would infect their bodies with sore sicknesses, and grievous diseases. And also those which should escape or overcome these difficulties, should yet be in danger of the savage people, who are cruel, barbarous and most treacherous, being most furious in their rage, and merciless where they overcome—not being content only to kill, and take away life, but delight to torment men in the most bloody manner that may be; flaying some alive with the shells of fishes, cutting off the members and joints of others by piecemeal, and broiling on the coals, eat the collops of their flesh in their sight whilst they live; with other cruelties horrible to be related. And surely it could not be thought but the very hearing of these things could not but move the very bowels of men to grate within them, and make the weak to quake and tremble. It was further objected, that it would require greater sums of money to furnish such a voyage, and to fit them with necessaries. . . . Also many precedents of ill success, and lamentable miseries befalling others in the like designs were easy to be found, and not forgotten to be alleged; besides their own experience. . . .

It was answered, that all great and honorable actions are accompanied with great difficulties, and must be both enterprised and overcome with answerable courage. It was granted the dangers were great, but not desperate; the difficulties were many, but not invincible. . . . True it was, that such attempts were not to be made and undertaken without good ground and reason; not rashly or lightly, as many have done for curiosity or hope of gain, etc. But their condition was not ordinary; their ends were good and honorable; their calling lawful and urgent; and therefore they might expect the blessing of God in their proceeding. Yea, though they should lose their lives in this action, yet might they have comfort in the same, and their endeavors would be honorable.

The Mayflower Compact, 1620

The New England colonies were more theocratic than democratic, and remained so for more than a century. Nevertheless, one of the essential principles of democracy—that government is formed by man—was applied at Plymouth in 1620. There, by extending the idea of church covenants to civil concerns, the Pilgrims fashioned a political compact: the beginning of written constitutions in America.

From William T. Davis (ed.), *Bradford's History of Plymouth Plantation* (New York, 1908), p. 107.

In the name of God, Amen. We whose names are underwritten, the loyal subjects of our dread sovereign Lord, King James, by the grace of God, of Great Britain, France and Ireland king, defender of the faith, etc., having undertaken, for the glory of God, and advancement of the Christian faith, and honor of our king and country, a voyage to plant the first colony in the Northern parts of Virginia, do by these presents solemnly and mutually in the presence of God, and one of another, covenant and combine ourselves together into a civil body politic, for our better ordering and preservation and furtherance of the ends aforesaid; and by virtue hereof to enact, constitute, and frame such just and equal laws, ordinances, acts, constitutions, and offices, from time to time, as shall be thought most meet and convenient for the general good of the Colony, unto which we promise all due submission and obedience. In witness thereof we have hereunder subscribed our names at Cape Cod the 11 of November, in the year of the reign of our sovereign Lord, King James, of England, France, and Ireland the eighteenth, and of Scotland the fifty fourth. Anno Dom 1620.

Law and order in Massachusetts Bay: excerpts from the records of the General Court, 1631–36

The Puritans sought to create a community dedicated to the glorification of God, and all transgressors—sexual, economic, or political—were punished severely in Massachusetts Bay: but no more so than that meted out for comparable crimes in London, Paris, Geneva, or Madrid.

March 1, 1631

Nicholas Knopp is fined 5 pounds for taking upon him to cure scurvy by a water of no worth nor value, which he sold at a very dear rate, to be imprisoned until he pay his fine, or give security for it, or else to be whipped, and shall be liable to any man's action to whom he had received money for the said water.

March 8, 1631

It was ordered that Thomas Fox, servant to Mr. Cradock, shall be whipped for uttering malicious and scandalous speeches, whereby he sought to traduce the Court, as if they had taken some bribe in the business concerning Walter Palmer.

From Nathaniel B. Shurtleff (ed.), *Records of the Governor and Company of the Massachusetts Bay in New England* (Boston, 1853), Vol. I, pp. 83–84, 86, 88, 91–92, 99–101, 103, 107, 112, 123, 132–33, 160–61, 163, 177.

May 3, 1631

Thomas Walford of Charlton, is fined 10 shillings, and is enjoined, he and his wife, to depart out of the limits of this patent before the 20th day of October next, under pain of confiscation of his goods, for his contempt of authority and confronting officers.

June 14, 1631

It is ordered that Philip Ratliffe shall be whipped, have his ears cut off, fined 40 pounds, and banished out of the limits of this jurisdiction, for uttering malicious and scandalous speeches against the government and the church of Salem.

September 6, 1631

It is ordered that Henry Lynn shall be whipped and banished [from] the plantation before the 6th day of October next for writing into England falsely and maliciously against the government and execution of justice here.

It is ordered John Dawe shall be severely whipped for enticing an Indian woman to lie with him.

September 27, 1631

It is ordered that Josias Plastowe shall (for stealing four baskets of corn from the Indians) return them eight baskets, be fined 5 pounds, and hereafter be called by the name of Josias and not Mr.

October 18, 1631

It is ordered that if any man shall have carnal copulation with another man's wife, they both shall be punished by death.

September 4, 1632

It is ordered that Richard Hopkins shall be severely whipped, and branded with a hot iron on one of his cheeks, for selling pieces and powder and shot to the Indians.

October 3, 1632

It is ordered that Nicholas Frost, for theft by him committed at Damerills Cove upon the Indians, for drunkenness and fornication, of all which he is convicted, shall be fined 5 pounds, shall be severely whipped, and branded in the hand with a hot iron, and after banished out of this patent, with penalty that if ever he be found within the limits of the said patent, he shall be put to death.

March 4, 1633

It is ordered that Thomas Dexter shall be set in the bilbows, disfranchised and fined 40 pounds for speaking reproachful and seditious words against the government here established, and finding fault . . . with the acts of the Court, saying this captious government will bring all to naught, adding that the best of them was but an attorney.

September 3, 1633

Robert Coles is fined 10 pounds and enjoined to stand with a white sheet of paper on his back, wherein a drunkard shall be written in great letters, and to stand therewith so long as the Court thinks meet, for abusing himself shamefully with drink, enticing John Shotswell's wife to incontinency, and other misdemeanors.

March 4, 1634

It is ordered that Robert Coles, for drunkenness by him committed at Roxbury, shall be disfranchised, wear about his neck and so to hang upon his outward garment, a D, made of red cloth and set upon white; to continue this for a year, and not to leave it off any time when he comes amongst company.

August 5, 1634

It was ordered that Katherine Gray shall be whipped for her filthy and unchaste behavior with Thomas Elkin.

October 6, 1634

It is ordered that John Lee shall be whipped and fined 40 pounds for speaking reproachfully of the Governor, saying he was but a lawyer's clerk, and what understanding had he more than himself; also taxing the Court for making laws to pick men's purses; as also for abusing a maid of the Governors, pretending love in the way of marriage, when himself professes he intended none; as also for enticing her to go with him into the cornfield.

September 3, 1635

Whereas Mr. Roger Williams, one of the elders of the church of Salem, has broached and divulged diverse new and dangerous opinions against the authority of magistrates, has also wrote letters of defamation, both of the magistrates and churches here ... and yet maintains the same without retraction, it is therefore ordered that the said Mr. Williams shall depart out of this jurisdiction within six weeks.

October 6, 1635

Whereas Benjamin Felton has brought into this country one Robert Scarlett, a known thief, who since his coming hither has committed diverse felonies. ... It is therefore ordered that the said Scarlett shall be severely whipped and branded in the forehead with a T, and after sent to his said Master, whom the Court enjoins to send the said Scarlett out of this jurisdiction.

September 6, 1636

Edward Woodley, for attempting a rape, swearing and breaking into a house, was censured to be severely whipped 30 stripes, a year's imprisonment, and kept to hard labor, with a course diet, and to wear a collar of iron.

Elizabeth, the wife of Thomas Applegate, was censured to stand with her tongue in a cleft stick, for swearing, railing, and reviling.

Roger Williams on toleration: letter to the town of Providence, 1655

The Puritans were not as ideologically authoritarian, and Roger Williams was not as politically democratic as some contemporaries and later scholars have imagined. Williams was banished by the Puritans, reluctantly, for his subversive doctrine which denied to the magistrates of Massachusetts Bay authority over religious matters. The Puritans continued to justify religious persecution while Williams pled for religious toleration. A most lucid statement of his beliefs appeared in his famous letter to the people of Providence.

That ever I should speak or write a tittle that tends to such an infinite liberty of conscience is a mistake, and which I have ever disclaimed and

From *Narragansett Club Publications* (Providence, Rhode Island, 1866–74), Vol. VI, pp. 278–79.

abhorred. To prevent such mistakes, I shall at present only propose this case: There goes many a ship to sea, with many hundred souls in one ship, whose weal and woe is common, and is a true picture of a commonwealth or a human combination of society. It hath fallen out sometimes that both Papists and Protestants, Jews, and Turks, may be embarked in one ship; upon which supposal I affirm that all the liberty of conscience that ever I pleaded for turns upon these two hinges: that none of the Papists, Protestants, Jews, or Turks be forced to come to the ship's prayers or worship, if they practice any. I further add that I never denied that, notwithstanding this liberty, the commander of this ship ought to command the ship's course, yea, and also command that justice, peace, and sobriety be kept and practiced, both among the seamen and all the passengers. If any of the seamen refuse to perform their services, or passengers to pay their freight; if any refuse to help, in person or purse, towards the common charges or defense; if any refuse to obey the common laws and orders of the ship concerning their common peace or preservation; if any shall mutiny and rise up against their commanders and officers; if any should preach or write that there ought to be no commanders or officers because all are equal in Christ, therefore no masters or officers, no laws nor orders, nor corrections nor punishments—I say, I never denied but in such cases, whatever is pretended, the commander or commanders may judge, resist, compel, and punish such transgressions according to their deserts and merits. This, if seriously and honestly minded, may, if it so please the Father of lights, let in some light to such as willingly shut not their eyes.

Baptism and slavery: the laws of Maryland (1664) and Virginia (1667)

The precise status of some blacks remained legally ambiguous until the colonial legislatures specified that they were slaves. Following are two of the earliest acts known.

Maryland

It is desired by the lower house that the upper house would be pleased to draw up an Act obliging Negroes to serve *durante vita* [during life], they thinking it very necessary for the prevention of the damage masters of such slaves may sustain by such slaves pretending to be Christened and so plead the law of England. . . .

From William H. Browne (ed.), *Archives of Maryland* (Baltimore, 1883), Vol. I, pp. 526–27, 533–34; William W. Hening, *The Statutes at Large; Being a Collection of all the Laws of Virginia* (New York, 1823), Vol. II, p. 260.

AN ACT CONCERNING NEGROES AND OTHER SLAVES

Be it enacted by the Right Honorable the Lord Proprietary, by the advice and consent of the upper and lower house of this present General Assembly, that all Negroes or other slaves already within the province, and all Negroes and other slaves to be hereafter imported into the province, shall serve Durante Vita [during life]. And all children born of any Negro or other slave shall be slaves as their fathers were, for the term of their lives. And forasmuch as diverse freeborn English women, forgetful of their free condition and to the disgrace of our nation, do intermarry with Negro slaves, by which also diverse suits may arise touching the issue of such women, and a great damage does befall the masters of such Negroes for prevention whereof for deterring such freeborn women from such shameful matches, Be it further enacted by the authority, advice and consent aforesaid, That whatsoever freeborn woman shall intermarry with any slave from and after the last day of this present assembly shall serve the master of such slave during the life of her husband, And that all the issue of such freeborn women so married shall be slaves as their fathers were, And be it further enacted that all the issues of English or other freeborn women that have already married Negroes shall serve the masters of their parents till they be thirty years of age and no longer.

Virginia

WHEREAS some doubts have risen whether children that are slaves by birth, and by the charity and piety of their owners made partakers of the blessed sacrament of baptism, should by virtue of their baptism be made free; *It is enacted and declared by this grand assembly, and the authority thereof,* that the conferring of baptism does not alter the condition of the person as to his bondage or freedom; that diverse masters, freed from this doubt, may more carefully endeavor the propagation of christianity by permitting children, though slaves, or those of greater growth if capable, to be admitted to that sacrament.

Bacon's Rebellion: his charge against Governor William Berkeley, 1676

The causes of Bacon's Rebellion, as one contemporary noted, are "not easy to be discovered, but 'tis certain there are many things that concurred toward it." An anti-elite feeling was one significant factor. Another was the deep-seated hostility to Indians, which the following document written by Bacon makes abundantly clear.

From "Proclamations of Nathaniel Bacon," *Virginia Magazine of History and Biography* (July 1893), Vol. I, pp. 59–61.

For having upon specious pretenses of public works raised unjust taxes upon the Commonalty for the advancement of private favorites and other sinister ends but no visible effects in any measure adequate.

For not having during the long time of his government in any measure advanced this hopeful colony either by fortification, towns or trade.

For having abused and rendered contemptible the majesty of Justice, of advancing to places of judicature scandalous and ignorant favorites.

For having wronged his Majesties prerogative and interest by assuming the monopoly of the beaver trade.

By having in that unjust game bartered and sold his Majesties country and the lives of his loyal subjects to the barbarous heathen.

For having protected, favored and emboldened the Indians against his Majesties most loyal subjects, never contriving, requiring or appointing any due or proper means of satisfaction for their many invasions, murders and robberies committed upon us.

For having, when the army of the English was just upon the track of the Indians, which now in all places burn, spoil and murder, and when we might with ease have destroyed them, who then were in open hostility; for having expressly countermanded and sent back our army by passing his word for the peaceable demeanor of the said Indians, who immediately prosecuted their evil intentions, committing murders and robberies in all places being protected by the said engagement and word passed of him, the said Sir William Berkeley; having ruined and made desolate a great part of his Majesties country, have now drawn themselves into such obscure and remote places and are by their successes so emboldened and confirmed, and by their Confederacy so strengthened, that the cries of blood are in all places and the terror and consternation of the people so great, that they are now become not only a difficult, but a very formidable enemy who might with ease have been destroyed. . . .

For having, with only the privacy of some few favorites, without acquainting the people, only by the alteration of a figure forged a commission by we know not what hand, not only without but against the consent of the people, for raising and effecting of civil wars and distractions, which being happily and without bloodshed prevented.

For having the second time attempted the same thereby, calling down our forces from the defense of the frontiers, and most weak exposed places, for the prevention of civil mischief and ruin amongst ourselves, whilst the barbarous enemy in all places did invade, murder and spoil us, his Majesty's most faithful subjects.

Of these the aforesaid Articles we accuse Sir William Berkeley, as guilty of each and every one of the same, and as one who has traitorously attempted, violated and injured his Majesty's interest here, by the loss of a great part of his colony, and many of his faithful and loyal subjects by him betrayed, and in a barbarous and shameful manner exposed to the incursions and murders of the heathen.

And we further declare these the ensuing persons in this list, to have been his wicked, and pernicious counsellors, aiders and assisters against the Commonalty in these our cruel commotions.

Sir Henry Chicherly	William Cole
Colonel Charles Wormley	Richard Whitacre
Philip Dalowell	Nicholas Spencer
Robert Beverly	Joseph Bridger
Robert Lee	William Clabourne
Thomas Ballard	Thomas Hawkins, Junior
William Sherwood	Hubberd Farrell
Joseph Page	John West
Joseph Cliffe	Thomas Reade

Mathew Kemp.

And we do further demand, that the said Sir William Berkeley, with all the persons in this list, be forthwith delivered up, or surrender themselves, within four days, after the notice hereof, or otherwise we declare as follows, that in whatsoever house, place, or ship, any of the said persons shall reside, be hide, or protected, we do declare, that the owners, masters, or inhabitants of the said places to be confederates and traitors to the people, and the estates of them, as also of all the aforesaid persons to be confiscated. This we the commons of Virginia do declare, desiring a prime union among ourselves, that we may jointly and with one accord defend ourselves against the common enemy. And let not the faults or crimes of the oppressors divide and separate us, who have suffered by their oppressions.

These are therefore in his Majesty's name, to command you forthwith to seize the persons above mentioned, as traitors to the King and Country; and them to bring to Middle Plantation, and there to secure them till further order, and in case of opposition, if you want any other assistance, you are forthwith to demand it in the name of the people of all the counties of Virginia.

William Penn's letter to the Delaware Indians, August 18, 1681

William Penn wrote the following letter from London, to be read by his commissioners in Pennsylvania to the Indians. Its spirit of trust and friendship should be contrasted with that of Nathaniel Bacon in the preceding document.

My friends—There is one great God and power that hath made the world and all things therein, to whom you and I, and all people owe their

From Samuel Hazard (ed.), *Annals of Pennsylvania, from the discovery of the Delaware* (Philadelphia, 1850), pp. 532–33.

being and well-being, and to whom you and I must one day give an account for all that we do in the world; this great God hath written his law
in our hearts, by which we are taught and commanded to live and help,
and do good to one another, and not to do harm and mischief one to
another. Now this great God hath been pleased to make me concerned in
your parts of the world, and the king of the country where I live hath given
unto me a great province, but I desire to enjoy it with your love and consent, that we may always live together as neighbors and friends, else what
would the great God say to us, who hath made us not to devour and destroy
one another, but live soberly and kindly together in the world? Now I
would have you well observe, that I am very sensible of the unkindness and
injustice that hath been too much exercised towards you by the people of
these parts of the world, who sought themselves, and to make great advantages by you, rather than be examples of justice and goodness unto you,
which I hear hath been matter of trouble to you, and caused great grudg-
ings and animosities, sometimes to the shedding of blood, which hath made
the great God angry; but I am not such a man, as is well known in my own
country; I have great love and regard towards you, and I desire to win and
gain your love and friendship, by a kind, just, and peaceful life, and the
people I send are of the same mind, and shall in all things behave themselves
accordingly; and if in anything any shall offend you or your people, you
shall have a full and speedy satisfaction for the same, by an equal number
of just men on both sides, that by no means you may have just occasion of
being offended against them. I shall shortly come to you myself, at what
time we may more largely and freely confer and discourse of these matters.
In the meantime, I have sent my commissioners to treat with you about
land, and a firm league of peace. Let me desire you to be kind to them and
the people, and receive these presents and tokens which I have sent to you,
as a testimony of my good will to you, and my resolution to live justly,
peaceably, and friendly with you.

William Snelgrave's account of two slave mutinies on the African coast, 1704 and 1721

*The dread possibilities of slave insurrections on shipboard forced slave traders
to be constantly alert. The danger was multiplied if the slaves belonged to a
single tribe, and especially if that tribe—such as the Coromantines from the
Gold Coast—was distinguished for its courage and independence. The Coromantines were highly regarded by the English and fetched a greater price in
America. But they were "ferocious and stubborn" as well, and frequently incited
other slaves to rebellion.*

From Elizabeth Donnan (ed.), *Documents Illustrative of the History of the Slave
Trade to America* (Washington, D.C., 1931), Vol. II, pp. 353–55. Reprinted by courtesy of the Carnegie Institution of Washington.

The first mutiny I saw among the Negroes, happened during my first voyage, in the year 1704. It was on board the *Eagle* galley of London, commanded by my father, with whom I was as purser. We had bought our Negroes in the river of Old Calabar in the Bay of Guinea. At the time of their mutinying we were in that river, having four hundred of them on board, and not above ten white men who were able to do service. For several of our ship's company were dead, and many more sick; besides, two of our boats were just then gone with twelve people on shore to fetch wood, which lay in sight of the ship. All these circumstances put the Negroes on consulting how to mutiny, which they did at four o'clock in the afternoon, just as they went to supper. But as we had always carefully examined the men's irons, both morning and evening, none had got them off, which in a great measure contributed to our preservation. Three white men stood on the watch with cutlaces in their hands. One of them who was on the forecastle, a stout fellow, seeing some of the men Negroes take hold of the chief mate, in order to throw him over-board, he laid on them so heartily with the flat side of his cutlace, that they soon quitted the mate, who escaped from them, and run on the quarter-deck to get arms. I was then sick with an ague, and lying on a couch in the great cabin, the fit being just come on. However, I no sooner heard the outcry, that the slaves were mutinying, but I took two pistols and run on the deck with them; where, meeting with my father and the chief mate, I delivered a pistol to each of them. Whereupon they went forward on the booms, calling to the Negro men that were on the forecastle; but they did not regard their threats, being busy with the sentry, (who had disengaged the chief mate,) and they would have certainly killed him with his own cutlace, could they have got it from him; but they could not break the line wherewith the handle was fastened to his wrist. And so, tho' they had seized him, yet they could not make use of his cutlace. Being thus disappointed, they endeavored to throw him over-board, but he held so fast by one of them that they could not do it. My father seeing this stout man in so much danger, ventured amongst the Negroes to save him; and fired his pistol over their heads, thinking to frighten them. But a lusty slave struck him with a billet so hard, that he was almost stunned. The slave was going to repeat his blow, when a young lad about seventeen years old, whom we had been kind to, interposed his arm, and received the blow, by which his arm-bone was fractured. At the same instant the mate fired his pistol, and shot the Negro that had struck my father. At the sight of this the mutiny ceased, and all the men-Negroes on the forecastle threw themselves flat on their faces, crying out for mercy.

Upon examining into the matter, we found, there were not above twenty men slaves concerned in this mutiny; and the two ringleaders were missing, having, it seems, jumped overboard as soon as they found their project defeated, and were drowned. This was all the loss we suffered on this occasion; for the Negro that was shot by the mate, the surgeon beyond all expectation cured. And I had the good fortune to lose my ague, by the fright and hurry I was put into. Moreover, the young man, who had received the blow on his arm to save my father, was cured by the surgeon in our passage to Virginia. At our arrival in that place we gave him his freedom; and a worthy gentleman, one Colonel Carter, took him into his service, till he became well enough acquainted in the country to provide for himself.

I have been several voyages, when there has been no attempt made by our Negroes to mutiny; which I believe was owing chiefly to their being kindly used, and to my Officers care in keeping a good watch. But sometimes we meet with stout stubborn people amongst them, who are never to be made easy; and these are generally some of the Cormantines, a nation of the Gold Coast. I went in the year 1721, in the *Henry* of London, a voyage to that part of the coast, and bought a good many of these people. We were obliged to secure them very well in irons, and watch them narrowly. Yet they nevertheless mutinied, tho' they had little prospect of succeeding. I lay at that time near a place called Mumfort on the Gold-Coast, having near five hundred Negroes on board, three hundred of which were men. Our ship's company consisted of fifty white people, all in health. And I had very good officers; so that I was very easy in all respects.

After we had secured these people, I called the linguists, and ordered them to bid the men-Negroes between decks be quiet; (for there was a great noise amongst them.) On their being silent, I asked, "What had induced them to mutiny?" They answered, "I was a great rogue to buy them, in order to carry them away from their own country, and that they were resolved to regain their liberty if possible." I replied, "That they had forfeited their freedom before I bought them, either by crimes or by being taken in war, according to the custom of their country; and they being now my property, I was resolved to let them feel my resentment if they abused my kindness. Asking at the same time, whether they had been ill used by the white men, or had wanted for any thing the ship afforded?" To this they replied, "They had nothing to complain of." Then I observed to them, "That if they should gain their point and escape to the shore, it would be no advantage to them, because their countrymen would catch them, and sell them to other ships." This served my purpose, and they seemed to be convinced of their fault, begging, "I would forgive them, and promising for the future to be obedient, and never mutiny again, if I would not punish them this time." This I readily granted, and so they went to sleep. When daylight came we called the men-Negroes up on deck, and examining their irons, found them all secure. So this affair happily ended, which I was very glad of; for these people are the stoutest and most sensible Negroes on the coast. Neither are they so weak as to imagine as others do, that we buy them to eat them; being satisfied we carry them to work in our plantations, as they do in their own country.

However, a few days after this, we discovered they were plotting again, and preparing to mutiny.

Advertisements for runaway indentured servants, 1736–39

White emigrants without funds could come to America as indentured servants, contracting to work a specified number of years—usually five—to repay their transportation costs. During this period the indentured servant received board and lodging, but no pay, nor did he possess full political or civil rights. Once the contract was successfully completed he became a free man, entitled to an "outfit" (clothes, tools, seed) and perhaps a small grant of land. But many servants found their work too hard or their masters too cruel, and fled before finishing the term of their indenture.

Virginia, 1736

Ran away lately from the Bristol Company's Iron Works, in King George County, a servant man named James Sumners, a West Country [i.e., Cornish] Man, and speaks thick, he is a short thick fellow, with short black hair and a ruddy complexion. Whoever secures the said servant and brings him to the said Iron Works, or to the Hon. John Taylor, Esq., in Richmond County, or gives notice of him, so as he may be had again, shall be well rewarded besides what the law allows.

Virginia, 1737

Ran away some time in June last, from William Pierce of Nansemond County, a servant man named James Sumners, a West Country [i.e., Cornamed Winifred Thomas. She is Welsh woman, short black hair'd and young; mark'd on the inside of her right arm with gunpowder W.T. and the date of the year underneath. She knits and spins, and is supposed to be gone into North Carolina by the way of Cureatuck and Roanoke Inlet. Whoever brings her to her master shall be paid a pistole besides what the law allows, paid by

WILLIAM PIERCE

Georgia, 1739

Run away on the 5th Instant from Robert William's Plantation in Georgia, 3 men servants, one named James Powell, is a bricklayer by trade about five feet 9 inches high, a strong made man, born in Wiltshire, talks broad, and when he went away he wore his own short hair, with a white cap: Among his comrades he was call'd Alderman.

From Ulrich B. Phillips (ed.), *A Documentary History of American Industrial Society* (Cleveland, 1910), Vol. I, pp. 346–48.

Another named Charles Gastril did formerly belong to the Pilot Boat at Pill near Bristol, is by trade a sawyer, about 5 feet 10 inches high, of a thin spare make, raw boned, and has a scar somewhere on his upper lip, aged about 25.

The 3rd named Jenkin James, a lusty young fellow, about the same height as Gastril, has a good fresh complexion, bred by trade a tailor, but of late has been used to sawing, talks very much Welshly, and had on when he went away a coarse red coat and waistcoat, the buttons and button holes of the coat black.

Any person or persons who apprehend them, or either of them, and bring them to Mr. Thomas Jenys in Charleston, or to the said Mr. Robert Williams in Savannah shall receive 10 pounds currency of South Carolina for each.

ROBERT WILLIAMS

Besides the above mentioned reward, there is a considerable sum allow'd by the Trustees [of the colony of Georgia] for taking run away servants.

Some problems of governing Georgia from England: excerpts from the Earl of Egmont's diary, 1733–40

The founders of Georgia—the thirteenth colony to be established by England —hoped to fashion a settlement without slavery, without strong liquor, and without great disparities in wealth. It was to be populated by sober, hardworking yeomen. From the beginning, however, the settlers complained, and in time Georgia followed the Carolina pattern with slaves, plantations, and even debtors and debtors' prisons.

November 19, 1733

Mr. Vernon showed me a letter from Mr. Oglethorp lately received, wherein he speaks of a mutiny among the persons we sent over, which was suppressed by sending away one Gray. He also writes that during his absence at Charlestown the people were fallen to drinking of rum, whereby we had lost twenty persons, and their sickness was grown contagious, so that those who attended them, nurses etc., were all dead, but a ship of forty Jews arriving with a physician, he entirely put a stop to it, so that

From R. A. Roberts *et al.* (eds.), *Manuscripts of the Earl of Egmont* (London, 1920– 23), Vol. I, pp. 440, 451; Vol. II, pp. 112, 121–23, 194, 286, 450–51, 481; Vol. III, pp. 65–66, 109.

not one died afterwards. He says twenty houses were already built, and nineteen more laid out with the names of streets etc., and that he has ordered four forts to be built, which will stop all avenues to the town, in case of attack or surprise from the Spaniards or Indians, their friends. . . .

November 29, 1733

This morning Captain Pury came to see me. . . . He said there were three things that made our people at Savannah uneasy. 1. That if they die without heirs male, their land falls back to the Trustees, and descends not to their wife and daughter. 2. That they are not allowed to keep slaves of blacks, as Carolina allows. 3. That there being many lazy fellows in the number, and others not able to work, those who work stoutly think it unreasonable the others should enjoy the fruits of their labor, and when the land is cleared, have an equal share and chance when lots are cast for determining each person's division.

June 19, 1734

One of the letters gave an account that an Englishman had by the present of a blanket seduced an Indian married woman to lie with him, of which the Indians complained, the punishment with them for that crime being to cut the adulterer's throat. That they had punished the woman by cutting off her ears and hair, but they would be contented if we whipped the man.

August 19, 1734

The seven Indians with their interpreter, Mr. Oglethorp, Mr. Vernon, and Mr. Verelts, came and dined with me. I diverted them in the best manner, walked them into the wood, had music and dancing. I made also some presents. They behaved with great decency, and were well pleased. At parting the King Tomachiki made me a speech to tell me he came down to see me in good will and returned in friendship. . . .

They were yesterday to see the Archbishop of Canterbury, and were extremely pleased with their visit. They had apprehensions that he was a conjuror, but the kind reception he gave them altered that imagination. The Archbishop would have put some questions to them concerning their notions of religion, but they have a superstition that it is unfortunate to disclose their thoughts of those matters, and refused to answer. . . .

The [Indian] King made a sensible reflection since he came over [to England]. He said he saw we knew a great many more things than they, but he thought we were not the better men for it, and that they were more happy and innocent in their ignorance. . . .

September 17, 1735

Mr. Burton informed us that two gentlemen, one a clergyman, bred at the University, and who have some substance, have resolved to go to Georgia out of a pious design to convert the Indians. They are brothers and their names Wesley. . . .

June 17, 1736

This very morning before I came to the Board, visiting Sir Robert Brown, who is a devoted man to Sir Robert Walpole . . . , he asked me in a very doubtful way whether indeed I thought our Georgia settlement advantageous to England. And when I replied, yes, giving him some reasons, he answered he believed indeed I thought so, which was as much as to say he did not. He added that our charter gave us, the Trustees, too much power and made us independent of the Crown, and that there was a spirit in all the Colonies to throw off their dependency on the Crown of England. I replied our charter was but for 21 years, after which our power was at an end, and the Colony fell under his Majesty's sole power, who might do with it as he pleased.

December 7, 1737

Williamson of Savannah complains heavily against Mr. John Wesley, the minister, for refusing his wife the Sacrament, and conversing with her contrary to his express command, to the disturbance of his wife and himself, and to the administering great scandal. He desires reparation of the said Mr. Wesley or he must leave the Colony. . . . Williamson also enclosed to us the copy of a letter wrote by Mr. Wesley to his wife, accusing her of lying, breach of faith etc.; and also enclosed his wife's deposition wherein she swears that he offered to marry her, and on that condition to make fasting and frequent communion easy to her, and to abandon his design of preaching among the Indians, but to fix himself in Savannah.

April 26, 1738

Mr. John Wesley, our minister at Savannah, left with us his license for performing ecclesiastical service at Savannah, which we took for a resignation, and therefore resolved to revoke his commission. In truth the Board did it with great pleasure, he appearing to us to be a very odd mixture of a man, an enthusiast and at the same time a hypocrite, wholly distasteful to the greater part of the inhabitants, and an incendiary of the people against the magistracy.

June 5, 1739

Robert Hows, late clerk of Savannah church, came this morning. . . . I made him several enquiries, to which he answered as follows. That he had long refused to sign the representation for Negroes, because he feared they would take the work from white men's hands and impoverish them, as in the case of Charlestown, where the tradesmen are all beggars by that means, and besides, there would be danger from Negroes rising and cutting their throats; but the promoters of that application said the Negroes should not be allowed to work at anything but producing rice (a labor too hard for white men), and in felling timber.

February 4, 1740

Mr. Stephens came to see me. . . . I said that as to Negroes he would not find one Trustee for allowing them, that we wanted them not for the works, labors or produces we intend to carry on, and our nearness to the Spaniards would endanger their cutting the throats of the white men . . . if they had lately rose in Carolina and cut the throats of 34 white men, for which 50 of them were put to death, as the last accounts inform us, how dangerous must it appear to suffer Negroes in Georgia, where there are so [few] white men, and at a time when Spain makes all free that fly to [Saint] Augustine.

He replied, he knew that without Negroes the colony must drop; that let our produces be what they will, they cannot turn to account but with their help . . . if an equal number of Negroes were allowed in Georgia to that of white men there would be no danger. That laying it down as fact that the colony cannot subsist without them, all arguments of danger should give way thereto.

A New York governor complains of legislative encroachments upon royal authority: George Clinton to the Lords of Trade, October 20, 1748

Gradually the colonial legislatures assumed greater prerogatives and powers. Most important, no taxes could be levied without their consent. Control of taxation gave the legislatures a degree of administrative power over public finances. They appointed treasurers and audited the accounts of public officers. Supervision of the pursestrings, in turn, gave these assemblies a major voice in military and judicial matters, in Indian relations, and in ecclesiastical policies. Governor Clinton's letter of complaint touches upon some of these matters, for

From E. B. O'Callaghan (ed.), *Documents Relative to the Colonial History of the State of New York* (Albany, 1855), Vol. VI, pp. 456–57.

it was his responsibility to apply England's decrees, which frequently conflicted with legislative enactments.

My Lords: I have in my former letters informed Your Lordships what encroachments the Assemblies of this province have from time to time made on His Majesty's prerogative and authority, in drawing an absolute dependence of all the Officers upon them for their salaries and reward for their services, and by their taking in effect the nomination to all Officers. . . .

That Your Lordships may the better comprehend the methods which the Assembly have taken, to draw unto themselves the executive powers of Government, I must observe to Your Lordships:

> 1. That the Assembly refuse to admit of any amendment to any money bill; so that the bill must pass as it comes from the Assembly, or all the supplies granted for the support of the government and the most urgent services must be lost.
>
> 2. It appears that they take the payment of the [military] forces, passing of Muster Rolls into their own hands, by naming the Commissaries for those purposes in the Act.
>
> 3. They, by granting the salaries of the Officers personally by name, and not to the Officer for the time being, intimate that if any person be appointed to any Office, his salary must depend upon their approbation of the appointment.
>
> 4. They issue the greatest part of the money granted to His Majesty without Warrant, though by His Majesty's commission to me it is directed that all monies raised by Act of Assembly shall be issued from the Treasury by my Warrant and not otherwise.
>
> 5. They have appointed an Agent for the Colony who is to take his directions from a Committee of Assembly (exclusive of the Council and of the Governor) and to be paid by Warrant from the Speaker of the Assembly.
>
> 6. In order to lay me under a necessity of passing the Bill for payment of the Officers' salaries and services in the manner the Assembly had formed it, they tacked to it the payment of the forces posted on the frontier for the defense thereof, so that I must either pass the bill or leave the colony defenseless and open to the enemies incursions.

This last laid me under great difficulties, in refusing my assent, and therefore I took the advice of His Majesty's Council for this province as to what may be proper for me to do on this occasion, who advised me, from the present urgency of affairs, to give my assent to the bill. . . .

I must now refer it to Your Lordships consideration whether it be not high time to put a stop to these usurpations of the Assembly on His

Majesty's authority in this Province, and for that purpose may it not be proper that His Majesty signify his disallowance of the Act, at least for the payment of salaries, though it has already in most parts taken its effect. There seems the more reason for this because the appointment of an Agent (exclusive of the Governor and Council) may be construed a perpetual clause, or at least may give ground for their insisting on the like cause in all future acts of Assembly, and for their likewise insisting on the same method of supporting the government. And I must in general beg of Your Lordships to take under your serious consideration what instruction or other method may be necessary to put a stop to these perpetually growing encroachments of the Assemblies of this province on the executive powers entrusted with me and His Majesty's other Officers.

2
Empire and Revolution

Captain Thomas Morris of His Majesty's XVII
Regiment of Infantry, on his expedition to Detroit, 1764

After the French were defeated in the Seven Years War, a massive rebellion of Indians led by the Ottawa chief, Pontiac, was crushed by English troops in 1763. Nevertheless, Pontiac's influence among the western tribes—as this excerpt from the journal of Captain Morris testifies—remained powerful. In the next decade the Northwest posed complex problems for the English government, in regulating the fur trade, in calming the deep-seated hostility of Indians, in providing for military defense, and in fashioning a policy of land settlement. These issues were never resolved to the satisfaction of colonials.

I set out in good spirits from Cedar Point, in Lake Erie, on the 26th of August, 1764, about four o'clock in the afternoon, at the same time that the army proceeded for Detroit. My escort consisted of Godefroy and another Canadian, two servants, twelve Indians, our allies, and five Mohawks, with a boat in which were our provisions. . . . I had with me likewise Warsong, the great Chippewaw chief, and Attawang, an Uttawaw chief, with some other Indians of their nations. . . . I was greatly delighted on observing the difference of temper betwixt these Indian strangers and those of my old acquaintance of the five nations. Godefroy was employed in interpreting to me all their pleasantries; and I thought them the most agreeable ralliers I had ever met with. As all men love those who resemble themselves, the sprightly manners of the French cannot fail to recommend them to these savages, as our grave deportment is an advantage to us among our Indian neighbors; for it is certain that a reserved Englishman differs not more from a lively Frenchman than does a stern Mohawk from a laughing Chippewaw. . . .

Passing by the encampment of the Miamis . . . I heard a yell, and found myself surrounded by Pontiac's army, consisting of six hundred savages, with tomahawks in their hands, who beat my horse, and endeavored to separate me from my Indians, at the head of whom I had placed myself on our discovering the village. By their malicious smiles, it was easy for me to guess their intention of putting me to death. They led me up to a person, who stood advanced before two slaves (prisoners of the Panis nation, taken in war and kept in slavery) who had arms, himself holding a fusil with the butt on the ground. By his dress, and the air he assumed, he appeared to be a French officer. I afterwards found that he was a native of old France, had been long in the regular troops as a drummer, and that his war-name was St. Vincent. This fine-dressed half French, half Indian figure desired me to dismount; a bear-skin was spread on the ground, and St. Vincent and I sat upon it, the whole Indian army, circle within circle, standing round us.

From Reuben G. Thwaites (ed.), *Early Western Travels* (Cleveland, 1904), Vol. I, pp. 303–08.

Godefroy sat a little distance from us; and presently came Pontiac, and squatted himself, after his fashion, opposite to me. This Indian has a more extensive power than ever was known among that people; for every chief used to command his own tribe: but eighteen nations, by French intrigue, had been brought to unite, and chose this man for their commander, after the English had conquered Canada; having been taught to believe that, aided by France, they might make a vigorous push and drive us out of North America. Pontiac asked me in his language, which Godefroy interpreted, "whether I was come to tell lies, like the rest of my countrymen." He said, "That Ononteeo (the French king) was not crushed as the English had reported, but had got upon his legs again." . . . The next day I went to the grand council, and addressed the chiefs. When I mentioned that their father, the king of France, had ceded those countries to their brother the king of England, (for so the two kings are called by the Indians) the great Miamis chief started up and spoke very loud, in his singular language, and laughed. Godefroy whispered to me that it was very lucky that he received my intelligence with contempt and not anger, and desired me to say no more, but sit down, and let my chief speak; accordingly I sat down, and he produced his belts, and spoke. . . . Pontiac said to my chief: "If you have made peace with the English, we have no business to make war on them. The war-belts came from you." He afterwards said to Godefroy, "I will lead the nations to war no more; let them be at peace, if they choose it; but I myself will never be a friend to the English. I shall now become a wanderer in the woods; and if they come to seek me there, while I have an arrow left, I will shoot at them." This I imagined he said in despair, and gave it as my opinion, that he might easily be won to our interest; and it afterwards proved so. He made a speech to the chiefs, who wanted to put me to death, which does him honor, and shows that he was acquainted with the law of nations: "We must not," said he, "kill ambassadors; do we not send them to the Flat-heads, our greatest enemies, and they to us? Yet these are always treated with hospitality." . . .

The greater part of the warriors got drunk; and a young Indian drew his knife, and made a stroke at me; but Godefroy seized his arm, threw him down, and took the knife from him. He certainly saved my life, for I was sitting, and could not have avoided the blow though I saw it coming. I was now concealed under my mattress, as all the young Indians were determined to murder me, was afterwards obliged to put on Indian shoes and cover myself with a blanket to look like a savage, and escape by fording the river into a field of Indian corn with St. Vincent and Godefroy. . . . Pontiac asked Godefroy, who returned to the village to see what was going on, "what he had done with the English man." And being told, he said, "you have done well." Attawang came to see me, and made his two sons guard me. Two Kickapoo chiefs came to me, and spoke kindly, telling me that they had not been at war with the English for seven years. Two Miamis came likewise, and told me that I need not be afraid to go to their village.

A Huron woman however abused me because the English had killed her son. Late at night I returned to Attawang's cabin, where I found my servant concealed under a blanket, the Indians having attempted to murder him; but they had been prevented by St. Vincent. There was an alarm in the night, a drunken Indian having been seen at the skirt of the wood. One of the Delaware nation, who happened to be with Pontiac's army, passing by the cabin where I lay, called out in broken English: "Damned son of a bitch."

Thomas Hutchinson's account of American resistance to the Stamp Act, 1765

The Stamp Act aroused an uproar of protest in the colonies. All across America colonial legislatures passed resolutions of protest, and royal officials and their supporters were intimidated by vigilante organizations. Nowhere could the Stamp Act be enforced.

Rather ironically, the Lieutenant-Governor of Massachusetts, Thomas Hutchinson, was opposed to the passage of the Stamp Act on the grounds that Parliament could not tax the colonies. But he also believed that the law, once enacted, must be obeyed. In the following account he describes how his house was ransacked by a Boston mob.

Upon the news of the intention to lay this duty [the Stamp Act] on the colonies, many people the last year had associated and engaged to forbear the importation, or consumption, of English goods; and particularly to break off from the custom of wearing black clothes, or other mourning, upon the death of relations. This agreement was then signed by some of the council, and representatives, and by great numbers of people in the town of Boston, and the disuse of mourning soon became general. This was intended to alarm the manufacturers in England. And now, an agreement was made, and signed by a great proportion of the inhabitants of Boston, to eat no lamb during the year. This was in order to increase the growth, and, of course, the manufacture of wool in the province. Neither of these measures much served the purpose for which they were professedly intended, but they served to unite the people in an unfavorable opinion of parliament as being biased by the immediate interest of the kingdom, separate and distinct from the interest of the colonies. Such a bias, they were taught, rendered it improper that the parliament should be the common legislature of both; and the advocates for its authority began to lose the favor of the people. . . .

Reprinted by permission of the publishers from Lawrence S. Mayo (ed.), *Thomas Hutchinson's History of the Colony and Province of Massachusetts Bay* (Cambridge, Mass.: Harvard University Press), pp. 84–85, 86–87, 88–89, 90. Copyright 1936 and 1964 by the President and Fellows of Harvard College.

The distributor of stamps for the colony of Connecticut arrived in Boston from London; and, having been agent for that colony, and in other respects of a very reputable character, received from many gentlemen of the town such civilities as were due to him. When he set out for Connecticut, Mr. [Andrew] Oliver, the distributor for Massachusetts Bay, accompanied him out of town. This occasioned murmuring among the people, and an inflammatory piece in the next *Boston Gazette*. A few days after, early in the morning, a stuffed image was hung upon a tree, called the great tree of the south part of Boston. Labels affixed denoted it to be designed for the distributor of stamps. People who were passing by stopped to view it, and the report caused others to gather from all quarters of the town, and many from the towns adjacent. The governor caused the council to be convened. Before they came to any determination the sheriff, with his deputies, had been to the place, but, by advice of some of the graver persons present, forbore any attempt to remove the image. The majority of the council, but not the whole, advised not to meddle with it; and urged as a reason, that the people were orderly and, if left alone, would take down the image and bury it without any disturbance; but an attempt to remove it would bring on a riot, the mischief designed to be prevented. . . .

Despairing of protection, and finding his family in terror and great distress, Mr. Oliver came to a sudden resolution to resign his office before another night, and immediately signified, by a writing under his hand to one of his friends, that he would send letters by a ship then ready to sail for London which should contain such resignation; and he desired that the town might be made acquainted with it, and with the strong assurances he had given, that he would never act in that capacity. This victory was a matter of triumph. The mob assembled in the evening; not to insult the distributor, but to give him thanks, and to make a bonfire upon the hill near his house.

It was hoped that the people, having obtained all that they desired, would return to order, but, having repeatedly assembled with impunity, a very small pretence served to induce them to reassemble. The next evening, the mob surrounded the house of the lieutenant-governor and chief justice [Thomas Hutchinson]. He was at Mr. Oliver's house when it was assaulted, and had excited the sheriff and the colonel of the regiment to attempt to suppress the mob. A report was soon spread, that he was a favorer of the stamp act, and had encouraged it by letters to the ministry. Upon notice of the approach of the people, he caused the doors and windows to be barred; and remained in the house. After attempting to enter, they called upon him to come into the balcony, and to declare that he had not written in favor of the act, and they would retire quite satisfied. This was an indignity to which he would not submit; and, therefore, he made no answer. An ancient reputable tradesman obtained their attention, and endeavoring to persuade them, not only of the unwarrantableness of their proceedings, but of the groundlessness of their suspicions of the lieutenant-governor, who might well enough wish the act of parliament had not passed, though he disapproved of the violent opposition to its execution. Some were for withdrawing, and others for continuing; when one of the neighbors called to them from his window and affirmed, that he saw the lieutenant-governor in his carriage, just before night, and that he was gone to lodge at his house in the country. Upon this, they dispersed, with only breaking some of the glass. . . .

[On] the evening of the 26th of August . . . a mob was [again] collected in King Street, drawn there by a bonfire, and well supplied with strong drink. After some annoyance to the house of the registrar of the admiralty, and somewhat greater to that of the comptroller of the customs, whose cellars they plundered of the wine and spirits in them, they came, with intoxicated rage, upon the house of the lieutenant-governor. The doors were immediately split to pieces with broad axes, and a way made there, and at the windows, for the entry of the mob; which poured in and filled in an instant every room in the house.

The lieutenant-governor had very short notice of the approach of the mob. He directed his children, and the rest of the family, to leave the house immediately, determining to keep possession himself. His eldest daughter, after going a little way from the house, returned, and refused to quit it, unless her father would do the like. This caused him to depart from his resolution, a few minutes before the mob entered. They continued their possession until daylight; destroyed, carried away, or cast into the street, everything that was in the house; demolished every part of it, except the walls, as far as lay in their power; and had begun to break away the brickwork. The damage was estimated at about twenty-five hundred pounds sterling, without regard to a great collection of public as well as private papers, in the possession and custody of the lieutenant-governor.

The town was, the whole night, under the awe of this mob; many of the magistrates, with the field officers of the militia, standing by as spectators; and nobody daring to oppose, or contradict.

William Pitt on the repeal of the Stamp Act, 1766

William Pitt, the Earl of Chatham, was undoubtedly the most distinguished statesman in England, and his support of American resistance to the Stamp Act was much appreciated in the colonies. Pitt's speech is a strong appeal for colonial self-taxation as an inalienable right enjoyed by all Englishmen. One should note, however, that Pitt also asserted the absolute authority of the English government over the colonies.

Parliament did repeal the Stamp Act (by a vote of 275 to 167 in the House of Commons), and then passed the Declaratory Act which concluded that

From T. C. Hansard, *The Parliamentary History of England from the Earliest Period to the Year 1803* (London, 1813), Vol. XVI, pp. 99–100, 107–08.

they might legislate for the colonies "in all cases whatsoever." In effect, Parlia-
ment had lost a skirmish with the colonists but refused to concede the battle.
Only one of the conflicting views of the empire could ultimately prevail. Either
the English government had to agree to a division of power, or the colonists had
to accept the sovereignty of Parliament.

It is my opinion that this kingdom has no right to lay a tax upon the colonies. At the same time, I assert the authority of this kingdom over the colonies to be sovereign and supreme, in every circumstance of government and legislation whatsoever. They are the subjects of this kingdom, equally entitled with yourselves to all the natural rights of mankind and the peculiar privileges of Englishmen, equally bound by its laws, and equally participating of the constitution of this free country. The Americans are the sons, not the bastards, of England. Taxation is no part of the governing or legislative power. . . . When, therefore, in this House we give and grant, we give and grant what is our own. But in an American tax, what do we do? We, your Majesty's Commons of Great Britain, give and grant to your Majesty, what? Our own property? No. We give and grant to your Majesty, the property of your Majesty's commons of America. It is an absurdity in terms. . . .

There is an idea in some, that the colonies are virtually represented in this House. I would fain know by whom an American is represented here? Is he represented by any knight of the shire, in any county in this kingdom? Would to God that respectable representation was augmented to a greater number! Or will you tell him, that he is represented by any representative of a borough—a borough, which perhaps, its own representative never saw. This is what is called 'the rotten part of the constitution.' It cannot continue the century; if it does not drop, it must be amputated. The idea of a virtual representation of America in this House is the most contemptible idea that ever entered into the head of a man; it does not deserve a serious refutation.

The Commons of America, represented in their several assemblies, have ever been in possession of the exercise of this, their constitutional right, of giving and granting their own money. They would have been slaves if they had not enjoyed it. At the same time, this kingdom, as the supreme governing and legislative power, has always bound the colonies by her laws, by her regulations, and restrictions in trade, in navigation, in manufactures, in everything except that of taking their money out of their pockets without their consent. . . .

A great deal has been said without doors, of the power, of the strength of America. It is a topic that ought to be cautiously meddled with. In a good cause, on a sound bottom, the force of this country can crush America to atoms. I know the valor of your troops. I know the skill of your officers. There is not a company of foot that has served in America, out of which you may not pick a man of sufficient knowledge and experience to make a governor of a colony there. But on this ground, on the Stamp Act, when so many here will think it a crying injustice, I am one who will lift up my hands against it.

In such a cause, your success would be hazardous. America, if she fell, would fall like a strong man. She would embrace the pillars of the state, and pull down the constitution along with her. Is this your boasted peace? Not to sheath the sword in its scabbard, but to sheath it in the bowels of your countrymen?

The Americans have not acted in all things with prudence and temper. They have been wronged. They have been driven to madness by injustice. Will you punish them for the madness you have occasioned? Rather let prudence and temper come first from this side. I will undertake for America, that she will follow the example. There are two lines in a ballad of Prior's, of a man's behavior to his wife, so applicable to you and your colonies, that I cannot help repeating them:

> Be to her faults a little blind;
> Be to her virtues very kind.

Upon the whole, I will beg leave to tell the House what is really my opinion. It is, that the Stamp Act be repealed absolutely, totally, and immediately. That the reason for the repeal be assigned, because it was founded on an erroneous principle. At the same time, let the sovereign authority of this country over the colonies be asserted in as strong terms as can be devised, and be made to extend to every point of legislation whatsoever. That we may bind their trade, confine their manufactures, and exercise every power whatsoever, except that of taking their money out of their pockets without their consent.

The "Boston Massacre" as recorded by Deacon John Tudor, 1770

Relations between the citizens of Boston and the British troops stationed there had been overheated for some time. Insults were a common matter. Fights frequently broke out. In October 1769 a mob attacked a small detachment of soldiers, but no shots were fired. However, five months later, on the night of March 5, 1770, the tense situation finally culminated in bloodshed. Five citizens died, and the event stirred Americans throughout the continent. Every year thereafter, on March 5, orations were delivered in Boston to commemorate that night of terror.

On Monday evening the fifth [of March], a few minutes after 9 o'clock [P.M.], a most horrid murder was committed in King Street....

From William Tudor (ed.), *Deacon Tudor's Diary* (Boston, 1896), pp. 30–34.

This unhappy affair began by some boys and young fellows throwing snow balls at the sentry placed at the Customhouse door. On which 8 or 9 soldiers came to his assistance. Soon after a number of people collected, when the Captain [Thomas Preston] commanded the soldiers to fire, which they did and 3 men were killed on the spot and several mortally wounded, one of which died next morning. The Captain soon drew off his soldiers up to the Main Guard, or the consequences might have been terrible, for on the guns firing the people were alarmed and set the bells a ringing as if for fire, which drew multitudes to the place of action. Lieutenant-Governor Hutchinson, who was commander in chief, was sent for and came to the Council chamber, where some of the Magistrates attended. The Governor desired the multitudes about 10 o'clock to separate and go home peaceably and he would do all in his power that justice should be done, etc., the 29th regiment being then under arms on the south side of the Townhouse. But the people insisted that the soldiers should be ordered to their barracks first before they would separate, which being done the people separated about 1 o'clock. Captain Preston was taken up by a warrant given to the high sheriff by Justices [Richard] Dana and [John] Tudor and came under examination about 2 o'clock, and we sent him to jail soon after 3, having evidence sufficient to commit him, on ordering the soldiers to fire. So about 4 o'clock the town became quiet. The next forenoon the 8 soldiers that fired on the inhabitants were also sent to jail. Tuesday morning the inhabitants met at Faneuil Hall and after some pertinent speeches, chose a committee of 15 gentlemen to wait on the Lieutenant-Governor in Council to request the immediate removal of the troops. The message was in these words: that it is the unanimous opinion of the meeting that inhabitants and soldiery can no longer live together in safety; that nothing can rationally be expected to restore the peace of the town and prevent blood and carnage but the removal of the troops; and that we most fervently pray his Honor that his power and influence may be exerted for their instant removal. His Honor's reply was: Gentlemen, I am extremely sorry for the unhappy difference and especially of the last evening, and signifying that it was not in his power to remove the troops, etc.

The above reply was not satisfactory to the inhabitants, as but one regiment should be removed to the Castle Barracks. In the afternoon the town adjourned to Dr. Sewell's meetinghouse [Old South Church], for Faneuil Hall was not large enough to hold the people, there being at least 3,000, some supposed near 4,000. They chose a committee to wait on the Lieutenant-Governor to let him and the Council know that nothing less will satisfy the people than a total and immediate removal of the troops out of the town. His Honor laid before the Council the vote of the town. The Council thereon expressed themselves to be unanimously of opinion that it was absolutely necessary for his Majesty's service, the good order of the town, etc., that the troops should be immediately removed out of the town. His Honor communicated this advice of the Council to Colonel Dalrymple and desired he would order the troops down to Castle Williams.

After the Colonel had seen the vote of the Council he gave his word and honor to the town's committee that both Regiments would be removed without delay. The Committee returned to the Town Meeting and Mr. [John] Hancock, chairman of the Committee, read their report as above, which was received with a shout and clap of hands, which made the Meetinghouse ring. So the meeting was dissolved and a great number of gentlemen appeared to watch the center of the town and the prison, which continued for 11 nights and all was quiet again, as the soldiers were all moved to the Castle.

(Thursday), agreeable to a general request of the inhabitants, were followed to the grave (for they were all buried in one) in succession the 4 bodies of Misters Sam Gray, Sam Maverick, James Caldwell and Crispus Attucks, the unhappy victims who fell in the bloody Massacre. On this sorrowful occasion most of the shops and stores in town were shut; all the bells were ordered to toll a solemn peal in Boston, Charlestown, Cambridge, and Roxbury. The several hearses forming a junction in King Street, the theatre of that inhuman tragedy, proceeded from thence through the main street, lengthened by an immense concourse of people, so numerous as to be obliged to follow in ranks of 4 and 6 abreast and brought up by a long train of carriages. The sorrow visible in the countenances, together with the peculiar solemnity, surpass description. It was supposed that the spectators and those that followed the corps amounted to 15,000, some supposed 20,000.

"Declaration of Rights" of the Continental Congress, 1774

The colonial delegates to the first Continental Congress represented a wide variety of political persuasions. The conservative end of the spectrum recommended conciliation with Britain. But their plan, suggested by Joseph Galloway, was defeated (six colonies opposed, five in favor), and thereafter the radicals led by John and Samuel Adams, Patrick Henry, Christopher Gadsden, and Richard Henry Lee, exercised control of the congress.

The "Declaration of Rights" they endorsed enumerated a long list of infringements and violations of colonial rights, including the Sugar Act, Stamp Act, Quartering Act, Tea Act, Quebec Act, and all the Coercive (Intolerable) Acts. The Declaration, in effect, represented a complete repudiation of parliamentary authority over the colonies. However, to indicate their willingness to compromise, the radicals promised to accept bona fide parliamentary regulation of external commerce.

Whereas, since the close of the last war, the British parliament, claiming a power of right to bind the people of America by statute in all cases

From Worthington C. Ford (ed.), *Journals of the Continental Congress,* 1774–89 (Washington, D.C., 1904), Vol. I, pp. 63–73.

whatsoever, hath in some acts expressly imposed taxes on them, and in others, under various pretences, but in fact for the purpose of raising a revenue, hath imposed rates and duties payable in these colonies, established a board of commissioners, with unconstitutional powers, and extended the jurisdiction of courts of Admiralty, not only for collecting the said duties, but for the trial of causes merely arising within the body of a county.

And whereas, in consequence of other statutes, judges who before held only estates at will in their offices, have been made dependent on the Crown alone for their salaries; and standing armies kept in times of peace; and it has lately been resolved in Parliament that colonists may be transported to England and tried there upon accusations for treasons. . . .

And whereas in the last session of parliament three statutes were made . . . which are impolitic, unjust, and cruel, as well as unconstitutional, and most dangerous and destructive of American rights.

And whereas, Assemblies have been frequently dissolved, contrary to the rights of the people, when they attempted to deliberate on grievances; and their dutiful, humble, loyal, and reasonable petitions to the crown for redress have been repeatedly treated with contempt by his majesty's ministers of state:

The good people of the several colonies . . . justly alarmed at these arbitrary proceedings of parliament and administration, have severally elected, constituted, and appointed deputies to meet and sit in general congress, in the city of Philadelphia, in order to obtain such establishment, as that their religion, laws, and liberties may not be subverted.

Whereupon the deputies so appointed now being assembled, in a full and free representation of these colonies, taking into their most serious consideration the best means of attaining the ends aforesaid, do, in the first place, as Englishmen, declare:

That the inhabitants of the English Colonies in North America, by the immutable laws of nature, the principles of the English constitution, and the several charters or compacts, have the following Rights:

Resolved, 1. That they are entitled to life, liberty, and property, and they have never ceded to any sovereign power whatever, a right to dispose of either without their consent.

Resolved, 2. That our ancestors, who first settled these colonies, were at the time of their emigration from the mother country, entitled to all the rights, liberties and immunities of free and natural-born subjects within the realm of England.

Resolved, 3. That by such emigration they by no means forfeited, surrendered or lost any of those rights, but that they were, and their descendants now are, entitled to the exercise and enjoyment of all such of them as their local and other circumstances enable them to exercise and enjoy.

Resolved, 4. That the foundation of English liberty, and of all free government, is a right in the people to participate in their legislative council; and as the English colonists are not represented, and from their local and other circumstances cannot properly be represented in the British parliament, they are entitled to a free and exclusive power of legislation in their several provincial legislatures, where their right of representation can alone be preserved, in all cases of taxation and internal polity, subject only to the negative of their sovereign, in such manner as has been hitherto used and accustomed. But, from the necessity of the case, and a regard to the mutual interest of both countries, we cheerfully consent to the operation of such acts of the British parliament as are bona fide, restrained to the regulation of our external commerce, for the purpose of securing the commercial advantages of the whole empire to the mother country and the commercial benefits of its respective members; excluding every idea of taxation, internal or external, for raising a revenue on the subjects in America without their consent.

Resolved, 5. That the respective colonies are entitled to the common law of England, and more especially to the great and inestimable privilege of being tried by their peers of the vicinage, according to the course of that law.

Resolved, 6. That they are entitled to the benefit of such of the English statutes as existed at the time of their colonization; and which they have, by experience, respectively found to be applicable to their several local and other circumstances.

Resolved, 7. That these, his majesty's colonies, are likewise entitled to all the immunities and privileges granted and confirmed to them by royal charters, or secured by their several codes of provincial laws.

Resolved, 8. That they have a right peaceably to assemble, consider of their grievances, and petition the King; and that all prosecutions, prohibitory proclamations, and commitments for the same, are illegal.

Resolved, 9. That the keeping a standing army in these colonies, in times of peace, without the consent of the legislature of that colony, in which such army is kept, is against law.

Resolved, 10. It is indispensably necessary to good government, and rendered essential by the English constitution, that the constituent branches of the legislature be independent of each other; that, therefore, the exercise of legislative power in several colonies, by a council appointed, during pleasure, by the crown, is unconstitutional, dangerous, and destructive to the freedom of American legislation. . . .

A Tory version of the skirmishes at Lexington and Concord, 1775

The British marched on Lexington and Concord to arrest rebel leaders and to search out hidden arms. Disdainful of the colonials, they could never have anticipated the fearful rout they would experience before the long day ended. At Lexington eight Americans were killed and ten wounded. But on their return from Concord to Boston the royal troops were sniped at with devastating effect by colonial sharpshooters. All told, there were 273 British and 95 American casualties. "Whoever looks upon them as an irregular mob," a British officer commented, "will find himself mistaken."

On the 18th [of April, 1775] at eleven at night, about eight hundred grenadiers and light infantry were ferried across the bay to Cambridge, from whence they marched to Concord, about twenty miles. The [provincial] congress had been lately assembled at that place, and it was imagined that the General [Thomas Gage] had intelligence of a magazine being formed there, and that they were going to destroy it.

The people in the country (who are all furnished with arms, and have what they call minute companies in every town ready to march on any alarm) had a signal, it is supposed, by a light from one of the steeples in town, upon the troops embarking. The alarm spread through the country so that before daybreak the people in general were in arms and on their march to Concord. About daybreak a number of the people appeared before the troops at Lexington. They were called to disperse, when they fired on the troops and ran off. Upon which the light infantry pursued them and brought down about fifteen of them. The troops went on to Concord and executed the business they were sent on, and on their return found two or three of their people lying in the agonies of death, scalped, and their noses and ears cut off, and eyes bored out, which exasperated the soldiers exceedingly. A prodigious number of people now occupied the hills, woods, and stone walls along the road. The light troops drove some parties from the hills, but all the road being enclosed with stone walls, served as a cover to the rebels, from whence they fired on the troops, running off whenever they had fired but still supplied by fresh numbers who came from many parts of the country. In this manner were the troops harassed in their return for seven or eight miles. They were almost exhausted and had expended near the whole of their ammunition when to their great joy they were relieved by a brigade of troops under the command of Lord Percy, with two pieces of artillery. The troops now combated with fresh ardor, and marched in their return with undaunted

Reprinted by permission of the publishers from Ann Hulton, *Letters of a Loyalist Lady* (Cambridge, Mass.: Harvard University Press), pp. 78–80. Copyright 1927 by the President and Fellows of Harvard College; copyright 1955 by Kenneth Ballard Murdock.

countenances, receiving sheets of fire all the way for many miles, yet having no visible enemy to combat with, for they never would face them in an open field, but always skulked and fired from behind walls and trees, and out of windows of houses. But this cost them dear for the soldiers entered those dwellings and put all the men to death. Lord Percy has gained great honor by his conduct through this day of severe service. He was exposed to the hottest of the fire and animated the troops with great coolness and spirit. Several officers are wounded, and about one hundred soldiers. The killed amount to near fifty. As to the enemy, we can have no exact account, but it is said there was about ten times the number of them engaged, and that near one thousand of them have fallen.

The troops returned to Charlestown about sunset, after having some of them marched near fifty miles, and being engaged from daybreak in action, without respite or refreshment, and about ten in the evening they were brought back to Boston. The next day the country poured down its thousands, and at this time from the entrance of Boston Neck at Roxbury, round by Cambridge to Charlestown, is surrounded by at least twenty thousand men, who are raising batteries on three or four different hills. We are now cut off from all communication with the country, and many people must soon perish with famine in this place. Some families have laid in a store of provisions against a siege. We are threatened, while the outlines are attacked, with a rising of the inhabitants within [Boston]. . . . Tomorrow is Sunday, and we may hope for one day of rest. At present a solemn dead silence reigns in the streets. Numbers have packed up their effects and quitted the town, but the General has put a stop to any more removing and there remains in town about nine thousand souls (besides the servants of the crown). These are the greatest security. The General declared that if a gun is fired within the town, the inhabitants shall fall a sacrifice.

Thomas Paine advocates American independence in his pamphlet *Common Sense*, 1776

A recent immigrant, Tom Paine had been in the colonies less than two years when he wrote and anonymously published the pamphlet Common Sense *(January 1776). Its reception was phenomenal. In three months over 120,000 copies were distributed, and several times that figure were eventually sold. American hostility had previously focused upon Parliament. Paine's pamphlet turned colonial resentment against the monarchy. Written in plain and forceful prose which any layman could understand, it argued against reconciliation and convinced many to a course of revolution.*

From Moncure D. Conway (ed.), *The Writings of Thomas Paine* (New York, 1894), Vol. I, pp. 84–87, 90–91, 100–01.

The sun never shone on a cause of greater worth. 'Tis not the affair of a city, a county, a province, or a kingdom; but of a continent—of at least one eighth part of the habitable globe. 'Tis not the concern of a day, a year, or an age; posterity are virtually involved in the contest, and will be more or less affected ever to the end of time, by the proceedings now. Now is the seed-time of continental union, faith and honor. The least fracture now will be like a name engraved with the point of a pin on the tender rind of a young oak; the wound would enlarge with the tree, and posterity read it in full grown characters.

By referring the matter from argument to arms, a new era for politics is struck—a new method of thinking has arisen. All plans, proposals, etc., prior to the nineteenth of April, i.e., to the commencement of hostilities, are like the almanacs of the last year; which though proper then, are superceded and useless now. Whatever was advanced by the advocates on either side of the question then, terminated in one and the same point, viz. a union with Great Britain; the only difference between the parties was the method of effecting it; the one proposing force, the other friendship; but it has so far happened that the first has failed, and the second has withdrawn her influence.

As much has been said of the advantages of reconciliation, which, like an agreeable dream, has passed away and left us as we were, it is but right that we should examine the contrary side of the argument, and inquire into some of the many material injuries which these colonies sustain, and always will sustain, by being connected with and dependent on Great Britain: to examine that connection and dependence, on the principles of nature and common sense; to see what we have to trust to, if separated, and what we are to expect, if dependent.

I have heard it asserted by some, that as America has flourished under her former connection with Great Britain, the same connection is necessary towards her future happiness, and will always have the same effect. Nothing can be more fallacious than this kind of argument. We may as well assert that because a child has thrived upon milk, that it is never to have meat, or that the first twenty years of our lives is to become a precedent for the next twenty. But even this is admitting more than is true; for I answer roundly, that America would have flourished as much, and probably much more, had no European power taken any notice of her. The commerce by which she hath enriched herself are the necessaries of life, and will always have a market while eating is the custom of Europe.

But she has protected us, say some. That she hath engrossed us is true, and defended the continent at our expense as well as her own, is admitted; and she would have defended Turkey from the same motive, viz. for the sake of trade and dominion.

Alas! we have been long led away by ancient prejudices and made large sacrifices to superstition. We have boasted the protection of Great Britain, without considering, that her motive was *interest* not *attachment;*

and that she did not protect us from *our enemies* on *our account;* but from *her enemies* on *her own account,* from those who had no quarrel with us on any *other account,* and who will always be our enemies on the *same account.* Let Britain waive her pretensions to the continent, or the continent throw off the dependence, and we should be at peace with France and Spain, were they at war with Britain. The miseries of Hanover's last war ought to warn us against connections. . . .

But Britain is the parent country, say some. Then the more shame upon her conduct. Even brutes do not devour their young, nor savages make war upon their families; wherefore, the assertion, if true, turns to her reproach; but it happens not to be true, or only partly so, and the phrase *parent* or *mother country* hath been jesuitically adopted by the king and his parasites, with a low papistical design of gaining an unfair bias on the credulous weakness of our minds. Europe, and not England, is the parent country of America. This new world hath been the asylum for the persecuted lovers of civil and religious liberty from *every part* of Europe. Hither have they fled, not from the tender embraces of the mother, but from the cruelty of the monster; and it is so far true of England, that the same tyranny which drove the first emigrants from home, pursues their descendants still. . . .

I challenge the warmest advocate for reconciliation to show a single advantage that this continent can reap by being connected with Great Britain. I repeat the challenge; not a single advantage is derived. Our corn will fetch its price in any market in Europe, and our imported goods must be paid for, buy them where we will.

But the injuries and disadvantages which we sustain by that connection are without number; and our duty to mankind at large, as well as to ourselves, instruct us to renounce the alliance: because, any submission to, or dependence on Great Britain, tends directly to involve this continent in European wars and quarrels, and set us at variance with nations who would otherwise seek our friendship, and against whom we have neither anger nor complaint. As Europe is our market for trade, we ought to form no partial connection with any part of it. It is the true interest of America to steer clear of European contentions, which she never can do, while, by her dependence on Britain, she is made the make-weight in the scale of British politics.

Europe is too thickly planted with kingdoms to be long at peace, and whenever a war breaks out between England and any foreign power, the trade of America goes to ruin, *because of her connection with Britain.* The next war may not turn out like the last, and should it not, the advocates for reconciliation now will be wishing for separation then, because neutrality in that case would be a safer convoy than a man of war. Every thing that is right or reasonable pleads for separation. The blood of the slain, the weeping voice of nature cries, 'TIS TIME TO PART. Even the distance at which the Almighty hath placed England and America is a strong and natural proof that the authority of the one over the other, was never the design of heaven. . . .

Men of passive tempers look somewhat lightly over the offences of Great Britain, and, still hoping for the best, are apt to call out, *Come, come, we shall be friends again for all this.* But examine the passions and feelings of mankind: bring the doctrine of reconciliation to the touchstone of nature, and then tell me whether you can hereafter love, honor, and faithfully serve the power that hath carried fire and sword into your land? If you cannot do all these, then are you only deceiving yourselves, and by your delay bringing ruin upon posterity. Your future connection with Britain, whom you can neither love nor honor, will be forced and unnatural, and being formed only on the plan of present convenience, will in a little time fall into relapse more wretched than the first. But if you say, you can still pass the violations over, then I ask, hath your house been burnt? Hath your property been destroyed before your face? Are your wife and children destitute of a bed to lie on, or bread to live on? Have you lost a parent or a child by their hands, and yourself the ruined and wretched survivor? If you have not, then you are not a judge of those who have. But if you have, and can still shake hands with the murderers, then you are unworthy the name of husband, father, friend, or lover, and whatever may be your rank or title in life, you have the heart of a coward, and the spirit of a sycophant. . . .

Ye that tell us of harmony and reconciliation, can ye restore to us the time that is past? Can ye give to prostitution its former innocence? Neither can ye reconcile Britain and America. The last cord now is broken; the people of England are presenting addresses against us. There are injuries which nature cannot forgive; she would cease to be nature if she did. As well can the lover forgive the ravisher of his mistress, as the continent forgive the murders of Britain. The Almighty hath implanted in us these inextinguishable feelings for good and wise purposes. They are the guardians of his image in our hearts. They distinguish us from the herd of common animals. The social compact would dissolve, and justice be extirpated from the earth, or have only a casual existence, were we callous to the touches of affection. The robber and the murderer would often escape unpunished, did not the injuries which our tempers sustain, provoke us into justice.

O! ye that love mankind! Ye that dare oppose not only the tyranny but the tyrant, stand forth! Every spot of the old world is overrun with oppression. Freedom hath been hunted round the globe. Asia and Africa have long expelled her. Europe regards her like a stranger, and England hath given her warning to depart. O! receive the fugitive, and prepare in time an asylum for mankind.

Two American ministers defend the loyalist cause, 1777

Church leaders, like other Americans, divided over the issue of rebellion. Generally, however, Congregational and Presbyterian ministers sided with the rebels. As early as 1750, for example, Reverend Jonathan Mayhew of Boston, in his "Discourse on Unlimited Submission," stated: "Britons will not be slaves." And Reverend John Witherspoon, president of the College of New Jersey (Princeton University), signed the Declaration of Independence.

Quaker leaders, Anglican ministers, and German pastors, on the other hand, tended to take the loyalist side. Presented below are two selections by Anglican ministers.

EXTRACT FROM A SERMON BY THE REVEREND CHARLES INGLIS TO LOYALIST TROOPS IN NEW YORK, SEPTEMBER 1777

Never, I will boldly and without hesitation pronounce it, never was a more just, more honorable or necessary cause for taking up arms than that which now calls you into the field. It is the cause of truth against falsehood, of loyalty against rebellion, of legal government against usurpation, of constitutional freedom against tyranny—in short, it is the cause of human happiness of millions against outrage and oppression. Your generous efforts are required to assert the rights of your amiable, injured sovereign. They are required to restore your civil constitution which was formed by the wisdom of the ages, and was the admiration and envy of mankind— under which we and our ancestors enjoyed liberty, happiness and security —but is now subverted to make room for a motley fabric that is perfectly adapted to popular tyranny. Your bleeding country, through which destitution and ruin are driving in full career, from which peace, order, commerce, and useful industry are banished—your loyal friends and relations groaning in bondage under the iron scourge of persecution and oppression —all these now call upon you for succour and redress.

It is not wild, insatiable ambition which sports with lives and fortunes of mankind that leads you forth, driven from your peaceful habitations for no other cause than honoring your King, as God hath commanded; you have taken up the sword to vindicate his just authority, to support your excellent constitution, to defend your families, your liberty, and property, to secure to yourselves and your posterity that inheritance of constitutional freedom to which you were born; and all this against the violence of usurped power, which would deny you even the right of judgment or of choice, which would rend from you the protection of your parent state, and eventually place you—astonishing infatuation and madness—place

From John W. Lydekker, *The Life and Letters of Charles Inglis* (London, 1936), p. 257. Reprinted by permission of the Society for Promoting Christian Knowledge.

you under the despotic rule of our inveterate Popish enemies, the inveterate enemies of our religion, our country and our liberties.

EXTRACT FROM A LETTER BY THE REVEREND JACOB DUCHÉ TO GEORGE WASHINGTON, OCTOBER 1777

Dear Sir, suffer me in the language of truth and real affection, to address myself to you. All the world must be convinced you are engaged in the service of your country from motives perfectly disinterested. You risked everything that was dear to you, abandoned the sweets of domestic life, which your affluent fortune can give the uninterrupted enjoyment of. But had you, could you have had, the least idea of matters being carried to such a dangerous extremity? Your most intimate friends shuddered at the thought of a separation from the mother country, and I took it for granted that your sentiments coincided with theirs. What, then, can be the consequence of this rash and violent measure? The most respectable characters have withdrawn themselves, and are succeeded by a great majority of illiberal and violent men. Take an impartial view of the present [Continental] Congress, and what can you expect from them? . . . From the New England provinces can you find one that, as a gentleman, you could wish to associate with? Are the dregs of Congress, then, still to influence a mind like yours? These are not the men you engaged to serve; these are not the men that America has chosen to represent her. Most of them were chosen by a little low faction, and the few gentlemen that are among them are well known to lie on the balance, and looking up to your hand alone to turn the beam. 'Tis you, Sir, and you only, that support the present Congress; of this you must be fully sensible. . . .

After this view of the Congress, turn to the army. The whole world knows that its existence depends upon you; that your death or captivity disperses it in a moment, and that there is not a man on that [revolutionary] side [of] the question, in America, capable of succeeding you. As to the army itself, what have you to expect from them? Have they not frequently abandoned you yourself, in the hour of extremity? Can you have the least confidence in a set of undisciplined men and officers, many of whom have been taken from the lowest of people, without principle, without courage? Take away them that surround your person, how very few are there that you can ask to sit at your table! As to your little navy, of that little, what is left? . . .

And now, where are your resources? Oh! My dear Sir, how sadly have you been abused by a faction devoid of truth, and void of tenderness to you and your country! They have amused you with hopes of a declaration of war on the part of France. Believe me, from the best authority, it

From Jared Sparks (ed.), *Correspondence of the American Revolution* (Boston, 1853), Vol. I, pp. 451–57.

was a fiction from the first. . . . From your friends in England you have nothing to expect. Their numbers have diminished to a cipher; the spirit of the whole nation is inactivity; a few sounding names among the nobility, though perpetually ringing in your ears, are without character, without influence. Disappointed ambition has made them desperate, and they only wish to make the deluded Americans instruments of revenge. . . .

How unequal the contest! How fruitless the expense of blood! Under so many discouraging circumstances, can virtue, can honor, can the love of your country, prompt you to proceed? Humanity itself, and surely humanity is no stranger to your breast, calls upon you to desist. Your army must perish for want of common necessaries, or thousands of innocent families must perish to support them; wherever they encamp, the country must be impoverished; wherever they march, the troops of Britain will pursue, and must complete the destruction which America herself has begun. Perhaps, it may be said, it is better to die than to be made slaves. This, indeed, is a splendid maxim in theory, and perhaps, in some instances, may be found experimentally true; but when there is the least probability of a happy accommodation, surely wisdom and humanity call for some sacrifices to be made, to prevent inevitable destruction. . . .

Oh! Sir, let no false ideas of worldly honor deter you from engaging in so glorious a task [i.e., giving up the revolution]. Whatever censure may be thrown out by mean, illiberal minds, your character will rise in the estimation of the virtuous and noble. It will appear with lustre in the annals of history, and form a glorious contrast to that of those who have fought to obtain conquest, and gratify their own ambition by the destruction of their species and the ruin of their country.

Excerpts from the General Orders and Farewell Orders of George Washington to the Army, 1775–83

Stirring the colonials to revolution was an easier task than sustaining their military effort for eight years. This was the supreme accomplishment of George Washington. When officers quarreled over rank and honors; when state governments were tardy and remiss in supplying food, clothing, and troop quotas; when men deserted; when currency became hopelessly inflated—Washington, though subject to occasional doubts and despair—persevered in the revolutionary cause.

These excerpts from his Orders to the Army show that while Washington worried over the larger issues of military battles, patriotism, independence, and the success of federal union, he was also concerned with more trivial subjects such as gambling, profanity, and soldiers swimming in the nude.

From John C. Fitzpatrick (ed.), *The Writings of George Washington* (Washington, D.C., 1931–44), Vol. III, pp. 340–41, 440; Vol. V, pp. 211–12, 337; Vol. VII, p. 46; Vol. VIII, pp. 28–29, 152–53, Vol. IX, pp. 178–79; Vol. XI, pp. 8–10; Vol. XX, p. 95; Vol. XXVII, pp. 223–27.

July 15, 1775

Notwithstanding the orders already given, the General hears with astonishment, that not only Soldiers, but Officers unauthorized are continually conversing with the Officers and Sentrys of the enemy; any Officer, Non-Commissioned Officer or Soldier, or any person whatsoever, who is detected holding any conversation, or carrying on any correspondence with any of the Officers or Sentrys of the advanced posts of the enemy, will be immediately brought before a General Court Martial, and punished with the utmost severity.

August 22, 1775

The General does not mean to discourage the practice of bathing whilst the weather is warm enough to continue it, but he expressly forbids any persons doing it at or near the bridge in Cambridge, where it has been observed and complained that many men, lost to all sense of decency and common modesty, are running about naked upon the bridge, whilst passengers, and even ladies of the first fashion in the neighborhood, are passing over it, as if they meant to glory in their shame.

July 2, 1776

The fate of unborn millions will now depend, under God, on the courage and conduct of this army. Our cruel and unrelenting enemy leaves us no choice but a brave resistance or the most abject submission. This is all we can expect. We have therefore to resolve to conquer or die. Our own country's honor, all call upon us for a vigorous and manly exertion, and if we now shamefully fall, we shall become infamous to the whole world. Let us therefore rely upon the goodness of the cause, and the side of the supreme Being, in whose hands victory is, to animate and encourage us to great and noble actions. The eyes of all our countrymen are now upon us, and we shall have their blessings, and praises, if happily we are the instruments of saving them from the tyranny meditated against them. Let us . . . show the world that a free man contending for LIBERTY on his own ground is superior to any slavish mercenary on earth.

July 25, 1776

It is with inexpressible concern, the General sees soldiers fighting in the cause of liberty and their country, committing crimes most destructive to the army, and which in all other armies are punished with death. What a shame and reproach will it be if [British] soldiers fighting to enslave us, for two pence, or three pence a day, should be more regular, watchful and sober, than men who are contending for everything that is dear and valuable in life.

January 21, 1777

The General is very sorry to find that the late order allowing . . . plunder . . . has been so mistaken by some and abused by others. This indulgence was granted to scouting parties only, as a reward for extraordinary fatigues, hardship, and danger they were exposed to upon those parties. The General never meant, nor had any idea, that any of our own or enemy's stores, found at any evacuated post, were to be considered as the property of those that first marched in.

May 8, 1777

As few vices are attended with more pernicious consequences in civil life, so there are none more fatal in a military one than that of GAM[BL]ING, which often brings disgrace and ruin upon officers, and injury and punishment upon the soldiery. And reports prevailing, which, it is to be feared are too well founded, that this destructive vice has spread its baneful influence in the army, and, in a peculiar manner, to the prejudice of the recruiting service—The Commander in Chief, in the most pointed and explicit terms, forbids ALL officers and soldiers, playing at cards, dice, or at any games, except those of EXERCISE, for diversion; it being impossible, if the practice be allowed at all, to discriminate between innocent play for amusement, and criminal gam[bl]ing for pecuniary and sordid purposes.

May 31, 1777

It is much to be lamented that the foolish and scandalous practice of *profane swearing* is exceedingly prevalent in the American army. Officers of every rank are bound to discourage it, first by their example, and then by punishing offenders. As a means to abolish this, and every other species of immorality, Brigadiers are enjoined to take effectual care to have divine service duly performed in their respective brigades.

September 4, 1777

Notwithstanding all the cautions, the earnest requests, and the positive orders of the Commander in Chief, to prevent *our own army* from plundering *our own friends* and *fellow citizens*, yet to his astonishment and grief, fresh complaints are made to him that so wicked, infamous and cruel a practice is still continued, and that too in circumstances most distressing: where the wretched inhabitants, dreading the enemy's vengeance for their adherence to our cause, have left all, and fled to us for refuge! We complain of the cruelty and barbarity of our enemies; but does it equal ours? They sometimes spare the property of their *friends*. But some amongst us, beyond expression barbarous, rob even *them!* Why did we assemble in arms? Was it not, in one capital point, to protect the property of our countrymen? And shall we to our eternal reproach, be the first to pillage and destroy? Will no motives of humanity, of zeal, interest and of honor, restrain the violence of the soldiers, or induce officers to keep so strict a watch over the ill-disposed, as effectually to prevent the execution of their evil designs and the gratification of their savage inclinations? Or if these powerful motives are too weak, will they pay no regard to their own safety? How many noble designs have miscarried, how many victories have been lost, how many armies ruined, by an indulgence of soldiers in plundering?

March 1, 1778

The Commander in Chief again takes occasion to return his warmest thanks to the virtuous officers and soldiery of this army for that persevering fidelity and zeal which they have uniformly manifested in all their conduct. Their fortitude not only under common hardships incident to a military life, but also under the additional sufferings to which the peculiar situation of these States have exposed them, clearly proves them worth the enviable privilege of contending for the rights of human nature, the *freedom and independence* of their country. The recent instance [at Valley Forge] of uncomplaining patience during the scarcity of provisions in camp is fresh proof that they possess in an eminent degree the spirit of soldiers and the magnanimity of patriots. The few refractory individuals who disgrace themselves by murmurs it is to be hoped have repented such unmanly behavior, and resolved to emulate the noble example of their associates upon every trial which the customary casualties of war may hereafter throw in their way.... Surely we who are free citizens in arms engaged in a struggle for everything valuable in society and partaking in the glorious task of laying the foundation of an *Empire,* should scorn effeminately to shrink under these accidents and rigors of war which mercenary hirelings fighting in the cause of lawless ambition, rapine and devastation, encounter with cheerfulness and alacrity. We should not be merely equal, we should be superior to them in every qualification that dignifies the man or the soldier in proportion as the motive from which we act and the final hopes of our toils are superior to theirs.

September 26, 1780

Treason of the blackest dye was yesterday discovered! General Arnold who commanded at West Point, lost to every sentiment of honor, or public and private obligation, was about to deliver up that important post into the hands of the enemy. Such an event must have given the American cause a deadly wound if not a fatal stab. Happily the treason has been timely discovered to prevent the fatal misfortune. The providential train of circumstances which led to it affords the most convincing proof that the liberties of America are the object of divine protection.

At the same time that the treason is to be regretted the General cannot help congratulating the Army on the happy discovery. Our enemies, despairing of carrying their point by force, are practicing every base art to effect by bribery and corruption what they cannot accomplish in a manly way.

Great honor is due to the American Army that this is the first instance of treason of the kind, where many were to be expected from the nature of the dispute, and nothing is so bright an ornament in the character of the American soldiers as their having been proof against all the arts and seduction of an insidious enemy.

Farewell Orders to the Armies of the United States   November 2, 1783

Every American officer and soldier must now console himself for any unpleasant circumstances which may have occurred by a recollection of the uncommon scenes in which he has been called to act no inglorious part, and the astonishing events of which he has been a witness, events which have seldom if ever before taken place on the stage of human action, nor can they probably ever happen again. For who has before seen a disciplined Army formed at once from such raw materials? Who, that was not a witness, could imagine that the most violent local prejudices would cease so soon, and that men who came from the different parts of the continent, strongly disposed, by the habits of education, to despise and quarrel with each other, would instantly become but one patriotic band of brothers; or who, that was not on the spot, can trace the steps by which such a wonderful revolution has been effected, and such a glorious period put to all our warlike toils?

It is universally acknowledged that the enlarged prospects of happiness, opened by the confirmation of our independence and sovereignty, almost exceeds the power of description. And shall not the brave men, who have contributed so essentially to these inestimable acquisitions, retiring victorious from the field of war to the field of agriculture, participate in all the blessings which have been obtained; in such a republic, who will exclude them from the rights of citizens and the fruits of their labor? In such a country, so happily circumstanced, the pursuits of commerce and the cultivation of the soil will unfold to industry the certain road to competence. To those hardy soldiers, who are actuated by the spirit of adventure, the fisheries will afford ample and profitable employment, and the extensive and fertile regions of the west will yield a most happy asylum to those, who, fond of domestic enjoyments, are seeking for personal independence. Nor is it possible to conceive that any one of the United States will prefer a national bankruptcy and a dissolution of the union, to a compliance with the requisitions of Congress and the payment of its just debts; so that the officers and soldiers may expect considerable assistance in recommencing their civil occupations from the sums due to them from the public which must and will most inevitably be paid.

In order to effect this desirable purpose and to remove the prejudices which may have taken possession of the minds of any of the good people of the States, it is earnestly recommended to all the troops that with strong attachments to the Union, they should carry with them into civil society the most conciliating dispositions; and that they should prove themselves not less virtuous and useful as citizens than they have been persevering and victorious as soldiers. Tho there should be some envious individuals who are unwilling to pay the debt the public has contracted, or to yield the tribute due to merit; yet, let such unworthy treatment produce no invective or any instance of intemperate conduct; let it be remembered that the unbiased voice of the free citizens of the United States has promised the just reward, and given the merited applause; let it be known and remembered, that the reputation of the federal Armies is established beyond the reach of malevolence; and let a consciousness of their achievements and fame still incite the men, who composed them, to honorable actions, under the persuasion that the private virtues of economy, prudence, and industry, will not be less amiable in civil life than the more splendid qualities of valor, perseverance, and enterprise were in the field. Every one may rest assured that much, very much of the future happiness of the officers and men will depend upon the wise and manly conduct which shall be adopted by them when they are mingled with the great body of the community. The General has frequently given it as his opinion, in the most public and explicit manner, that, unless the principles of the federal government were properly supported and the powers of the union increased, the honor, dignity, and justice of the nation would be lost forever. Yet he cannot help repeating on this occasion so interesting a sentiment, and leaving it as his last injunction to every officer and every soldier who may view the subject in the same serious point of light, to add his best endeavors to those of his worthy fellow citizens towards effecting these great and valuable purposes on which our very existence as a nation so materially depends.

Benjamin Franklin's "Information to those who would remove to America," 1784

The United States was the first revolutionary country to win independence; the first modern nation to reject monarchy; the first to predicate her government on the equality of mankind. The new nation also proffered to newcomers what the old world never could: an opportunity for economic advancement. In America, Franklin informed prospective emigrants, the laws were equitable, the land was cheap, and social distinctions were minimal. "Strangers are welcome," wrote Franklin, who are willing and able to work. Industry was rewarded and even sanctified as idleness was condemned. "The people have a saying," Franklin noted, "that God Almighty is himself a mechanic, the greatest in the universe; and he is respected and admired more for the variety, ingenuity, and utility of his handiworks than for the antiquity of his family."

Many persons in Europe, having directly or by letters, expressed to the writer, who is well acquainted with North America, their desire of transporting and establishing themselves in that country; but who appear to have formed, through ignorance, mistaken ideas and expectations of what is to be obtained there; he thinks it may be useful, and prevent inconvenient, expensive, and fruitless removals and voyages of improper persons, if he gives some clearer and truer notions of that part of the world, than appear to have hitherto prevailed.

He finds it is imagined by numbers, that the inhabitants of North America are rich, capable of rewarding, and disposed to reward, all sorts of ingenuity; that they are at the same time ignorant of all the sciences, and, consequently, that strangers, possessing talents in the belles-lettres, fine arts, etc., must be highly esteemed, and so well paid, as to become easily rich themselves; that there are also abundance of profitable offices to be disposed of, which the natives are not qualified to fill; and that having few persons of family among them, strangers of birth must be greatly respected, and of course easily obtain the best of those offices, which will make all their fortunes; that the governments too, to encourage emigration from Europe, not only pay the expense of personal transportation, but give land gratis to strangers, with Negroes to work for them, utensils of husbandry, and stocks of cattle. These are all wild imaginations; and those who go to America with expectations founded upon them, will surely find themselves disappointed.

The truth is, that though there are in that country few people so miserable as the poor of Europe, there are also very few that in Europe would be called rich; it is rather a general happy mediocrity that prevails. There are few great proprietors of the soil, and few tenants; most people cultivate

From Jared Sparks (ed.), *The Works of Benjamin Franklin* (Boston, 1836), Vol. II, pp. 467–77.

their own lands, or follow some handicraft or merchandise; very few rich enough to live idly upon their rents or incomes, or to pay the highest prices given in Europe for painting, statues, architecture, and the other works of art, that are more curious than useful. Hence the natural geniuses that have arisen in America with such talents have uniformly quitted that country for Europe, where they can be more suitably rewarded. It is true that letters and mathematical knowledge are in esteem there, but they are at the same time more common than is apprehended; there being already existing nine colleges or universities, viz. four in New England, and one in each of the provinces of New York, New Jersey, Pennsylvania, Maryland, and Virginia, all furnished with learned professors; besides a number of smaller academies; these educate many of their youth in the languages, and those sciences that qualify men for the professions of divinity, law, or physic. Strangers are by no means excluded from exercising these professions; and the quick increase of inhabitants everywhere gives them a chance of employ[ment], which they have in common with the natives. Of civil offices, or employments, there are few; no superfluous ones, as in Europe; and it is a rule established in some of the States, that no office should be so profitable as to make it desirable. . . .

These ideas prevailing more or less in all the United States, it cannot be worth any man's while, who has a means of living at home, to expatriate himself in hopes of obtaining a profitable civil office in America; and, as to military offices, they are at an end with the war, the armies being disbanded. Much less is it advisable for a person to go thither who has no other quality to recommend him but his birth. In Europe it has indeed its value; but it is a commodity that cannot be carried to a worse market than that of America, where people do not inquire concerning a stranger, *What is he?* but, *What can he do?* If he has any useful art, he is welcome; and if he exercises it, and behaves well, he will be respected by all who know him; but a mere man of quality, who, on that account, wants to live upon the public by some office or salary, will be despised and disregarded. The husbandman is in honor there, and even the mechanic, because their employments are useful. The people have a saying, that God Almighty is himself a mechanic, the greatest in the universe; and he is respected and admired more for the variety, ingenuity, and utility of his handiworks than for the antiquity of his family. They are pleased with the observation of a Negro, and frequently mention it, that *Boccarora* (meaning the white man) *make de black man workee, make de horse workee, make de ox workee, make ebery ting workee; only de hog. He, de hog, no workee; he eat, he drink, he walk about, he go to sleep when he please, he live like a gempleman.* According to these opinions of the Americans, one of them would think himself more obliged to a genealogist, who could prove for him that his ancestors and relations for ten generations had been ploughmen, smiths, carpenters, turners, weavers, tanners, or even shoemakers, and consequently that they were useful members of society; than if he could only prove that they were gentlemen, doing nothing of value, but living

idly on the labor of others, mere *fruges consumere nati,* (. . . born merely
to eat up the corn) and otherwise *good for nothing,* till by their death their
estates, like the carcass of the Negro's gentleman-hog, come to be *cut up. . . .*

The almost general mediocrity of fortune that prevails in America
obliging its people to follow some business for subsistence, those vices that
arise usually from idleness are in a great measure prevented. Industry and
constant employment are great preservatives of the morals and virtue of a
nation. Hence bad examples to youth are more rare in America, which
must be a comfortable consideration to parents. To this may be truly added,
that serious religion, under its various denominations, is not only tolerated,
but respected and practised. Atheism is unknown there; infidelity rare and
secret; so that persons may live to a great age in that country, without having their piety shocked by meeting with either an atheist or an infidel. And
the Divine Being seems to have manifested his approbation of the mutual
forbearance and kindness with which the different sects treat each other,
by the remarkable prosperity with which He has been pleased to favor the
whole country.

Shays' Rebellion: Henry Knox sounds the alarm in a letter to George Washington, October 1786

*Henry Knox, according to one scholar, reacted to news of the uprising in west-
ern Massachusetts "with the poise of an old maid who has heard a burglar." His
letters—of which the following is but one example—indicated that a full-scale
rebellion was under way, consisting of twelve to fifteen thousand well-armed
and well-disciplined men, whose real aim was to hang every creditor. Such was
hardly the case. Ezra Stiles of Connecticut warned George Washington that the
rebellion was "doubtless magnified at a distance."*

*Yet Washington chose to believe Knox, as did many others. The tale grew
with the telling, men of property everywhere became frightened, and the net
result was salutary: state after state, previously reluctant to participate in the
Philadelphia convention, decided to send delegates.*

On the first impression of faction and licentiousness the fine theoretic
government of Massachusetts has given way, and its laws arrested and
trampled under foot. . . . High taxes are the ostensible cause of the commotions, but that they are the true cause is as far remote from truth as light
from darkness. The people who are the insurgents have never paid any or
but very little taxes. But they see the weakness of government. They feel at
once [the lack of] their own property, compared with the opulent, and
their own force, and they are determined to make use of the latter in order
to remedy the former. Their creed is, "that the property of the United

Henry Knox to George Washington, October 23, 1786, Washington Papers, Library
of Congress.

States has been protected from the confiscations of Britain by the joint exertions of all, and therefore ought to be the common property of all, and he that attempts opposition to this creed is an enemy to equity and justice, and ought to be swept from off the face of the earth." In a word, they are determined to annihilate all debts public and private, and have agrarian laws which are easily effected by the means of unfunded paper money, which shall be a tender in all cases whatever.

The numbers of these people may amount in mass actually to about one-fifth part of [the inhabitants in] populous counties, and to them may be collected people of similar sentiments from the states of Rhode Island, Connecticut and New Hampshire, so as to constitute a body of 12 or 15,000 desperate and unprincipled men. They are chiefly of the young and active part of the community, more easily collected than perhaps kept together afterward. But they will probably commit overt acts of terror which will compel them to embody for their own safety. . . . Having proceeded to this length for which they are now ripe, we shall have a formidable rebellion against reason, the principle of all government, and the very name of liberty. This dreadful situation has alarmed every man of principle and property in New England. They start as from a dream, and ask what has been the cause of our delusion? What is to give us security against the violence of lawless men? Our government must be braced, changed or altered to secure our lives and property. We imagined that the mildness of our government and the virtue of the people were so correspondent that we were not as other nations, requiring force to support the laws. But we find that we are men, actual men, possessing all the turbulent passions belonging to that animal, and that we must have a government proper and adequate for him. The people of Massachusetts, for instance, are far advanced in this doctrine, and the men of reflection, of principle, are determined to endeavor to establish a government which shall have the power to protect them in their lawful pursuits, and which shall be efficient in case of internal commotions or foreign invasions. They mean that liberty shall be the basis, a liberty resulting from the equal and firm administration of the laws. They wish for a general government of unity as they see the local legislatures must naturally and necessarily tend to retard and frustrate all general government.

We have arrived at that point of time in which we are forced to see our national humiliation, and that a progression in this line cannot be productive of happiness, either public or private. Something is ·vanting, and something must be done or we shall be involved in the horror of faction and civil war without a prospect of its termination. Every tried friend to the liberty of his country is bound to reflect, and to step forward to prevent the dreadful consequences which will result from a government of events. Unless this is done we shall be liable to be ruled by an arbitrary . . . armed tyranny, whose want and will must be law.

Shays' Rebellion: the reaction of Thomas Jefferson, January–February 1787

Jefferson, residing in Paris, refused to be alarmed by reports of the insurgency in Massachusetts. Shays' rebellion led him to philosophize upon rebellion in general. The one in Massachusetts was "absolutely unjustified," he believed, as would be the case where governments were honest and representative, where elections were free and frequent, and where the public were educated and well informed by the press. But rebellions were also valuable—he likened them to a "storm in the atmosphere"—even in a republic, and he hoped the authorities would treat the rebels with leniency.

To Edward Carrington   January 16, 1787

The tumults in America, I expected would have produced in Europe an unfavorable opinion of our political state. But it has not. On the contrary, the small effect of these tumults seems to have given more confidence in the firmness of our governments. . . .

I am persuaded myself that the good sense of the people will always be found to be the best army. They may be led astray for a moment, but will soon correct themselves. The people are the only censors of their governors; and even their errors will tend to keep these to the true principles of their institution. To punish these errors too severely would be to suppress the only safeguard of the public liberty. The way to prevent these irregular interpositions of the people is to give them full information of their affairs through the channel of the public papers, and to contrive that those papers should penetrate the whole mass of the people. The basis of our governments being the opinion of the people, the very first object should be to keep that right; and were it left to me to decide whether we should have a government without newspapers or newspapers without a government, I should not hesitate a moment to prefer the latter. But I should mean that every man should receive those papers and be capable of reading them.

To James Madison   January 30, 1787

I am impatient to learn your sentiments on the late troubles in the eastern states. So far as I have yet seen, they do not appear to threaten serious consequences. Those states have suffered by the stoppage of the channels of their commerce, which have not yet found other issues. This must render money scarce, and make the people uneasy. This uneasiness

From Paul L. Ford (ed.) *The Works of Thomas Jefferson* (New York, 1904–5), Vol. V, pp. 252–53, 254–56, 263.

has produced acts absolutely unjustifiable; but I hope they will provoke no severities from their governments. A consciousness of those in power that their administration of the public affairs has been honest, may perhaps produce too great a degree of indignation; and those characters wherein fear predominates over hope, may apprehend too much from these instances of irregularity. They may conclude too hastily that nature has formed man insusceptible of any other government but that of force, a conclusion not founded in truth nor experience. Societies exist under three forms sufficiently distinguishable. 1. Without government, as among our Indians. 2. Under governments wherein the will of everyone has a just influence, as is the case in England in a slight degree, and in our states in a great one. 3. Under governments of force: as is the case in all other monarchies and in most of the other republics. To have an idea of the curse of existence under these last, they must be seen. It is a government of wolves over sheep. It is a problem, not clear in my mind, that the first condition is not the best. But I believe it to be inconsistent with any great degree of population. The second state has a great deal of good in it. The mass of mankind under that enjoys a precious degree of liberty and happiness. It has its evils too: the principal of which is the turbulence to which it is subject. But weigh this against the oppressions of monarchy, and it becomes nothing. *Malo periculosam libertatem quam quietam servitutem.* [I prefer perilous liberty to quiet servitude]. Even this evil is productive of good. It prevents the degeneracy of government, and nourishes a general attention to public affairs. I hold it that a little rebellion now and then is a good thing, and as necessary in the political world as storms in the physical. Unsuccessful rebellions indeed generally establish the encroachments on the rights of the people which have produced them. An observation of this truth should render honest republican governors so mild in their punishment of rebellions as not to discourage them too much. It is a medicine necessary for the sound health of government.

To Abigail Adams   February 22, 1787

The spirit of resistance to government is so valuable on certain occasions, that I wish it to be always kept alive. It will often be exercised when wrong, but better so than not to be exercised at all. I like a little rebellion now and then. It is like a storm in the atmosphere.

An American Jew writes to the federal convention on the issue of religious equality: letter from Jonas Phillips, September 7, 1787

The meaning of the following letter from Jonas Phillips, a Jewish resident of Philadelphia, is plain enough: the constitution of his state, Pennsylvania, was contradictory—affording religious toleration to all in one section, but denying it in another section which required a religious oath Phillips could not take. The letter asks the convention delegates, then preparing the federal Constitution, to remove such inequities.

In fact, the founding fathers had already decided to do what Phillips had requested. The Constitution of the United States guaranteed freedom of religion, provided for the separation of church and state, and specifically stated that "no religious test shall ever be required as a qualification to any office or public trust under the United States." Unfortunately, state laws did not have to conform to national law, and many states maintained discriminatory codes well into the nineteenth century. New York State, as early 1777, and Virginia by its famous "Act for Establishing Religious Freedom" passed in 1786, were the first to remove political inequalities based on religion. Within the next half-dozen years four other states—Georgia, Pennsylvania, South Carolina, and Delaware—did the same. In Massachusetts, on the other hand, the legal stipulation that all elected officials had to declare a belief in Christianity was kept until 1821. Rhode Island maintained its system of political preference for Christians only until 1842; and New Hampshire, until 1876.

Sires: With leave and submission I address myself to those in whom there is wisdom, understanding and knowledge. They are the honorable personages appointed and made overseers of a part of the terrestrial globe of the earth, namely the 13 United States of America, in convention assembled, the Lord preserve them amen.

I, the subscriber, being one of the people called Jews, of the city of Philadelphia, a people scattered and dispersed among all nations, do behold with concern that among the laws in the Constitution of Pennsylvania, there is a clause, Section 10, to wit—'I do believe in one God, the Creator and governor of the Universe and Rewarder of the good and punisher of the wicked; and I do acknowledge the Scriptures of the Old and New Testament to be given by divine inspiration.' To swear and believe that the New Testament was given by divine inspiration is absolutely against the religious principles of a Jew, and is against his conscience to take any such oath. By the above law a Jew is deprived of holding any public office, or place of government, which is contradictory to the bill of rights [of Pennsylvania], Section 2—'That all men have a natural and unalienable right to

From Herbert Friedenwald (ed.), "A Letter of Jonas Phillips to the Federal Convention," *American Jewish Historical Society Publications* (New York, 1894), Vol. II, pp. 108–10.

worship almighty God according to the dictates of their own conscience and understanding; that no man ought or of right can be compelled to attend any religious worship or creed, or support any place of worship or maintain any minister contrary to or against his own free will and consent; nor can any man who acknowledges the being of a God be justly deprived or abridged of any civil right as a citizen on account of his religious sentiments or peculiar mode of religious worship; and that no authority can or ought to be vested in or assumed by any power whatever that shall in any case interfere or in any manner control the right of conscience in the free exercise of religious worship.'

It is well known among all the citizens of the 13 United States that the Jews have been true and faithful whigs, and during the late contest with England they have been foremost in aiding and assisting the states with their lives and fortunes. They have supported the cause, have bravely fought and bled for liberty which they cannot enjoy.

Therefore, if the honorable convention shall in their wisdom think fit, and alter the said oath and leave out the words, to wit—'and I do acknowledge the scripture of the New Testament to be given by divine inspiration' —then the Israelites will think themselves happy to live under a government where all religious societies are on an equal footing. I solicit this favor for myself, my children and posterity, and for the benefit of all the Israelites throughout the 13 United States of America.

My prayers are unto the Lord. May the people of these states rise up as a great and young lion. May they prevail against their enemies. May the degrees of honor of his Excellency, the president of the Convention, George Washington, be exalted and raised up. May everyone speak of his glorious exploits. May God prolong his days among us in this land of liberty. May he lead the armies against his enemies as he has done heretofore. May God extend peace unto the United States. May they get up to the highest prosperities. May God extend peace to them and their seed after them, so long as the sun and moon endureth. May the almighty God of our father, Abraham, Isaac and Jacob, indue this noble Assembly with wisdom, judgment and unanimity in their counsels. And may they have the satisfaction to see that their present toil and labor for the welfare of the United States may be approved of through all the world and particularly by the United States of America—is the ardent prayer of

Your most devoted obedient servant, Jonas Phillips

Alexander Hamilton attacks the Articles of Confederation: selections from *The Federalist*, No. 15, December 1787

Written in the main by Alexander Hamilton and James Madison (John Jay contributed but five of the eighty-five numbers) as explanatory essays in defense of the Constitution, "The Federalist" has quite properly come to be regarded as one of America's unique contributions to Western political theory. Thomas Jefferson considered it "the best commentary on the principles of government which ever was written." Scores of editions have appeared since its initial publication, and translations into a dozen languages have carried its reasoning throughout the world.

In the fifteenth essay Alexander Hamilton presented a review of the "national humiliation" America experienced under the Articles of Confederation, and of the absolute necessity of ratifying the new Constitution to rectify these conditions.

We may indeed with propriety be said to have reached almost the last stage of national humiliation. There is scarcely any thing that can wound the pride or degrade the character of an independent nation which we do not experience. Are there engagements to the performance of which we are held by every tie respectable among men? These are the subjects of constant and unblushing violation. Do we owe debts to foreigners and to our own citizens contracted in a time of imminent peril for the preservation of our political existence? These remain without any proper or satisfactory provision for their discharge. Have we valuable territories and important posts in the possession of a foreign power which, by express stipulations, ought long since to have been surrendered? These are still retained, to the prejudice of our interests, not less than of our rights. Are we in a condition to resent or to repel the aggression? We have neither troops, nor treasury, nor government. Are we even in a condition to remonstrate with dignity? The just imputations on our own faith, in respect to the same treaty, ought first to be removed. Are we entitled by nature and compact to a free participation in the navigation of the Mississippi? Spain excludes us from it. Is public credit an indispensable resource in time of public danger? We seem to have abandoned its cause as desperate and irretrievable. Is commerce of importance to national wealth? Ours is at the lowest point of declension. Is respectability in the eyes of foreign powers a safeguard against foreign encroachments? The imbecility of our government even forbids them to treat with us. Our ambassadors abroad are the mere pageants of mimic sovereignty. Is a violent and unnatural decrease in the value of land a symptom of national distress? The price of improved land in most parts of the country is much lower than can be accounted for by the quantity of

From *The Federalist, No. 15.*

waste land at market, and can only be fully explained by that want of private and public confidence, which are so alarmingly prevalent among all ranks, and which have a direct tendency to depreciate property of every kind. Is private credit the friend and patron of industry? That most useful kind which relates to borrowing and lending is reduced within the narrowest limits, and this still more from an opinion of insecurity than from the scarcity of money. To shorten an enumeration of particulars which can afford neither pleasure nor instruction, it may in general be demanded, what indication is there of national disorder, poverty, and insignificance that could befall a community so peculiarly blessed with natural advantages as we are, which does not form a part of the dark catalogue of our public misfortunes?

This is the melancholy situation to which we have been brought by those very maxims and councils which would now deter us from adopting the proposed Constitution; and which, not content with having conducted us to the brink of a precipice, seem resolved to plunge us into the abyss that awaits us below. Here, my countrymen impelled by every motive that ought to influence an enlightened people, let us make a firm stand for our safety, our tranquility, our dignity, our reputation. Let us at last break the fatal charm which has too long seduced us from the paths of felicity and prosperity. . . .

The great and radical vice in the construction of the existing Confederation is in the principle of LEGISLATION for STATES or GOVERNMENTS, in their CORPORATE or COLLECTIVE CAPACITIES, and as contradistinguished from the INDIVIDUALS of which they consist. Though this principle does not run through all the powers delegated to the Union, yet it pervades and governs those on which the efficacy of the rest depends. Except as to the rule of apportionment, the United States has an indefinite discretion to make requisitions for men and money; but they have no authority to raise either, by regulations extending to the individual citizens of America. The consequence of this is, that though in theory their resolutions concerning those objects are laws, constitutionally binding on the members of the Union, yet in practice they are mere recommendations which the States observe or disregard at their option.

It is a singular instance of the capriciousness of the human mind, that after all the admonitions we have had from experience on this head, there should still be found men who object to the new Constitution, for deviating from a principle which has been found the bane of the old, and which is in itself evidently incompatible with the idea of GOVERNMENT; a principle, in short, which, if it is to be executed at all, must substitute the violent and sanguinary agency of the sword to the mild influence of the magistracy.

There is nothing absurd or impracticable in the idea of a league or alliance between independent nations for certain defined purposes precisely stated in a treaty regulating all the details of time, place, circumstance, and quantity; leaving nothing to future discretion; and depending for its execution on the good faith of the parties. Compacts of this kind exist among all civilized nations, subject to the usual vicissitudes of peace and war, of observance and non-observance, as the interests or passions of the contracting powers dictate. In the early part of the present century there was an epidemical rage in Europe for this species of compacts, from which the politicians of the times fondly hoped for benefits which were never realized. With a view to establishing the equilibrium of power and the peace of that part of the world, all the resources of negotiations were exhausted, and triple and quadruple alliances were formed; but they were scarcely formed before they were broken, giving an instructive but afflicting lesson to mankind, how little dependence is to be placed on treaties which have no other sanction than the obligations of good faith, and which oppose general considerations of peace and justice to the impulse of any immediate interest or passion.

If the particular States in this country are disposed to stand in a similar relation to each other, and to drop the project of a general DISCRETIONARY SUPERINTENDENCE, the scheme would indeed be pernicious, and would entail upon us all the mischiefs which have been enumerated under the first head; but it would have the merit of being, at least, consistent and practicable. Abandoning all views towards a confederate government, this would bring us to a simple alliance offensive and defensive; and would place us in a situation to be alternate friends and enemies of each other, as our mutual jealousies and rivalships, nourished by the intrigues of foreign nations, should prescribe to us.

But if we are unwilling to be placed in this perilous situation; if we still will adhere to the design of a national government, or, which is the same thing, of a superintending power, under the direction of a common council, we must resolve to incorporate into our plan those ingredients which may be considered as forming the characteristic difference between a league and a government; we must extend the authority of the Union to the persons of the citizens,—the only proper objects of government.

Anti-Federalists oppose the ratification of the Constitution, 1788

The Anti-Federalists were in substantial agreement among themselves on many basic principles. Almost to a man they insisted on a bill of rights. They feared consolidated government, opposed unlimited taxing power, disapproved of Shays' rebellion, and warned against standing armies in peacetime. But the Anti-Federalists, for two reasons, were at a disadvantage: they were unorganized, and they had no constructive alternative to offer except to retain the Articles of Confederation.

From Morton Borden (ed.), *The Antifederalist Papers* (East Lansing, Mich., 1965), pp. 11–12, 109–12, 247–49.

*Three examples of Anti-Federalist criticism follow: from a letter in a
Massachusetts newspaper; from a pamphlet published in New York; and from
a speech by Patrick Henry before the Virginia ratifying convention.*

*A LETTER SIGNED "THE YEOMANRY OF MASSACHU-
SETTS" IN THE MASSACHUSETTS GAZETTE, JANUARY
25, 1788*

Another thing they tell us, that the Constitution must be good from
the characters which composed the Convention that framed it. It is graced
with the names of a Washington and a Franklin. Illustrious names, we
know—worthy characters in civil society. Yet we cannot suppose them to
be infallible guides; neither yet that a man must necessarily incur guilt to
himself merely by dissenting from them in opinion.

We cannot think the noble general has the same ideas with ourselves,
with regard to the rules of right and wrong. We cannot think he acts a very
consistent part, or did through the whole of the contest with Great Britain.
Notwithstanding he wielded the sword in defense of American liberty, yet
at the same time was, and is to this day, living upon the labors of several
hundreds of miserable Africans, as free born as himself; and some of them
very likely, descended from parents who, in point of property and dignity
in their own country, might cope with any man in America. We do not
conceive we are to be overborne by the weight of any names, however
revered.

*MELANCTON SMITH, AN ADDRESS TO THE PEOPLE OF
THE STATE OF NEW YORK: SHOWING THE NECESSITY
OF MAKING AMENDMENTS TO THE CONSTITUTION,
PROPOSED FOR THE UNITED STATES, PREVIOUS TO ITS
ADOPTION, 1788.*

All the powers of rhetoric and arts of description are employed to
paint the condition of this country in the most hideous and frightful
colors. We are told that agriculture is without encouragement; trade is
languishing; private faith and credit are disregarded, and public credit is
prostrate; that the laws and magistrates are condemned and set at naught;
that a spirit of licentiousness is rampant, and ready to break over every
bound set to it by the government; that private embarrassments and distresses invade the house of every man of middling property, and insecurity
threatens every man in affluent circumstances—in short, that we are in a
state of the most grievous calamity at home, and that we are contemptible
abroad, the scorn of foreign nations, and the ridicule of the world. From
this high-wrought picture one would suppose that we were in a condition
the most deplorable of any people upon earth. But suffer me, my country-

men, to call your attention to a serious and sober estimate of the situation in which you are placed, while I trace the embarrassments under which you labor, to their true sources. What is your condition? Does not every man sit under his own vine and under his own fig-tree, having none to make him afraid? Does not every one follow his own calling without impediments and receive the reward of his well-earned industry? The farmer cultivates his land, and reaps the fruit which the bounty of heaven bestows on his honest toil. The mechanic is exercised in his art, and receives the reward of his labor. The merchant drives his commerce, and none can deprive him of the gain he honestly acquires; all classes and callings of men amongst us are protected in their various pursuits, and secured by the laws in the possession and enjoyment of the property obtained in those pursuits. The laws are as well executed as they ever were, in this or any other country. Neither the hand of private violence, nor the more to be dreaded hand of legal oppression, are reached out to distress us.

It is true, many individuals labor under embarrassments, but these are to be imputed to the unavoidable circumstances of things, rather than to any defect in our governments. We have just emerged from a long and expensive war. During its existence few people were in a situation to increase their fortunes, but many to diminish them. Debts contracted before the war were left unpaid while it existed, and these were left a burden too heavy to be borne at the commencement of peace. Add to these, that when the war was over too many of us, instead of reassuming our old habits of frugality and industry, by which alone every country must be placed in a prosperous condition, took up the profuse use of foreign commodities. The country was deluged with articles imported from abroad, and the cash of the country has been sent to pay for them, and still left us laboring under the weight of a huge debt to persons abroad. These are the true sources to which we are to trace all the private difficulties of individuals. . . .

With regard to our public and national concerns, what is there in our condition that threatens us with any immediate danger? We are at peace with all the world; no nation menaces us with war; nor are we called upon by any cause of sufficient importance to attack any nation. The state governments answer the purposes of preserving the peace, and providing for present exigencies. Our condition as a nation is in no respect worse than it has been for several years past. Our public debt has been lessened in various ways, and the western territory, which has been relied upon as a productive fund to discharge the national debt, has at length been brought to market, and a considerable part actually applied to its reduction. I mention these things to show that there is nothing special in our present situation, as it respects our national affairs, that should induce us to accept the proffered system, without taking sufficient time to consider and amend it. . . .

PATRICK HENRY BEFORE THE VIRGINIA
RATIFYING CONVENTION, 1788

The [Articles of] Confederation, this despised government, merits in my opinion the highest encomium—it carried us through a long and dangerous war; it rendered us victorious in that bloody conflict with a powerful nation; it has secured us a territory greater than any European monarch possesses—and shall a government which has been thus strong and vigorous, be accused of imbecility and abandoned for want of energy? Consider what you are about to do before you part with the government. Take longer time in reckoning things; revolutions like this have happened in almost every country in Europe; similar examples are to be found in ancient Greece and ancient Rome—instances of the people losing their liberty by their own carelessness and the ambition of a few. We are cautioned . . . against faction and turbulence. I acknowledge that licentiousness is dangerous, and that it ought to be provided against. I acknowledge, also, the new form of government may effectually prevent it. Yet there is another thing it will as effectually do—it will oppress and ruin the people. . . .

And here I would make this inquiry of those worthy characters who composed a part of the late federal convention. I am sure they were fully impressed with the necessity of forming a great consolidated government, instead of a confederation. That this is a consolidated government is demonstrably clear; and the danger of such a government is, to my mind, very striking. I have the highest veneration for those gentlemen; but, sir, give me leave to demand: What right had they to say, *We, the people?* My political curiosity, exclusive of my anxious solicitude for the public welfare, leads me to ask: Who authorized them to speak the language of, *We, the people,* instead of, *We, the states?* States are the characteristics and the soul of a confederation. If the states be not the agents of this compact, it must be one great, consolidated, national government, of the people of all the states. . . . Sir, on this great occasion, I would demand the cause of their conduct. Even from that illustrious man [Washington] who saved us by his valor, I would have a reason for his conduct. . . . The federal Convention ought to have amended the old system; for this purpose they were solely delegated; the object of their mission extended to no other consideration. You must, therefore, forgive the solicitation of one unworthy member to know what danger could have arisen under the present Confederation, and what are the causes of this proposal to change our goverment.

3
Problems of a New Nation

"Advice and consent": a conflict between President Washington and the Senate as described in the diary of Senator William Maclay, August 22, 1789

The new government of the United States was launched in a mood of optimism, even exuberance. George Washington's trip from Mount Vernon to New York was delayed by constant celebrations en route. Nevertheless, there were those watchdogs of democracy, like Senator "Billy" Maclay of Pennsylvania, who feared the possibility of aristocratic domination. If a monarchy was ever to govern America, he believed, it would develop through the executive office. Thus, when Washington, in perfectly good faith, and acting in accord with the express provision of the Constitution, came to the Senate to obtain its "advice and consent" on an Indian treaty, he was both mortified and angered at their nervous reluctance to proceed while he was present.

August 22nd, Saturday

The doorkeeper . . . told us of the arrival of the President. The President was introduced, and took our Vice-President's chair. He rose and told us bluntly that he had called on us for our advice and consent to some propositions respecting the treaty to be held with the Southern Indians. Said he had brought General [Henry] Knox, [Secretary of War], with him, who was well acquainted with the business. He then turned to General Knox, who was seated on the left of the chair. General Knox handed him a paper, which he handed to the President of the Senate, who was seated on a chair on the floor to his right. Our Vice-President, [John Adams], hurried over the paper. Carriages were driving past, and such a noise, I could tell it was something about "Indians," but was not master of one sentence of it. Signs were made to the doorkeeper to shut down the sashes. Seven heads, as we have since learned, were stated at the end of the paper which the Senate were to give their advice and consent to. They were so framed that this could not be done by aye or no. . . .

Mr. [Robert] Morris rose. Said the noise of carriages had been so great that he really could not say that he had heard the body of the paper which had been read, and prayed that it might be read again. It was so [read]. It was no sooner read than our Vice-President immediately read the first head over again and put the question: Do you advise and consent, etc.? There was a dead pause. Mr. Morris whispered to me, "We will see who will venture to break the silence first." Our Vice-President was proceeding, "As many as—" I rose reluctantly, indeed, and, from the length of the pause, the hint given by Mr. Morris, and the proceeding of our Vice-President, it appeared to me that if I did not no other one would, and we should have these advices and consents ravished, in a degree, from us: "Mr.

From Edgar S. Maclay (ed.), *Journal of William Maclay* (New York, 1890), pp. 128–31.

President: The paper which you have now read to us appears to have for its basis sundry treaties and public transactions between the Southern Indians and the United States and the States of Georgia, North Carolina, and South Carolina. The business is new to the Senate. It is of importance. It is our duty to inform ourselves as well as possible on the subject. I therefore call for the reading of the treaties and other documents alluded to in the paper before us."

I cast an eye at the President of the United States. I saw he wore an aspect of stern displeasure. . . . I rose and said, when I considered the newness and importance of the subject, that one article had already been postponed; that General Lincoln, the first named of the commissioners, would not be here for a week; the deep interest Georgia had in this affair—I could not think it improper that the Senators from the State should be indulged in a postponement until Monday; and more especially as I had not heard any inconvenience pointed out that could possibly flow from it. The question was put and actually carried; but [Oliver] Ellsworth immediately began a long discourse on the merits of the business. He was answered by Lee, who appealed to the Constitution with regard to the power of making war. [Pierce] Butler and [Ralph] Izard answered, and Mr. Morris at last informed the disputants that they were debating on a subject that was actually postponed. Mr. Adams denied, in the face of the House, that it had been postponed. This very trick has been played by him and his New England men more than once. The question was, however, put a second time and carried.

I had at an early stage of the business whispered to Mr. Morris that I thought the best way to conduct the business was to have all the papers committed. My reasons were, that I saw no chance of a fair investigation of subjects while the President of the United States sat there, with his Secretary of War, to support his opinions and overawe the timid and neutral part of the Senate. Mr. Morris hastily rose and moved that the papers communicated to the Senate by the President of the United States should be referred to a committee of five, to report as soon as might be to them. He was seconded by Mr. [James] Gunn. Several members grumbled some objections. Mr. Butler rose; made a lengthy speech against commitment; said we were acting as a council. No council ever committed anything; committees were an improper mode of doing business; it threw business out of the hands of the many into the hands of the few, etc.

I rose and supported the mode of doing business by committees; that committees were used in all public deliberative bodies, etc. I thought I did the subject justice, but concluded the commitment can not be attended with any possible inconvenience. Some articles are already postponed until Monday. Whoever the committee are, if committed, they must make their report on Monday morning. I spoke through the whole in a low tone of voice. Peevishness itself, I think, could not have taken offense at anything I said.

As I sat down, the President of the United States started up in a violent fret. *"This defeats every purpose of my coming here,"* were the first words that he said. He then went on that he had brought his Secretary of War with him to give every necessary information; that the Secretary knew all about the business, and yet he was delayed and could not go on with the matter. He cooled, however, by degrees. Said he had no objection to putting off this matter until Monday, but declared he did not understand the matter of commitment. He might be delayed; he could not tell how long. He rose a second time, and said he had no objection to postponement until Monday at ten o'clock. By the looks of the Senate this seemed agreed to. A pause for some time ensued. We waited for him to withdraw. He did so with a discontented air. Had it been any other man than the man whom I wish to regard as the first character in the world, I would have said, with sullen dignity.

I can not now be mistaken. The President wishes to tread on the necks of the Senate. Commitment will bring the matter to discussion, at least in the committee, where he is not present. He wishes us to see with the eyes and hear with the ears of his Secretary only. The Secretary to advance the premises, the President to draw the conclusions, and to bear down our deliberations with his personal authority and presence. Form only will be left to us. This will not do with Americans. But let the matter work; it will soon cure itself.

Excerpts from Alexander Hamilton's "Report on Public Credit," January 1790

Three months after Congress requested him to prepare a report on the best means of providing for the support of public credit, Secretary of the Treasury Alexander Hamilton submitted his proposals. The prompt payment of the Revolutionary War debt, he reasoned, was not only morally indisputable but economically indispensable if the credit of the country was to be maintained. To pay the old debt, the nation would have to accept a new debt—though Hamilton specifically denied that he considered permanent national indebtedness a benefit. He did believe, however, that if the rich and powerful part of the American community were given a stake in the government—by their purchase of bonds —they would be committed by economic self-interest to support the union. In that sense the debt would be a blessing.

If the maintenance of public credit, then, be truly so important, the next enquiry which suggests itself is, by what means it is to be effected?

From Harold C. Syrett and Jacob E. Cooke (eds.) *The Papers of Alexander Hamilton* (New York: Columbia University Press, 1962,) Vol. VI, pp. 68–71, 106, 110. Reprinted by permission.

The ready answer to which question is, by good faith, by a punctual performance of contracts. States, like individuals, who observe their engagements, are respected and trusted; while the reverse is the fate of those who pursue an opposite conduct. . . .

While the observance of that good faith, which is the basis of public credit, is recommended by the strongest inducements of political expediency, it is enforced by considerations of still greater authority. There are arguments for it which rest on the immutable principles of moral obligation. And in proportion as the mind is disposed to contemplate, in the order of Providence, an intimate connection between public virtue and public happiness, will be its repugnancy to a violation of those principles. This reflection derives additional strength from the nature of the debt of the United States. It was the price of liberty. The faith of America has been repeatedly pledged for it, and with solemnities, that give peculiar force to the obligation. There is indeed reason to regret that it has not hitherto been kept; that the necessities of war, conspiring with inexperience in the subjects of finance, produced direct infractions; and that the subsequent period has been a continued scene of negative violation, or noncompliance. But a diminution of this regret arises from the reflection that the last seven years have exhibited an earnest and uniform effort, on the part of the government of the union, to retrieve the national credit, by doing justice to the creditors of the nation; and that the embarrassments of a defective constitution, which defeated this laudable effort, have ceased. . . .

It cannot but merit particular attention, that among ourselves the most enlightened friends of good government are those whose expectations are the highest. To justify and preserve their confidence; to promote the increasing respectability of the American name; to answer the calls of justice; to restore landed property to its due value; to furnish new resources both to agriculture and commerce; to cement more closely the union of the states; to add to their security against foreign attack; to establish public order on the basis of an upright and liberal policy—these are the great and invaluable ends to be secured by a proper and adequate provision, at the present period, for the support of public credit. To this provision we are invited, not only by the general considerations which have been noticed, but by others of a more particular nature. It will procure to every class of the community some important advantages, and remove some no less important disadvantages.

The advantage to the public creditors from the increased value of that part of their property which constitutes the public debt, needs no explanation. But there is a consequence of this, less obvious, though not less true, in which every other citizen is interested. It is a well known fact, that in countries in which the national debt is properly funded, and an object of established confidence, it answers most of the purposes of money. Transfers of stock or public debt are there equivalent to payments in specie; or in other words, stock, in the principal transactions of business, passes current as specie. The same thing would, in all probability happen here, under the like circumstances.

The benefits are various and obvious.

First. Trade is extended by it; because there is a larger capital to carry it on, and the merchant can at the same time afford to trade for smaller profits; as his stock, which, when unemployed, brings him in an interest from the government, [and] serves him also as money when he has a call for it in his commercial operations.

Secondly. Agriculture and manufactures are also promoted by it for the like reason, that more capital can be commanded to be employed in both; and because the merchant, whose enterprise in foreign trade, gives to them activity and extension, has greater means for enterprise.

Thirdly. The interest of money will be lowered by it; for this is always in a ratio to the quantity of money, and to the quickness of circulation. This circumstance will enable both the public and individuals to borrow on easier and cheaper terms. And from the combination of these effects, additional aids will be furnished to labor, to industry, and to arts of every kind. . . .

Persuaded as the Secretary is, that the proper funding of the present debt will render it a national blessing; yet he is so far from acceding to the position, in the latitude in which it is sometimes laid down, that "public debts are public benefits," a position inviting to prodigality, and liable to dangerous abuse—that he ardently wishes to see it incorporated, as a fundamental maxim, in the system of public credit of the United States, that the creation of debt should always be accompanied with the means of extinguishment. This he regards as the true secret for rendering public credit immortal. . . .

Deeply impressed, as the Secretary is, with a full and deliberate conviction, that the establishment of public credit upon the basis of a satisfactory provision for the public debt, is, under the present circumstance of this country, the true desideratum towards relief from individual and national embarrassments; that without it, these embarrassments will be likely to press still more severely upon the community—he cannot but indulge an anxious wish, that an effectual plan for that purpose may, during the present session, be the result of the united wisdom of the legislature.

A Republican attack and Federalist defense of the Hamiltonian system, 1793–94

Hamilton's recommendations for the funding of the national debt, for the assumption of state debts, for the establishment of a national bank, and for a federal excise tax, created partisan divisions in America which ran fever high in the 1790's. Out of this division, political parties emerged. But many contemporaries seriously doubted whether the nation could survive the deep sectional and economic rivalries Hamilton's reports had stimulated. The following are two particularly articulate examples of contemporary feelings.

JOHN TAYLOR'S ATTACK

An immense debt has been accumulated, from every region of the union and of every possible description, constituted into funds of almost perpetual duration, and subject from its nature upon the slightest incidents to constant fluctuation, with a power in the Secretary of the Treasury, through the medium of the sinking fund to raise it at pleasure. And upon the basis of this debt, a bank of discount has been formed, allied by its charter to the government itself, and in a great measure subjected to the direction of the same officer.

The experience of other countries has shown that the dealers in the public funds, and especially those whose fortunes consist principally in that line, have no interest and of course feel but little concern in all those questions of fiscal policy which particularly affect the landholder, the merchant, and the artisan. Although these classes should groan under the burdens of government, yet the public creditor will be not otherwise affected by the pressure, than as he receives what has been gleaned from their industry. . . . They are the tenants of the farm, he the landlord and the man of revenue. The disparity of their interests, and the difference of their sensations, respecting the objects to which they point, in a great measure separate them in society.

Knowing that they live upon the labor of the other classes, the public creditors behold them with jealousy, suspect a thousand visionary schemes against their welfare, and are always alarmed and agitated with every trifling incident which happens. And having one common interest, which consists simply in the imposition of high taxes and their rigid collection, they form a compact body and move always in concert. Whilst the administration finds the means to satisfy their claims, they are always devoted to it, and support all its measures. They therefore may be considered in every country, where substantial funds are established and their demands are

From two pamphlets by John Taylor, *An Examination of the Late Proceedings in Congress Respecting the Official Conduct of the Secretary of the Treasury* (1793), and *Inquiry into the Principles and Tendencies of Certain Public Measures* (1794).

punctually paid, as a ministerial corps, leagued together upon principles to a certain degree hostile to the rest of the community. . . .

The proprietors of bank stock are still more subservient to this policy than any other class of public creditors. The institution itself being founded on the same paper system must communicate the same interest to those within its sphere. And in other respects, it possesses a strength and energy to which the common members of the fiscal corps are strangers. The superiority of its gains invigorates the principle common to them all; but the constitutional subordination to the head of that department sanctifies under the cloak of authority, that degree of subservience which a sense of shame, among independent men, might occasionally forbid. The bank, however, should not be considered simply in the light of an institution, uniting together with greater force, the members of the fiscal corps. As an engine of influence, capable under management authorized by its principles, of polluting every operation of the government, it is entitled to particular attention. . . .

If we take an impartial review of the measures of the government from its adoption to the present time, we shall find . . . that a faction of monarchic speculators seized upon its legislative functions in the commencement and have directed all its operations since. We shall find that to the views of this faction, an apt instrument has been obtained in the Secretary of the Treasury. . . . If the public debt has been accumulated by every possible contrivance, buoyed up by means of the sinking fund, made in a great measure perpetual, and formed into a powerful monied machine, dependent on the fiscal administration, to this combination it is due. If by means of this sudden elevation of fortune, a dangerous inequality of rank has been created among the citizens of these states, thereby laying the foundation for the subversion of the government itself, by undermining its true principles, to this combination it is due. If those sound and genuine principles of responsibility which belong to representative government and constitute its bulwark and preserve its harmony, have been annulled or weakened; if a practicable means of influence, whereby the members of the legislature may be debauched from the duty they owe their constituents has been formed; if, by implication and construction, the obvious sense of the Constitution has been perverted and its powers enlarged, so as to pave the way for the conversion of the government from a limited into an unlimited one, to this combination they are due. . . .

A design for erecting aristocracy and a monarchy is subsisting—a *money impulse,* and not the *public good,* is operating on Congress; taxes are imposed upon motives other than the general welfare. A portion of the rich class of citizens are the proprietors of the device [the Bank], whilst labor supports it. An annuity to a great amount is suddenly conjured up by law, which is received exclusively by the rich, that is the aristocracy. Will it not make them richer? It is paid out of labor, and labor in all countries falls on the poor. Will it not make this class poorer? . . . Banking in its *best* view is only a fraud whereby labor suffers the imposition of paying an

interest upon the circulating medium; whereas if specie only were circu-
lated, the medium would, in passing among the rich, often lie in the pockets
of the aristocracy without gaining interest. But the aristocracy, as cunning
as rapacious, have contrived this device to inflict upon labor a tax, constantly working for their emolument. . . . Labor is deprived of its hard
earned fruits. A portion of these is gotten from it and bestowed upon ease
and affluence. The loss is the same, whether a daring robber extorts your
property with his pistol at your breast or whether a midnight thief secretly
filches it away. . . .

Which is most to be dreaded: titles without wealth, or exorbitant
wealth without titles? Have the words *prince, lord, highness,* or *protector*
a magical influence upon our minds, or can they lay a spell upon our exertions? . . . Who are most to be dreaded, the nominal or *real* lords of
America? It is evident that exorbitant wealth constitutes the substance and
danger of aristocracy. Money in a state of civilization is power. If we
execrate the shadow, what epithet is too hard for an administration which
is laboring to introduce the substance? . . . A democratic republic is endangered by an immense disproportion in wealth. In a state of nature,
enormous strength possessed by one or several individuals would constitute
a monarchy or an aristocracy—in a state of civilization similar consequences
will result from enormous wealth. . . . The acquisitions of *honest industry*
can seldom become dangerous to public or private happiness whereas the
accumulations of *fraud* and *violence* constantly diminish both.

Did labor intend to place itself under the whip of an avaricious, insatiable, and luxurious aristocracy? Labor, in the erection of a government,
after deducting the necessary expense of supporting it, designed to secure
safety to itself in the enjoyment of its own fruits. The stimulating system
[of Hamilton] frustrates this object and changes government into its master,
brandishing the lash of legislation and leaving to labor what measure of
sustenance it pleases. . . . An aristocracy, therefore, have good reason to
exclaim "a national debt is a national blessing," and in pursuance of their
maxim, to create one that is fictitious, payable to themselves out of the hard
earned fruits of labor. To them it is a mine, yielding gold without work.

A FEDERALIST DEFENSE

Men devoted to the laborious and honorable occupations of agriculture, at a distance from the seat of information, without the means of
inquiring or the leisure to make deep researches and to investigate complex
principles and obscure facts—however virtuous (and in all nations they
are to be regarded as the most virtuous part of the society)—are liable
from these circumstances to be imposed on and misled by the artifices of
the wicked and ambitious. . . .

From a pamphlet by "Marcellus," *Letters from the Virginia Gazette* (1794), the above
excerpts taken from Charles Beard, *Economic Origins of Jeffersonian Democracy,*
paperback edition (New York, 1965), pp. 197–200, 204–05, 207–09, 234–36.

What is aristocracy? If aristocracy in this meaning [hereditary] does not exist [in America] let those who so frequently use the terms *aristocrat* and *democrat*, define them. . . . Do they mean by the term *aristocrat*, a *rich man*, contradistinguished from a *poor man?* If by the term *aristocrat*, they mean the rich and by the term *democrat*, the poor; by vilifying the first and exalting the last do they mean to censure industry by which wealth is acquired and commend idleness which is the cause of poverty and the fruitful source of every vice? If they make it a crime to be rich, men will cease to make any efforts to better their condition, to provide for the education and comforts of their families, and add to their own wealth as well as the riches of their country by honest industry, and from a civilized society we shall become a horde of savages. To this deplorable condition would their system gradually reduce us. But it cannot be expected that such haughty dictators would wait for the slow operation of time. They may attempt to reduce all property at once to a level; abolition of debt, agrarian laws and emancipation of slaves may be expected among their first *coups de main*. For, if by the term *democrat* they mean the poor, who so poor as our slaves, who therefore so fit to participate in the spoils of the rich and to direct the affairs of the nation? I ask again, whence proceeds the danger of the growth of aristocratic orders amongst us? Certainly not from the accumulations of landed property. I may be answered from the funding system. I may be told in the same cant, indefinite, and unintelligible language of the existence of a *paper nobility*. . . . It will be sufficient to say that we owed the debt—that if we were honest we were bound to pay it.

That much speculation existed at the commencement of the system is true; and perhaps much property acquired by fraud, but are not all other negotiations also subject to fraud? Has not land risen almost as rapidly in value as stock in the funds? If a man makes a fortunate purchase of land is he censured for it? If he buys the bond of an individual for half its nominal value is he censured for it? Why then load with opprobrious epithets those . . . who have purchased the obligations of the public?

If instead of meaning the poor by the term democrat, they [Republicans] denominate a friend of that kind of government in which each person in his individual capacity exercises those functions which in our society are delegated to representatives, such as were some of the petty tumultuous commonwealths of old, this would be a government so hostile to the happiness of our citizens and so counter to the habits and practice of the American people that no man would deem it honorable to assume the name, as in this sense it would be regarded as another term for anarchist.

I could wish that the doctrines of the times and justice to the subject would permit me to draw a veil over certain peculiarities. But when we hear so much about *liberty* and *equality* we are obliged to consider how far the application of these principles in their *most extensive meaning* to our situation would be promotive of our happiness and consistent with our peace. . . . It can hardly be necessary to tell a Virginian that two-fifths of the inhabitants of our state are slaves; and that even part of the free men have no share in the management of public affairs. What do those who preach *liberty* and *equality* mean? Do they mean to raise the blacks to equal social rights with the whites? Do they mean to remove the existing discrimination amongst the whites themselves? . . . Perhaps nothing is meant but frothy declamation.

Criticisms of George Washington from the newspaper Philadelphia *Aurora*, September–October 1795

George Washington, it should be remembered, was a controversial figure. Most Americans venerated him as their incorruptible and indispensable leader. But many others considered him a fallible human who should have died before he became President, when—they believed—he virtually allied America to Britain by endorsing Jay's treaty, became increasingly authoritarian, and was little more than a popular idol manipulated by Hamilton and the Federalists for partisan purposes.

September 15, 1795

Believe me, Sir, your fellow citizens are not mere moulds of wax, calculated to receive any impression which the *dicta* of a magistrate may attempt to make upon them; neither are they too timid to resist, or too shortsighted to detect the imposition; and however you may attempt to clothe your responses to their applications in mystery and empiricism, they will not regard you as a priest, a prophet, or a demigod. . . . Stript of the mantle of infallibility, and possessing nought of the *jus divinum*, you appear before them a frail mortal, whose passions and weaknesses are like those of other men. "Belisarius"

September 18, 1795

It is said the President values himself in his *firmness*, and that as he began the treaty, this quality would prompt him to go through with it. But it will be remembered that what may be called firmness in a good cause is obstinacy in a bad one, and that perseverance in virtue may command respect, but a pertinacity in wrong must ensure disgust and detestation. "Pittachus"

September 30, 1795

At the dissolution of the American army, you had declared that you would not accept of any office under the government. This no doubt was your determination—America had no office to give worthy of your acceptance. A

From the Philadelphia *Aurora,* September 15, 18, 30, October 23, 1795.

Governor of a State was beneath the dignity of a Commander in Chief, and a President of Congress was still more contemptible. You retired from public life perhaps because public life could not gratify your ambition; for this country did not yet offer the opportunity of imitating monarchical splendor, or of exercising regal power. It was, however, to this resignation that you owed so great an increase of your popularity. It was supposed that he who could forego an opportunity of placing himself on the throne must be more than man. It was imagined that the late army would and could have declared you a king. . . . You rejected the temptation, perhaps from the danger of the attempt; and to secure the fame which your forebearance gave was one probable reason for your refusal to receive any compensation for your military services, other than defraying the expenses of your camp family. Is virtue then so scarce? Is human nature so debased that a man is exalted into a demigod because he was not an open traitor? An endeavor to enslave us by the army might have produced civil war, but must have ended in the deserved punishment of the Commander who would attempt it. If avoiding a hazardous enterprise entitles a man to any character for virtue, it is for the virtue of prudence. You are, perhaps, the only person who ever acquired fame by shrinking from an attempt which must have been unsuccessful. "Portius"

October 23, 1795

The House of Representatives must either impeach [Washington] or renounce their sacred duties. . . . I will examine what charges will probably compose his impeachment, as a matter of curious speculation.

1st. Instead of exercising the qualified veto entrusted to him for the preservation of liberty, so as to restrain aristocratical innovations, and to prevent dangerous institutions, he expressly sanctioned the Funding System, the Assumption, the Bank, and all the rest of the long train of legislative evils, of which we complain so justly.

2nd. He has patronized the enemies of the people with an ardor which appears to demonstrate congeniality of sentiment and unity of design.

3rd. He has formed a close and suspicious union with the despot whose Generals he vanquished in the field, and whose machinations he ought ever to have opposed in the Cabinet.

4th. He has manifested a hostility to the brave Republic which has contended for the Rights of Man against all the tyrants of the earth. . . .

5th. He proscribed the Democratic Societies, those centinels of liberty, nearly at the same moment George the Third repeated the philippic taught him with much difficulty by Mr. Pitt, against the "self-created societies" in England.

6th. He exercised legislative power through the medium of a proclamation [of neutrality], justifiable only under absurd pretexts, and most criminal in its real motives.

7th. He forced the philosophic patriot [Jefferson] who first occupied the Department of State to abandon the service of his country and to seek a humble retirement.

8th. He has administered the executive department upon principles incompatible with the spirit of republican constitution, and on precedents derived from the corrupt government of England, a government contrived to produce the greatest possible quantity of wealth, splendor, and power for the *governors,* and to excite the superlative degree of credulity and ignorance in the *governed.*

9th. He indirectly superseded the various resolutions brought forward in Congress to obtain compensation for British injustice by unconstitutionally appointing our Chief Justice [Jay] minion and parasite extraordinary and plenipotentiary to the Court of St. James.

10th. He secured the adoption of the Treaty procured by the complaisance of this most honorable ambassador by tenderly concealing its hideous features from the public eye.

11th. He saw without one single emotion of "sensibility," without one single sensation of patriotism, his country before him in the humblest attitude of entreaty, earnestly supplicating him not to surrender her property, her hopes, and her liberty, to the tyrant from whose chains she had just escaped.

12th. He has destroyed the Constitution by the ratification of a Treaty which could only have been signed upon the principle that all those powers were vested in the President and Senate which were given to Congress.

13th. He has submitted to the insults and to the injuries which his country has received with a passiveness which would have dishonored the administration of an Oriental Queen.

14th. He shrunk from a contest in which his country would have obtained glory, to wage a despicable war with the savages of the desert, that might employ the attention and expand the debt of his country.

15th. He ostentatiously exerted that military force against a few deluded citizens [the Whiskey Rebellion], whom reason would soon have brought back to their duty, which he ought to have directed against the haughty enemy who had invaded our territory, and plundered our merchants in every part of the globe.

16th. He maintained a standing army under the absurd pretext of preventing a return of that spirit of insurrection which has been extinguished forever by the genius of Republican virtue.

17th. The firmness which he once possessed has degenerated into haughtiness to his fellow citizens and their allies, and the caution which once saved his country is degenerated into cowardice to his inveterate enemies.

When all these circumstances are combined, an awful conclusion bursts upon the understanding. . . . An impeachment must appear requisite. "Casca."

October 23, 1795

Will not the world be led to conclude that the mask of hypocrisy has been alike worn by a CAESAR, a CROMWELL, and a WASHINGTON? "A Calm Observer"

George Washington's advice to a nation: extracts from his Farewell Address, September 1796

The criticisms he endured as president, the rise of political parties, the division of Americans into "French" and "English" factions, the insurrections in Pennsylvania which had challenged established order—all disturbed Washington and hastened his desire to escape further political abuse by retiring to the quiet of Mount Vernon. His Farewell Address was in effect a warning to Americans to steer clear of permanent foreign entanglements, to forsake violent methods and to have reverence for law and authority, to cease "the spirit of party" which threatened the nation. Few could quarrel with such advice, but it failed to resolve the issues. "The President is fortunate to get off just as the bubble is bursting," Jefferson noted, "leaving others to hold the bag."

The basis of our political systems is the right of the people to make and to alter their Constitutions of Government. But the Constitution which at any time exists, 'till changed by an explicit and authentic act of the whole people, is sacredly obligatory upon all. The very idea of the power and the right of the people to establish Government presupposes the duty of every individual to obey the established Government.

All obstructions to the execution of the laws, all combinations and associations, under whatever plausible character, with the real design to direct, control, counteract, or awe the regular deliberation and action of the constituted authorities are destructive of this fundamental principle and of fatal tendency. They serve to organize faction, to give it an artificial and extraordinary force; to put in the place of the delegated will of the nation, the will of a party; often a small but artful and enterprising minority of the community; and, according to the alternate triumphs of different parties, to make the public administration the mirror of the ill concerted and incongruous projects of faction, rather than the organ of consistent and wholesome plans digested by common councils and modified by mutual interests. However combinations or associations of the above description may now and then answer popular ends, they are likely, in the course of time and things, to become potent engines, by which cunning, ambitious and unprincipled men will be enabled to subvert the power of the people, and to usurp for themselves the reins of Government; destroying afterwards the very engines which have lifted them to unjust dominion.

From John C. Fitzpatrick (ed.), *The Writings of George Washington* (Washington, D.C., 1931–44), Vol. XXXV, pp. 224–38.

Towards the preservation of our Government and the permanency of your present happy state, it is requisite, not only that you steadily discountenance irregular oppositions to its acknowledged authority, but also that you resist with care the spirit of innovation upon its principles however specious the pretexts. One method of assault may be to effect, in the forms of the Constitution, alterations which will impair the energy of the system, and thus to undermine what cannot be directly overthrown. In all the changes to which you may be invited, remember that time and habit are at least as necessary to fix the true character of Governments, as of other human institutions; that experience is the surest standard by which to test the real tendency of the existing Constitution of a country; that facility in changes upon the credit of mere hypotheses and opinion exposes to perpetual change, from the endless variety of hypotheses and opinion; and remember, especially, that for the efficient management of your common interests, in a country so extensive as ours, a Government of as much vigor as is consistent with the perfect security of liberty is indispensable. . . .

I have already intimated to you the danger of parties in the state, with particular reference to the founding of them on geographical discriminations. Let me now take a more comprehensive view, and warn you in the most solemn manner against the baneful effects of the spirit of party, generally:

This spirit, unfortunately, is inseparable from our nature, having its root in the strongest passions of the human mind. It exists under different shapes in all Governments, more or less stifled, controlled, or repressed; but, in those of the popular form it is seen in its greatest rankness and is truly their worst enemy.

The alternate domination of one faction over another, sharpened by the spirit of revenge natural to party dissension, which in different ages and countries has perpetrated the most horrid enormities, is itself a frightful despotism. But this leads at length to a more formal and permanent despotism. The disorders and miseries which result, gradually incline the minds of men to seek security and repose in the absolute power of an individual; and sooner or later the chief of some prevailing faction more able or more fortunate than his competitors, turns this disposition to the purposes of his own elevation, on the ruins of public liberty. . . .

So likewise, a passionate attachment of one nation for another produces a variety of evils. Sympathy for the favorite nation, facilitating the illusion of an imaginary common interest, in cases where no real common interest exists, and infusing into one the enmities of the other, betrays the former into a participation in the quarrels and wars of the latter, without adequate inducement or justification. It leads also to concessions to the favorite nation of privileges denied to others, which is apt doubly to injure the nation making the concessions; by unnecessarily parting with what ought to have been retained; and by exciting jealously, ill will, and a disposition to retaliate, in the parties from whom equal privileges are withheld. And it gives to ambitious, corrupted, or deluded citizens (who devote themselves to the favorite nation) facility to betray, or sacrifice the interests of their own country, without odium, sometimes even with popularity; gilding with the appearances of a virtuous sense of obligation a commendable deference for public opinion, or a laudable zeal for public good, the base or foolish compliances of ambition, corruption or infatuation. . . .

Against the insidious wiles of foreign influence (I conjure you to believe me fellow citizens), the jealousy of a free people ought to be constantly awake; since history and experience prove that foreign influence is one of the most baneful foes of Republican Government. But that jealousy to be useful must be impartial; else it becomes the instrument of the very influence to be avoided, instead of a defence against it. Excessive partiality for one foreign nation and excessive dislike of another, cause those whom they actuate to see danger only on one side, and serve to veil and even second the arts of influence on the other. Real patriots, who may resist the intrigues of the favorite, are liable to become suspected and odious; while its tools and dupes usurp the applause and confidence of the people, to surrender their interests.

The great rule of conduct for us, in regard to foreign nations is in extending our commercial relations to have with them as little political connection as possible. So far as we have already formed engagements let them be fulfilled, with perfect good faith. Here let us stop.

Abigail Adams on France and Francophiles: letters to her sister, January–April 1798

In March 1798, Congress requested and John Adams released the diplomatic papers of the American mission to France. They told of a complex attempt at international blackmail—the XYZ affair—on the part of the French foreign minister, Talleyrand. Americans responded to the news with an outburst of anti-Gallic sentiment. "It is gratifying to behold," wrote one Federalist, "the military spirit which prevails. . . . While we are united and true to each other no nation on earth can make an impression on us." The Federalists had been respected; now they experienced the heady sensation of popularity. From Philadelphia the President's wife, Abigail, kept her sister informed of events, particularly the change in public opinion which resulted from the XYZ disclosures.

January 20, 1798

I am at a loss to know how the people who were formerly so much alive to the usurpation of one nation [England] can crouch so tamely to a much

From Stewart Mitchell (ed.), *New Letters of Abigail Adams* (Boston: Houghton Mifflin Co. 1947), pp. 124, 140–41, 148, 151–52, 154, 156, 161. Reprinted by permission of the American Antiquarian Society.

more dangerous and daring one, to one which aims not only at our independence and liberty but a total annihilation of the Christian religion; whose laws, all which they have, are those of Draco; who are robbers, murderers, scoffers, backbiters. In short, [there is] no crime however black or horrid to which they have not become familiar. America must be punished, punished for having amonst her legislatures men who sanction these crimes, who justify France in all her measures, and who would rejoice to see fire, sword and massacre carried into the island of Great Britain until she becomes as miserable as France is wretched.

March 5, 1798

You will learn that at length dispatches have arrived from our commissioners [to France], but with them, no prospect of success.... We shall now see how the American pulse beat. I fear we shall be driven to war, but to *defend* ourselves is our duty. War the French have made upon us a long time.

March 27, 1798

There is an attempt in this city [Philadelphia] to get a petition signed to Congress declaring their determination not to go to war with France, and they hope to set this measure in operation through the different states. Is it possible that any person can suppose this country wish for war, by which nothing is to be obtained, much to be expended and hazarded, in preference to peace? *But in self defense* we may be involved in war; and for that we ought to be prepared, and that is what the President means. What benefit can war be to him? He has no ambition for military glory. He cannot add by war, to his peace, comfort or happiness. It must accumulate upon him an additional load of care, toil, trouble, malice, hatred, and I dare say revenge. But for all this he will not sacrifice the honor and independence of his country to any nation, and if in support of that, we are involved in war, we must and we ought to meet it, with firmness, with resolution, and with union of sentiment.

April 4, 1798

Out of fears for the safety of our Envoy's ... [their dispatches]would not have yet been published, if the House of Representatives had not called for them. [Albert] Gallatin, the sly, the artful, the insidious Gallatin knew better than to join in the call. [William B.] Giles was heard to say to his friends in the House, "You are doing wrong to call for those dispatches. They will injure us." These men knew that the President would not have expressed himself in such strong terms in his Message, if he had not possessed convincing evidence. ... The Jacobins in the Senate and House were struck dumb, and opened not their mouths, not having their cue, not having received their lessons from those emissaries which Talleyrand made no secret of telling our Envoys are spread all over our country; and from whence they drew their information. I believe Talleyrand is not too scrupulous to take a *fee*. We are ensnared. We shall be destroyed unless the snare is broken, and that speedily.

April 13, 1798

The public opinion is changing here very fast, and the people begin to see who have been their firm unshaken friends, steady to their interests and defenders of their rights and liberties. The merchants of this city have had a meeting to prepare an address of thanks to the President for his firm and steady conduct as it respects their interests. I am told that the French cockade so frequent in the streets here, is not now to be seen, and the common people say if Jefferson had been our President, and Madison & Burr our negotiators, we should all have been sold to the French.

April 22, 1798

As the French have boasted of having more influence in the United States, than our own government, the men who now espouse their cause against their own country, and justify their measures, ought to be carefully marked. They ought to be brought into open light. Addresses from the merchants, traders, and underwriters have been presented and signed by more than 500 men, of the greatest property here in this city, highly approving the measures of the Executive. A similar one from the Grand Jurors, one from York Town, and yesterday, one from the Mayor, Aldermen, and common counsel of the city, a very firm and manly address. Others are coming in from New York, from Baltimore, and I presume Boston will be no longer behind than time to consult upon the measure. They must in this way show the haughty tyrants that we are not that divided people we have appeared to be.

An episode of mistaken identity during the quasi-war with France, September–October 1798

An undeclared naval war with France developed quickly after the XYZ affair. American naval vessels were ordered to comb the Caribbean of French warships and privateers. That task was accomplished quickly and effectively—before the quasi-war ended in 1800 the fledgling American navy had defeated the French in eight of nine engagements—but not without some understandable errors. The following three letters tell the story of an embarrassing mistake committed by an over-eager American officer, Samuel Nicholson, captain of the Constitution. *The first letter, written by Nicholson, explains his reasons for making the seizure; the second gives the account by the captured officers; and the third letter, written by Secretary of State Timothy Pickering, is a request that the whole affair be speedily terminated. So it was. The ship was returned, and the American government by court order paid damages.*

CAPTAIN SAMUEL NICHOLSON TO SECRETARY OF THE NAVY BENJAMIN STODDERT, FROM HAMPTON ROAD, SEPTEMBER 12, 1798

Sir: I have the pleasure to inform you that I arrived here yesterday evening. . . . On the 8th Instant at 6 A.M. in the Latitude 33:10 North & Longitude 74:00 West a man from our mast-head made [out] a sail. . . . We soon perceived him to be a Ship of War . . . when I fired a shot over him and hoisted my colors. He then the first time showed me an English ensign and fired one gun to leeward. He then kept by the wind, all sail set, and endeavored to get the wind of us. . . . I had from his maneuvering every reason to expect a broadside from him every moment until my 3rd Lieutenant, Mr. Beal, was actually on board of him and ordered and drove his men from their quarters, who were constantly trailing and pointing their guns into us, as we altered our positions. We were then within pistol shot of each other, and if he had caught me one instant off our guard I am convinced he would have fired his broadside into us. I hailed them and was answered very impertinently in broken English by their boatswain. . . . I ordered them to hoist out their boats and for their Captain to come on board the *Constitution* with his papers. They at first refused. I repeated my request and told them if they . . . gave me any further trouble by attempting to get away I would absolutely fire into them, sink them, and give them no quarters. I was convinced they were pirates. . . .

Their Captain had the French national uniform on. They said they were French-royalists and bound from Jamaica to Philadelphia, and had a Commission from the English government, and a Register and Clearance from Jamaica, all of which I believe to be counterfeits. They have no articles, shipping papers or Log-book, etc. . . . The crew is made up of 7 French officers, Frenchmen, Spaniards, 3 English, Portuguese, Italians, 1 American, Dutch, Negroes—in all about 75 men. A British officer and an American gentleman, belonging to Baltimore, passengers. The Ship is called the *Niger,* built by the Spanish government, taken by the British and sold at Jamaica 2 or 3 years since. They have a great deal of money on board, and I am informed a large sum under the magazine. The crew have their pockets full. There was a disturbance amongst them a few nights ago,

From Dudley W. Knox (ed.), *Naval Documents Related to the Quasi-War between the United States and France* (Washington, D.C., 1935), Vol. I, pp. 393–95, 414–17, 555–56.

fighting with knives, etc. I ordered them to be searched and deprived of their knives, money, watches etc. Every one of those people have one or two trunks American made full of good clothes, etc., which I have no doubt have been plundered from the Americans. The French Captain was very solicitous on his first coming on board to have his French boatswain excused being put in irons with the rest of his people but one of my men named Martin Rose swears that seven months ago he was on board a schooner from Portsmouth, bound to the West Indies and was taken by a French schooner of which this same man was boatswain. . . . We are really put on our guard by these people for of all beings I ever beheld in human shape, I declare I never saw so impudent and daring a set of rascals, and I have had a great many to take care of in my time. It is my real opinion if they could get an opportunity they would blow our ship up by way of revenge. They are fit for and capable of anything be it ever so desperate. . . .

This ship was certainly cruising (and is not consigned to any person in Philadelphia) and capturing our American homeward bound East and West India-men. I have no doubt but different sets of papers and various methods will be made use of whenever any of those people fall into our hands. . . . It is certain they cleared from Jamaica and said they were bound to Philadelphia, but that they ever meant to go there with that crew, before they had disposed of the greater part of them in prizes, I cannot conceive; or believe at any rate I had a duty to do, which I thought obliged me to see this ship into port. . . . I have taken care of her and brought her into Virginia. I shall deliver the prisoners into the hands of the Marshall and have no doubt that the District Judge with my agent under your orders will take the necessary steps to have her condemned to us.

GEORGE DU PETIT-THOUARS (MASTER OF THE NIGER*) AND DU BOUETIER (FIRST MATE ON THE* NIGER*), ACCOUNT OF THE CAPTURE OF THEIR SHIP BY THE AMERICAN FRIGATE* CONSTITUTION

On the 8th of September, at 7 in the morning . . . I perceived a vessel to windward. The weather was very black and stormy in the north, which caused her to be hidden from me for some time. . . . For a few moments I was uncertain as to what this vessel was, but shortly thereafter I made her out to be a warship and judged her to be American. Having approached me within cannon-shot, she hoisted the American colors, and fired a shot. Whereupon I hoisted the English colors and fired a shot to leeward.

I had hardly climbed to the forecastle of the frigate, when I was surrounded by great numbers of men armed with sabers and pistols. *The Captain asked me whence I came?* From Kingston, I told him. *When did you leave?* The 11th of August. . . . *Very well, where are your papers?* You have them. Here is my general clearance which I forgot to send you. *I do not want these papers; I want your French commission.* I have none. I have been in the service of the English for five years. I command English ships. I have been in command of this vessel for three years. She belongs to a merchant of Jamaica. *Let me have your dagger.* No, sir, I am English, and a friend of your nation. I should not be disarmed. *Give it to me, or I shall have it taken from you.* . . . Then I gave it to him.

. . . Presently they fetched Mr. Belmont and Mr. Demanes, both commissioned officers in the service of His Britannic Majesty who showed him their commissions. He asked by what chance they were to be found on my ship, since I and my lieutenant were wearing French uniforms; they answered him that we had no uniforms and that these were the clothes we always wore. . . . I told him again that my ship was English; that a part of my cargo belonged to Philadelphia merchants; that since I fell under his suspicion, nothing was simpler than to detain me and to convoy my ship to the nearest port; but I begged him to leave on board one of my officers with ten of my crew in order to look after the cargo and the various things belonging to me, to my passengers and to my crew. . . . He answered me, that I was not to teach him his trade and that he did not need my advice. . . . Captain Nicholson took possession of all my papers, such as my Log Book of this voyage and preceding voyages, my register . . . my two war commissions, my general clearance, all my bills of lading, my charter party issued by the government for chartering my vessel, all the orders of various Santo Domingo Generals, all my private papers, such as letters and accounts relative to my dealings with the various merchants of Jamaica, and more than one hundred letters, which were entrusted to me at Kingston to be delivered to various merchants in Philadelphia. . . .

[Captain Nicholson] treated me like a pirate; he told me that he would have me hanged, and used a hundred thousand still more insulting epithets, such as rascal, abominable wretch, etc., which he also applied to my unfortunate passengers. Bring me, I said to him, before a court of justice; if I am a pirate, I will be hanged; you are not my judge, and your position obliges you to treat me well, and to respect the flag under which it pleases you to arrest me. On the morrow of this horrible scene, they took my servant away from me, and quartered us aft, with seven paces walking space and a sentinel, who followed us wherever our needs obliged us to go; at night we had two sentinels at the door of our cabins.

TIMOTHY PICKERING, SECRETARY OF STATE, TO THOMAS NELSON, UNITED STATES ATTORNEY, VIRGINIA DISTRICT, OCTOBER 22, 1798

The case appeared to me, and I believe to the Secretary of the Navy, to warrant an immediate discharge of the *Niger;* but Captain Nicholson's letters to him manifested his conviction that she was a good prize. . . . Indeed the eagerness of Captain Nicholson to procure a condemnation savored of rapacity. And in the very letter in which he informed of the death of his son . . . his thoughts seemed wholly engrossed with his prize and the means of ensuring, if possible, a condemnation. The captain and other officers of the *Niger* complain bitterly of the rough ungentlemanly treatment they experienced from Captain Nicholson, while they speak in handsome and grateful terms of his officers and of the Artillery officers at Norfolk to whose care they were committed. Upon the whole view of the case, 1 am inclined to think that there is not another captain in the American Navy who with the evidence of the ship's papers and the information of the passengers (one of them an American citizen) would have imagined the *Niger* a subject of capture. But it would seem that Captain Nicholson made no inquiry whatever of the passengers; for word of information from them; although, as above mentioned, one was an American gentleman, and the other an English Officer with his lady and children. Such characters were peculiarly qualified, and, one would suppose, inclined to give correct information. I expect it will appear on the trial that the capture was wholly unwarrantable; and consequently that damages must be decreed to the captured. Nevertheless, I have thought it expedient that the trial should be had, in order not only to prevent any complaint on the part of Captain Nicholson and ship's company, that a good prize was improperly given up, of which they would have been entitled to one half—but by clearly ascertaining the facts, to enable the President to form a correct opinion of Captain Nicholson's conduct. . . .

The British Minister has written to me concerning the *Niger*, declaring her to be a British vessel, and desiring she may be immediately restored. A copy of this letter is enclosed. Mr. Bond, the British Consul at Philadelphia, had before written to me on the same subject. I have now only to express my hopes that the trial will be finished at the time appointed. . . . Any further delay will swell the bill of damages and costs. . . . The case being a clear one, any adjournment of the cause will appear to the owners and officers very vexatious.

The sedition trial of Thomas Cooper, 1799–1800

Between May and July 1798, the Federalist-dominated Congress enacted a series of alien and sedition laws designed to silence their political opposition. The sedition law specified that true statements could not be considered seditious. Moreover, even if false, the intent of the statement had to be scandalous and malicious before a man was found guilty. But Republican newspaper owners and editors, who became prime targets for prosecution, found it difficult to demonstrate the truth or the nonmalicious intent of their published opinions, particularly when their cases were heard before biased judges. Thomas Cooper, owner of the Northumberland Gazette, *a Pennsylvania newspaper, was tried in 1800 for criticisms of the Adams administration that he had written the previous*

From Francis Wharton (ed.), *State Trials of the United States during the Administrations of Washington and Adams* (Philadelphia, 1849), pp. 663–65, 670–77.

*year. In his speech to the jury Cooper attempted to demonstrate that such crit-
icisms were hardly seditious, but an honest exercise of an opposition newspaper
in a free society; Judge Samuel Chase believed otherwise, and in his closing
charge to the jury practically ordered them to return a vote for conviction.*

*Cooper was found guilty, but the Alien and Sedition acts proved a serious
political blunder. They "operated," noted Thomas Jefferson, "as powerful seda-
tives of the XYZ inflammation."*

INTRODUCTORY REMARKS OF THOMAS COOPER TO THE JURY

If it were true, as it is not true that, in the language of the attorney-
general, I have been guilty of publishing with the basest motives a foul and
infamous libel on the character of the President; of exciting against him
the hatred and contempt of the people of this country, by gross and malicious falsehoods—then, indeed, would it be his duty to bring me before
this tribunal, it would be yours to convict, and the duty of the court to
punish me. But I hope, in the course of this trial, I shall be enabled to
prove to your satisfaction, that I have published nothing which truth will
not justify; that the assertions for which I am indicted are free from malicious imputation; and that my motives have been honest and fair.

You will observe, gentlemen of the jury, that the law requires it to be
proved as a necessary part of the charge, that the passages for which I
am indicted should be false and scandalous, and published from malicious
motives; and before you will be able, consistently with your oaths, to convict upon this indictment, you must be thoroughly satisfied that both
these parts of the charge are well founded. Nor does it appear to me that
the expression of the act, to bring the President into contempt, can be fulfilled, if the accusation, as in the present instance, is related to an examination of his public conduct, and no improper motives are imputed to him.
And that I have carefully avoided imputing any impropriety of intention to
the President, even in the very paper complained of; that the uniform
tenor of my conduct and language has been to attribute honesty of motive
even where I have strongly disapproved of the tendency of his measures, I
can abundantly show.

You, and all who hear me, will know that this country is divided, and
almost equally divided, into two grand parties: usually termed, whether
properly or improperly, *Federalists* and *Anti-Federalists;* and that the
governing powers of the country are ranked in public opinion under the
former denomination—of these divisions, the one wishes to increase,
the other to diminish, the powers of the executive; the one thinks that the
people (the democracy of the country) has too much, the other too little,
influence on the measures of government; the one is friendly, the other
hostile, to a standing army and a permanent navy; the one thinks them
necessary to repel invasions and aggressions from without, and commotions

within; the other, that a well-organized militia is a sufficient safeguard for all that an army could protect, and that a navy is more dangerous and expensive than any benefit derived from it can compensate; the one thinks the liberties of our country endangered by the licentiousness, the other, by the restrictions of the press. Such are some among the leading features of these notorious divisions of political party. It is evident, gentlemen of the jury, that each will view with a jealous eye the positions of the other, and that there cannot but be a bias among the partisans of the one side, against the principles and doctrines inculcated by the other. In the present instance, I fear it cannot but have its effects; for, without impeaching the integrity of any person directly concerned in the progress of the present trial, I may fairly state that, under the Sedition Law, a defendant, such as I stand before you, is placed in a situation unknown in any other case.

Directly or indirectly, the public, if not the private, character of the President of the United States is involved in the present trial. Who nominates the judges who are to preside? The juries who are to judge of the evidence? The marshal who has the summoning of the jury? The President. Suppose a case of arbitration concerning the property of any one of you, where the adverse party should claim the right of nominating the persons whose legal opinions are to decide the law of the question, and of the very man who shall have the appointment of the arbitrators—what would you say to such a trial? And yet in fact such is mine, and such is the trial of every man who has the misfortune to be indicted under this law. But although I have a right to presume something of political bias against my opinions, from the court who try me, to you who sit there as jurymen, I am still satisfied you will feel that you have some character to support and some character to lose; and whatever your opinions may be on the subjects alluded to in the indictment, you will reverence as you ought the sacred obligation of the oath you have taken.

Gentlemen of the jury, I acknowledge, as freely as any of you can, the necessity of a certain degree of confidence in the executive government of the country. But this confidence ought not to be unlimited, and need not be paid up in advance; let it be earned before it be reposed; let it be claimed by the evidence of benefits conferred, of measures that compel approbation, of conduct irreproachable. It cannot be exacted by the guarded provisions of sedition laws, by attacks on the freedom of the press, by prosecutions, pains and penalties on those which boldly express the truth, or who may honestly and innocently err in their political sentiments. Let this required confidence be the meed of desert, and the public will not be backward to pay it.

But in the present state of affairs, the press is open to those who will praise, while the threats of the law hang over those who blame the conduct of the men in power. Indiscriminate approbation of the measures of the executive is not only unattacked, but fostered, and received with the utmost avidity; while those who venture to express a sentiment of opposition must do it in fear and trembling, and run the hazard of being dragged like myself before the frowning tribunal, erected by the Sedition Law. Be it so; but surely this anxiety to protect public character must arise from fear of attack. That conduct which will not bear investigation will naturally shun it; and whether my opinions are right or wrong, as they are stated in the charge, I cannot help thinking they would have been better confuted by evidence and argument than by indictment. Fines and imprisonment will produce conviction neither in the mind of the sufferer nor of the public.

JUDGE SAMUEL CHASE'S CHARGE TO THE JURY

Thomas Cooper, the traverser, stands charged with having published a false, scandalous and malicious libel against the President of the United States, in his official character as President. There is no civilized country that I know of that does not punish such offenses; and it is necessary to the peace and welfare of this country, that these offenses should meet with their proper punishment, since ours is a government founded on the opinions and confidence of the people. The Representatives and the President are chosen by the people. It is a government made by themselves; and their officers are chosen by themselves; and, therefore, if any improper law is enacted, the people have it in their power to obtain the repeal of such law, or even of the Constitution itself, if found defective, since provision is made for its amendment. Our government, therefore, is really republican; the people are truly represented, since all power is derived from them. It is a government of representation and responsibility: all officers of the government are liable to be displaced or removed, or their duration in office limited by elections at fixed periods. There is one department only, the judiciary, which is not subject to such removal; their offices being held "during good behavior," and therefore they can only be removed for misbehavior.

All governments which I have ever read or heard of punish libels against themselves. If a man attempts to destroy the confidence of the people in their officers, their supreme magistrate, and their legislature, he effectually saps the foundation of the government. A republican government can only be destroyed in two ways: the introduction of luxury, or the licentiousness of the press. This latter is the more slow, but most sure and certain means of bringing about the destruction of the government. The legislature of this country, knowing this maxim, has thought proper to pass a law to check this licentiousness of the press . . . . [Judge Chase read the second section of the Sedition Law]. It must, therefore, be observed, gentlemen of the jury, that the *intent* must be plainly manifest; it is an important word in the law; for if there is no such intent to defame, etc., there is no offense created by that law. . . .

[Thomas Cooper] states in his defense that he does not arraign the motives of the President, yet he has boldly avowed that his own motives in this publication were to censure the conduct of the President, which his conduct, as he thought, deserved. Now, gentlemen, the motives of the President, in his official capacity, are not a subject of inquiry with you. Shall we say to the President, you are not fit for the government of this country? It is no apology for a man to say that he believes the President to be honest, but that he has done acts which prove him unworthy the confidence of the people, incapable of executing the duties of his high station, and unfit for the important office to which the people have elected him. The motives and intent of the traverser, not of the President, are the subject to be inquired into by you.

Now we will consider this libel as published by the defendant, and observe what were his motives. You will find the traverser speaking of the President in the following words: "Even those who doubted his capacity, thought well of his intentions." This the traverser might suppose would be considered as a compliment to the intentions of the President; but I have no doubt that it was meant to carry a sting with it which should be felt; for it was in substance saying of the President, "you may have good intentions, but I doubt your capacity." He then goes on to say—"Nor were we yet saddled with the expense of a permanent navy, nor threatened, under his auspices, with the existence of a standing army. Our credit was not yet reduced so low as to borrow money at eight per cent in *time of peace*." Now, gentlemen, if these things were true, can any one doubt what effect they would have on the public mind? If the people believed those things, what would be the consequence? What! The President of the United States saddle us with a permanent navy, encourage a standing army, and borrow money at a large premium? And are we told, too, that this is in time of peace? If you believe this to be true, what opinion can you, gentlemen, form of the President? One observation must strike you, i.e., that these charges are made not only against the President, but against yourselves who elect the House of Representatives, for these acts cannot be done without first having been approved of by Congress. Can a navy be built, can an army be raised, or money borrowed, without the consent of Congress?

The President is further charged, for "the unnecessary violence of his official expressions might *justly* have provoked a war." This is a very serious charge indeed. What! The President, by unnecessary violence, plunge this country into a war! It cannot be—I say, gentlemen, again, if you believe this, what opinion can you form of the President? Certainly the worst you can form: you would certainly consider him totally unfit for the high station which he has so honorably filled, and with such benefit to his country.

The traverser states that, under the auspices of the President, "our credit is so low that we are obliged to borrow money at eight per cent in time of peace." I cannot suppress my feelings at this gross attack upon the

President. Can this be true? Can you believe it? Are we now in time of peace? Is there no war? No hostilities with France? Has she not captured our vessels and plundered us of our property to the amount of millions? Have we not armed our vessels to defend ourselves, and have we not captured several of her vessels of war? Although no formal declaration of war has been made, is it not notorious that actual hostilities have taken place? And is this, then, a time of peace? The very expense incurred, which rendered a loan necessary, was in consequence of the conduct of France. The traverser, therefore, has published an untruth, knowing it to be an untruth. . . .

Take this publication in all its parts, and it is the boldest attempt I have known to poison the minds of the people. . . . You will please to notice, gentlemen, that the traverser in his defense must prove every charge he has made to be true; he must prove it to the marrow. If he asserts three things, and proves but one, he fails; if he proves but two, he fails in his defense, for he must prove the whole of his assertions to be true. . . . If he fails in this proof, you must then consider whether his intention in making these charges were malicious or not. You must judge for yourselves—you must find the publication, and judge of the intent with which that publication was made, whether it was malice or not. . . .

Extracts from the original draft of Thomas Jefferson's first inaugural address, 1801

Jefferson's presidential victory in 1801 confirmed his faith in the peaceful methods of the democratic process rather than in the use of revolutionary means. "We in America," he once wrote, "deal in ink only," while European nations effect their political changes "in blood." Nevertheless, the bitter political fights of the previous decade had brought the country to the edge of civil dissension and disunion, and Jefferson believed it was imperative to halt or quiet such rabid partisanship. His inaugural address, in effect, was a peace offering to the opposition and a plea for the unity of all citizens, but it also contained a paean to America's achievements and potential, as well as a magnificent statement of republican principles.

During the contest of opinion through which we have passed, the animation of discussions and of exertions has sometimes worn an aspect which might impose on strangers unused to think freely, and to speak and to write what they think. But this being now decided by the voice of the nation, announced according to the rules of the Constitution, all will of course arrange themselves under the will of the law, and unite in common

From Paul L. Ford (ed.), *The Works of Thomas Jefferson* (New York, 1905), Vol. IX, pp. 194–97, 199–200.

efforts for the common good. All too will bear in mind this sacred principle, that though the will of the majority is in all cases to prevail, that will, to be rightful, must be reasonable: that the minority possess their equal rights, which equal laws must protect, and to violate would be oppression.

Let us then, fellow citizens, unite with one heart and one mind; let us restore to social intercourse that harmony and affection without which liberty, and even life itself, are but dreary things. And let us reflect that having banished from our land that religious intolerance under which mankind so long bled and suffered, we have yet gained little, if we countenance a political intolerance, as despotic as wicked, and capable of as bitter and bloody persecution.

During the throes and convulsions of the ancient world, during the agonized spasms of infuriated man, seeking through blood and slaughter his long lost liberty, it was not wonderful that the agitation of the billows should reach even this distant and peaceful shore; that this should be more felt and feared by some, and less by others, and should divide opinions as to measures of safety. But every difference of opinion is not a difference of principle. We have called, by different names, brethren of the same principle. We are all republicans; we are all federalists. If there be any among us who wish to dissolve this union, or to change its republican form, let them stand undisturbed, as monuments of the safety with which error of opinion may be tolerated where reason is left free to combat it.

I know indeed that some honest men have feared that a republican government cannot be strong; that this government is not strong enough. But would the honest patriot, in the full tide of successful experiment, abandon a government which has so far kept us free and firm on the theoretic and visionary fear that this government, the world's best hope may, by possibility, want energy to preserve itself? I trust not. I believe this, on the contrary, the strongest government on earth. I believe it the only one where every man, at the call of the law, would fly to the standard of the law; would meet invasions of public order, as his own personal concern. Sometimes it is said that man cannot be trusted with the government of himself. Can he then be trusted with the government of others? Or have we found angels in the form of kings to govern him? Let history answer this question.

Let us then pursue with courage and confidence our own federal and republican principles, our attachment to union and representative government. Kindly separated by nature and a wide ocean from the exterminating havoc of one quarter of the globe; too high-minded to endure the degradations of the others; possessing a chosen country, with room enough for all descendants to the 1,000th ... generation; entertaining a due sense of our equal right, to the use of our own faculties, to the acquisitions of our own industry, to honor and confidence from our fellow citizens resulting not from birth, but from our actions and their sense of them; enlightened by a benign religion, professed indeed and practiced in various forms, yet all of them inculcating honesty, truth, temperance, gratitude, and the love of man; acknowledging and adoring an overruling providence, which by all its dispensations proves that it delights in the happiness of man here, and his greater happiness hereafter; with all these blessings, what more is necessary to make us a happy and prosperous people? Still one thing more, fellow citizens, a wise and frugal government, which shall restrain men from injuring one another, shall leave them otherwise free to regulate their own pursuits of industry and improvement, and shall not take from the mouth of labor the bread it has earned. This is the sum of good government, and this is necessary to close the circle of our felicities. . . .

A Federalist moves from hope to despair: the letters of Fisher Ames, 1801–04

Jefferson's first administration was one of the most successful in American history. Despite the laments and cries and forebodings of Federalist leaders, the nation prospered, no blood baths took place, the Bank of the United States continued to operate, and peace was maintained. Jefferson proved an enormously capable politician, and in 1804 he was victorious over his Federalist opponent in all but two states (Connecticut and Delaware). As Republican power and popularity grew, Federalist hopes of regaining power changed to despair.

To Theodore Dwight   March 19, 1801

To encourage Mr. Jefferson to act right, and to aid him against his violent Jacobin adherents, we [Federalists] must make it manifest that we act on principle, and that we are deeply alarmed for the public good; that we are identified with the public. We must speak in the name and with the voice of the good and the wise, the lovers of liberty and the owners of property. By early impressing the preciousness, if I may use the word, of certain principles, and of the credit, commerce, and arts, that depend on adhering to them, and by pointing out the utter ruin of the commercial States by a Virginia or democratic system, may we not consolidate the Federalists, and check the licentiousness of the Jacobin administration?

To Thomas Dwight   April 16, 1802

The angels of destruction at Washington are making haste, as if they knew their time is short. . . . The French from 1789 to 1792, in like man-

From Seth Ames (ed.), *Works of Fisher Ames* (Boston, 1854), Vol. I, pp. 293, 297–98, 309–10, 317–18, 323–24, 328–32, 336–38.

ner, established a democracy of the wildest and wickedest sort, and thought they could have a king at the head of it. A monarchical mobocracy was their philosophical plan. It answered just as we might expect from joining contradictions together. A like issue must attend our Democrats, and the next thing will be, as in France, anarchy, then Jacobinism organized with energy enough to plunder and shed blood. The only chance of safety lies in the revival of the energy of the Federalists, who alone will or can preserve liberty, property or Constitution.

To Christopher Gore   December 13, 1802

Our ruin advances like a ship-launch, very slow at first, so that you can scarcely see motion, then quicker, and then so quick as to fire the ways. Congress is sitting, and we are expecting the gracious message from the throne.... They will probably change the places of doing the financial business of the government from the United States Bank to the State banks. They will thus hope to organize a faction in each State, devoted to themselves....

To prevent this utter destruction of all that is worth saving, we must animate the Federalists. We must try to raise their zeal high enough to defend, on principle, what the others would seize by violence. The Federalists must entrench themselves in the State governments, and endeavor to make State justice and State power a shelter of the wise, and good, and rich, from the wild destroying rage of the southern Jacobins.

To Christopher Gore   October 3, 1803

As to Louisiana ... [I] say that the acquiring of territory with money is mean and despicable.... The merchants at the southward look with eyes of favor to the opening of the port of New Orleans. The western settlers also like the thing, and care not what mean compliances, nor how many millions it costs. The Mississippi was a boundary.... We were confined within some limits. Now, by adding an unmeasured world beyond that river, we rush like a comet into infinite space. In our wild career, we may jostle some other world out of its orbit, but we shall, in every event, quench the light of our own.

To Thomas Dwight   October 26, 1803

Our country is too big for union, too sordid for patriotism, too democratic for liberty. What is to become of it, he who made it best knows. Its vice will govern it, by practicing upon its folly.... Yet we are told, the *vox populi* is the *vox dei;* and our demagogues claim a right divine to reign over us.

To Christopher Gore   November 16, 1803

What can be expected from a country where Tom Paine is invited to
come by the chief man, as Plato was by Dionysius; where the whiskey
secretary [Albert Gallatin] is Secretary of the Treasury; and where such
men as the English laws confine in jail for sedition, make the laws, and
unmake the judges? . . . Our people care not much for these things. To
get money is our business; the measures of government and political events,
are only our amusements.

To Thomas Dwight   November 29, 1803

I think the government will last my time. For that reason, I will fatten my
pigs, and prune my trees; nor will I any longer be at the trouble to govern
this country. I am no Atlas, and my shoulders ache. . . . You Federalists
are only lookers-on.

To Thomas Dwight   January 25, 1804

Democracy is a troubled spirit, fated never to rest, and whose dreams, if
it sleeps, present only visions of hell. I have long thought justice one of
the most refined luxuries of the most refined society; that ours is too gross,
too nearly barbarous, to have it. Justice, to be anything, must be stronger
than government, or at least stronger than the popular passions. Nothing
in the United States is half so strong as these passions; indeed the government itself has no other strength. I have contemplated an essay to show
that democracy and justice are incompatible.

An episode during the Lewis and Clark expedition, July 27, 1806

*Thomas Jefferson was probably the most Western-minded of early American
statesmen. Even before the purchase of Louisiana he had requested and Congress had approved a secret appropriation for an exploration "to the Western
Ocean." The two men Jefferson selected as leaders—Meriwether Lewis and
William Clark—started up the Missouri river in 1804, reached the Pacific in
1805, and returned in 1806. Their narrative of the journey is one of the greatest
adventure stories in American history. The following is a dramatic episode, recorded by Lewis, of his encounter with some Indians during their return trip.*

From Reuben G. Thwaites (ed.), *Original Journals of the Lewis and Clark Expedition*
(New York, 1905), Vol. V, pp. 223–25.

This morning at daylight the Indians got up and crowded around the fire. J. Fields, who was on post, had carelessly laid his gun down behind him near where his brother was sleeping. One of the Indians, the fellow to whom I had given the medal last evening, slipped behind him and took his gun and that of his brother unperceived by him. At the same instant two others advanced and seized the guns of Drewyer and myself. J. Fields, seeing this, turned about to look for his gun and saw the fellow just running off with her [the gun] and his brother's. He called to his brother who instantly jumped up and pursued the Indian with him, whom they overtook at the distance of 50 or 60 paces from the camp, seized their guns, and wrested them from him. R. Fields, as he seized his gun, stabbed the Indian to the heart with his knife. The fellow ran about 15 steps and fell dead; of this I did not know until afterwards.

Having recovered their guns they ran back instantly to the camp; Drewyer, who was awake, saw the Indian take hold of his gun and instantly jumped up and seized her and wrested her from him but the Indian still retained his pouch. His jumping up and crying "Damn you, let go my gun," awakened me. I jumped up and asked what was the matter, which I quickly learned when I saw Drewyer in a scuffle with the Indian for his gun. I reached to seize my gun but found her gone. I then drew a pistol from my holster and turning myself about saw the Indian making off with my gun. I ran at him with my pistol and bid him lay down my gun, which he was in the act of doing, when the Fieldses returned and drew up their guns to shoot him, which I forbid as he did not appear to be about to make any resistance or commit any offensive act. He dropped the gun and walked slowly off. I picked her up instantly. Drewyer having about this time recovered his gun and pouch, asked me if he might not kill the fellow, which I also forbid as the Indian did not appear to wish to kill us.

As soon as they found us all in possession of our arms they ran and endeavored to drive off all the horses. I now hollered to the men and told them to fire on them if they attempted to drive off our horses. They accordingly pursued the main party who were driving the horses up the river, and I pursued the man who had taken my gun, who with another was driving off a part of the horses which were to the left of the camp. I pursued them so closely that they could not take twelve of their own horses, but continued to drive one of mine with some others; at the distance of three hundred paces they entered one of those steep nitches in the bluff, with the horses before them. Being nearly out of breath I could pursue no further. I called to them, as I had done several times before, that I would shoot them if they did not give me my horse and raised my gun. One of them jumped behind a rock and spoke to the other who turned around and stopped at the distance of 30 steps from me, and I shot him through the belly. He fell to his knees and on his right elbow, from which position he partly raised himself up and fired at me, and turning himself about crawled in behind a rock which was a few feet from him. He overshot me. Being bareheaded I felt the wind of his bullet very distinctly. Not having my shotpouch I could not reload my piece, and as there were two of them behind good shelters from me I did not think it prudent to rush on them with my pistol which I had discharged. I had not the means of reloading until I reached camp; I therefore returned leisurely towards camp. On my way I met with Drewyer who having heard the report of the guns had returned in search of me and left the Fieldses to pursue the Indians. I desired him to hasten to the camp with me and assist in catching as many of the Indian horses as were necessary. . . . We reached the camp and began to catch the horses and saddle them and put on the packs. The reason I had not my pouch with me was that I had not time to return about 50 yards to camp after getting my gun before I was obliged to pursue the Indians or suffer them to collect and drive off all the horses. We had caught and saddled the horses and began to arrange the packs when the Fieldses returned with four of our horses and took four of the best of those of the Indians. While the men were preparing the horses I put four shields and two bows and quivers of arrows which had been left by the fire, with sundry other articles; they left all their baggage at our mercy.

An act laying an embargo on all ships and vessels in the ports and harbors of the United States, December 22, 1807

The problem of foreign affairs bedeviled Jefferson's second term. Both England and France violated America's rights as a neutral nation, but England's paramount position as a naval power caused Americans to be most conscious of her actions—illegal blockades, the confiscation of cargoes, the impressment of sailors. In 1807 there occurred an immediate provocation which might have resulted in war, when the British frigate, HMS Leopard, fired three broadsides at close range into the side of an American naval ship, the Chesapeake. But Jefferson regarded war as an admission of diplomatic bankruptcy, and he wished to try a policy of economic coercion to force both England and France to respect American sovereign rights. Precisely six months after the Leopard's attack, Jefferson signed the Embargo Act. Supplemented four times by additional legislation to enforce its provisions, the embargo proved both ineffective and unpopular, and was finally abandoned by Jefferson before he left the presidency.

Be it enacted by the Senate and House of Representatives of the United States of America in Congress assembled, that an embargo be, and hereby is laid on all ships and vessels in the ports and places within the limits or jurisdiction of the United States, cleared or not cleared, bound to

From Richard Peters (ed.), *The Public Statutes at Large of the United States of America* (Boston, 1845), Vol. II, pp. 451–53.

any foreign port or place; and that no clearance be furnished to any ship or vessel bound to such foreign port or place, except vessels under the immediate direction of the President of the United States: and that the President be authorized to give such instructions to the officers of the revenue, and of the navy and revenue cutters of the United States, as shall appear best adapted for carrying the same into full effect: *Provided,* that nothing herein contained shall be construed to prevent the departure of any foreign ship or vessel, either in ballast, or with the goods, wares and merchandise on board of such foreign ship or vessel, when notified of this act.

SEC. 2. *And it be further enacted,* that during the continuance of this act, no registered, or sea letter vessel, having on board goods, wares and merchandise, shall be allowed to depart from one port of the United States to any other within the same, unless the master, owner, consignee or factor of such vessel shall first give bond, with one or more sureties to the collector of the district from which she is bound to depart, in a sum of double the value of the vessel and cargo, that the said goods, wares, or merchandise shall be relanded in some port of the United States, dangers of the seas excepted, which bond, and also a certificate from the collector where the same may be relanded, shall by the collector respectively be transmitted to the Secretary of the Treasury. All armed vessels possessing public commissions from any foreign power, are not to be considered as liable to the embargo laid by this act.

Speeches in Congress for and against war with England, December 10–11, 1811

Jefferson's presidential actions postponed rather than resolved the issue of American grievances against England; his successor, James Madison, fared far worse. After the embargo, United States policy shifted from that of economic coercion to economic bribery—to no avail. War-hawking politicians in Congress demanded that national honor be redeemed by a declaration of hostilities. And Madison—whose diplomatic blunders, ironically, resulted from his zealous desire for peace—succumbed to these pressures. In December 1811, he requested additional military forces, which evoked the following speeches from John Randolph, Jr. of Virginia and Richard M. Johnson of Kentucky. The final declaration of war came in June 1812.

JOHN RANDOLPH, JR. OF VIRGINIA AGAINST WAR, DECEMBER 10, 1811

Go! March to Canada! Leave the broad bosom of the Chesapeake and her hundred tributary rivers—the whole line of seacoast from Machias to

From *The Debates and Proceedings in the Congress of the United States, Twelfth Congress, First Session* (Washington, D.C., 1853), pp. 447–51, 454–60.

St. Mary's, unprotected! You have taken Quebec—have you conquered England? Will you seek for the deep foundations of her power in the frozen deserts of Labrador? . . . Will you call upon her to leave your ports and harbors untouched, only just till you can return from Canada, to defend them? The coast is to be left defenseless, whilst men of the interior are revelling in conquest and spoil. But grant for a moment, for mere argument's sake, that in Canada you touched the sinews of [England's] strength. . . . In what situation would you then place some of the best men of the nation? As Chatham and Burke, and the whole band of her patriots, prayed for her defeat in 1776, so must some of the truest friends to their country deprecate the success of our arms against the only power that holds in check the archenemy of mankind. . . .

Our people will not submit to be taxed for this war of conquest and dominion. The Government of the United States was not calculated to wage offensive foreign war—it was instituted for the common defense and general welfare; and whosoever should embark it in a war of offense, would put it to a test which it was by no means calculated to endure. Make it out that Great Britain had instigated the Indians on the late occasion, and he was ready for battle; but not for dominion. He was unwilling, however, under present circumstances, to take Canada, at the risk of the Constitution —to embark in a common cause with France and be dragged at the wheels of the car of some Burr or Bonaparte. For a gentleman from Tennessee or Gennessee, or Lake Champlain, there may be some prospect of advantage. Their hemp would bear a great price by the exclusion of foreign supply. In that too the great importers were deeply interested. The upper country on the Hudson and the Lakes would be enriched by the supplies for the troops, which they alone could furnish. They would have the exclusive market; to say nothing of the increased preponderance from the acquisition of Canada. . . .

Mr. Randolph dwelt on the danger arising from the black population. He said he would touch this subject as tenderly as possible—it was with reluctance that he touched it at all—but in cases of great emergency, the State physician must not be deterred by a sickly, hysterical humanity from probing the wound of his patient—he must not be withheld by a fastidious and mistaken humanity from representing his true situation to his friends, or even to the sick man himself, where the occasion called for it. What was the situation of the slaveholding States? During the war of the Revolution, so fixed were their habits of subordination, that when the whole Southern country was overrun by the enemy, who invited them to desert, no fear was ever entertained of an insurrection of the slaves. . . . But should we therefore be unobservant spectators of the progress of society within the last twenty years—of the silent but powerful change wrought by time and chance, upon its composition and temper? When the fountains of the great deep of abomination were broken up, even the poor slaves had not escaped the general deluge. The French Revolution had polluted even them. Nay, there had not been wanting men in [the French Assembly] . . . to preach upon that floor to a crowded audience of blacks in the galleries —teaching them that they are equal to their masters; in other words, advising them to cut their throats. Similar doctrines were disseminated by peddlers from New England and elsewhere, throughout the Southern country—and masters had been found so infatuated, as by their lives and conversation, by a general contempt of order, morality, and religion, unthinkingly to cherish these seeds of self-destruction to them and their families. What was the consequence? Within the last ten years, repeated alarms of insurrection among the slaves—some of them awful indeed. From the spreading of this infernal doctrine, the whole Southern country had been thrown into a state of insecurity. Men dead to the operation of moral causes, had taken away from the poor slave his habits of loyalty and obedience to his master, which lightened his servitude by a double operation; beguiling his own cares and disarming his master's suspicions and severity; and now, like true empirics in politics, you are called upon to trust to the mere physical strength of the fetter which holds him in bondage. You have deprived him of all moral restraint, you have tempted him to eat of the fruit of the tree of knowledge, just enough to perfect him in wickedness; you have opened his eyes to his nakedness; you have armed his nature against the hand that has fed him, that has clothed him, that has cherished him in sickness; that hand, which before he became a pupil of your school, he had been accustomed to press with respectful affection. You have done all this—and then show him the gibbet and the wheel, as incentives to a sullen, repugnant obedience. God forbid, sir, that the Southern States should ever see an enemy on their shores, with these infernal principles of French fraternity in the van! While talking of taking Canada, some of us were shuddering for our own safety at home. He spoke from facts, when he said that the nightbell never tolled for fire in Richmond that the mother did not hug her infant more closely to her bosom. . . .

Before this miserable force of ten thousand men was raised to take Canada, he begged them to look at the state of defense at home—to count the cost of the enterprise before it was set on foot, not when it might be too late—when the best blood of the country should be spilt, and nought but empty coffers left to pay the cost . . . . He would beseech the House, before they ran their heads against this post, Quebec, to count the cost. His word for it, Virginia planters would not be taxed to support such a war—a war which must aggravate their present distresses; in which they had not the remotest interest. . . . He called upon those professing to be Republicans to make good the promises held out by their Republican predecessors when they came into power—promises, which for years afterwards they had honestly, faithfully fulfilled. We had vaunted of paying off the national debt, of retrenching useless establishments; and yet had now become as infatuated with standing armies, loans, taxes, navies, and war, as ever were the Essex Junto. What Republicanism is this?

RICHARD M. JOHNSON OF KENTUCKY FOR WAR,
DECEMBER 11, 1811

I feel rejoiced that the hour of resistance is at hand, and that the President, in whom the people have so much confidence, has warned us of the perils that await them, and has exhorted us to put on the armor of defense, to gird on the sword, and assume the manly and bold attitude of war. ... For the first time since my entrance into this body, there now seems to be but one opinion with a great majority—that with Great Britain war is inevitable; that the hopes of the sanguine as to a returning sense of British justice have expired; that the prophecies of the discerning have failed; and, that her infernal system has driven us to the brink of a second revolution, as important as the first. Upon the Wabash, through the influence of British agents, and within our territorial sea by the British navy, the war has already commenced. Thus, the folly, the power, and the tyranny of Great Britain, have taken from us the last alternative of longer forbearance.

We must now oppose the further encroachments of Great Britain by war, or formally annul the Declaration of our Independence, and acknowledge ourselves her devoted colonies. The people whom I represent will not hesitate which of the two courses to choose; and, if we are involved in war, to maintain our dearest rights, and to preserve our independence, I pledge myself to this House, and my constituents to this nation, that they will not be wanting in valor, nor in their proportion of men and money to prosecute the war with effect. Before we relinquish the conflict, I wish to see Great Britain renounce the piratical system or paper blockade; to liberate our captured seamen on board her ships of war; to relinquish the practice of impressment on board our merchant vessels; to repeal her Orders in Council; and cease, in every other respect, to violate our neutral rights; to treat us as an independent people. The gentleman from Virginia [Mr. Randolph] has objected to the destination of this auxiliary force—the occupation of the Canadas, and the other British possessions upon our borders where our laws are violated, the Indians stimulated to murder our citizens, and where there is a British monopoly of the peltry and fur trade. I should not wish to extend the boundary of the United States by war if Great Britain would leave us to the quiet enjoyment of independence; but, considering her deadly and implacable enmity, and her continued hostility, I shall never die contented until I see her expulsion from North America, and her territories incorporated with the United States. It is strange that the gentleman would pause before refusing this force, if destined to keep the Negroes in subordination—who are not in a state of insurrection as I understand—and he will absolutely refuse to vote this force to defend us against the lawless aggressions of Great Britain—a nation in whose favor he had said so much. ...

The gentleman from Virginia says we are identified with the British in religion, in blood, in language, and deeply laments our hatred to that country, who can boast of so many illustrious characters. This deep rooted enmity to Great Britain arises from her insidious policy, the offspring of her perfidious conduct towards the United States. Her disposition is unfriendly; her enmity is implacable; she sickens at our prosperity and happiness. If obligations of friendship do exist, why does Great Britain rend those ties asunder, and open the bleeding wounds of former conflicts? Or does the obligation of friendship exist on the part of the United States alone? I have never thought that the ties of religion, of blood, of language, and of commerce, would justify or sanctify insult and injury—on the contrary, that a premeditated wrong from the hand of a friend created more sensibility, and deserved the greater chastisement and the higher execration. What would you think of a man, to whom you were bound by the most sacred ties, who would plunder you of your substance, aim a deadly blow at your honor, and in the hour of confidence endeavor to bury a dagger in your bosom? Would you, sir, proclaim to the world your affection for this miscreant of society, after this conduct, and endeavor to interest your audience with the ties of kindred that bound you to each other? So let it be with nations, and there will be neither surprise nor lamentation that we execrate a government so hostile to our independence —for it is from the government that we meet with such multiplied injury, and to that object is our hatred directed. ... The records of that government are now stained with the blood of ... martyrs in freedom's cause, as vilely as with the blood of American citizens; and certainly we shall not be called upon to love equally the murderer and the victim. For God's sake let us not again be told of the ties of religion, of laws, of blood, and of customs, which bind the two nations together, with a view to extort our love for the English government, and more especially, where the same gentleman [Randolph], has acknowledged that we have ample cause of war against that nation—let us not be told of the freedom of that corrupt government, whose hands are washed alike in the blood of her own illustrious statesmen, for a manly opposition to tyranny, and the citizens of every other clime.

Twenty-eight years have elapsed, and the only remedy which we have attempted against these crying enormities has been negotiation and remonstrance, and so far from producing any beneficial effect, Great Britain has made new innovations and urged new pretensions, until the neutral rights of the United States are entirely destroyed. ... May the wrath of this nation kindle into a flame and become a consuming fire! Though slow to anger, may her indignation be like the rushing of mighty waters and the volcanic eruptions of Hecla!

Sedition in New England, 1814–15

The war was hardly popular in New England. Federalist governors in those states openly defied the national administration, refusing to permit their militia to fight outside state boundaries. Boston financiers did not subscribe to requests for loans to finance the war. Northern newspapers teemed with inflammatory appeals to resist the war effort. The possibility of secession seemed real. James Madison "looks miserably shattered and woebegone," a visitor reported. "His mind is full of the New England sedition." Fortunately, the Hartford Convention of 1814–15 was controlled by moderates rather than extremists. Instead of secession, they passed a series of proposals for constitutional amendments.

The first chapter of Mathew Carey's The Olive Branch—*first published in November 1814, and reprinted in many subsequent editions—contains an account of the dangers America faced from the internal division and seditious upheaval in New England.*

In the year 1814, the situation of the United States was highly critical. Party and faction, the bane and destruction of the ancient republics, were carried to such an extravagant extent as to endanger the public tranquility —and menace us with civil war, the greatest scourge that ever afflicted mankind. Unceasing efforts were used to excite our citizens to open resistance of the government. The principal scenes of these disorders lay in the eastern states; but in almost every portion of the union, persons were constantly employed in inflaming the public mind, and preparing it for commotions. Thousands and tens of thousands of our citizens, upright, honest, and honorable in private life, were so deluded by the madness of party and faction as to believe that the defeat, the disgrace, and the disasters of our armies . . . were all "a consummation devoutly to be wished" —and the certain means of procuring a speedy and honorable peace which we could not fail to obtain from the magnanimity of Great Britain, provided we removed those public officers, whom, according to them, she has so much reason to execrate. . . .

It was said, that those who had for years urged the propriety, and necessity, and advantages to the eastern states, of a dissolution of the union, did not intend to proceed thus far; and that they held out these threats *in terrorem* to awe the administration. There is the strongest possible reason to believe that this was a pernicious, a fatal error—and that the leaders of the malcontents were perfectly serious in their views of a separation. . . . To vindicate myself from the charge of folly, in those gloomy apprehensions and anticipations, I submit to the reader a few specimens of the unceasing efforts which for years had been made to enkindle the flames of civil war. . . . Never was more activity displayed—never was a cause more sedulously

From Mathew Carey, *The Olive Branch: Or, Faults on Both Sides, Federal and Democratic,* tenth edition (Philadelphia, 1818), pp. 37–43.

or ably advocated. And never was there less scruple about the means, provided the end could be accomplished.

On or before the fourth of July, if James Madison is not out of office, *a new form of government will be in operation in the Eastern section of the union. Instantly after, the contest in many of the states will be, whether to adhere to the old, or join the new government.* Like everything else foretold years ago, and which is verified every day, this warning will be also ridiculed as visionary. Be it so. But Mr. Madison cannot complete his term of service, if the war continues. It is not possible; and if he knew human nature, he would see it.

Is there a federalist, a patriot in America, who conceives it his duty to shed his blood for Bonaparte, for Madison, for Jefferson, and that HOST OF RUFFIANS *in Congress,* who have set their faces against US for years, and spirited up the BRUTAL PART OF THE POPULACE to destroy us? Not one. Shall we then any longer be held in slavery, and driven to desperate poverty, by such a graceless faction? Heaven forbid.

If at the present moment, no symptoms of civil war appear, THEY CERTAINLY WILL SOON, *unless the courage of the war party fail them.*

A CIVIL WAR *becomes as certain as the events that happen according to the known laws and established course of nature.*

If we would preserve the liberties, by that struggle [the American revolution] so dearly purchased, *the call for* RESISTANCE *against the usurpations of our own government is as urgent as it was formerly against those of our mother country.*

If the impending negotiation with Great Britain is defeated by insidious artifice; if the friendly and conciliatory proposals of the enemy should not, from French subserviency, or views of sectional ambition, be met throughout with a spirit of moderation and sincerity, so as to terminate the infamous war which is scattering its horrors around us, and arrest the calamities and distress of a disgraced country, *it is necessary to apprise you that such conduct will be no longer borne with. The injured States will be compelled, by every motive of duty, interest and honor, by one manly exertion of their strength to dash into atoms the bonds of tyranny. It will then be too late to retreat. The die will be cast. Freedom preserved.*

A SEPARATION OF THE STATES *will be an inevitable result. Motives numerous and urgent will demand that measure. As they originate in oppression, the oppressors must be responsible for the momentous and contingent events, arising from the* DISSOLUTION OF THE PRESENT CONFEDERACY, *and the erection of* SEPARATE GOVERNMENTS. It will be their work. While posterity will admire the independent spirit of the Eastern section of our country, and with sentiments of gratitude, enjoy the fruits of their firmness and wisdom, the descendants of the South and West will have reason to curse the infatuation and folly of your councils.

Bold and resolute, when they step forth in the sacred cause of freedom and independence, the Northern people will secure their object. No obstacle can impede them. No force can withstand their powerful arm. The most numerous armies will melt before their manly strength. Does not the pages of history instruct you, that the feeble debility of the South never could face the vigorous activity of the North? Do not the events of past ages remind you of the valuable truth, *that a single spark of Northern liberty, especially when enlightened by congenial commerce, will explode a whole atmosphere of sultry Southern despotism?*

The aggregate strength of the South and West, if brought against the North, would be driven into the ocean, or back to their own sultry wilds; and they might think themselves fortunate if they escaped other punishment than a defeat, which their temerity would merit. While the one would strive to enslave, the other would fight for freedom. While the councils of the one would be distracted with discordant interests; the decisions of the other would be directed by one soul. Beware! Pause! before you take the fatal plunge.

You have carried your oppressions to the utmost stretch. *We will no longer submit.* Restore the Constitution to its purity. Give us security for the future, indemnity for the past. Abolish every tyrannical law. Make an immediate and honorable peace. Revive our commerce. Increase our navy. Protect our seamen. *Unless you comply with these just demands, without delay, we will withdraw from the Union, scatter to the winds the bonds of tyranny, and transmit to posterity that Liberty purchased by the Revolution.*

Americans! PREPARE YOUR ARMS: *you will soon be called to use them.* We must use them for the emperor of France, OR FOR OURSELVES. It is but an individual who now points to this ambiguous alternative. But Mr. Madison and his cabal may rest assured, there is in the hearts of many thousands in this abused and almost ruined country, a sentiment and energy to illustrate the distinction when his madness shall call it into action.

Old Massachusetts is as terrible to the American, now, as she was to the British cabinet in 1775; for America, too, has her Butes and Norths. Let then the commercial states breast themselves to the shock, and know that to themselves they must look for safety. All party bickerings must be sacrificed on the altar of patriotism. *Then, and not till then, shall they humble the pride and ambition of Virginia, whose strength lies in their weakness; and chastise the insolence of those madmen of Kentucky and Tennessee, who aspire to the government of these states, and threaten to involve the country in all the horrors of war.*

The language of the writers is plain and unequivocal. It admits of no mistake or misconstruction. That they intended to produce insurrection and dissolution of the union, unless they and their friends were enabled to seize upon the government, regardless of the frightful consequences, it would require consummate impudence to deny it; it would be folly, or insanity to disbelieve.

Peace and predictions for the future: a letter of Samuel Taggart, February 19, 1815

While Americans celebrated the peace treaty of 1815 as a monumental victory, an astute New England observer, Samuel Taggart, noted that it failed utterly to settle any of the outstanding grievances for which the United States went to war. Taggart also predicted that the Republican party would capitalize politically upon this peace, as indeed they did. The Federalists, tainted by the stigma of disloyalty, soon vanished entirely. Most important, Taggart foresaw that Britain would benefit economically from the peace by making capital investments in the American market, which yielded higher returns. In later years British investors bought up sizable proportions of stock in banks (including the second Bank of the United States), in canals (especially the Erie Canal), as well as in state bonds, railroad ventures, and western land speculations.

The treaty [of Ghent] I call a good one, because it secures to us the blessing of peace, which is beyond all price; and even if it was much less advantageous than it is, I should rejoice in it. I think it is as good as we had any right to expect, and better than I expected we could obtain. But it falls far short of the extravagant demands of our government at the commencement of the war, and what they would have still continued to be had Bonaparte continued all-powerful in Europe. As good, and probably a better, treaty might have been obtained when a cessation of arms was asked for by Admiral Warren, and an immense saving both of blood and treasure have been made. Our war-hawks, some of them at least, affect to speak of it as a glorious war and an honorable peace; but the treaty guaranties no one object for which the war was commenced. It is entirely silent about free-trade and sailor's rights, or the doctrine of blockades and impressment. . . .

There is another consequence of this war, which I think I clearly foresee. I do not know whether it strikes others in the same light it does me, i.e., this war which was waged for the express purpose of humbling Great Britain, and to compel her to do us justice, according to the common slang

From Samuel Taggart to Manasseh Cutler, February 19, 1815, in William Parker Cutler and Julia Perkins Cutler, *Life, Journals and Correspondence of Rev. Manasseh Cutler* (Cincinnati, 1888), Vol. II, pp. 332–34.

of the day, will render this country tributary to her, for perhaps half a century to come, in this way. Interest on public stocks is low in England, averaging not more than four per cent. Great numbers of the holders of American stocks wish to avail themselves of it as a mercantile capital. It will be either so or exchanged for British goods. This stock, on account of its bearing a higher interest, will be eagerly sought after by the moneyed capitalists of Europe, and it would not be strange if within three years much the largest portion of our public stocks should be owned in Great Britain. The interest will have to be paid in a foreign country in specie, and this will make a constant drain of the precious metals. But with all these and greater inconveniences peace is a blessing beyond all price.

There is one observation farther, which has occurred to me. We live in an eventful period. Probably there has not been so long, so destructive, and so extensive a war in the civilized world as has been during the last 20 or 25 years. How sudden and how great is the change within the last 18 months. Perhaps there has not been a period within the recollection of any person now living in which the European world has been so generally at peace as at this moment. The United States were the last getting into the vortex, and they have been the last in tasting the blessings of peace. May this peace among the nations prove the happy prelude of the universal reign of him who is the Prince of peace.

What the effect of peace will be on the state of political parties in this country, it will be impossible to foresee on any other grounds than conjecture. There is no doubt but endeavors will be used to make the public believe that it is an advantageous peace, and that Great Britain has been compelled to yield to us a great deal, and the credit of the whole will be claimed for the administration. Indeed, I can see this game begun already, and it will probably be attended with some success.

4

Jacksonian Enterprise

Speech of John C. Calhoun on internal improvements before the House of Representatives, February 4, 1817

After the War of 1812, Republican party leaders continued to address the nation with Jeffersonian rhetoric, but their actions were plainly Hamiltonian. A second Bank of the United States was chartered. A protective tariff was enacted. And spokesmen such as Henry Clay of Kentucky and John C. Calhoun of South Carolina endorsed federal programs of internal improvements. One of the most quoted speeches—deservedly so—was Calhoun's appeal to national security and future greatness by binding the country with a vast gridwork of roads and canals. His speech is particularly fascinating since Calhoun later became the most prominent advocate of states' rights.

At peace with all the world, abounding in pecuniary means, and, what was of the most importance, and at what he rejoiced as most favorable to the country, party and sectional feelings merged in a liberal and enlightened regard to the general concerns of the nation—such are the favorable circumstances under which we are now deliberating. Thus situated, to what can we direct our resources and attention more important than internal improvements? What can add more to the wealth, the strength, and the political prosperity of our country? The manner in which facility and cheapness of intercourse, added to the wealth of a nation, has been so often and ably discussed by writers on political economy, that he presumed the House to be perfectly acquainted with the subject. It was sufficient to observe that every branch of national industry—agricultural, manufacturing, and commercial—was greatly stimulated and rendered by it more productive. The result is that it tends to diffuse universal opulence. It gives to the interior the advantages possessed by the parts most eligibly situated for trade. It makes the country price, whether in the sale of the raw produce or in the purchase of the articles for consumption, approximate to that of the commercial towns. In fact, if we look into the nature of wealth, we will find that nothing can be more favorable to its growth than good roads and canals. An article, to command a price, must not only be useful, but must be the subject of demand; and the better the means of commercial intercourse the larger is the sphere of demand. The truth of these positions is obvious, and has been tested by all countries where the experiment has been made. It has particularly been strikingly exemplified in England, and if the result there, in a country so limited and so similar in its products, has been to produce a most uncommon state of opulence, what may we not expect from the same cause in our country, abounding as it does in the greatest variety of products, and presenting the greatest facility for improvements? Let it not be said that internal improvements

From the *Annals of the Congress of the United States,* Fourteenth Congress, Second Session (Washington, D.C., 1854), pp. 851–54.

may be wholly left to the enterprise of the States and of individuals. He knew that much might justly be expected to be done by them; but in a country so new and so extensive as ours, there is room enough for all the General and State governments and individuals in which to exert their resources. But many of the improvements contemplated are on too great a scale for the resources of the States or individuals; and many of such a nature, that the rival jealousy of the States, if left alone, might prevent. They required the resources and the general superintendence of this Government to effect and complete them.

But there are higher and more powerful considerations why Congress ought to take charge of this subject. If we were only to consider the pecuniary advantages of a good system of roads and canals, it might indeed admit of some doubt whether they ought not to be left wholly to individual exertions; but when we come to consider how intimately the strength and political prosperity of the Republic are connected with this subject, we find the most urgent reasons why we should apply our resources to them. In many respects, no country of equal population and wealth possesses equal materials of power with ours. The people, in muscular power, in hardy and enterprising habits, and in a lofty and gallant courage, are surpassed by none. In one respect, and, in my opinion, in one only, are we materially weak. We occupy a surface prodigiously great in proportion to our numbers. The common strength is brought to bear with great difficulty on the point that may be menaced by an enemy. It is our duty, then, as far as in the nature of things it can be effected, to counteract this weakness. Good roads and canals judiciously laid out, are the proper remedy. In the recent war, how much did we suffer for the want of them! Besides the tardiness and the consequential inefficacy of our military movements, to what an increased expense was the country put for the article of transportation alone! In the event of another war, the saving in this particular would go far towards indemnifying us for the expense of constructing the means of transportation. . . .

On this subject of national power, what can be more important than a perfect unity in every part, in feelings and sentiments? And what can tend more powerfully to produce it, than overcoming the effects of distance? No country, enjoying freedom, ever occupied anything like as great an extent of country as this Republic. One hundred years ago, the most profound philosophers did not believe it to be even possible. They did not suppose it possible that a pure Republic could exist on as great a scale even as the island of Great Britain. What then was considered as chimerical we now have the felicity to enjoy; and, what is most remarkable, such is the happy mould of our Government, so well are the State and general powers blended, that much of our political happiness draws its origin from the extent of our Republic. It has exempted us from most of the causes which distracted the small Republics of antiquity. Let it not, however, be forgotten; let it be forever kept in mind, that it exposes us to the greatest of all calamities, next to the loss of liberty, and even to that in its consequence—*disunion*. We are great, and rapidly—I was about to say fearfully—growing. This is our pride and danger—our weakness and our strength. Little does he deserve to be intrusted with the liberties of this people who does not raise his mind to these truths. We are under the most imperious obligation to counteract every tendency to disunion. The strongest of all cements is, undoubtedly, the wisdom, justice, and, above all, the moderation of this House; yet the great subject on which we are now deliberating, in this respect, deserves the most serious consideration. Whatever impedes the intercourse of the extremes with this, the center of the Republic, weakens the Union. The more enlarged the sphere of commercial circulation, the more extended that of social intercourse; the more strongly are we bound together; the more inseparable are our destinies. Those who understand the human heart best know how powerfully distance tends to break the sympathies of our nature. Nothing, not even dissimilarity of language, tends more to estrange man from man. Let us then bind the Republic together with a perfect system of roads and canals. Let us conquer space. It is thus the most distant parts of the Republic will be brought within a few days travel of the center; it is thus that a citizen of the West will read the news of Boston still moist from the press. The mail and the press are the nerves of the body politic. By them the slightest impression made on the most remote parts is communicated to the whole system; and the more perfect the means of transportation, the more rapid and true the vibration. To aid us in this great work, to maintain the integrity of this Republic, we inhabit a country presenting the most admirable advantages. Belted around, as it is, by lakes and oceans, intersected in every direction by bays and rivers, the hand of industry and art is tempted to improvement. So situated, blessed with a form of Government at once combining liberty and strength, we may reasonably raise our eyes to a most splendid future, if we only act in a manner worthy of our advantages. If, however, neglecting them, we permit a low, sordid, selfish, and sectional spirit to take possession of this House, this happy scene will vanish. We will divide, and in its consequences will follow misery and despotism.

Two suggestions for the education of females:
Thomas Jefferson and Emma Willard, 1818–19

Educational academies were first opened to females in the 1790's, though their curriculum was less rigorous than that for males. Timothy Dwight noted that "girls sink down to songs, novels, and plays." Thomas Jefferson also complained that females were too preoccupied with novels, "a poison which infects the mind" and "destroys its tone." Jefferson, however, liberal as he was, did not conceive that education for females should be on a par with that of males.

From Paul L. Ford (ed.), *The Works of Thomas Jefferson* (New York, 1905), Vol. XII, pp. 90–93; Emma Willard, *An Address to the Public, particularly to the Members of the Legislature of New York, Proposing a Plan for Improving Female Education* (Middlebury, Vermont, 1819), pp. 19–24.

Emma Willard who founded a Female Seminary in Troy, New York, was one of the first to propose a training equally demanding for both sexes.

THOMAS JEFFERSON TO NATHANIEL BURWELL, MARCH 14, 1818

A plan of female education has never been a subject of systematic contemplation with me. It has occupied my attention so far only as the education of my own daughters occasionally required. Considering that they would be placed in a country situation, where little aid could be obtained from abroad, I thought it essential to give them a solid education, which might enable them, when [they had] become mothers, to educate their own daughters, and even to direct the course for sons, should their fathers be lost, or incapable, or inattentive. . . .

A great obstacle to good education is the inordinate passion prevalent for novels, and the time lost in that reading which should be instructively employed. When this poison infects the mind, it destroys its tone and revolts against wholesome reading. Reason and fact, plain and unadorned, are rejected. Nothing can engage attention unless dressed in all the figments of fancy, and nothing so bedecked comes amiss. The result is a bloated imagination, sickly judgment, and disgust towards all the real business of life. This mass of trash, however, is not without some distinction; some few modelling their narratives, although fictitious, on the incidents of real life, have been able to make them interesting and useful vehicles of sound morality. . . . For a like reason, too, much poetry should not be indulged. Some is useful for forming style and taste. Pope, Dryden, Thompson, Shakespeare, and of the French, Molière, Racine, the Corneilles, may be read with pleasure and improvement. The French language [has] become that of the general intercourse of nations, and from their extraordinary advances, now the depository of all science, is an indispensable part of education for both sexes. . . .

The ornaments too, and the amusements of life, are entitled to their portion of attention. These, for a female, are dancing, drawing, and music. The first is a healthy exercise, elegant and very attractive for young people. Every affectionate parent would be pleased to see his daughter qualified to participate with her companions, and without awkwardness at least, in the circles of festivity, of which she occasionally becomes a part. It is a necessary accomplishment, therefore, although of short use, for the French rule is wise, that no lady dances after marriage. This is founded in solid physical reasons, gestation and nursing leaving little time to a married lady when this exercise can be either safe or innocent. Drawing is thought less of in this country than in Europe. It is an innocent and engaging amusement, often useful, and a qualification not to be neglected in one who is to become a mother and an instructor. Music is invaluable where a person has an ear. Where they have not, it should not be attempted. It furnishes a delightful recreation for the hours of respite from the cares of the day, and lasts us through life. The taste of this country, too, calls for this accomplishment more strongly than for either of the others.

I need say nothing of household economy, in which the mothers of our country are generally skilled, and generally careful to instruct their daughters. We all know its value, and that diligence and dexterity in all its processes are inestimable treasures. The order and economy of a house are as honorable to the mistress as those of the farm to the master, and if either be neglected, ruin follows, and children destitute of the means of living.

AN EXTRACT FROM EMMA WILLARD'S ADDRESS TO THE NEW YORK LEGISLATURE, 1819

Not even is youth considered in our sex, as in the other, a season which should be wholly devoted to improvement. Among families, so rich as to be entirely above labor, the daughters are hurried through the routine of boarding school instructions, and at an early period introduced into the gay world, and, thenceforth, their only object is amusement. Mark the different treatment which the sons of these families receive. While their sisters are gliding through the mazes of the midnight dance, they employ the lamp to treasure up for future use the riches of ancient wisdom; or to gather strength and expansion of mind, in exploring the wonderful paths of philosophy. When the youth of these two sexes has been spent so differently, is it strange, or is nature in fault, if more mature age has brought such a difference of character, that our sex have been considered by the other, as the pampered, wayward, babies of society, who must have some rattle put into our hands to keep us from doing mischief to ourselves or others?

Another difference in the treatment of the sexes is made in our country, which, though not equally pernicious to society, is more pathetically unjust to our sex. How often have we seen a student, who, returning from his literary pursuits, finds a sister, who was his equal in acquirements, while their advantages were equal, of whom he is now ashamed. While his youth was devoted to study, and he was furnished with the means, she, without any object of improvement, drudged at home, to assist in the support of the father's family, and perhaps to contribute to her brother's subsistence abroad; and now, being of a lower order, the rustic innocent wonders and weeps at his neglect.

Not only has there been a want of system concerning female education, but much of what has been done, has proceeded upon mistaken principles. One of these is, that, without a regard to the different periods of life, proportionate to the importance, the education of females has been too exclusively directed to fit them for displaying to advantage the charms of youth and beauty. Though it may be proper to adorn this period of life, yet, it is incomparably more important to prepare for the serious duties of maturer years. Though well to decorate the blossom, it is far better to prepare for the harvest. In the vegetable creation, nature seems but to sport when she embellishes the flower; while all her serious cares are directed to perfect the fruit.

Another error is that it has been made the first object in educating our sex to prepare them to please the other. But reason and religion teach that we too are primary existences; that it is for us to move in the orbit of our duty, around the Holy Center of perfection, the companions not the satellites of men; else, instead of shedding around us an influence that may help to keep them in their proper course, we must accompany them in the wildest deviations. Neither would I be understood to mean, that our sex should not seek to make themselves agreeable to the other. The error complained of, is that the taste of men, whatever it might happen to be, has been made a standard for the formation of the female character. In whatever we do, it is of the utmost importance that the rule, by which we work, be perfect. For if otherwise what is it but to err upon principle? A system of education which leads one class of human beings to consider the approbation of another, as their highest object, teaches that the rule of their conduct should be the will of beings, imperfect and erring like themselves, rather than the will of God, which is the only standard of perfection.

James Tallmadge, Jr., speaks against slavery in Missouri, February 16, 1819

When Missouri applied for statehood Congressman James Tallmadge, Jr., of New York proposed an amendment to the enabling act which would have prohibited "the further introduction of slavery" into Missouri, and which would have freed all slaves born there at the age of twenty-five. His proposal elicited a short but fiery dispute which, Jefferson said, "like a fire bell in the night, awakened and filled me with terror." Ultimately an agreement was reached— the Compromise of 1820—which settled the problem temporarily. The argument over slavery in Missouri, John Quincy Adams predicted with uncommon accuracy, was merely the "title page to a great tragic volume."

Sir, the honorable gentleman from Missouri, (Mr. John Scott), who has just resumed his seat, has told us of the *ides of March,* and has cautioned us to *"beware of the fate of Caesar and of Rome."* Another gentleman, (Mr. Thomas Cobb), from Georgia, in addition to other expressions of great warmth, has said "that, if we persist, the Union will be dissolved"; and, with a look fixed on me, has told us, "we have kindled a fire which all the waters of the ocean cannot put out, which seas of blood can only extin-

From the *Annals of the Congress of the United States,* Fifteenth Congress, Second Session (Washington, D.C., 1855), pp. 1204–06, 1211.

guish." Sir, language of this sort has no effect on me; my purpose is fixed, it is interwoven with my existence, its durability is limited with my life, it is a great and glorious cause, setting bounds to a slavery the most cruel and debasing the world ever witnessed; it is the freedom of man; it is the cause of unredeemed and unregenerated human beings.

Sir, if a dissolution of the Union must take place, let it be so! If civil war, which gentlemen so much threaten, must come, I can only say, let it come! My hold on life is probably as frail as that of any man who now hears me; but, while that hold lasts, it shall be devoted to the service of my country—to the freedom of man. If blood is necessary to extinguish any fire which I have assisted to kindle, I can assure gentlemen, while I regret the necessity, I shall not forbear to contribute my might. Sir, the violence to which gentlemen have resorted to on this subject will not move my purpose, nor drive me from my place. I have the fortune and the honor to stand here as the representative of freemen, who possess intelligence to know their rights, who have the spirit to maintain them. Whatever might be my own private sentiments on this subject, standing here as the representative of others, no choice is left me. I know the will of my constituents, and, regardless of consequences, I will avow it; as their representative, I will proclaim their hatred to slavery in every shape; as their representative, here will I hold my stand, until this floor, with the Constitution of my country which supports it, shall sink beneath me. If I am doomed to fall, I shall at least have the painful consolation to believe that I fall, as a fragment, in the ruins of my country. . . .

Sir, has it already come to this; that in the Congress of the United States—that, in the legislative councils of republican America, the subject of slavery has become a subject of so much feeling—of such delicacy—of such danger, that it cannot safely be discussed? . . . Are we to be told of the dissolution of the Union; of civil war, and of seas of blood? And yet, with such awful threatenings before us, do gentlemen, in the same breath, insist upon the encouragement of this evil; upon the extension of this monstrous scourge of the human race? An evil so fraught with such dire calamities to us as individuals, and to our nation, and threatening, in its progress, to overwhelm the civil and religious institutions of the country, with the liberties of the nation, ought at once to be met and to be controlled. If its power, its influence, and its impending dangers have already arrived at such a point that it is not safe to discuss it on this floor, and it cannot now pass under consideration as a proper subject for general legislation, what will be the result when it is spread through your widely extended domain? Its present threatening aspect, and the violence of its supporters, so far from inducing me to yield to its progress, prompts me to resist its march. Now is the time. It must now be met, and the extension of the evil must now be prevented, or the occasion is irrecoverably lost, and the evil can never be contracted.

Sir, extend your view across the Mississippi, over your newly acquired territory; a territory so far surpassing in extent the limits of your present country, that that country which gave birth to your nation, which achieved your Revolution, consolidated your Union, formed your Constitution, and has subsequently acquired so much glory, hangs but as an appendage to the extended empire over which your Republican government is now called to bear sway. Look down the long vista of futurity. See your empire, in extent unequalled; in advantageous situation without a parallel; and occupying all the valuable part of our continent. Behold this extended empire, inhabited by the hardy sons of American freemen— knowing their rights, and inheriting the will to protect them—owners of the soil on which they live, and interested in the institutions which they labor to defend—with two oceans having your shores, and tributary to your purposes bearing on their bosoms the commerce of your people. Compared to yours, the governments of Europe dwindle into insignificance, and the whole world is without a parallel. But, sir, reverse this scene; people this fair dominion with the slaves of your planters; extend slavery—this bane of man, this abomination of heaven—over your extended empire, and you prepare its dissolution; you turn its accumulated strength into positive weakness; you cherish a canker in your breast; you put poison in your bosom; you place a vulture on your heart—nay, you whet the dagger and place it in the hands of a portion of your population, stimulated to use it, by every tie, human and divine. The envious contrast between your happiness and their misery, between your liberty and their slavery, must constantly prompt them to accomplish your destruction. Your enemies will learn the source and the cause of your weakness. As often as internal dangers shall threaten, or internal commotions await you, you will then realize, that, by your own procurement, you have placed amidst your families, and in the bosom of your country, a population producing at once the greatest cause of individual danger and of national weakness. With this defect, your government must crumble to pieces, and your people become the scoff of the world. . . .

Sir, on this subject the eyes of Europe are turned upon you. You boast of the freedom of your Constitution and your laws; you have proclaimed, in the Declaration of Independence, "That all men are created equal; that they are endowed by their Creator with certain inalienable rights; that amongst these are life, liberty, and the pursuit of happiness"; and yet you have slaves in your country. The enemies of your government, and the legitimates of Europe, point to your inconsistencies, and blazon your supposed defects. If you allow slavery to pass into territories where you have the lawful power to exclude it, you will justly take upon yourself all the charges of inconsistency; but, confine it to the original slaveholding states, where you found it at the formation of your government, and you stand acquitted of all imputation.

Economic depression in the West, described in the letters of a foreign traveler, May–June 1820

If the debates over slavery in Missouri were the first signs of discord during the so-called "Era of Good Feelings," the depression of 1819 shattered the window-dressing of national harmony. The depression was most acute in the urban West. There an anti-eastern, anti-Bank of the United States prejudice developed and persisted. James Flint's letters, written from Jeffersonville, Indiana, and Cincinnati, Ohio, describe the economic conditions which prevailed.

May 4, 1820

The money in circulation is puzzling to traders, and more particularly to strangers; for besides the multiplicity of banks, and the diversity in supposed value, fluctuations are so frequent, and so great, that no man who holds it in his possession can be safe for a day. The merchant, when asked the price of an article, instead of making a direct answer, usually puts the question, "What sort of money have you got?" Supposing that a number of bills are shown, and one or more are accepted, it is not till then that the price of the goods is declared; and an additional price is uniformly laid on, to compensate for the supposed defect in the quality of the money. Trade is stagnated—produce cheap—and merchants find it difficult to lay in assortments of foreign manufactures. . . .

Agriculture languishes—farmers cannot find profit in hiring laborers. The increase of produce in the United States is greater than any increase of consumption that may be pointed out elsewhere. To increase the quantity of provisions, then, without enlarging the numbers of those who eat them, will only be diminishing the price farther. Land in these circumstances can be of no value to the capitalist who would employ his funds in farming. The spare capital of farmers is here chiefly laid out in the purchase of lands.

Laborers and mechanics are in want of employment. I think that I have seen upwards of 1500 men in quest of work within eleven months past, and many of these declared, that they had no money. . . . You have no doubt heard of emigrants returning to Europe without finding the prospect of a livelihood in America. Some who have come out to this part of the country do not succeed well. Laborers' wages are at present a dollar and an eighth part per day. Board costs them two and three-fourths or three dollars per week, and washing three-fourths of a dollar for a dozen of pieces. On these terms, it is plain that they cannot live two days by the

From James Flint, *Letters from America* (Edinburgh, Scotland, 1822), reprinted in Reuben G. Thwaites (ed.), *Early Western Travels: 1748–1846* (Cleveland, 1904), Vol. IX, pp. 225–28, 238, 241.

labor of one, with the other deductions which are to be taken from their wages. . . . And the poor laborer is almost certain of being paid in depreciated money; perhaps from thirty to fifty per cent under par. I have been several men turned out of boarding houses, where their money would not be taken. They had no other recourse left but to lodge in the woods, without any covering except their clothes. They set fire to a decayed log, spread some boards alongside of it for a bed, laid a block of timber across for a pillow, and pursued their labor by day as usual. A still greater misfortune than being paid with bad money is to be guarded against, namely, that of not being paid at all. Public improvements are frequently executed by subscription, and subscribers do not in every case consider themselves dishonored by nonpayment of the sum they engage for. . . . Employers are also in the habit of deceiving their workmen, by telling them that it is not convenient to pay wages in money, and that they run accounts with the storekeeper, the tailor, and the shoemaker, and that from them they may have all the necessaries they want very cheap. The workman who consents to this mode of payment, procures orders from the employer, on one or more of these citizens, and is charged a higher price for the goods than the employer actually pays for them. This is called *paying in trade.*

June 26, 1820

Cincinnati suffers much now from the decline in business. The town does not present anything like the stir that animated it about a year and a half ago. Building is in a great measure suspended, and the city which was lately over-crowded with people, has now a considerable number of empty houses. Rents are lowered, and the price of provisions considerably reduced. Many mechanics and laborers find it impossible to procure employment. The same changes have taken place in the other towns of the western country. Numbers of people have deserted them, and commenced farming in the woods. They will there have it in their power to raise produce enough for their families, but, with the present low markets, and the probability of a still greater reduction, they can have no inducement but necessity for cultivating a surplus produce. . . .

Of four provincial banks in town, the paper of three is reduced to about one-third part of the specie sums on the face of their notes, and the people are making a brisk run on the fourth. This paper shop is not paying in specie, but merely giving *money like its own.* When the barter can be no longer continued, the house must be shut, and the holders of the *pictures* find them of no value.

John Marshall's opinion, for the Supreme Court, in the case of *McCulloch* v. *Maryland*, 1819

Sectionalism began to predominate in the third decade of the nineteenth century, but the Supreme Court—persuaded by John Marshall—so defined the federal system as to enhance national power and to limit state authority. One of the most famous cases involved Maryland's attempt to tax a branch of the Bank of the United States located in Baltimore. Following Hamilton's logic, and even paraphrasing his prose, Marshall declared that Congress had the right to use any appropriate means—such as the Bank—to exercise its legitimate powers. Those powers were supreme. A state could not be permitted to tax and perhaps thereby to destroy an instrument of the federal government. The state law was struck down. Following are significant excerpts taken from the Supreme Court decision.

Incorporating the [first] Bank of the United States did not steal upon an unsuspecting legislature, and pass unobserved. Its principle was completely understood, and was opposed with equal zeal and ability. After being resisted, first, in the fair and open field of debate, and afterwards, in the executive cabinet, with as much persevering talent as any measure has ever experienced, and being supported by arguments which convinced minds as pure and intelligent as this country can boast, it became a law. The original act was permitted to expire; but a short experience of the embarrassments to which the refusal to revive it exposed the government, convinced those who were most prejudiced against the measure of its necessity, and induced the passage of the present law. It would require no ordinary share of intrepidity, to assert that a measure adopted under these circumstances, was a bold and plain usurpation, to which the Constitution gave no countenance. . . .

In discussing this question, the counsel for the state of Maryland have deemed it of some importance, in the construction of the Constitution, to consider that instrument, not as emanating from the people, but as the act of sovereign and independent states. The powers of the general government, it has been said, are delegated by the states, who alone are truly sovereign; and must be exercised in subordination to the states, who alone possess supreme dominion. It would be difficult to sustain this proposition. The convention which framed the Constitution was indeed elected by the state legislatures. But the instrument when it came from their hands, was a mere proposal, without obligation, or pretensions to it. It was reported to the then existing Congress of the United States, with a request that it might "be submitted to a convention of delegates, chosen in each state by the people thereof, under the recommendation of its legislature, for their

From Henry Wheaton, *A Digest of the Decisions of the Supreme Court of the United States from 1789 to February Term, 1820* (New York, 1821), Vol. IV, p. 316 ff.

assent and ratification." This mode of proceeding was adopted; and by the convention, by congress, and by the state legislatures, the instrument was submitted to the *people*. They acted upon it in the only manner in which they can act safely, effectively, and wisely, on such a subject, by assembling in convention. It is true, they assembled in their several states—and where else should they have assembled? No political dreamer was ever wild enough to think of breaking down the lines which separate the states, and of compounding the American people into one common mass. Of consequence, when they act, they act in their states. But the measures they adopt do not, on that account, cease to be the measures of the people themselves, or become the measures of the state governments.

From these conventions, the Constitution derives its whole authority. The government proceeds directly from the people; is "ordained and established," in the name of the people; and is declared to be ordained "in order to form a more perfect union, establish justice, insure domestic tranquility, and secure the blessings of liberty to themselves and to their posterity." The assent of the states, in their sovereign capacity, is implied, in calling a convention, and thus submitting that instrument to the people. But the people were at perfect liberty to accept or reject it; and their act was final. It required not the affirmance, and could not be negatived, by the state governments. The Constitution, when thus adopted, was of complete obligation, and bound the state sovereignties. The government of the Union, then, ... is emphatically and truly a government of the people. In form, and in substance, it emanates from them. Its powers are granted by them, and for their benefit. . . .

Among the enumerated powers, we do not find that of establishing a bank or creating a corporation. But there is no phrase in the instrument which, like the articles of confederation, excludes incidental or implied powers. . . . A constitution, to contain an accurate detail of all the subdivisions of which its great powers will admit, and of all the means by which they may be carried into execution, would partake of the prolixity of a legal code, and could scarcely be embraced by the human mind. It would, probably, never be understood by the public. Its nature, therefore, requires, that only its great outlines should be marked, its important objects designated, and the minor ingredients which compose those objects, be deducted from the nature of the objects themselves. That this idea was entertained by the framers of the American Constitution is not only to be inferred from the nature of the instrument, but from the language. Why else were some of the limitations, found in the 9th section of the 1st article, introduced? It is also, in some degree, warranted, by their having omitted to use any restrictive term which might prevent its receiving a fair and just interpretation. In considering this question, then, we must never forget that it is a *constitution* we are expounding. . . .

We admit, as all must admit, that the powers of the government are limited, and that its limits are not to be transcended. But we think the sound construction of the Constitution must allow to the national legislature that discretion, with respect to the means by which the powers it confers are to be carried into execution, which will enable that body to perform the high duties assigned to it, in the manner most beneficial to the people. Let the end be legitimate, let it be within the scope of the Constitution, and all means which are appropriate, which are plainly adapted to that end, which are not prohibited, but consist with the letter and spirit of the Constitution, are constitutional. . . . After the most deliberate consideration, and all means which are appropriate, which are plainly adapted to incorporate the Bank of the United States is a law made in pursuance of the Constitution, and is a part of the supreme law of the land. . . .

The states have no power, by taxation or otherwise, to retard, impede, burden, or in any manner control, the operations of the constitutional laws enacted by congress to carry into execution the powers vested in the general government. This is, we think, the unavoidable consequence of that supremacy which the Constitution has declared. We are unanimously of opinion, that the law passed by the legislature of Maryland, imposing a tax on the Bank of the United States, is unconstitutional and void.

The essence of the Monroe Doctrine, 1823

The immediate occasion for the principles which James Monroe announced in 1823 was the proposal by Great Britain for a joint Anglo-American declaration on Latin America. Jefferson and Madison both advised their old associate and fellow Virginian to accept the British offer. John Quincy Adams, however, persuaded Monroe to make a foreign policy statement which would be purely American. In fact, some of the ideas included in the Monroe Doctrine—which was actually part of a presidential message to Congress—stemmed from the mind of Adams.

At the proposal of the Russian Imperial Government . . . a full power and instructions have been transmitted to the minister of the United States at St. Petersburg to arrange by amicable negotiation the respective rights and interests of the two nations on the northwest coast of this continent. A similar proposal has been made . . . to the Government of Great Britain, which has likewise been acceded to. The Government of the United States has been desirous by this friendly proceeding of manifesting. . . their solicitude to cultivate the best understanding with his [the Russian] Government. In the discussions to which this interest has given rise and in the arrangements by which they may terminate, the occasion has been judged proper for asserting, *as a principle in which the rights and interests of the*

From James D. Richardson (ed.), *A Compilation of the Messages and Papers of the Presidents* (Washington, D.C., 1897), Vol. II, pp. 207 ff. Italics added.

*United States are involved, that the American continents, by the free and
independent condition which they have assumed and maintain, are henceforth not to be considered as subjects for future colonization by any
European powers. . . .*

*In the wars of the European powers, in matters relating to themselves,
we have never taken any part, nor does it comport with our policy so to do.
It is only when our rights are invaded or seriously menaced that we resent
injuries or make preparations for our defense.* With the movements in this
hemisphere we are of necessity more immediately connected, and by causes
which must be obvious to all enlightened and impartial observers. The
political system of the allied powers is essentially different in this respect
from that of America. This difference proceeds from that which exists in
their respective Governments; and to the defense of our own, which has
been achieved by the loss of so much blood and treasure, and matured by
the wisdom of their most enlightened citizens, and under which we have
enjoyed unexampled felicity, this whole nation is devoted. *We owe it,
therefore, to candor, and to the amicable relations existing between the
United States and those powers, to declare that we should consider any
attempt on their part to extend their system, to any portion of this hemisphere, as dangerous to our peace and safety. With the existing colonies or
dependencies of any European power we have not interfered and shall not
interfere. But with the Governments who have declared their independence and maintained it, and whose independence we have, on great consideration and on just principles, acknowledged, we could not view any
interposition for the purpose of oppressing them, or controlling in any
other manner their destiny, by any European power, in any other light
than as the manifestation of an unfriendly disposition toward the United
States.*

The relations of Henry Clay and John Quincy Adams: from Adams's *Memoirs*, March 1824 to February 1825

*By 1824 the facade of political unity had crumbled completely, and at least
five "favorite sons," representing different geographical sections, sought the
presidency. There were "coalitions of every description, without the least regard
to principle," Albert Gallatin complained. "I see nothing but . . . the fulfillment
of personal views and passions." Though Andrew Jackson received a plurality of
electoral votes, and Adams ran a close second, with Crawford and Clay lagging
far behind, without a majority the choice fell to the House of Representatives.
There Clay's supporters voted for Adams, which gave him the presidency, and
Adams later appointed Clay as Secretary of State. A glimpse of the proceedings
is revealed in the following excerpts taken from the diary of John Quincy Adams.*

From Charles F. Adams (ed.), *Memoirs of John Quincy Adams* (Philadelphia, 1875),
Vol. VI, pp. 258, 265, 315, 446–47, 457, 464–65, 478, 483, 501, 506–09.

March 15, 1824

I dined at General Jackson's, with a company of about twenty-five—heads of Departments, members of Congress, and officers of the army and navy. Clay and Calhoun were there. It was the General's birthday, and apparently the occasion upon which he gave the dinner. Clay had been arguing [a case] in the Supreme Court . . . against the Government, and had taken the opportunity of being, as he professed, very severe upon me. At the dinner he became warm, vehement, and absurd upon the tariff, and persisted in discussing it, against two or three attempts of Eaton to change the subject of conversation. He is so ardent, dogmatical, and overbearing that it is extremely difficult to preserve the temper of friendly society with him.

March 23, 1824

The mining and countermining upon this presidential election is an admirable study of human nature. The mist into which Calhoun's bubble broke settles upon Jackson, who is now taking the fragments of Clinton's party. Those of Clay will also fall chiefly to him and his sect, and Crawford's are now working chiefly for mine. They both consider my prospects as desperate and are scrambling for my spoils. I can do no more than satisfy them that I have no purchasable interest. My friends will go over to whomever they may prefer—some to one and some to another.

May 2, 1824

Clay . . . is now quite flushed with hopes, and told Crowningshield that he was already sure of eight states, and should be elected. He plays brag, as he has done all his life.

December 17, 1824

The account was yesterday received of the choice of electors in Louisiana. . . . This leaves Mr. Crawford with forty-one and Mr. Clay with thirty-seven, electoral votes. Mr. Crawford, therefore, will, and Mr. Clay will not, be one of the three persons from whom the House of Representatives, voting by states, will be called to choose a President. Mr. Letcher is an intimate friend of Mr. Clay's and lodges at the same house with him. He expects that after the result is known, that Mr. Clay cannot be voted for in the House, there will be meetings of the people in the several counties instructing their members to vote for Jackson. . . .

The drift of all Letcher's discourse was much the same as Wyer had told me, that Clay would willingly support me if he could thereby serve himself, and the substance of his *meaning* was, that if Clay's friends could *know* that he would have a prominent share in the administration, that might induce them to vote for me, even in the face of instructions. But Letcher did not profess to have any authority from Clay for what he said, and he made no definite propositions. He spoke of his interview with me as altogether confidential, and in my answers to him I spoke in mere general terms.

January 1, 1825

... [Clay] told me that he should be glad to have with me soon some confidential conversation upon public affairs. I said I should be happy to have it whenever it might suit his convenience.

January 9, 1825

Mr. Clay came at six, and spent the evening with me in a long conversation explanatory of the past and prospective of the future. He said that the time was drawing near when the choice must be made in the House of Representatives of a President from the three candidates presented by the electoral college; that he had been much urged and solicited with regard to the part in that transaction that he should take, and had not been five minutes landed at his lodgings before he had been applied to by a friend of Mr. Crawford's, in a manner so gross that it had disgusted him; that some of my friends, also, disclaiming, indeed, to have any authority from me, had repeatedly applied to him, directly or indirectly, urging considerations personal to himself as motives to his cause. He had thought it best to reserve for some time his determination to himself: first, to give a decent time for his own funeral solemnities as a candidate; and, secondly, to prepare and predispose all his friends to a state of neutrality between the three candidates who would be before the House, so that they might be free ultimately to take that course which might be most conducive to the public interest. The time had now come at which he might be explicit in his communication with me, and he had for that purpose asked this confidential interview. He wished me, as far as I might think proper, to satisfy him with regard to some principles of great public importance, but without any personal considerations for himself. In the question to come before the House between General Jackson, Mr. Crawford, and myself, he had no hesitation in saying that his preference would be for me.

January 25, 1825

There is at this moment a very high state of excitement in the House, Mr. Clay and the majority of the Ohio and Kentucky delegations having yesterday unequivocally avowed their determination to vote for me. This immediately produced an approximation of the Calhoun, Crawford, and Jackson partisans.

January 29, 1825

On my return home, Mr. Clay came in, and sat with me a couple of hours, discussing all the prospects and probabilities of the presidential election. He spoke to me with the utmost freedom of men and things; intimated doubts and prepossessions concerning individual friends of mine, to all which I listened with due consideration.

February 9, 1825

May the blessings of God rest upon the event of this day!—the second Wednesday in February, when the election of a President of the United States for the term of four years, from the 4th of March next, was consummated. Of the votes in the electoral college, there were ninety-nine for Andrew Jackson, of Tennessee; eighty-four for John Quincy Adams, of Massachusetts; forty-one for William Harris Crawford, of Georgia; and thirty-seven for Henry Clay, of Kentucky: in all, two hundred and sixty-one. This result having been announced, on opening and counting the votes in joint meeting of the two Houses, the House of Representatives immediately proceeded to vote by ballot from the three highest candidates, when John Quincy Adams received the votes of thirteen, Andrew Jackson of seven, and William H. Crawford of four states. The election was thus completed, very unexpectedly, by a single ballot.

February 11, 1825

G. Sullivan . . . said he would tell me what the Calhounites said: that if Mr. Clay should be appointed Secretary of State, a determined opposition to the Administration would be organized from the outset; that the opposition would use the name of General Jackson as its head; that the Administration would be supported only by the New England States—New York being doubtful, the West much divided and strongly favoring Jackson as a Western man, Virginia already in opposition, and all the South decidedly adverse. The Calhounites had also told him what Administration would satisfy him: namely, Joel R. Poinsett, Secretary of State; Langdon Cheves, Secretary of the Treasury; John McLean, now Postmaster General, Secretary of War; and Southard, of the Navy.

I asked Sullivan with whom he had held these conversations. He said, with Calhoun himself, and with Poinsett. I told Sullivan that I would some day call on him to testify to these facts in a Court of Justice. He said, surely not. I insisted that I would, and told him that he would find it necessary under this threatened opposition of Mr. Calhoun; that I had no doubt Mr. Calhoun, in holding this language to him, intended it should come to me, and that its object was to intimidate me, and deter me from the nomination of Mr. Clay; that I had heard the same intimations from him through other channels; and, in all probability, at some future day some occasion would arise of necessity for proving the facts judicially, in which case I should certainly call upon him.

He said he should certainly then refuse to answer. . . .

[Later that day] I told the President . . . that I should offer the Department of State to Mr. Clay, considering it due to his talents and services, to the Western section of the Union, whence he comes, and to the confidence in me manifested by their delegations.

February 12, 1825

General Brown entered this morning into an argument to convince me that it would not be expedient that Mr. Clay should be Secretary of State. He had a high opinion of Mr. Clay, but if I should offer him the Department he hoped he would not accept it, and he believed it would be better if I should not offer it to him.

The case of Peggy (O'Neale) Eaton: from the letters of Margaret Bayard Smith, 1829–31

Senator John Henry Eaton, old friend, close political associate and biographer of Andrew Jackson, squired the notorious Peggy O'Neale while she was married to a ship's purser, Timberlake. When Timberlake died at sea, Eaton decided— at Jackson's insistence—to marry Peggy. Stories and rumors of her promiscuous behavior multiplied, and the Eatons were snubbed by Washington society. Jackson came to her defense, as did Martin Van Buren, who used the episode to advance his own political fortunes. A hostile observer was the wife of a Washington newspaper owner, Margaret Bayard Smith. She felt that Jackson's "weakness originates in an amiable cause—his devoted and ardent friendship for General Eaton."

To Mrs. Kirkpatrick   **January 1829**

Tonight General Eaton, the bosom friend and almost adopted son of General Jackson, is to be married to a lady whose reputation, her previous connection with him both before and after her husband's death, had been totally destroyed. She is the daughter of O'Neal who kept a large tavern and boarding house. . . . She has never been admitted into good society,

From Gaillard Hunt (ed.), *The First Forty Years of Washington Society* (New York, 1906), pp. 252–53, 282, 287–89, 305–06, 310–11, 318–19.

is very handsome and of not an inspiring character and violent temper. She is, it is said, irresistible and carries whatever point she sets her mind on. The General's personal and political friends are very much disturbed about it; his enemies laugh and divert themselves with the idea of what a suitable lady in waiting Mrs. Eaton will make to Mrs. Jackson and repeat the old adage, "birds of a feather will flock together."

To J. Bayard H. Smith   **February 25, 1829**

Every one acknowledges General Eaton's talents and virtues—but his late unfortunate connection is an obstacle to his receiving a place of honor, which it is apprehended even General Jackson's firmness cannot resist. It is a pity. Every one that knows esteems, and many love him for his benevolence and amiability. Oh, woman, woman! The rumor of yesterday was, that he was to have no place at home, but be sent abroad—so it was added (though evidently only for the joke of it) that he was to be minister to *Hayti,* that being the most proper Court for *her* to reside in—I repeat these are rumors.

To Mrs. Boyd   **Spring of 1829**

A stand, a *noble* stand, I may say, since it is a stand taken against power and favoritism, has been made by the ladies of Washington, and not even the President's wishes, in favor of his dearest, personal friend, can influence them to violate the respect due to virtue, by visiting one who has left her straight and narrow path. With the exception of two or three timid and rather insignificant personages, who trembled for their husband's offices, not a lady has visited her, and so far from being inducted into the President's house, she is, I am told, scarcely noticed by the females of his family. On Inauguration day, when they went in company with the Vice-President's lady, the lady of the Secretary of the Treasury and those of two distinguished Jacksonian Senators, Hayne and Livingston, this New Lady never approached the party, either in the Senate chamber, at the President's house, where by the President's express request, they went to receive the company, nor at night at the Inaugural Ball. On these three public occasions she was left alone, and kept at a respectful distance from these virtuous and distinguished women, with the sole exception of a seat at the supper table, where, however, notwithstanding her proximity, she was not spoken to by them. These are facts you may rely on, not rumors—facts, greatly to the honor of our sex.

To Mrs. Kirkpatrick   **1829**

Mrs. Eaton continues excluded from society, except the houses of some of the foreigners, the President's and Mr. Van Buren's. The Dutch Minister's family have openly declared against her admission into society. The other evening at a grand fete at the Russian Minister's, Mrs. Eaton was led first to the supper table, in consequence of which Mrs. Heugans and family would not go to the table and was quite enraged—for the whole week you heard scarcely anything else. And it is generally asserted that if Mr. Van Buren, our Secretary, persists in visiting her, our ladies will not go to his house. We shall see.

To Mrs. Kirkpatrick   **January 26, 1830**

One woman has made sad work here; to be, or not to be, her friend is the test of presidential favor. Mr. Van Buren sided with her and is consequently the right hand man, the constant riding, walking and visiting companion of the President and his friend General Eaton, while the other members of the cabinet are looked on coldly—some say unkindly, and enjoy little share in the councils of state. Mr. Calhoun, Ingham, his devoted friend, Branch and Berrian form one party; the President, Van Buren, General Eaton and Mr. Barry the other. It is generally supposed that, as they cannot sit together, some change in the Cabinet must take place. Meanwhile, the lady who caused this division is forced, notwithstanding the support and favor of such high personages, to withdraw from society. She is not received in any private parties, and since the 8th of January has withdrawn from public assemblies. At the ball given on that occasion, she was treated with such marked and universal neglect and indignity, that she will not expose herself again to such treatment. General Eaton, unable to clear his wife's fair name, has taken his revenge by blackening that of other ladies, one of whose husbands has resented it in such a manner, that it was universally believed he would receive a challenge. But General Eaton has very quietly pocketed the abuse lavished on him. This affair was for two weeks the universal topic of conversation. Mr. Campbell, as the original cause of all this uproar and difficulty, felt so miserable for a whole week, while a duel was daily expected, that he said it wholly unfitted him for everything else.

To Mrs. Kirkpatrick   **August 29, 1831**

The papers do not exaggerate, nay, do not detail one half of [the President's] imbecilities. He is completely under the government of Mrs. Eaton, one of the most ambitious, violent, malignant, yet silly women you ever heard of. You will soon see the recall of the Dutch minister announced. Madam Huygen's spirited conduct in refusing to visit Mrs. Eaton is undoubtedly the cause. The new Cabinet, if they do not yield to the President's will on the point, will, it is supposed, soon be dismissed. Several of them in order to avoid this dilemma, are determined not to keep house or bring on their families. Therefore, not keeping house, they will not give parties and may thus avoid the disgrace of entertaining the favorite. It was hoped, on her husband's going out of office, she would have left the city, *but she will not.* She hopes for a complete triumph and is not satisfied with having the Cabinet broken up and a virtuous and intelligent minister recalled, and many of our best citizens frowned upon by the President. Our society is in a sad state. Intrigues and parasites in favor, divisions and animosity existing. As for ourselves, we keep out of the turmoil, seldom speak and never take any part in this troublesome and shameful state of things. Yet no one can deny, that the President's weakness originates in an amiable cause—his devoted and ardent friendship for General Eaton.

Andrew Jackson's veto of the bill to recharter the Bank of the United States, July 10, 1832

With no appreciation and little understanding of the function of banks, Andrew Jackson's hatred centered on the largest financial institution of all—the Bank of the United States—which in 1830 held one-third of all the deposits and specie in American banks. Determined to destroy this monopolistic "monster," Jackson vetoed its recharter, and won the election of 1832 by appealing directly to the people for support. The Jacksonian rhetoric—against the rich and powerful— is distinctly Jeffersonian in tone; but the results of the veto served the interests of state bankers and other entrepreneurs who had long chaffed under the financial restraints imposed by the federal Bank.

A bank of the United States is in many respects convenient for the Government and useful to the people. Entertaining this opinion, and deeply impressed with the belief that some of the powers and privileges possessed by the existing bank are unauthorized by the Constitution, subversive of the rights of the States, and dangerous to the liberties of the people, I felt it my duty at an early period of my administration to call the attention of Congress to the practicability of organizing an institution combining all its advantages and obviating these objections. I sincerely regret that in the act before me I can perceive none of those modifications of the bank charter which are necessary, in my opinion, to make it compatible with justice, with sound policy, or with the Constitution of our country. . . .

More than eight million of the stock of this bank are held by foreigners. By this act the American Republic proposes virtually to make them a present of some millions of dollars. For these gratuities to foreigners and to some of our own opulent citizens the act secures no equivalent whatever. They are the certain gains of the present stockholders under the operation of this act, after making full allowance for the payment of the bonus. . . .

From James D. Richardson (ed.), *A Compilation of the Messages and Papers of the Presidents* (Washington, D.C., 1897), Vol. II, pp. 1139–40, 1144, 1153–54.

Is there no danger to our liberty and independence in a bank that in its nature has so little to bind it to our country? The president of the bank has told us that most of the State banks exist by its forbearance. Should its influence become concentered, as it may under the operation of such an act as this, in the hands of a self-elected directory whose interests are identified with those of the foreign stockholders, will there not be cause to tremble for the purity of our elections in peace and for the independence of our country in war? . . . Should the stock of the bank principally pass into the hands of the subjects of a foreign country, and we should unfortunately become involved in a war with that country, what would be our condition? Of the course which would be pursued by a bank almost wholly owned by the subjects of a foreign power, and managed by those whose interests, if not affections, would run in the same direction, there can be no doubt. All its operations within would be in aid of the hostile fleets and armies without. Controlling our currency, receiving our public moneys, and holding thousands of our citizens in dependence, it would be more formidable and dangerous than the naval and military power of the enemy.

If we must have a bank with private stockholders, every consideration of sound policy and every impulse of American feeling admonishes that it should be *purely American*. Its stockholders should be composed exclusively of our own citizens, who at least ought to be friendly to our Government and willing to support it in times of difficulty and danger. So abundant is domestic capital that competition in subscribing for the stock of local banks has recently led almost to riots. To a bank exclusively of American stockholders, possessing the powers and privileges granted by this act, subscriptions for $200,000,000 could be readily obtained. Instead of sending abroad the stock of the bank in which the Government must deposit its funds and on which it must rely to sustain its credit in times of emergency, it would rather seem to be expedient to prohibit its sale to aliens under the penalty of absolute forfeiture. . . .

It is to be regretted that the rich and powerful too often bend the acts of government to their selfish purposes. Distinctions in society will always exist under every just government. Equality of talents, of education, or of wealth cannot be produced by human institutions. In the full enjoyment of the gifts of Heaven and the fruits of superior industry, economy and virtue, every man is equally entitled to protection by law; but when the laws undertake to add to these natural and just advantages artificial distinctions, to grant titles, gratuities, and exclusive privileges, to make the rich richer and the potent more powerful, the humble members of society—the farmers, mechanics, and laborers—who have neither the time nor the means of securing like favors to themselves, have a right to complain of the injustice of their Government. There are no necessary evils in government. Its evils exist only in its abuses. If it would confine itself to equal protection, and, as Heaven does its rains, shower its favors alike on the high and the low, the rich and the poor, it would be an unqualified blessing. In the act before me there seems to be a wide and unnecessary departure from these just principles.

Nor is our Government to be maintained or our Union preserved by invasions of the rights and powers of the several States. In thus attempting to make our General Government strong we make it weak. Its true strength consists in leaving individuals and States as much as possible to themselves —in making itself felt, not in its power, but in its beneficence; not in its control, but in its protection; not in binding the States more closely to the center, but leaving each to move unobstructed in its proper orbit. . . .

Many of our rich men have not been content with equal protection and equal benefits, but have besought us to make them richer by act of Congress. By attempting to gratify their desires we have in the results of our legislation arrayed section against section, interest against interest, and man against man, in a fearful commotion which threatens to shake the foundations of our Union. It is time to pause in our career to review our principles, and if possible revive that devoted patriotism and spirit of compromise which distinguished the sages of the Revolution and the fathers of our Union. If we cannot at once, in justice to interests vested under improvident legislation, make our Government what it ought to be, we can at least take a stand against all new grants of monopolies and exclusive privileges, against any prostitution of our Government to the advancement of the few at the expense of the many, and in favor of compromise and gradual reform in our code of laws and system of political economy.

The Bank war: from the correspondence of Nicholas Biddle, 1832–33

Nicholas Biddle, president of the Bank of the United States, was everything Andrew Jackson was not: urbane, educated, and sophisticated, he was equally at home in the worlds of poetry and business. But, influenced by Henry Clay and Daniel Webster, he miscalculated public opinion and lost. A large majority of Americans applauded Jackson's veto, and sustained his actions in placing government funds in "pet" banks.

Biddle to Charles J. Ingersoll   February 11, 1832

Here am I, who have taken a fancy to this Bank, and having built it up with infinite care, am striving to keep it from being destroyed to the infinite wrong as I most sincerely and conscientiously believe of the whole country. To me all other considerations are insignificant—I mean to stand by it and defend it with all the small faculties which Providence has assigned to me. I care for no party in politics or religion. . . . I am for the Bank and the

From Reginald C. McGrane (ed.), *The Correspondence of Nicholas Biddle* (Boston, 1919), pp. 179, 195–96, 199–200, 207, 209.

Bank alone.... Well then, here comes Mr. Jackson who takes it into his head to declare that the Bank had failed, and that it ought to be superceded by some rickety machinery of his own contrivance.

Biddle to William G. Bucknor   July 13, 1832

The Bank is fairly before the country and large majorities of both houses of Congress have decided in its favor. One individual has however opposed his will to the deliberate reflections of the representatives of the people— and the question now is whether the Bank ought to exert itself to defeat the re-election of that person who is now the only obstacle to its success. On that question I have made up my mind that to interfere in the election would be a departure from the duty which the Bank owes to the country. The first law of its existence is entire and unqualified abstinence from all political connections and exertions. This it has hitherto practiced, and whatever may be the consequences, must continue to practice. The temptations to a contrary course are I feel very great, but I believe it to be the duty of the Bank to resist them.

Biddle to Henry Clay   August 1, 1832

You ask what is the effect of the Veto. My impression is that it is working as well as the friends of the Bank and of the country could desire. I have always deplored making the Bank a party question, but since the President will have it so, he must pay the penalty of his own rashness. As to the Veto message I am delighted with it. It has all the fury of a chained panther biting the bars of his cage. It is really a manifesto of anarchy—such as Marat or Robespierre might have issued to the mob of the faubourg St. Antoine; and my hope is that it will contribute to relieve the country from the dominion of these miserable people. You are destined to be the instrument of that deliverance, and at no period of your life has the country ever had a deeper stake in you. I wish you success most cordially, because I believe the institutions of the Union are involved in it.

R. L. Colt to Biddle   December 8, 1832

It is astonishing what a change the message has produced. No one doubts for a moment had this message come out 6 weeks ago that Jackson would have lost his election. And yet, in 6 weeks more, it will be the flinging up of caps and hurrah for Jackson—he is all right—the Bank must be put down —the Tariff must be put down—so must the Supreme Court—the lands given to the Western states—and internal improvements is worse than bad. I really think you ought to curtail your discount in Tennessee, Mobile, Charleston, Savannah, and Virginia. I would let these people feel a pressure, but not of course so as to cause failures.

Biddle to J. S. Barbour   April 16, 1833

The fact is that the real sin of the Bank in the eyes of the executive is, that it is refractory and unmanageable. When these people first came to power on a current of overwhelming popularity, to which they thought everything should yield, they considered the Bank a part of the spoils, and one of their first efforts was to possess themselves of the institution for the benefit of their partisans. . . . This is the whole secret of the opposition.

Biddle to Thomas Cooper   May 6, 1833

The truth is, that the question is no longer between this Bank and no Bank. It is a mere contest between Mr. Van Buren's Government Bank and the present institution—between Chestnut St. and Wall St.—between a Faro Bank and a National Bank.

Andrew Jackson and the doctrine of nullification, December 10–20, 1832

For some years South Carolinians were disturbed by high protective tariffs which they felt penalized Southern economic interests to the benefit of Northern ones. In 1828, John C. Calhoun had secretly authored the South Carolina Exposition and Protest which declared that Southern inhabitants were "the serfs" of the tariff system. Four years later the legislature of South Carolina declared the tariff acts "null and void," and that no federal duties would be collected within the state after February 1, 1833. Jackson was incensed. Privately he referred to Calhoun as demented, and threatened to hang South Carolina nullifiers for treason. But publicly his position was remarkably well tempered. The first excerpt consists of part of the long proclamation Jackson issued on December 10, 1832, which was actually drafted by his Secretary of State, Edward Livingston. The second excerpt contains the resolutions of the South Carolina legislature, adopted ten days later, in response to Jackson's proclamation.

PROCLAMATION OF ANDREW JACKSON ADDRESSED TO THE PEOPLE OF SOUTH CAROLINA, DECEMBER 10, 1832

I consider . . . the power to annul a law of the United States, assumed by one State, *incompatible with the existence of the Union, contradicted expressly by the letter of the Constitution, unauthorized by its spirit, inconsistent with every principle on which it was founded and destructive of the great object for which it was formed.* . . .

From James D. Richardson (ed.), *A Compilation of the Messages and Papers of the Presidents* (Washington, D.C., 1897), Vol. II, pp. 1206, 1217–19; *Statutes at Large of South Carolina*, Vol. I, 356–57.

Contemplate the condition of that country of which you still form an important part. Consider its Government, uniting in one bond of common interest and general protection so many different States, giving to all their inhabitants the proud title of *American citizen,* protecting their commerce, securing their literature and their arts, facilitating their intercommunication, defending their frontiers, and making their name respected in the remotest parts of the earth. Consider the extent of its territory, its increasing and happy population, its advance in arts which render life agreeable, and the sciences which elevate the mind! See education spreading the lights of religion, morality, and general information into every cottage in this wide extent of our territories and states. Behold it as the asylum where the wretched and the oppressed find a refuge and support. Look on this picture of happiness and honor and say, *We too are citizens of America.* Carolina is one of these proud States; her arms have defended, her best blood has cemented, this happy Union. And then add, if you can, without horror and remorse: this happy Union we will dissolve; this picture of peace and prosperity we will deface; this free intercourse we will interrupt; these fertile fields we will deluge with blood; the protection of that glorious flag we renounce; the very name of Americans we discard. And for what, mistaken men? For what do you throw away these inestimable blessings? For what would you exchange your share in the advantages and honor of the Union? For the dream of a separate independence—a dream interrupted by bloody conflicts with your neighbors and a vile dependence on a foreign power. If your leaders could succeed in establishing a separation, what would be your situation? Are you united at home? Are you free from the apprehension of civil discord, with all its fearful consequences? Do our neighboring republics, every day suffering some new revolution or contending with some new insurrection, do they excite your envy? But the dictates of a high duty oblige me solemnly to announce that you cannot succeed. The laws of the United States must be executed. I have no discretionary power on the subject; my duty is emphatically pronounced in the Constitution. Those who told you that you might peaceably prevent their execution deceived you; they could not have been deceived themselves. They know that a forcible opposition could alone prevent the execution of the laws, and they know that such opposition must be repelled. Their object is disunion. But be not deceived by names. Disunion by armed force is treason. Are you really ready to incur its guilt? If you are, on the heads of the instigators of the act be the dreadful consequences; on their heads be the dishonor, but on yours may fall the punishment. On your unhappy State will inevitably fall all the evils of the conflict you force upon the Government of your country. It cannot accede to the mad project of disunion, of which you would be the first victims. Its First Magistrate cannot, if he would, avoid the performance of his duty. The consequence must be fearful for you, distressing to your fellow-citizens here, and to the friends of good government throughout the world. Its enemies have beheld our prosperity with a vexation they could not conceal; it was a standing refutation of their slavish doctrines, and they will point to our discord with the triumph of malignant joy. It is yet in our power to disappoint them. There is yet time to show that the descendants of the Pinckneys, the Sumpters, the Rutledges, and of the thousand other names which adorn the pages of your Revolutionary history, will not abandon that Union to support which so many of them fought and bled and died. I adjure you, as you honor their memory, as you love the cause of freedom, to which they dedicated their lives, as you prize the peace of your country, the lives of its best citizens, and your own fair fame, to retrace your steps. Snatch from the archives of your State the disorganizing edict of its convention; bid its members to reassemble and promulgate the decided expressions of your will to remain in the path which alone can conduct you to safety, prosperity, and honor. Tell them that compared to disunion all other evils are light, because that brings with it an accumulation of all. Declare that you will never take the field unless the star-spangled banner of your country shall float over you; that you will not be stigmatized when dead, and dishonored and scorned while you live, as the authors of the first attack on the Constitution of your country. Its destroyers you cannot be. You may disturb its peace, you may interrupt the course of its prosperity, you may cloud its reputation for stability; but its tranquillity will be restored, its prosperity will return, and the stain upon its national character will be transferred and remain an eternal blot on the memory of those who caused the disorder.

RESPONSE OF THE SOUTH CAROLINA LEGISLATURE TO JACKSON'S PROCLAMATION, DECEMBER 20, 1832

Resolved, That the power vested by the Constitution and laws in the President of the United States, to issue his proclamation, does not authorize him in that mode to interfere whenever he may think fit in the affairs of the respective states, or that he should use it as a means of promulgating executive expositions of the Constitution, with the sanction of force thus superseding the action of other departments of the general government.

Resolved, That it is not competent to the President of the United States to order by proclamation the constituted authorities of a state to repeal their legislation, and that the late attempt of the President to do so is unconstitutional, and manifests a disposition to arrogate and exercise a power utterly destructive of liberty.

Resolved, That the opinions of the President in regard to the rights of the States are erroneous and dangerous, leading not only to the establishment of a consolidated government in the stead of our free confederacy, but to the concentration of all powers in the chief executive. . . .

Resolved, That each state of the Union has the right, whenever it may deem such a course necessary for the preservation of its liberties or vital interests, to secede peaceably from the Union, and that there is no constitutional power in the general government, much less in the executive department of that government, to retain by force such state in the Union.

Resolved, That the primary and paramount allegiance of the citizens of this state, native or adopted, is of right due to this state.

Resolved, That the declaration of the President of the United States in his said proclamation, of his personal feelings and relations towards the State of South Carolina, is rather an appeal to the loyalty of subjects, than to the patriotism of citizens, and is a blending of official and individual character, heretofore unknown in our state papers, and revolting to our conception of political propriety. . . .

Resolved, That the principles, doctrines and purposes, contained in the said proclamation are inconsistent with any just idea of a limited government, and subversive of the rights of the states and liberties of the people, and if submitted to in silence would lay a broad foundation for the establishment of monarchy.

Resolved, That while this legislature has witnessed with sorrow such a relaxation of the spirit of our institutions, that a President of the United States dare venture upon this high handed measure, it regards with indignation the menaces which are directed against it, and the concentration of a standing army on our borders—that the state will repel force by force, and relying upon the blessings of God, will maintain its liberty at all hazards.

Resolved, That copies of these resolutions be sent to our members in Congress, to be laid before that body.

The character of Martin Van Buren according to a political opponent, 1835

David Crockett, the colorful but somewhat phony frontiersman, did not write— but let his name be used as the author of—the hostile biography of Martin Van Buren which appeared in 1835. It was actually written by Augustin S. Clayton, a congressman from Georgia. The volume portrays Van Buren as a politician without principle, and as a rather aristocratic and effeminate individual. The satirization failed to keep Van Buren from the presidency in 1837 but was used quite effectively by the Whigs in the election of 1841.

Mr. Van Buren's parents were humble, plain, and not much troubled with book knowledge; and so were mine. His father hung out his sign on a

From David Crockett, *The Life of Martin Van Buren, Heir-Apparent to the "Government," and the Appointed Successor of General Jackson* (Philadelphia, 1835), pp. 26–32, 80–81. On the title page is the following poem: "Good Lord! What is VAN! for though simple he looks,/ Tis a task to unravel his looks and his crooks;/ With his depths and his shallows, his good and his evil,/ All in all, he's a *Riddle* must puzzle the devil."

post, with a daub on it, intended for a horse, and with the words *"entertainment for man and horse";* so did mine—for both kept little village taverns. He has become a great man without any good reason for it; and so have I. He has been nominated for president without the least pretensions; and so have I. But here the similarity stops—from his cradle he was of the *non-committal* tribe; I never was. He had always two ways to do a thing; I never had but one. He was generally half bent; I tried to be as straight as a gun-barrel. He couldn't bear his rise; I never minded mine. He forgot all his old associates because they were poor folks; I stuck to the people that made me. I would not have mentioned his origin, because I like to see people rise from nothing; but when they try to hide it, I think it ought to be thrown up to them; for a man that hasn't soul enough to own the friends that have started him, and to acknowledge the means by which he has climbed into notice, ought once-in-a-while to be reminded of the mire in which he used to wallow. . . .

The world is generally curious to know, when they read the life of a great man, what kind of a boy he was; whether he gave early signs of what he has turned out to be. About this there are many rumors; but as I do not wish to deal in the marvellous, my readers must excuse me if I decline giving any of the prodigies of my hero in his youth, especially as authentic. I do not wish to risk the credibility of my narrative, by relating any of these wonders as true. For instance, it is said that at a year old he could laugh on one side of his face and cry on the other, at one and the same time; and so by his eating, after he was weaned he could chew his bread and meat separately on the opposite sides of his mouth; plainly showing, as all the old women said, that he had a *turn* for anything. While at school, he was remarkable for his aptness; it is said—but I do not vouch for the truth of the report—that at six years old he could actually tell when his book was wrong end upwards; and at twelve, he could read it just as well *up-side-down* as *right-side-up,* and that he practiced it both ways, to acquire a shifting *knack* for business, and a ready turn for doing things more ways than one. . . .

Mr. Van Buren became a politician at an early period of his life, and has pushed it as a *trade,* from the begining to the present hour; and no man has done a better business. He has met with as few losses and bad debts in his dealings, as any adventurer that ever commenced *bartering;* but he never believed in the doctrine "that honesty was the best policy," and now thinks the maxim entirely falsified in his success. To *his* notion *principle* had nothing to do with *traffic* of any kind; and he is astonished when any person talks to him of the impropriety of two prices to things, of two kinds of weights and *measures,* of altering the quality of articles, and shifting their places, if necessary, as often as a man's interest may dictate. His rule is, as there is no "friendship in trade," so there is none in politics. A pleasant anecdote is related of him when he was quite young. It is truly like him, and planted the principle upon which he has acted ever since. A warmly-contested election was coming on, and the friends on both sides, being men of influence, used great exertions, and became much excited; our hero applied to quite a knowing politician for his opinion as to the result. The answer expressing much doubt, young Martin, casting his eyes wishfully towards the ground, said, "I do wish I knew which party would succeed, as I want to take a side, but don't like to be in the minority."

... [Sometime ago] Mr. Van Buren was just beginning to *creep* into what he now calls "*genteel society.*" He was then contented to eat and to drink and to associate with plain men, with honest hearts and clean hands. If he was travelling, and stopped at a house, he was willing to sit down among the people, and did not feel himself degraded by riding in a comfortable country wagon. Then, anybody could tell by his looks that he was not a *woman;* but the signs of the times are woefully changed.

Now, he travels about the country and through the cities in an English coach; has English servants, dressed in uniform—I think they call it livery; they look as big as most of our members of Congress, and fully as fine as the higher officers in the army; no longer mixes with the sons of little tavernkeepers; forgets all his old companions and friends in the humbler walks of life; eats in a room by himself; and is so stiff in his gait, and prim in his dress, that he is what the English call a dandy. When he enters the Senate-chamber in the morning, he struts and swaggers like a crow in a gutter. He is laced up in corsets, such as women in a town wear, and, if possible, tighter than the best of them. It would be difficult to say, from his personal appearance, whether he was man or woman, but for his large red and gray whiskers.

A hostile view of American business and society, 1836

By the end of the 1830's a ferment for reform touched many literate Americans in the Northern states. William Leggett, who worked for seven years with William C. Bryant on the New York Evening Post, *is an excellent example of those who fought for a better society. Like other Jacksonians, he attacked financial monopolies. He also waged a struggle against slavery, against limited suffrage, and against the suppression of trade unions. In the following essay, published in* The Plaindealer *on December 31, 1836, Leggett spoke out against the conditions of social inequality which existed in America.*

Look through society, and tell us who and what are our most affluent men? Did they derive their vast estates from inheritance? There are scarcely a dozen wealthy families in this metropolis whose property descended to them by bequest. Did they accumulate it by patient industry?

From William Leggett, *A Collection of the Political Writings of William Leggett* (New York, 1840), Vol. II, pp. 162–65.

There are few to whom the affirmative answer will apply. Was it the reward of superior wisdom? Alas, that is a quality which has not been asserted as a characteristic of our rich. Whence, then, have so many derived the princely fortunes, of which they display the evidences in their spacious and elegant dwellings, in their costly banquets, their glittering equipages, and all the luxurious appliances of wealth? The answer is plain. They owe them to special privileges; to that system of legislation which grants peculiar facilities to the opulent, and forbids the use of them to the poor; to that pernicious code of laws which considers the rights of property as an object of greater moment than the rights of man.

Cast yet another glance on society, in the aspect it presents when surveying those of opposite condition. What is the reason that such vast numbers of men groan and sweat under a weary life, spending their existence in incessant toil, and yet accumulating nothing around them, to give them hope of respite, and a prospect of comfort in old age? Has nature been less prodigal to them, than to those who enjoy such superior fortune? Are their minds guided by less intelligence, or their bodies nerved with less vigor? Are their morals less pure, or their industry less assiduous? In all these respects they are at least the equals of those who are so far above them in prosperity. The disparity of condition, a vast multitude of instances, may be traced directly to the errors of our legislation; to that wretched system, at war with the fundamental maxim of our government, which, instead of regarding the equality of human rights, and leaving all to the full enjoyment of natural liberty in every respect not inconsistent with public order, bestows privileges on one, and denies them to another, and compels the many to pay tribute and render homage to the few. Take a hundred ploughmen promiscuously from their fields, and a hundred merchants from their desks, and what man, regarding the true dignity of his nature, could hesitate to give the award of superior excellence, in every main intellectual, physical, and moral respect, to the band of hardy rustics over that of the lank and sallow accountants, worn out with the sordid anxieties of traffic and the calculations of gain? Yet the merchant shall grow rich from participation in the unequal privileges which a false system of legislation has created, while the ploughman, unprotected by the laws, and dependent wholly on himself, shall barely earn a frugal livelihood by continued toil.

In as far as inequality of human condition is the result of natural causes it affords no just topic of complaint, but in as far as it is brought about by the intermeddling of legislation, among a people who proclaim, as the foundation maxim of all their political institutions, the equality of the rights of man, it furnishes a merited reprehension. That this is the case with us, to a very great extent, no man of candor and intelligence can look over our statute books and deny. We have not entitled ourselves to be excepted from the condemnation which Sir Thomas More pronounces on other governments. "They are a conspiracy of the rich, who, on pretense of managing the public, only pursue their private ends, and devise all the

ways and arts they can find out, first, that they may, without danger, preserve all that they have so acquired, and then that they may engage the
poor to toil and labor for them, at as low rates as possible, and oppress
them as much as they please."

A friendly view of American business and society, 1837

*Francis J. Grund was still another of those hundreds of nineteenth century
European visitors and immigrants who felt impelled to describe and explain
America to the world. Unlike Charles Dickens, Francis Trollope, and other
hostile recorders, Grund fell in love with what he saw. He arrived in the United
States in 1827, and worked as a teacher, correspondent, and editor. A staunch
Jacksonian politically, he thought of the United States as the antithesis of
Europe, a country destined to control the Western hemisphere. Business enter-
prise and economic freedom, he believed, constituted the core of America's
strength.*

There is, probably, no people on earth with whom business constitutes
pleasure, and industry amusement, in an equal degree with the inhabitants
of the United States of America. Active occupation is not only the principal
source of their happiness, and the foundation of their national greatness,
but they are absolutely wretched without it, and instead of the "*dolce far
niente,*" know but the *horrors* of idleness. Business is the very soul of an
American. He pursues it, not as a means of procuring for himself and his
family the necessary comforts of life, but as the foundation of all human
felicity; and shows as much enthusiastic ardor in his application to it as any
crusader ever evinced for the conquest of the Holy Land, or the followers
of Mohammed for the spreading of the Koran.

From the earliest hour in the morning till late at night, the streets,
offices, and warehouses of the large cities are thronged by men of all trades
and professions, each following his vocation like a *per petuum mobile*, as
if he never dreamed of cessation from labor, of the possibility of becoming
fatigued. If a lounger should happen to be parading the street, he would
be sure to be jostled off the side-walk, or to be pushed in every direction,
until he keeps time with the rest. Should he meet a friend, he will only talk
to him on business . . . and if he retires to some house of entertainment, he
will again be entertained with *business*. Wherever he goes, the hum and
bustle of *business* will follow him; and when he finally sits down to his dinner, hoping there, at least, to find an hour of rest, he will discover, to his
sorrow that the Americans treat that as a *business* too, and dispatch it in
less time than he is able to stretch his limbs under the mahogany. In a very

From Francis J. Grund, *The Americans, in Their Moral, Social, and Political Relations*
(Boston, 1837), pp. 202–04, 238.

few minutes, the clang of steel and silver will cease, and he will again be left to his solitary reflections, while the rest are about their *business*. In the evenings, if he has no friends or acquaintances, none will intrude on his retirement; for the people are either at home with their families, or preparing for the *business* of the next day.

Whoever goes to the United States for the purpose of settling there must resolve, in his mind, to find pleasure in business, and business in pleasure, or he will be disappointed and wish himself back to the sociable idleness of Europe. Nor can any one travel in the United States without making a *business* of it. In vain would he hope to proceed at his ease. He must prepare to go at the rate of fifteen or twenty miles an hour, or conclude to stay quietly at home. He must not expect to stop, except at the places fixed upon by the proprietors of the road or the steamboat; and if he happens to take a friend by the hand an instant after the sign of departure is given, he is either left behind or carried on against his intention, and has to inquire after his luggage in another state or territory. The habit of posting being unknown, he is obliged to travel in company with the large caravans which are daily starting from, and arriving at, all the large cities, under convoy of a thousand puffing and clanking engines, where all thoughts of pleasure are speedily converted into sober reflections on the safety of property and persons. He must resign the gratification of his own individual tastes to the wishes of the majority who are traveling on *business*, and with whom speed is infinitely more important than all that contributes to pleasure; he must eat, drink, sleep, and wake, when they do, and has no other remedy for the catalogue of his distresses but the hope of their speedy termination. Arrived at the period of his sufferings he must be cautious how he gives vent to his joy, for he must *stop quickly* if his *busy* conductor shall not hurl him on again on a new journey.

Neither is this hurry of business confined to the large cities, or the method of travelling; it communicates itself to every village and hamlet, and extends to, and penetrates, the western forests. Town and country rival with each other in the eagerness of industrious pursuits. Machines are invented, new lines of communication established, and the depths of the sea explored to afford scope for the spirit of enterprise; and it is as if all America were but one gigantic workshop, over the entrance of which there is the blazing inscription *"No admission here, except on business."*

The position of a man of leisure in the United States is far from being enviable; for unless he takes delight in literary and scientific pursuits, he is not only left without companions to enjoy his luxuriant ease, but, what is worse, he forfeits the respect of his fellow-citizens, who, by precept and example, are determined to discountenance idleness. . . . There is no distinct line of demarcation between the rich and the poor, as in Europe; the deserters from both ranks, but especially from the latter, being more numerous than those who remain; and the number of newcomers putting computation altogether out of the question. Neither is there that envy amongst the laboring classes which characterizes the *"canaille"* of Europe, and manifests itself by an indiscriminate hatred of all whose fortunes are superior to their own. Exemption from labor, the *beau ideal* of the French and Italians, is not even *desired* by the industrious population of America; and the poor are willing to protect the possessions of the rich, because they expect themselves to need that protection at some future period. In all the hues and cries against the Bank, there was not the least manifestation of a desire to despoil the rich of their property. All that the people contended for was, in their opinion, an equal chance for acquiring it. They wished to put down that which they deemed a monopoly and an impediment to the progress of the small merchant; but never dreamed of plunder. This question has been sadly misrepresented in Europe, and accompanied by pictures of the cupidity of the lower classes, to which it would be difficult to find the originals in the United States of America.

A patrician analysis of Martin Van Buren and William Henry Harrison; from the letters of Justice Joseph Story, 1837–40

Joseph Story was one of the last of an old breed: a natural aristocrat and genuine conservative, he viewed the changes wrought during the Jacksonian era with characteristic pessimism. Ironically, he saw hope for the future in the figure of General William H. Harrison, not because of his intellectual achievements or political capacity or other extraordinary talents, but precisely because he was reputed to be a plain, common, and honest man.

To Harriet Martineau   April 7, 1837

Mr. Van Buren is President. Things look ill in all our money concerns, and public confidence is greatly shaken. But after a while, notwithstanding all our political blunders, we shall go ahead again; such is the recuperative power of a young country, however badly governed.

To Justice John McLean   May 10, 1837

Our country is in a state of unexampled distress and suffering. Credit, and confidence, and business are everywhere at a stand. The experiments of General Jackson, from his interference in removing the deposits and annihilating the Bank of the United States, down to the last infatuated act of the Treasury Circular, have produced their natural effects. They have

From William W. Story (ed.), *Life and Letters of Joseph Story* (Boston, 1851), Vol. II, pp. 273, 277, 281, 298, 307–08, 327–28.

swept over the country with the violence and destruction of a hurricane. Will the people awake to their rights and duties? I fear not. They have become stupefied, and are led on to their ruin by the arts of demagogues and the corrupted influences of party.

To Harriet Martineau   November 3, 1837

The reformers in America are a very different class from the reformers in England. If you had been in America the last six months and seen the whole country thrown into the utmost confusion, and suffering the most irretrievable losses from the violence of party spirit, and the rash and extravagant projects of the administration, you would have learned, I think, that there may be a despotism exercised in a republic, as irresistible and as ruinous as in any form of monarchy.

To Charles Sumner   August 11, 1838

The last session of Congress ended disgracefully for the administration, which has persisted with a most perverse and rash obstinacy in its financial projects, ruinous to the country. The sub-treasury scheme, one of the worst measures, in my judgment, which could have been fastened on the country, and which would have been the source of the most mischievous corruptions of the country, was defeated after a terrible struggle. The administration did all it could to carry it, and it was lost by a majority of about twenty only in the House, though in my conscience I do not believe that there were thirty members who really approved it.

To Harriet Martineau   January 19, 1839

I presume you may wish to know what Congress are doing. . . . The refusal to act upon the abolition petitions, being in effect a denial of the Constitutional right of petition, has created a good deal of excitement; and the question of slavery is becoming more and more an absorbing one, and will, if it continues to extend its influence, lead to a dissolution of the Union. At least, there are many of our soundest statesmen who look to this as a highly probable event.

The only other subject of general interest now before Congress is the sub-treasury scheme, (as it is called) substituting a machinery of the Government itself for the usual agency of banks, as depositaries and remittants of the public money, which is strongly opposed by the whole Whig party, as a measure designed to concentrate in the executive department the whole power over the currency of the country, and thus by its patronage and its arbitrary measures, to subject the commerce of the country to an irresistible influence. It will probably be defeated.

To Simon Greenleaf, Esq.   February 6, 1840

The nomination of Harrison runs like wildfire on the prairies. It aston-ishes all persons, friends and foes. The general impression here is that he will certainly be chosen President. Mr. Webster told me last evening that there was not the slightest doubt of it. The administration party are evi-dently in great alarm, and some are preparing to leap overboard before the ship sinks. In the meantime, the farmers in the West are beginning to feel the public pressure most severely. All their produce is at a very low price, money is exceedingly scarce, and business at a dead stand. I confess, that, desponding as I habitually am on all such subjects, I feel more encour-agement than I have felt for a long time.

To Mrs. Joseph Story   February 9, 1840

It is wonderful how the nomination of General Harrison has taken. In the western States it has been received with acclamations. He is a very honest man, whose public services have been great, and whose military achieve-ments have given him considerable honor. But his talents are not of a high order, and at this hour he is filling the office of clerk of a County Court in Ohio. What, however, seems to give him great strength is, that he is poor and honest, or, as Mr. Abbott Lawrence said the other day to me "the peo-ple believe that he won't lie, and won't steal." The real truth is, that the people are best pleased with a man whose talents do not elevate him so much above the mass, as to become an object of jealousy, or envy. The prospect of his being President is quite encouraging. Webster thinks it cer-tain. I am not so sanguine. What I most anxiously desire is, to see a Presi-dent who shall act as President of the country, and not as a mere puppet of party.

5
Freedom and Slavery

Excerpts from the introduction to Theodore Weld's *American Slavery As It Is: Testimony of a Thousand Witnesses*, 1839–40

To most contemporaries and to many later scholars, William Lloyd Garrison symbolized the antislavery crusade. Actually, a second center of abolitionism existed in upstate New York, western Pennsylvania, and Ohio. This movement stemmed from and borrowed the techniques of religious revivalism. It was at once more practical, more moderate, more influential and more politically oriented than the Garrisonians. A volume by one of their better-known leaders, Theodore Weld's American Slavery As It Is, *sold more than 100,000 copies in the year following its publication in 1839.*

Reader, you are empannelled as a juror to try a plain case and bring in an honest verdict. The question at issue is not one of law, but of fact: "What is the actual condition of the slaves in the United States?" A plainer case never went to a jury. Look at it. TWENTY-SEVEN HUNDRED THOUSAND PERSONS in this country, men, women, and children, are in SLAVERY. Is slavery, as a condition for human beings, good, bad, or indifferent? We submit the question without argument. You have common sense, and conscience, and a human heart: pronounce upon it. You have a wife, or a husband, a child, a father, a mother, a brother or a sister—make the case your own, make it theirs, and bring in your verdict. The case of Human Rights against slavery has been adjudicated in the court of conscience times innumerable. The same verdict has always been rendered—"Guilty"; the same sentence has always been pronounced, "Let it be accursed"; and human nature, with her million echoes, has rung it round the world in every language under heaven, "Let it be accursed. Let it be accursed." His heart is false to human nature, who will not say "Amen." There is not a man on earth who does not believe that slavery is a curse. Human beings may be inconsistent, but human *nature* is true to herself. She has uttered her testimony against slavery with a shriek ever since the monster was begotten; and till it perishes amidst the execrations of the universe, she will traverse the world on its track, dealing her bolts upon its head, dashing against it her condemning brand. We repeat it, every man knows that slavery is a curse. Whoever denies this, his lips libel his heart. Try him; clank the chains in his ears, and tell him they are for *him;* give him an hour to prepare his wife and children for a life of slavery; bid him make haste and get ready their necks for the yoke, and their wrists for the coffle chains, then look at his pale lips and trembling knees, and you have *nature's* testimony against slavery.

Two million seven hundred thousand persons in these States are in

From Theodore Weld, *American Slavery As It Is: Testimony of a Thousand Witnesses* (New York, 1839), pp. 7–10.

this condition. They were made slaves and are held such by force, and by being put in fear, and this for no crime! Reader, what have you to say of such treatment? Is it right, just, benevolent? Suppose I should seize you, rob you of your liberty, drive you into the field, and make you work without pay as long as you live, would that be justice and kindness, or monstrous injustice and cruelty? Now, everybody knows that the slaveholders do these things to the slaves every day, and yet it is stoutly affirmed that they treat them well and kindly, and that their tender regard for their slaves restrains the masters from inflicting cruelties upon them. We shall go into no metaphysics to show the absurdity of this pretense. . . . Are slaveholders dunces, or do they take all the rest of the world to be, that they think to bandage our eyes with such thin gauzes? Protesting their kind regard for those whom they hourly plunder of all they have and all they get! What! when they have seized their victims, and annihilated all their *rights,* still claim to be the special guardians of their *happiness!* Plunderers of their liberty, yet the careful suppliers of their wants? Robbers of their earnings, yet watchful sentinels round their interests, and kind providers for their comfort? Filching all their time, yet granting generous donations for rest and sleep? Stealing the use of their muscles, yet thoughtful of their ease? Putting them under *drivers,* yet careful that they are not hard-pushed? Too humane forsooth to stint the stomachs of their slaves, yet force their *minds* to starve, and brandish over them pains and penalties, if they dare to reach forth for the smallest crumb of knowledge, even a letter of the alphabet! . . .

As slaveholders and their apologies are volunteer witnesses in their own cause, and are flooding the world with testimony that their slaves are kindly treated; that they are well fed, well clothed, well housed, well lodged, moderately worked, and bountifully provided with all things needful for their comfort, we propose—first, to disprove their assertions by the testimony of a multitude of impartial witnesses, and then to put slaveholders themselves through a course of cross-questioning which shall draw their condemnation out of their own mouths. We will prove that the slaves in the United States are treated with barbarous inhumanity; that they are overworked, underfed, wretchedly clad and lodged, and have insufficient sleep; that they are often made to wear round their necks iron collars armed with prongs, to drag heavy chains and weights at their feet while working in the field, and to wear yokes, and bells, and iron horns; that they are often kept confined in the stocks day and night for weeks together, made to wear gags in their mouths for hours or days, have some of their front teeth torn out or broken off, that they may be easily detected when they run away; that they are frequently flogged with terrible severity, have red pepper rubbed into their lacerated flesh, and hot brine, spirits of turpentine, etc., poured over the gashes to increase the torture; that they are often stripped naked, their backs and limbs cut with knives, bruised and mangled by scores and hundreds of blows with the paddle, and terribly torn by the claws of cats, drawn over them by their tormentors; that they are often hunted with blood-hounds and shot down like beasts, or torn in pieces by dogs; that they are often suspended by the arms and whipped and beaten till they faint, and when revived by restoratives, beaten again till they faint, and sometimes till they die; that their ears are often cut off, their eyes knocked out, their bones broken, their flesh branded with red hot irons; that they are maimed, mutilated and burned to death over slow fires. . . . We will establish all these facts by the testimony of scores and hundreds of eye witnesses, by the testimony of *slaveholders* in all parts of the slave states, by slaveholding members of Congress and of state legislatures, by ambassadors to foreign courts, by judges, by doctors of divinity, and clergymen of all denominations, by merchants, mechanics, lawyers and physicians, by presidents and professors in colleges and *professional* seminaries, by planters, overseers and drivers. We shall show, not merely that such deeds are committed, but that they are frequent; not done in corners, but before the sun; not in one of the slave states, but in all of them; not perpetrated by brutal overseers and drivers merely, but by magistrates, by legislators, by professors of religion, by preachers of the gospel, by governors of states, by "gentlemen of property and standing," and by delicate females moving in the "highest circles of society." We know, full well, the outcry that will be made by multitudes, at these declarations; the multiform cavils, the flat denials, the charges of "exaggeration" and "falsehood" so often bandied, the sneers of affected contempt at the credulity that can believe such things, and the rage and imprecations against those who give them currency. We know, too, the threadbare sophistries by which slaveholders and their apologists seek to evade such testimony. If they admit that such deeds are committed, they tell us that they are exceedingly rare, and therefore furnish no grounds for judging of the general treatment of slaves; that occasionally a brutal wretch in the *free* states barbarously butchers his wife, but that no one thinks of inferring from that, the general treatment of wives at the North and West.

They tell us, also, that the slaveholders of the South are proverbially hospitable, kind and generous, and it is incredible that they can perpetrate such enormities upon human beings; further, that it is absurd to suppose that they would thus injure their own property, that self-interest would prompt them to treat their slaves with kindness, as none but fools and madmen wantonly destroy their own property; further, that Northern visitors at the South come back testifying to the kind treatment of the slaves, and the slaves themselves corroborate such representations. All these pleas, and scores of others, are bruited in every corner of the free States; and who that hath eyes to see, has not sickened at the blindness that saw not, at the palsy of heart that felt not, or at the cowardice and sycophancy that dared not expose such shallow fallacies. We are not to be turned from our purpose by such vapid babblings.

An aristocratic New Yorker's account of the Texas issue and the election of 1844: from the diary of Philip Hone, June 1844 to March 1845

Philip Hone, an affluent and perhaps typical New York businessman, was anti-slavery, but also anti-abolitionist. On one hand he condemned abolitionist activity as "a most mischievous undertaking, which may bring destruction upon their own heads and civil war into the bosom of our hitherto happy country." On the other, he resisted the extension of Southern power and influence, considered the annexation of Texas abominable, and lamented the defeat of Henry Clay by James K. Polk.

Tuesday, June 11, 1844

Mr. Tyler's infamous treaty, by which he hoped to rob Mexico of her province of Texas, against the consent of the people of the United States, to promote his political ends with the Southern States, at the risk of plunging the country into an unjust and discreditable war, and to force the country to assume thereby the enormous debts of a set of vagabond adventurers, has received its quietus in the Senate, where it was discussed in secret session several days, and finally rejected on Saturday.

Friday, November 8, 1844

Yesterday's news from the West and the North has settled the question. The State of New York has gone for Polk and Dallas by a majority of five or six thousand. This result, which makes them President and Vice President of the Unitd States, has been brought about by foreign votes made for the purpose. Mr. Clay is again defeated; the people have rejected their best friend, and repudiated the principles by which alone national prosperity and individual happiness might have been secured. So let it be! We must submit, and have only to pray that the Almighty will avert from the country the evils which, from present appearances, the people have brought upon themselves, and that the administration may turn out better than some of us now anticipate.

There is a Whig loss in the State since the election of General Harrison in 1840 of about 20,000. The slaveholders of the South and the Abolitionists of the North have gone equally against us. Free trade and protection have voted for Polk and Dallas. Mr. Clay's talents, public services, and sound principles are too much for this perverse leveling generation. The beauty of his character forms too strong a contrast to their deformity.

Reprinted by permission of Dodd, Mead & Co., Inc. from Allan Nevins (ed.), *The Diary of Philip Hone* (New York, 1936), pp. 706–07, 719–20, 726–27.

158

Saturday, March 1, 1845

The great question of the annexation of Texas, which has kept the public mind in an unprecedented state of excitement, and the result of which was doubtful until the last moment, was carried in the Senate by means the most unconstitutional on Thursday evening. The party who elected Mr. Polk were determined to carry it through all hazards, and the foundations of the republic have been broken up to accomplish the object. The measure was carried by a vote of 27 to 25. These twenty-five are all Whigs, and three of the majority are also Whigs. If their consciences are satisfied, so be it. The end of all these things is at hand. The Constitution is a dead letter, the ark of safety is wrecked, the wall of separation which has hitherto restrained the violence of popular rage is broken down, the Goths are in possession of the Capitol, and if the Union can stand the shock it will only be another evidence that Divine Providence takes better care of us than we deserve.

President Polk asks for war: an extract from his diary, May 9, 1846

Texas insisted that its southern boundary extended to the Rio Grande river, a rather specious claim which President Polk took seriously. But even before the first shots were fired in the disputed region (between the Rio Grande and Nueces rivers), Polk had decided to ask for a declaration of war against Mexico. The following entry in Polk's famous diary, for May 9, 1846, records the reactions of various cabinet members to Polk's request.

The Cabinet held a regular meeting to-day; all the members present. I brought up the Mexican question, and the question of what was the duty of the administration in the present state of our relations with that country. The subject was very fully discussed. All agreed that if the Mexican forces at Matamoras committed any act of hostility on General Taylor's forces I should immediately send a message to Congress recommending an immediate declaration of war. I stated to the Cabinet that up to this time, as they knew, we had heard of no open act of aggression by the Mexican army, but that the danger was imminent that such acts would be committed. I said that in my opinion we had ample cause of war, and that it was impossible that we could stand in *statu quo,* or that I could remain silent much longer; that I thought it was my duty to send a message to Congress very soon and recommend definitive measures. I told them that I thought I ought to make such a message by Tuesday next, that the coun-

From Milo M. Quaife (ed.), *The Diary of James K. Polk* (New York, 1910), Vol. I, pp. 384–86.

try was excited and impatient on the subject, and if I failed to do so I would not be doing my duty. I then propounded the distinct question to the Cabinet and took their opinions individually, whether I should make a message to Congress on Tuesday, and whether in that message I should recommend a declaration of war against Mexico. All except the Secretary of the Navy gave their advice in the affirmative. Mr. Bancroft dissented but said if any act of hostility should be committed by the Mexican forces he was then in favor of immediate war. Mr. Buchanan said he would feel better satisfied in his course if the Mexican forces had or should commit any act of hostility, but that as matters stood we had ample cause of war against Mexico, and he gave his assent to the measure. It was agreed that the message should be prepared and submitted to the Cabinet in their meeting on Tuesday. . . .

About 6 o'clock P.M. General R. Jones, the Adjutant General of the army, called and handed to me dispatches received from General Taylor by the Southern mail which had just arrived, giving information that a part of the Mexican army had crossed the Del Norte, and attacked and killed and captured two companies of dragoons of General Taylor's army consisting of 63 officers and men. The dispatch also stated that he had on that day (26th April) made a requisition on the Governors of Texas and Louisiana for four Regiments each, to be sent to his relief at the earliest practicable period. . . . I immediately summoned the Cabinet to meet at 7½ O'Clock this evening. The Cabinet accordingly assembled at that hour; all the members present. The subject of the dispatch received this evening from General Taylor, as well as the state of our relations with Mexico, were fully considered. The Cabinet was unanimously of opinion, and it was so agreed, that a message should be sent to Congress on Monday laying all the information in my possession before them and recommending vigorous and prompt measures to enable the Executive to prosecute the war.

Thomas Corwin's speech against the Mexican War, February 11, 1847

As Polk's imperialistic war aims became clearer, an increasing number of Northerners spoke out against the conflict. Abraham Lincoln, Daniel Webster, and Horace Greeley, rebuked the administration. Henry Thoreau went to jail in protest, and was inspired to write his essay on "Civil Disobedience." The state legislature of Massachusetts declared the war an unconstitutional action designed to strengthen "the slave power." James Russell Lowell, in the Biglow Papers, took up the theme of the war as part of a Southern conspiracy:

From *Congressional Globe*, Twenty-ninth Congress, Second Session, pp. 216–17.

> *"They just want this Californy*
> *So's to lug new slave-states in*
> *To abuse ye, an' to scorn ye,*
> *An' to plunder ye like sin."*

One of the strongest anti-war speeches was delivered by Thomas Corwin, an antislavery Whig from Ohio.

I did hope . . . we might get peace, and avoid the slaughter, the shame, the crime, of an aggressive unprovoked war. But now you have overrun half of Mexico—you have exasperated and irritated her people—you claim indemnity for all expenses incurred in doing this mischief, and boldly ask her to give up New Mexico and California; and, as a bribe to her patriotism, seizing on her property, you offer three millions to pay the soldiers she has called out to repel your invasion, on condition that she will give up to you at least one-third of her whole territory. . . .

What is the territory, Mr. President, which you propose to wrest from Mexico? It is consecrated to the heart of the Mexican by many a well-fought battle with his old Castilian master. His Bunker Hills, and Saratogas, and Yorktowns, are there! The Mexican can say, "There I bled for liberty! And shall I surrender that consecrated home of my affections to the Anglo-Saxon invaders? What do they want with it? They have Texas already. They have possessed themselves of the territory between the Nueces and the Rio Grande. What else do they want? To what shall I point my children as memorials of that independence which I bequeath to them when those battlefields shall have passed from my possession?"

Sir, had one come and demanded Bunker Hill of the people of Massachusetts, had England's Lion ever showed himself there, is there a man over thirteen and under ninety who would not have been ready to meet him? Is there a river on this continent that would not have run red with blood? Is there a field but would have been piled high with the unburied bones of slaughtered Americans before these consecrated battlefields of liberty should have been wrested from us? But this same American goes into a sister republic and says to poor, weak Mexico, "Give up your territory, you are unworthy to possess it; I have got one-half already, and all I ask of you is to give up the other!" England might as well, in the circumstances I have described, have come and demanded of us, "Give up the Atlantic slope—give up this trifling territory from the Alleghany Mountains to the sea; it is only from Maine to St. Mary's—only about one-third of your republic, and the least interesting portion of it." What would be the response? They would say, we must give this up to John Bull. Why? "He wants room." The Senator from Michigan says he must have this. Why, my worthy Christian brother, on what principle of justice? "I want room!"

Sir, look at this pretence of want of room. With twenty millions of people, you have about one thousand millions of acres of land, inviting settlement by every conceivable argument, bringing them down to a quarter of a dollar an acre, and allowing every man to squat where he pleases. But the Senator from Michigan says we will be two hundred millions in a few years, and we want room. If I were a Mexican I would tell you, "Have you not room in your own country to bury your dead men? If you come into mine, we will greet you with bloody hands, and welcome you to hospitable graves."

Why, says the chairman of this Committee on Foreign Relations, it is the most reasonable thing in the world! We ought to have the Bay of San Francisco. Why? Because it is the best harbor on the Pacific! It has been my fortune, Mr. President, to have practised a good deal in criminal courts in the course of my life, but I never yet heard a thief, arraigned for stealing a horse, plead that it was the best horse that he could find in the country! We want California. What for? Why, says the Senator from Michigan, we will have it; and the Senator from South Carolina, with a very mistaken view, I think, of policy, says you can't keep our people from going there. I don't desire to prevent them. Let them go and seek their happiness in whatever country or clime it pleases them. All I ask of them is, not to require this Government to protect them with that banner consecrated to war waged for principles—eternal, enduring truth. Sir, it is not meet that our old flag should throw its protecting folds over expeditions for lucre or for land. But you will say you want room for your people. This has been the plea of every robber chief from Nimrod to the present hour.

Daniel Webster defends a strong fugitive slave act: from his speech of March 7, 1850, in behalf of the Compromise of 1850

In 1850 it appeared that the American genius for compromise had settled the issue of slavery in the territories. President Pierce expressed the hope "that no sectional or ambitious or fanatical excitement may again threaten the durability of our institutions or obscure the light of our prosperity." Fashioned by Henry Clay, the compromise was ably defended by Daniel Webster in his "Seventh of March" speech which obtained immediate national renown. "The speech continues in demand," Webster noted a few weeks later. "One hundred and twenty thousand copies have gone off. I am sending a handsome copy to each member of the [state] legislature, and shall send the speech also pretty generally to the clergy of Massachusetts."

But Webster was severely scorned and censured by the intellectuals of New England for his defense of a stringent fugitive slave act. Webster's course, wrote Theodore Parker, "was as crooked as the Missouri." He has "been on all sides of moral questions, save the winning side." John Greenleaf Whittier expressed this bitterness towards Webster in "Ichabod":

From *Congressional Globe,* Thirty-first Congress, First Session, pp. 476–84.

"Of all we loved and honored, naught
Save power remains—
A fallen angel's pride of thought,
Still strong in chains.

"All else is gone, from those great eyes,
The soul is fled;
When faith is lost, when honor dies;
The man is dead!"

I wish to speak today, not as a Massachusetts man, nor as a Northern man, but as an American, and a member of the Senate of the United States. . . . It is not to be denied that we live in the midst of strong agitations, and are surrounded by very considerable dangers to our institutions and government. The imprisoned winds are let loose. The East, the North, and the stormy South combine to throw the whole sea into commotion, to toss its billows to the skies, and disclose its profoundest depths. I do not affect to regard myself . . . as holding, or as fit to hold, the helm in this combat with the political elements; but I have a duty to perform, and I mean to perform it with fidelity, not without a sense of existing dangers, but not without hope. I have a part to act, not for my own security or safety, for I am looking out for no fragment upon which to float away from the wreck, if wreck there must be, but for the good of the whole, and the preservation of all; and there is that which will keep me to my duty during this struggle, whether the sun and the stars shall appear, or shall not appear for many days. I speak today for the preservation of the Union. "Hear me for my cause." I speak today, out of a solicitous and anxious heart, for the restoration to the country of that quiet and that harmony which make the blessings of this Union so rich and so dear to us all. . . .

There has been found at the North, among individuals and among legislators, a disinclination to perform fully their constitutional duties in regard to the return of persons bound to service who have escaped into the free States. In that respect, the South, in my judgment, is right, and the North is wrong. Every member of every Northern legislature is bound by oath, like every other officer in the country, to support the Constitution of the United States; and the article of the Constitution which says to these States that they shall deliver up fugitives from service is as binding in honor and conscience as any other article. . . . When the subject, some years ago, was before the Supreme Court of the United States, the majority of the judges held that power to cause fugitives from service to be delivered up was a power to be exercised under the authority of this government. I do not know, on the whole, that it may not have been a fortunate decision. My habit is to respect the result of judicial deliberations and the solemnity of judicial decisions. As it now stands, the business of seeing that these fugitives are delivered up resides in the power of Congress and the national judicature, and my friend at the head of the Judiciary Committee has a bill on the subject now before the Senate, which, with some amendments to it, I propose to support, with all its provisions, to the fullest extent. And I desire to call the attention of all sober-minded men at the North, of all conscientious men, of all men who are not carried away by some fanatical idea or some false impression, to their constitutional obligations. I put it to all the sober and sound minds at the North as a question of morals and a question of conscience. What right have they, in their legislative capacity or any other capacity, to endeavor to get round this Constitution, or to embarrass the free exercise of the rights secured by the Constitution to the persons whose slaves escape from them? None at all; none at all. Neither in the forum of conscience, nor before the face of the Constitution, are they, in my opinion, justified in such an attempt. Of course it is a matter for their consideration. They probably, in the excitement of the times, have not stopped to consider of this. They have followed what seemed to be the current of thought and of motives, as the occasion arose, and they have neglected to investigate fully the real question, and to consider their constitutional obligations; which, I am sure, if they did consider, they would fulfill with alacrity. I repeat, therefore, Sir, that here is a well-founded ground of complaint against the North, which ought to be removed, which it is now in the power of the different departments of this government to remove; which calls for the enactment of proper laws authorizing the judicature of this government, in the several States, to do all that is necessary for the recapture of fugitive slaves and for their restoration to those who claim them. Wherever I go, and whenever I speak on the subject, and when I speak here I desire to speak to the whole North, I say that the South has been injured in this respect, and has a right to complain; and the North has been too careless of what I think the Constitution peremptorily and emphatically enjoins upon her as duty. . . .

A letter of Stephen A. Douglas to the editor of the Concord, New Hampshire, *State Capitol Reporter*, February 16, 1854

In 1854 Senator Stephen Douglas reopened the whole question of slavery in the territories by championing the Kansas-Nebraska bill, which left to the settlers— rather than Congress—the question of deciding whether or not slavery would be permitted. Excoriated by many Northerners, Douglas defended his ideas as the most democratic and pragmatic solution to a vexing problem. The following letter was addressed to a New Hampshire newspaper which had contained an article attacking the principles of his bill.

The [Nebraska] bill rests upon, and proposes to carry into effect, the great fundamental principle of self-government upon which our republican

From Robert W. Johannsen (ed.), *The Letters of Stephen A. Douglas* (Urbana, Ill.: University of Illinois Press, 1961), pp. 284–90. Reprinted by permission.

institutions are predicated. It does not propose to legislate slavery into the Territories, nor out of the Territories. It does not propose to establish institutions for the people, nor to deprive them of the right of determining for themselves what kind of domestic institutions they may have. It presupposes that the people of the Territories are as intelligent, as wise, as patriotic, as conscientious as their brethren and kindred whom they left behind them in the States, and as they were before they emigrated to the Territories. By creating a territorial government we acknowledge that the people of the Territory ought to be erected into a distinct political organization. By giving them a territorial legislature, we acknowledge their capacity to legislate for themselves. Now, let it be borne in mind that every abolitionist and freesoiler, who opposes the Nebraska bill, avows his willingness to support it, provided that slavery shall be forever prohibited therein. The objection, therefore, does not consist in a denial of the necessity for a territorial government, nor of the capacity of the people to govern themselves, so far as white men are concerned. They are willing to allow the people to legislate for themselves in relation to husband and wife, parent and child, master and servant, and guardian and ward, so far as white persons are to be affected; but seem to think that it requires a higher degree of civilization and refinement to legislate for the Negro race than can reasonably be expected the people of a Territory to possess. Is this position well founded? Does it require any greater capacity or keener sense of moral rectitude to legislate for the black man than for the white man? Not being able to appreciate the force of this theory on the part of the abolitionists, I propose, by the express terms of the Nebraska bill, to leave the people of the Territories "perfectly free to form and regulate their domestic institutions in their own way, subject only to the Constitution of United States. . . ."

The bill provides in words as specific and unequivocal as our language affords, that the *true intent and meaning* of the act is NOT to legislate slavery into any Territory or State. The bill, therefore, does not introduce slavery; does not revive it; does not establish it; does not contain any clause designed to produce that result, or which by any possible construction can have that legal effect. . . . The cry of the extension of slavery has been raised for mere party purposes by the abolition confederates and disappointed office-seekers. All candid men who understand the subject admit that the laws of climate, and production, and of physical geography, (to use the language of one of New England's greatest statesmen,) have excluded slavery from that country. . . . Mr. Badger of North Carolina [declared] . . . that he and his southern friends did not expect that slavery would go there; that the climate and productions were not adapted to slave labor; but they insisted upon it as a matter of principle, and of principle alone. In short, all candid and intelligent men make the same admission, and present the naked question as a matter of principle, whether the people shall be allowed to regulate their domestic concerns in their own way or not. In conclusion, I may be permitted to add, that the Democratic party, as well as the country, have a deep interest in this matter. Is our party to be again divided and rent asunder upon this vexed question of slavery?

Frederick Douglass on the Dred Scott decision, May 14, 1857

One of the most poorly reasoned and subjective judgments of the Supreme Court was recorded in the Dred Scott case. Despite ample historical precedents to the contrary, the Court maintained (a) that blacks could not be American citizens, and (b) that Congress could not forbid slaves from entering any territory, since such an action would amount to depriving Americans of their property without due process of law.

Frederick Douglass, an ex-slave and an altogether extraordinary individual, delivered this angry speech against the Dred Scott decision before an abolitionist meeting.

We are now told, in tones of lofty exultation, that the day is lost—all lost—and that we might as well give up the struggle. The highest authority has spoken. The voice of the Supreme Court has gone out over the troubled waves of the National Conscience, saying peace, be still. This infamous decision of the slaveholding wing of the Supreme Court maintains that slaves are within the contemplation of the Constitution of the United States, property; that slaves are property in the same sense that horses, sheep, and swine are property; that the old doctrine that slavery is a creature of local law is false; that the right of the slaveholder to his slave does not depend upon the local law, but is secured wherever the Constitution of the United States extends; that Congress has no right to prohibit slavery anywhere; that slavery may go in safety anywhere under the star-spangled banner; that colored persons of African descent have no rights that white men are bound to respect; that colored men of African descent are not and cannot be citizens of the United States.

You will readily ask me how I am affected by this devilish decision —this judicial incarnation of wolfishness? My answer is, and no thanks to the slaveholding wing of the Supreme Court, my hopes were never brighter than now. I have no fear that the National Conscience will be put to sleep by such an open, glaring, and scandalous tissue of lies as that decision is, and has been, over and over, shown to be.

The Supreme Court of the United States is not the only power in this world. It is very great, but the Supreme Court of the Almighty is greater. Judge Taney can do many things, but he cannot perform impossibilities. He cannot bail out the ocean, annihilate this firm old earth, or pluck the silvery star of liberty from our Northern sky. He may decide, and decide again;

From *Two Speeches by Frederick Douglass* (Rochester, N.Y., 1857), pp. 31–35.

but he cannot reverse the decision of the Most High. He cannot change the essential nature of things—making evil good, and good, evil.

Happily for the whole human family, their rights have been defined, declared, and decided in a court higher than the Supreme Court. . . . Such a decision cannot stand. God will be true though every man be a liar. We can appeal from this hell-black judgment of the Supreme Court, to the court of common sense and common humanity. We can appeal from man to God. If there is no justice on earth, there is yet justice in heaven. You may close your Supreme Court against the black man's cry for justice, but you cannot, thank God, close against him the ear of a sympathizing world, nor shut up the Court of Heaven. All that is merciful and just, on earth and in Heaven, will execrate and despise this edict of Taney.

If it were at all likely that the people of these free States would tamely submit to this demoniacal judgment, I might feel gloomy and sad over it, and possibly it might be necessary for my people to look for a home in some other country. But as the case stands, we have nothing to fear. In one point of view, we, the abolitionists and colored people, should meet this decision, unlooked for and monstrous as it appears, in a cheerful spirit. This very attempt to blot out forever the hopes of an enslaved people may be one necessary link in the chain of events preparatory to the downfall, and complete overthrow of the whole slave system. . . .

Step by step we have seen the slave power advancing; poisoning, corrupting, and perverting the institutions of the country; growing more and more haughty, imperious, and exacting. The white man's liberty has been marked out for the same grave with the black man's. The ballot box is desecrated, God's law set at nought, armed legislators stalk the halls of Congress, freedom of speech is beaten down in the Senate. The rivers and highways are infested by border ruffians, and white men are made to feel the iron heel of slavery. This ought to arouse us to kill off the hateful thing. They are solemn warnings to which the white people, as well as the black people, should take heed.

If these shall fail, judgment, more fierce or terrible, may come. The lightning, whirlwind, and earthquake may come. Jefferson said that he trembled for his country when he reflected that God is just, and his justice cannot sleep forever. The time may come when even the crushed worm may turn under the tyrant's feet. Goaded by cruelty, stung by a burning sense of wrong, in an awful moment of depression and desperation, the bondman and bondwoman at the South may rush to one wild and deadly struggle for freedom. Already slaveholders go to bed with bowie knives, and apprehend death at their dinners. Those who enslave, rob, and torment their cooks, may well expect to find death in their dinner-pots.

A Southern defense of the slave system: from Fitzhugh's *Cannibals All!*, 1857

George Fitzhugh, a Virginia lawyer, went one step further than other pro-slavery spokesmen. Previous writers had focussed attention on the evils of Northern capitalism, maintaining that the slave was better cared for during sickness and old age than the white industrial worker. Fitzhugh repeated this argument, and predicted that the competitive system in the North, as in Europe, would lead inevitably to economic depressions, to strikes, and to socialism. Southern society, on the other hand, because of slavery, would possess stability and balance. Northern abolitionists, he argued, hated slavery because they hated blacks; while the slave-owner, without such hatred, took a paternal interest in his charges.

The Negro slaves of the South are the happiest, and, in some sense, the freest people in the world. The children and the aged and infirm work not at all, and yet have all the comforts and necessaries of life provided for them. They enjoy liberty, because they are oppressed neither by care nor labor. The women do little hard work, and are protected from the despotism of their husbands by their masters. The negro men and stout boys work, on the average, in good weather, not more than nine hours a day. The balance of their time is spent in perfect abandon. Besides, they have their Sabbaths and holidays. White men, with so much of license and liberty, would die of ennui; but negroes luxuriate in corporeal and mental repose. With their faces upturned to the sun, they can sleep at any hour; and quiet sleep is the greatest of human enjoyments. "Blessed be the man who invented sleep." 'Tis happiness itself—and results from contentment with the present, and confident assurance of the future. We do not know whether free laborers ever sleep. They are fools to do so; for, whilst they sleep, the wily and watchful capitalist is devising means to ensnare and exploite them. The free laborer must work or starve. He is more of a slave than the negro, because he works longer and harder for less allowance than the slave, and has no holiday, because the cares of life with him begin when its labors end. He has no liberty, and not a single right. We know, 'tis often said, air and water, are common property, which all have equal right to participate and enjoy; but this is utterly false. The appropriation of the lands carries with it the appropriation of all on or above the lands. . . . A man cannot breathe the air, without a place to breathe it from, and all places are appropriated. All water is private property "to the middle of the stream," except the ocean, and that is not fit to drink.

Free laborers have not a thousandth part of the rights and liberties of negro slaves. Indeed, they have not a single right or a single liberty, unless it be the right or liberty to die. But the reader may think that he and other

From George Fitzhugh, *Cannibals All! Or, Slaves Without Masters* (Richmond, Va., 1857), pp. 29–31, 297–98.

capitalists and employers are freer than negro slaves. Your capital would soon vanish, if you dared indulge in the liberty and abandon of negroes. You hold your wealth and position by the tenure of constant watchfulness, care and circumspection. You never labor; but you are never free.

Where a few own the soil, they have unlimited power over the balance of society, until domestic slavery comes in, to compel them to permit this balance of society to draw a sufficient and comfortable living from "terra mater." Free society, asserts the right of a few to the earth—slavery, maintains that it belongs, in different degrees, to all. . . .

Our Southern slavery has become a benign and protective institution, and our negroes are confessedly better off than any free laboring population in the world. How can we contend that white slavery is wrong, whilst all the great body of free laborers are starving; and slaves, white or black, throughout the world, are enjoying comfort?

We write in the cause of Truth and Humanity, and will not play the advocate for master or for slave. The aversion to negroes, the antipathy of race, is much greater at the North than at the South; and it is very probable that this antipathy to the person of the negro, is confounded with or generates hatred of the institution with which he is usually connected. Hatred to slavery is very generally little more than hatred of negroes.

There is one strong argument in favor of negro slavery over all other slavery: that he, being unfitted for the mechanic arts, for trade, and all skillful pursuits, leaves those pursuits to be carried on by the whites; and does not bring all industry into disrepute, as in Greece and Rome, where the slaves were not only the artists and mechanics, but also the merchants. Whilst, as a general and abstract question, negro slavery has no other claims over other forms of slavery, except that from inferiority, or rather peculiarity, of race, almost all negroes require masters, whilst only the children, the women, the very weak, poor, and ignorant, etc., among the whites, need some protective and governing relation of this kind; yet as a subject of temporary, but world-wide importance, negro slavery has become the most necessary of all human institutions.

A Northern black in defense of his race, March 1858

Scarcely known to students, John S. Rock was perhaps the most well-educated black of his age. During his lifetime Rock had been a teacher, dentist, doctor, and lawyer. At the close of the Civil War he became the first black person to be admitted before the United States Supreme Court. In 1858, at a meeting in Faneuil Hall to commemorate the Boston Massacre, when he was but thirty-three years of age, Rock delivered an address on black pride which is as relevant and applicable today as it was then.

From John S. Rock, *Liberator*, March 12, 1858, reprinted in Thomas R. Frazier (ed.), *Afro-American History: Primary Sources* (New York: Harcourt Brace Jovanovich, Inc., 1970), pp. 120–24.

White Americans have taken great pains to try to prove that we are cowards. We are often insulted with the assertion that if we had the courage of the Indians or the white man, we would never have submitted to be slaves. I ask if Indians and white men have never been slaves? The white man tested the Indian's courage here when he had his organized armies, his battle-grounds, his places of retreat, with everything to hope for and everything to lose. The position of the African slave has been very different. Seized a prisoner of war, unarmed, bound hand and foot, and conveyed to a distant country among what to him were worse than cannibals; brutally beaten, half-starved, closely watched by armed men, with no means of knowing their own strength or the strength of their enemies, with no weapons, and without a probability of success. But if the white man will take the trouble to fight the black man in Africa or in Haiti, and fight him as fair as the black man will fight him there—if the black man does not come off victor, I am deceived in his prowess. But, take a man, armed or unarmed, from his home, his country, or his friends, and place him among savages, and who is he that would not make good his retreat? "Discretion is the better part of valor," but for a man to resist where he knows it will destroy him, shows more fool-hardiness than courage. There have been many Anglo-Saxon and Anglo-Americans enslaved in Africa, but I have never heard that they successfully resisted any government. . . .

The courage of the Anglo-Saxon is best illustrated in his treatment of the negro. A score or two of them can pounce upon a poor negro, tie and beat him, and then call him a coward because he submits. Many of their most brilliant victories have been achieved in the same manner. But the greatest battles which they have fought have been upon paper. We can easily account for this; their trumpeter is dead. He died when they used to be exposed for sale in the Roman market, about the time that Cicero cautioned his friend Atticus not to buy them, on account of their stupidity. A little more than half a century ago, this race, in connection with their Celtic neighbors, who have long been considered (by themselves, of course,) the bravest soldiers in the world, so far forgot themselves, as to attack a few cowardly, stupid negro slaves, who, according to their accounts, had not sense enough to go to bed. And what was the result? Why, sir, the negroes drove them out from the island like so many sheep, and they have never dared to show their faces, except with hat in hand.

Our true and tried friend, Rev. Theodore Parker, said, in his speech at the State House, a few weeks since, that "the stroke of the axe would have settled this question long ago, but the black man would not strike." Mr. Parker makes a very low estimate of the courage of his race, if he means that one, two or three millions of these ignorant and cowardly black slaves could, without means, have brought to their knees five, ten, or twenty millions of intelligent, brave white men, backed up by a rich oligarchy. But I know of no one who is more familiar with the true character of the Anglo-Saxon race than Mr. Parker. I will not dispute this point with him, but I will thank him or anyone else to tell us how it could have been done. . . . But when he says that "the black man *would not* strike," I am prepared to say that he does us great injustice. The black man is not a coward. The history of the bloody struggles for freedom in Haiti, in which the blacks whipped the French and the English, and gained their independence, in spite of the perfidy of that villainous First Consul, will be a lasting refutation of the malicious aspersions of our enemies. The history of the struggles for the liberty of the United States ought to silence every American calumniator. I have learned that even so late as the Texas war, a number of black men were silly enough to offer themselves as living sacrifices for our country's shame. . . .

Now, it would not be surprising if the brutal treatment which we have received for the past two centuries should have crushed our spirits. But this is not the case. Nothing but a superior force keeps us down. And when I see the slaves rising up by the hundreds annually, in the majesty of human nature, bidding defiance to every slave code and its penalties, making the issue Canada or death, and that too while they are closely watched by paid men armed with pistols, clubs, and bowie-knives, with the army and navy of this great Model Republic arrayed against them, I am disposed to ask if the charge of cowardice does not come with ill-grace. . . .

The prejudice which some white men have, or affected to have, against my color gives me no pain. If any man does not fancy my color, that is his business, and I shall not meddle with it. I shall give myself no trouble because he lacks good taste. If he judges my intellectual capacity by my color, he certainly cannot expect much profundity, for it is only skin deep, and is really of no very great importance to any one but myself. I will not deny that I admire the talents and noble characters of many white men. But I cannot say that I am particularly pleased with their physical appearance. . . . When I contrast the fine tough muscular system, the beautiful, rich color, the full broad features, and the gracefully frizzled hair of the negro, with the delicate physical organization, wan color, sharp features, and lank hair of the Caucasian, I am inclined to believe that when the white man was created, nature was pretty well exhausted—but determined to keep up appearances, she pinched up his features, and did the best she could under the circumstances. I would have you understand, that I not only love my race, but am pleased with my color; and while many colored persons may feel degraded by being called negroes, and wish to be classed among other races more favored, I shall feel it my duty, my pleasure and my pride, to concentrate my feeble efforts in elevating to a fair position a race to which I am especially identified by feelings and by blood.

My friends, we can never become elevated until we are true to ourselves. We can come here and make brilliant speeches, but our field of duty is elsewhere. Let us go to work—each man in his place determined to do what he can for himself and his race. . . . If we do this, friends will spring up in every quarter, and where we least expect them. But we must not

rely on them. They cannot elevate us. Whenever the colored man is elevated, it will be by his own exertions. Our friends can do what many of
them are nobly doing, assist us to remove the obstacles which prevent our
elevation, and stimulate the worthy to persevere. The colored man who,
by dint of perseverance and industry, educates and elevates himself, prepares the way for others, gives character to the race, and hastens the day
of general emancipation. While the negro who hangs around the corners
of the streets, or lives in the grog-shops or by gambling, or who has no
higher ambition than to serve, is by his vocation forging fetters for the
slave, and is "to all intents and purposes" a curse to his race. It is true, considering the circumstances under which we have been placed by our white
neighbors, we have a right to ask them not only to cease to oppress us, but
to give us that encouragement which our talents and industry may merit.
... In this country, where money is the great sympathetic nerve which
ramifies society, and has a ganglia in every man's pocket, a man is respected
in proportion to his success in business. When the avenues to wealth are
opened to us, we will then become educated and wealthy, and then the
roughest looking colored man that you ever saw, or ever will see, will be
pleasanter than the harmonies of Orpheus, and black will be a very pretty
color. It will make our jargon, wit—our words, oracles; flattery will then
take the place of slander, and you will find no prejudice in the Yankee
whatever. We do not expect to occupy a much better position than we
now do, until we shall have our educated and wealthy men, who can wield
a power that cannot be misunderstood. Then, and not till then, will the
tongue of slander be silenced, and the lip of prejudice sealed. Then, and not
till then, will we be able to enjoy true equality, which can exist only
among peers.

Abraham Lincoln on blacks and on slavery: from his speeches of 1858

*"It must be admitted, truth compels me to admit, even here in the presence of
the monument we have erected to his memory," Frederick Douglass said in
1876, "Abraham Lincoln was not, in the fullest sense of the word, either our
man or our model. In his interests, in his associations, in his habits of thought,
and in his prejudices, he was a white man. He was preeminently the white man's
President, entirely devoted to the welfare of white men." Lincoln's position in
1858 was quite clear: he wished slavery restricted from the territories, and he
looked forward to that day when it would eventually disappear from the states.
For "no man," he wrote, "is good enough to govern another man without that
other's consent." But if Lincoln believed in personal freedom for all, he was
never an advocate—as his speeches in the senatorial campaign against Stephen
Douglas in 1858 make plain—of social equality for blacks.*

From *The Speeches of Abraham Lincoln* (New York, 1908), pp. 52–53, 72, 91–92,
94–95, 151–52, 163, 185–86, 200, 204.

At Springfield, Illinois   June 16, 1858

We are now far into the fifth year since a policy was initiated with the avowed object and confident promise of putting an end to slavery agitation. Under the operation of that policy, that agitation has not only not ceased, but has constantly augmented. In my opinion, it will not cease until a crisis shall have been reached and passed. "A house divided against itself cannot stand." I believe this government cannot endure permanently half slave and half free. I do not expect the Union to be dissolved—I do not expect the house to fall—but I do expect it will cease to be divided. It will become all one thing, or all the other. Either the opponents of slavery will arrest the further spread of it, and place it where the public mind shall rest in the belief that it is in the course of ultimate extinction; or its advocates will push it forward till it shall become alike lawful in all the States, old as as well as new, North as well as South.

At Chicago, Illinois   July 10, 1858

I protest, now and forever, against that counterfeit logic which presumes that because I do not want a negro woman for a slave, I do necessarily want her for a wife. My understanding is that I need not have her for either; but, as God made us separate, we can leave one another alone, and do one another much good thereby. There are white men enough to marry all the white women, and enough black men to marry all the black women, and in God's name let them be so married. The judge [Stephen Douglas] regales us with the terrible enormities that take place by the mixture of races; that the inferior race bears the superior down. Why, judge, if we do not let them get together in the Territories, they won't mix there. [A voice: "Three cheers for Lincoln!" The cheers were given with a hearty good will.] I shall say at least that that is a self-evident truth.

At Springfield, Illinois   July 17, 1858

My declaration upon this subject of negro slavery may be misrepresented, but cannot be misunderstood. I have said that I do not understand the Declaration [of Independence] to mean that all men were created equal in all respects. They are not our equal in color; but I suppose that it does mean to declare that all men are equal in some respects; they are equal in their right to "life, liberty, and the pursuit of happiness." Certainly the negro is not our equal in color—perhaps not in many other respects; still, in the right to put into his mouth the bread that his own hands have earned, he is the equal of every other man, white or black. In pointing out that more has been given you, you cannot be justified in taking away the little which has been given him. All I ask for the negro is that if you do not like him, let him alone. If God gave him but little, that little let him enjoy.

At Ottawa, Illinois   **August 21, 1858**

I have no purpose to introduce political and social equality between the white and the black races. There is a physical difference between the two, which, in my judgment, will probably forever forbid their living together upon the footing of perfect equality; and inasmuch as it becomes a necessity that there must be a difference, I, as well as Judge Douglas, am in favor of the race to which I belong having the superior position. I have never said anything to the contrary, but I hold that, notwithstanding all this, there is no reason in the world why the negro is not entitled to all the natural rights enumerated in the Declaration of Independence—the right to life, liberty, and the pursuit of happiness. I hold that he is as much entitled to these as the white man. I agree with Judge Douglas he is not my equal in many respects—certainly not in color, perhaps not in moral or intellectual endowment. But in the right to eat the bread, without the leave of anybody else, which his own hand earns, he is my equal and the equal of Judge Douglas, and the equal of every living man.

At Charleston, Illinois   **September 18, 1858**

Judge Douglas has said to you that he has not been able to get from me an answer to the question whether I am in favor of negro citizenship. So far as I know, the judge never asked me the question before. He shall have no occasion to ever ask it again, for I tell him very frankly that I am not in favor of negro citizenship. . . . My opinion is that the different States have the power to make a negro citizen under the Constitution of the United States, if they choose. The Dred Scott decision decides that they have not that power. If the State of Illinois had that power, I should be opposed to the exercise of it. That is all I have to say about it.

At Galesburg, Illinois   **October 7, 1858**

The judge has alluded to the Declaration of Independence, and insisted that negroes are not included in that Declaration; and that it is a slander upon the framers of that instrument to suppose that negroes were meant therein; and he asks you: Is it possible to believe that Mr. Jefferson, who penned the immortal paper, could have supposed himself applying the language of that instrument to the negro race, and yet held a portion of that race in slavery? Would he not at once have freed them? I only have to remark upon this part of the judge's speech, . . . that I believe the entire records of the world, from the date of the Declaration of Independence up to within three years ago, may be searched in vain for one single affirmation, from one single man, that the negro was not included in the Declaration of Independence; . . . I will remind Judge Douglas and his audience that while Mr. Jefferson was the owner of slaves, as undoubtedly he was, in speaking upon this very subject, he used the strong language that "he trembled for his country when he remembered that God was just."

At Quincy, Illinois October 13, 1858

I suggest that the difference of opinion, reduced to its lowest terms, is no other than the difference between the men who think slavery is a wrong and those who do not think it wrong. The Republican party think it wrong —we think it is a moral, a social, and a political wrong. We think it is a wrong not confining itself merely to the persons or the States where it exists, but that it is a wrong which in its tendency, to say the least, affects the existence of the whole nation. Because we think it wrong, we propose a course of policy that shall deal with it as a wrong. We deal with it as with any other wrong, in so far as we can prevent its growing any larger, and so deal with it that in the run of time there may be some promise of an end to it.

John Brown's last words to the court, November 2, 1859

"It was so absurd," was Abraham Lincoln's later comment about John Brown's raid on the arsenal at Harpers Ferry, Virginia, "that the slaves, with all their ignorance, saw plainly enough it could not succeed." Both Republican and Democratic political leaders denounced the attack, and anti-Brown meetings were well attended in Northern cities. Northern and European intellectuals, on the other hand—with their noted propensity for idolizing and romanticizing the man of action—practically canonized John Brown. His death wrote Emerson, "will make the gallows as glorious as the cross."

Whether one approves or disapproves of his actions, none can deny Brown's courage. He was, according to a witness, "the coolest and firmest man I ever saw in defying danger and death. With one son dead by his side, and another shot through, he felt the pulse of his dying son with one hand and held his rifle with the other and commanded his men with the utmost composure, encouraging them to be firm and to sell their lives as dearly as they could." Tried and convicted of murder, criminal conspiracy, and treason against the State of Virginia, Brown died on the scaffold as bravely as he had fought.

I have, may it please the Court, a few words to say. In the first place, I deny everything but what I have all along admitted—a design on my part to free slaves. I intended certainly to have made a clear thing of that matter, as I did when I went last winter into Missouri and there took slaves without the snapping of a gun on either side, moved them through the

From the *National Intelligencer*, November 5, 1859. This varies slightly from the version in F. B. Sanford (ed.), *Life and Letters of John Brown* (Boston, 1885), pp. 584-85.

country, and finally left them in Canada. I designed to have done the same thing again on a larger scale. That was all I intended. I never did intend murder, or treason, or the destruction of property, or to incite slaves to rebellion, or to make insurrection.

I have another objection, and that is, it is unjust that I should suffer such a penalty. Had I interfered in the manner which I admit, and which I admit has been fairly proved . . . had I so interfered on behalf of the rich and powerful, the intelligent, the so-called great, or in behalf of any of their friends, . . . and suffered and sacrificed what I have in this interference, it would have been all right, and every man in this Court would have deemed it an act worthy of reward rather than punishment.

This Court acknowledges too, as I suppose, the validity of the law of God. I see a book kissed here which I suppose to be the Bible, or at least the New Testament. That teaches me that all things "whatsoever I would men should do to me, I should do even so to them." It teaches me, further, to "remember them that are in bonds, as bound with them." I endeavored to act up to these instructions. I say, I am yet too young to understand that God is any respecter of persons. I believe that to have interfered as I have done, in behalf of His despised poor, was not wrong but right. Now, if it is deemed necessary that I should forfeit my life for the furtherance of the ends of justice, and mingle my blood further with the blood of my children, and with the blood of millions in this slave country whose rights are disregarded by wicked, cruel, and unjust enactments, I submit. So let it be done!

Let me say one word further. I feel entirely satisfied with the treatment I have received on my trial. Considering the circumstances, it has been more generous than I expected, but I feel no consciousness of guilt. I have stated from the first what was my intention, and what was not. I have never had any design against the life of any person, nor any disposition to commit treason, or excite slaves to rebel, or make any general insurrection. I never encouraged any man to do so, but always discouraged any idea of that kind.

Let me say also a word in regard to the statements made by some of those connected with me. I hear that it has been stated by some of them that I have induced them to join me. But the contrary is true. I do not say this to injure them, but as regretting their weakness. There is not one of them but joined me of his own accord, and the greater part of them at their own expense. A number of them I never saw, and never had a word of conversation with till the day they came to me, and that was for the purpose I have stated.

Now I have done.

The Southern attitude toward the North: an editorial
from a New Orleans newspaper, November 13, 1860

John Brown's raid raised Southern fears of Northern invasion, of slaves rioting, raping, burning, and killing, of abolitionist conspiracies to poison whites. It was widely rumored that the Vice President, Hannibal Hamlin, was actually a mulatto. And though Lincoln swore that he had no intention of interfering with slavery in the states, most Southerners were inclined to believe the contrary. They equated Republicanism with abolitionism, and Lincoln's election—as the following editorial states—"capped the mighty pyramid of unfraternal enormities."

The history of the Abolition or Black Republican party of the North is a history of repeated injuries and usurpations, all having in direct object the establishment of absolute tyranny over the slave-holding States. And all without the smallest warrant, excuse or justification. We have appealed to their generosity, justice and patriotism, but all without avail. From the beginning, we have only asked to be let alone in the enjoyment of our plain, inalienable rights, as explicitly guaranteed in our common organic law. We have never aggressed upon the North, nor sought to aggress upon the North. Yet every appeal and expostulation has only brought upon us renewed insults and augmented injuries. They have robbed us of our property, they have murdered our citizens while endeavoring to reclaim that property by lawful means, they have set at naught the decrees of the Supreme Court, they have invaded our States and killed our citizens, they have declared their unalterable determination to exclude us altogether from the Territories, they have nullified the laws of Congress, and finally they have capped the mighty pyramid of unfraternal enormities by electing Abraham Lincoln to the Chief Magistracy, on a platform and by a system which indicates nothing but the subjugation of the South and the complete ruin of her social, political and industrial institutions.

All these statements are not only true, but absolutely indisputable. The facts are well known and patent. Under these circumstances, in view of the dark record of the past, the threatening aspect of the present, and the very serious contingencies which the future holds forth, we submit and appeal to a candid and honorable world, whether the Southern people have not been astonishingly patient under gross provocation—whether they have not exhibited remarkable forbearance—whether they have not been long suffering, slow to anger and magnanimous, on numerous occasions where indignation was natural, and severe measures of retaliation justifiable? There can be no doubt on this point. For the sake of peace, for

From the New Orleans *Daily Crescent*, November 13, 1860, reprinted in Dwight L. Dumond (ed.), *Southern Editorials on Secession* (New York: The Century Co., 1931), pp. 235–38. Reprinted by permission.

the sake of harmony, the South has compromised until she can compromise no farther, without she is willing to compromise away character, political equality, social and individual interest, and every right and franchise which freemen hold dear.

Abraham Lincoln's appeal for union: from his first inaugural address, March 4, 1861

Before Lincoln was inaugurated as America's sixteenth president, seven states had seceded from the union, the Confederate States of America had been established, and Jefferson Davis selected as its provisional president. Federal forts and arsenals were seized and declared to be Confederate property. Diplomats selected by the secessionist government were preparing to sail. Meanwhile, eight other slave states decided to wait and see what Lincoln would do. In his inaugural address Lincoln renewed the Republican pledge to respect slavery in the states, and he promised that the government would not assail the South; but he also warned that the question of war or peace rested with the South. If they chose war, he would be forced by his oath of office to "preserve, protect, and defend" the national government.

Physically speaking, we cannot separate. We cannot remove our respective sections from each other, nor build an impassable wall between them. A husband and wife may be divorced and go out of the presence and beyond the reach of each other; but the different parts of our country cannot do this. They cannot but remain face to face, and intercourse, either amicable or hostile, must continue between them. Is it possible, then, to make that intercourse more advantageous or more satisfactory after separation than before? Can aliens make treaties easier than friends can make laws? Can treaties be more faithfully enforced between aliens than laws can among friends? Suppose you go to war, you cannot fight always; and when, after much loss on both sides, and no gain on either, you cease fighting, the identical old questions as to terms of intercourse are again upon you. . . .

My countrymen, one and all, think calmly and well upon this whole subject. Nothing valuable can be lost by taking time. If there be an object to hurry any of you in hot haste to a step which you would never take deliberately, that object will be frustrated by taking time; but no good object can be frustrated by it. Such of you as are now dissatisfied still have the old Constitution unimpaired, and, on the sensitive point, the laws of your own framing under it; while the new administration will have no immediate power, if it would to change either. If it were admitted that you

From *The Speeches of Abraham Lincoln* (New York, 1908), pp. 316–19.

who are dissatisfied hold the right side in the dispute, there still is no single good reason for precipitate action. Intelligence, patriotism, Christianity, and a firm reliance on Him who has never yet forsaken this favored land, are still competent to adjust in the best way all our present difficulty.

In your hands, my dissatisfied fellow-countrymen, and not in mine, is the momentous issue of civil war. The government will not assail you. You can have no conflict without being yourselves the aggressors. You have no oath registered in heaven to destroy the government, while I shall have the most solemn one to "preserve, protect, and defend" it.

I am loath to close. We are not enemies, but friends. We must not be enemies. Though passion may have strained, it must not break, our bonds of affection. The mystic chords of memory, stretching from every battle-field and patriot grave to every living heart and hearthstone all over this broad land, will yet swell the chorus of the Union when again touched, as surely they will be, by the better angels of our nature.

Karl Marx and Frederick Engels on the causation of the American Civil War: essay in the Vienna *Presse*, written from London, October 20, 1861

What caused the Civil War? Was it the inevitable result of economic conflict between the industrial North and the agricultural South? Was it the result of mediocre political leadership during the decade of the 1850's? Was it the result of a mass emotional misunderstanding and distrust of the two sections toward each other? Was it slavery, or deeper yet, was the issue racism? Contemporaries disagreed, and scholars ever since have posed, rebutted and surrebutted the issue until it has become an historiographical nightmare. Marx and Engels were intensely interested in American affairs. Together they wrote essays for the New York Tribune as well as for papers in England and Europe. The following is taken from a Vienna paper which presents their (surprisingly simple and non-Marxian) analysis of its cause.

London, October 20, 1861

For months the leading weekly and daily papers of the London press have reiterated the same litany on the American Civil War. While they insult the free states of the North, they anxiously defend themselves against the suspicion of sympathizing with the slave states of the South. . . . In essence the extenuating arguments read: The war between the North and South is a tariff war. The war is, further, not for any principle, does not touch the

From Richard Enmale (ed.), *The Civil War in the United States, by Karl Marx and Frederick Engels* (New York, 1937), pp. 58–61. Reprinted by permission of International Publishers Co., Inc.

question of slavery and in fact turns on Northern lust for sovereignty. Finally, even if justice is on the side of the North, does it not remain a vain endeavor to want to subjugate eight million Anglo-Saxons by force! Would not the separation of the South release the North from all connection with Negro slavery and assure to it, with its twenty million inhabitants and its vast territory, a higher, hithero scarcely dreamt of, development? Accordingly must not the North welcome secession as a happy event, instead of wanting to put it down by a bloody and futile civil war? . . .

The war between North and South—so runs the first excuse—is a mere tariff war, a war between a protection system and a free trade system, and England naturally stands on the side of free trade. Shall the slaveowner enjoy the fruits of slave labor in their entirety or shall he be cheated of a portion of these by the protectionists of the North? That is the question which is at issue in this war. . . . It is characteristic of this discovery that it was made, not in Charleston, but in London. Naturally, in America every one knew that from 1846 to 1861 a free trade system prevailed, and that Representative Morrill carried his protectionist tariff in Congress only in 1861, after the rebellion had already broken out. Secession, therefore, did not take place because the Morrill tariff had gone through Congress, but, at most, the Morrill tariff went through Congress because secession had taken place. When South Carolina had her first attack of secession in 1831, the protectionist tariff of 1828 served her, to be sure, as a pretext. . . . This time, however, the old pretext has in fact not been repeated. In the Secession Congress at Montgomery all reference to the tariff question was avoided, because the cultivation of sugar in Louisiana, one of the most influential Southern States, depends entirely on protection.

But, the London press pleads further, the war of the United States is nothing but a war for the maintenance of the Union by force. The Yankees cannot make up their minds to strike fifteen stars from their standard. They want to cut a colossal figure on the world stage. Yes, it would be different, if the war was waged for the abolition of slavery! The question of slavery, however, as, among others, *The Saturday Review* categorically declares, has absolutely nothing to do with this war.

It is above all to be remembered that the war did not emanate from the North, but from the South. The North finds itself on the defensive. For months it had quietly looked on, while the secessionists appropriated to themselves the Union's forts, arsenals, shipyards, custom houses, pay offices, ships and supplies of arms, insulted its flag and took prisoner bodies of its troops. Finally the secessionists resolved to force the Union government out of its passive attitude by a sensational act of war, and *solely for this reason* proceeded to the bombardment of Fort Sumter near Charleston. On April 11 (1861) their General Beauregard had learnt in a parley with Major Anderson, the commander of Fort Sumter, that the fort was only supplied with provisions for three days more and accordingly must be peacefully surrendered after this period. In order to forestall this peaceful surrender, the secessionists opened the bombardment early on the following morning (April 12), which brought about the fall of the place in a few hours. News of this had hardly been telegraphed to Montgomery, the seat of the Secession Congress, when War Minister Walter publicly declared in the name of the new Confederacy: "No man can say where *the war opened today* will end." At the same time he prophesied "that before the first of May the flag of the Southern Confederacy would wave from the dome of the old Capitol in Washington and within a short time perhaps also from the Faneuil Hall in Boston." Only now ensued the proclamation in which Lincoln summoned 75,000 men to the protection of the Union. The bombardment of Fort Sumter cut off the only possible constitutional way out, namely, the summoning of a general convention of the American people, as Lincoln had proposed in his inaugural address. For Lincoln there now remained only the choice of fleeing from Washington, evacuating Maryland and Delaware and surrendering Kentucky, Missouri, and Virginia, or of answering war with war.

The question of the principle of the American Civil War is answered by the battle slogan with which the South broke the peace. Stephens, the Vice-President of the Southern Confederacy, declared in the Secession Congress, that what essentially distinguished the Constitution newly hatched at Montgomery from the Constitution of the Washingtons and Jeffersons was that now for the first time slavery was recognized as an institution good in itself, and as the foundation of the whole state edifice, whereas the revolutionary fathers, men steeped in the prejudices of the eighteenth century, had treated slavery as an evil imported from England and to be eliminated in the course of time. Another matador of the South, Mr. Spratt, cried out: "For us it is a question of the foundations of a great slave republic." If, therefore, it was indeed only in defense of the Union that the North drew the sword, had not the South already declared that the continuance of slavery was no longer compatible with the continuance of the Union?

The end of the Civil War: contrary hopes for the American future, March–April 1865

The legacy of a war which lasted four years, which took the lives of 620,000 soldiers, and which caused enormous devastation, was bound to linger for generations. Opinions cannot be changed by force, and defeat itself seemed to intensify Southern bitterness as victory confirmed Northern demands for punishment and retribution. Lincoln realized this, and in his second inaugural address, delivered a month before his assassination, he pled for a course of moderation and national reunification. Edmund Ruffin, on the other hand, who was given the honor of firing the first Southern gun on Fort Sumter in 1861,

From *The Speeches of Abraham Lincoln* (New York, 1908), pp. 410–11.

made a vow of eternal enmity to all Northerners. It was the last entry Ruffin made in his diary, in April 1865. He then committed suicide.

FROM LINCOLN'S SECOND INAUGURAL ADDRESS, MARCH 4, 1865

Neither party expected for the war the magnitude or the duration which it has already attained. Neither anticipated that the cause of the conflict might cease with, or even before, the conflict itself should cease. Each looked for an easier triumph, and a result less fundamental and astounding. Both read the same Bible, and pray to the same God; and each invokes his aid against the other. It may seem strange that any men should dare to ask a just God's assistance in wringing their bread from the sweat of other men's faces; but let us judge not, that we be not judged. The prayers of both could not be answered—that of neither has been answered fully. . . .

With malice toward none; with charity for all; with firmness in the right, as God gives us to see the right, let us strive on to finish the work we are in; to bind up the nation's wounds; to care for him who shall have borne the battle, and for his widow, and his orphan—to do all which may achieve and cherish a just and lasting peace among ourselves, and with all nations.

FROM THE LAST PAGE OF EDMUND RUFFIN'S DIARY, APRIL 1865

I here declare my unmitigated hatred to Yankee rule—to all political, social and business connections with the Yankees and to the Yankee race. Would that I could impress these sentiments, in their full force, on every living Southerner and bequeath them to every one yet to be born! May such sentiments be held universally in the outraged and down-trodden South, though in silence and stillness, until the now far-distant day shall arrive for just retribution for Yankee usurpation, oppression and atrocious outrages, and for deliverance and vengeance for the now ruined, subjugated and enslaved Southern States! And now with my latest writing and utterance, and with what will be near my latest breath, I here repeat and willingly proclaim my unmitigated hatred to Yankee rule—to all political, social and business connections with Yankees, and the perfidious, malignant and vile Yankee race.

From the diary of Edmund Ruffin, April 1865.

6
The Search for Justice

Testimony before the Joint Committee on Reconstruction: interrogation of James D. B. De Bow, March 28, 1866

Had Lincoln lived, could he have mastered the postwar problems as superbly as he had directed the nation in war? Or would his image have been sullied in the muddy waters of Reconstruction? The radical Republicans in Congress, for a variety of reasons—political, emotional, economic—believed that Lincoln and his successor, Andrew Johnson, were too lenient toward the defeated South. Congress refused to admit the provisional governments formed under the Johnson plan; and a joint committee consisting of six senators and nine members of the House of Representatives was formed to investigate the true condition of the South and the position of the black in Southern society.

One of the many witnesses called before the committee was James D. B. De Bow, publisher of the very influential periodical, De Bow's Review of the Southern and Western States, *which preached the doctrines of economic diversification and Southern nationalism.*

QUESTION: What are the views and feelings of the people [in Louisiana] as to the late war and its results, and as to the future condition of that State in its relations to the federal government?

ANSWER: There seems to be a general—you may say universal—acquiescence in the results. There is a great deal of dissatisfaction as to the course in reference to their condition pursued by the federal government. I think the people having fairly tried the experiment of secession are perfectly satisfied with the result, and that there is no disposition in any quarter, in any shape or form, to embarrass the United States government, or to refrain from the most complete performance of all the duties of citizenship. I saw nothing of that sort. All parties, those who were opposed to the war and those who were in favor of the war, are now agreed that it is for the best interest of the State to perform all the duties of citizenship, and to accept whatever the government has effected in reference to the negro, as well as in reference to other questions.

QUESTION: What are the alleged grounds of dissatisfaction among the people as to the action of the federal government?

ANSWER: The Freedman's Bureau is very largely complained of, and the delay in admitting their representatives. They confidently expected a very early restoration of their civil condition and political rights from the promises which were made. I think that feeling of hostility has grown up since the surrender. I think at the period of the surrender the feeling was very much more kindly, and the attitude and condition of the country more favorable than it is now. This constant irritation has produced the feeling.

From the testimony of James D. B. De Bow in *Report of the Joint Committee on Reconstruction at the First Session, Thirty-ninth Congress* (Washington, D.C., 1866), Part IV, pp. 132–36.

I do not think it is very serious, but still it exists; it would be dissipated immediately on the passage of liberal measures, such as, for instance, an order restoring the States to their status under the Constitution, restoring their political rights, the removal of the Freedman's Bureau, or some such regulation which would be fair to both parties.

QUESTION: What do they say there as to the necessity or advantage of retaining a military force in the State?

ANSWER: There is no one who thinks any such force necessary. I believe the condition of the State is such that the people would preserve all the order necessary. There is a general indisposition to have any military force there.

QUESTION: Is there or not a bitter feeling between those who supported the rebellion and those who supported the general government during the war in Louisiana?

ANSWER: I think those parties who have remained in the State and who were assuming they were good Union men during the war, perhaps making more claims in that regard than they are entitled to, are received with hostility. I think those who went away honestly for those reasons, and have returned, are respected, and receive very much consideration. I know of many cases of this kind, of men who went away, did not take part in the war, and have since returned. But there is a feeling in my State against those who remained there during the war and profess now that they were Union men all the time, but that their rights were taken away. There is a feeling against them, though not of any such hostile character as to endanger their personal safety or condition in any way. . . .

QUESTION: Do you think those who have been, or profess to have been, Union men in Louisiana would be perfectly safe there with the military protection of the government withdrawn?

ANSWER: Perfectly safe. I have no idea anybody would be disturbed at all. There might be some little unkindness of look or expression towards them. They would not be received, of course, on the same terms with those who have been in sympathy with the great body of the people there. They would respect those who were with them much more than they would that class of persons; but there would be no physical hostility, or any attempt to interfere with their rights—none whatever.

QUESTION: Do not those who were in the rebel army, or supported the rebel cause, make distinctions in social intercourse and business transactions between those who co-operated with them and those who favored the cause of the Union, as well as men who came there from the north?

ANSWER: The secession men, the men who were in the war, are generally ruined, their families are destitute, and there is a great disposition to sustain them, if they undertake any business at all. I think a great deal grows out of that, and a great deal grows, of course, out of actual sympathy with these men. Although, on the other hand, I can point in New Orleans to men who were not in sympathy with the south during the war, but the very opposite, who are doing a large and successful business. . . . I do not think the discrimination made is anything more than a social discrimination. I think that is well marked at present. There is a disposition on the part of those who have been with the south during the war not to mix a great deal with those who have remained in the south (as they say) as Union men; and the feeling extends, more or less, to northern men, though very little towards the great majority of northern people. Some who come there a little disposed to talk, etc. receive the cold shoulder; that is about all. I have known of balls and parties, where there was a mixture of all classes, and where certain ladies would say they would not associate with federal officers; but the party would go on all the same, all in the same room. That feeling is now stronger than it was. It is the result of political causes. I think it will wear away. . . .

QUESTION: Do the people there feel as though they ought to have any pay for their slaves who have been emancipated during the war?

ANSWER: I have spoken of that at various places where I have been, as a measure the United States might eventually take up, but I found among the people of the south themselves a very great difference of opinion on the subject. They said that would be making an unfair discrimination. "Why pay for slaves, and not pay for the property of the men who had no slaves destroyed by the war? Why will you pay the planter and nobody else, for his losses?" I think feeling would neutralize any such idea of paying for slaves, even if there were such expectation, which I do not think there is. . . .

QUESTION: Would the people there, in political matters, in elections that might take place, probably choose men who had been distinguished for their services in the rebellion, or would they be more likely to prefer men who had been attached to the Union cause during the war?

ANSWER: The choice is so meagre, there are so few men from whom the choice could be made on the Union side, the proportion of men of talent and worth who have been on the other side is so overwhelmingly large, that they would of necessity take men from that side. And I have no doubt that, other things being equal, they would prefer men, perhaps, who have been very decided on that side. There are exceptions to the rule, however. I have known men who were very decided in their opposition to the war selected.

QUESTION: What is your judgment as to the advantages of keeping up a military force in Louisiana, on the part of the United States?

ANSWER: I think it tends to produce irritation, and to perpetuate the disorder of the times. I think it leads to a return of the past, and that the sooner the military arm is removed the better. It irritates, annoys, and frets, without doing any good. And I may add, I think the same remark is applicable pretty generally where I travelled all over the south.

QUESTION: Do you think the people there, if left to themselves, would pretty generally settle down, fraternize, and become restored to good order?

ANSWER: The country is so devastated, there is so much distress, so

much want and suffering among the people of the south, that they have no
time for politics. I think they are disposed to go to work to restore their
broken fortunes. If these exciting, irritating, and annoying causes were
removed, it would not be six months, in my judgment, before this feeling
between northern and southern men there would in large part vanish, and
an entire restoration of harmony would begin to take place. The very necessities of their condition require it. They would find northern men bringing
their capital and industry among them, and they would invite them. The
labor they must have. The negro is defective as a laborer. Under the old
system, with all the negroes employed, there has always been a deficiency
of labor in the south.

QUESTION: What is your opinion of the necessity or utility of the
Freedman's Bureau, or of any agency of that kind?

ANSWER: I think if the whole regulation of the negroes, or freedmen,
were left to the people of the communities in which they live, it will be
administered for the best interest of the negroes as well as of the white men.
I think there is a kindly feeling on the part of the planters towards the
freedmen. They are not held at all responsible for anything that has happened. They are looked upon as the innocent cause. In talking with a number of planters, I remember some of them telling me they were succeeding
very well with their freedmen, having got a preacher to preach to them and
a teacher to teach them, believing it was for the interest of the planter to
make the negro feel reconciled; for to lose his services as a laborer for even
a few months would be very disastrous. The sentiment prevailing is, that it
is for the interest of the employer to teach the negro, to educate the children, to provide a preacher for him, and to attend to his physical wants.
And I may say I have not seen any exception to that feeling in the south.
Leave the people to themselves, and they will manage very well. The
Freedman's Bureau, or any agency to interfere between the freedman and
his former master, is only productive of mischief. . . .

QUESTION: Do you think the white men of the south would do justice
by the negroes in making contracts and in paying them for their labor?

ANSWER: Before these negroes were freed, there were some two or
three hundred thousand free negroes in the south, and some four or five
hundred thousand of them in the country. There were a great many in
Louisiana. There were in New Orleans some free negroes among the
wealthiest men we had. I made a comparison when I was superintendent of
the United States census in 1850, and found that the condition of the free
negroes in the south, their education, etc., was better; that as a class they
were immeasurably better off than the free people of the north. I never
heard any cause of complaint of our treatment of these people in the south
before the war, even from northern sources, and I do not presume there
would be more cause of complaint now. If we performed our duty to this
same class of population when the great mass of negroes were held by us
as slaves, I think it should go very far to indicate that we should not be
lacking in our duties to them now. . . .

QUESTION: What is your opinion as to the relative advantages to the blacks of the present system of free labor, as compared with that of slavery as it heretofore existed in this country?

ANSWER: If the negro would work, the present system is much cheaper. If we can get the same amount of labor from the same persons, there is no doubt of the result in respect to *economy*. Whether the same amount of labor can be obtained, it is too soon yet to decide. We must allow one summer to pass first. They are working now very well on the plantations. That is the general testimony. The negro women are not disposed to field work as has been in the past. The men are rather inclined to get their wives into other employment, and I think that will be the constant tendency, just as it is with the whites. Therefore, the real number of agricultural laborers will be reduced. . . . If we can only keep up their efficiency to the standard before the war, it will be better for the south, without doubt, upon the mere money question, because it is cheaper to hire the negro than to own him. Now a plantation can be worked without outlay of capital by hiring the negro and hiring the plantation.

QUESTION: What, in your opinion, is to be the effect upon the blacks?

ANSWER: I think it will be disastrous to them. I judge that because of the experience of other countries, and not from any experience we have had ourselves. I judge by their shiftless character, and their disposition to crowd into the cities. It is what I see all over the south. You will find large numbers of them in every city, crowded together in miserable shanties, eking out a very uncertain subsistence; and, so far, the mortality has been very great among them. . . .

QUESTION: What arrangements are generally made among the landholders and the black laborers in the south?

ANSWER: I think they generally get wages. A great many persons, however, think it better to give them an interest in the crops. That is getting to be very common.

QUESTION: What do you find the disposition of the people as to the extension of civil rights to the blacks—the right to sue and enforce their contracts and to hold property, real and personal, like white people?

ANSWER: I think there is a willingness to give them every right except the right of suffrage. It is believed they are unfit to exercise that. The idea is entertained by many that they will eventually be endowed with that right. It is only a question of time; but the universal conviction is that if it ever be conceded, it will be necessary to prepare for it by slow and regular means, as the white race was prepared. I believe everybody unites in the belief that it would be disastrous to give the right of suffrage now. Time and circumstances may alter the case. There is no difference of opinion upon this subject now.

QUESTION: Suppose the negroes were to vote now, what would be the influences operating upon them as to the exercise of that vote?

ANSWER: The negro would be apt to vote with his employer if he was treated well. That is his character. They generally go with their employer;

but it is probable they would be tampered with a great deal. There would be emissaries sent among them to turn their minds; so that, although I understand some prominent men think the negro would generally vote with his master, I doubt it. I think the tendency would be in that direction; but that they would be drawn off by emissaries sent there for malicious purposes, though a great many would, no doubt, go with their masters. You cannot make any rule. I find that northern men who have come to the south, purchased land, and gone to cultivating cotton or anything else, talk now very much as we do on these questions. Their views upon all these questions, with the little experience they have had, are very much the same as those of southern men. They say our experience, in regard to these questions, is worth more than their theories.

QUESTION: What facilities are the people disposed to give the freedmen in becoming educated?

ANSWER: I think they generally laugh at the idea of the negro learning. They have been accustomed to the idea that the negroes are pretty stupid. I do not think there would be any opposition to their becoming educated. We have schools all about for them, but the people sometimes laugh at the idea of the negroes learning much. Under the institution of slavery we used to teach them everything nearly except to read. On almost every plantation they were taught the Bible, the catechism, prayers, hymns, etc. But in regard to their being educated, so far as they are capable, I think the people regard it as for their best interest to afford them every facility— that is, the better informed people.

QUESTION: Do the employers of negroes in the south claim or exercise the right of physical compulsion to enforce their contracts?

ANSWER: No, sir, I know of no such claim—nothing of the kind. . . .

QUESTION: Are you satisfied that the people of the south have given up all ideas of secession under any circumstances?

ANSWER: *I am perfectly satisfied of that. The leaders, and the people of all classes of opinion, agree upon that subject.*

Ten questions asked of all prospective members of the Ku Klux Klan, 1868

By 1868 Johnson had been impeached, and the South was being reconstructed according to the plans of the radical Republicans. Instead of rekindling a love for the Union, military occupation delayed reconciliation and, in part, provoked the reactionary violence of such organizations as the Ku Klux Klan and the Knights of the White Camelia.

Every prospective member of the Klan had to answer correctly the ten

From "Revised and Amended Prescript of the Order of the Ku Klux Klan," adopted in 1868, in Walter L. Fleming (ed.), *Ku Klux Klan: Its Origin, Growth and Disbandment by J. C. Lester and D. L. Wilson* (New York, 1905), pp. 171–72.

questions posed below before he took a "final oath" and was "admitted to the
benefits, mysteries, secrets and purposes of the Order."

1st. Have you ever been rejected, upon application for membership
in the Ku Klux Klan, or have you ever been expelled from the same?

2d. Are you now, or have you ever been, a member of the Radical
Republican party, or either of the organizations known as the "Loyal
League" and the "Grand Army of the Republic?"

3d. Are you opposed to the principles and policy of the Radical
party, and to the Loyal League, and the Grand Army of the Republic,
so far as you are informed of the character and purposes of those
organizations?

4th. Did you belong to the Federal army during the late war, and
fight against the South during the existence of the same?

5th. Are you opposed to negro equality, both social and political?

6th. Are you in favor of a white man's government in this country?

7th. Are you in favor of Constitutional liberty, and a Government of
equitable laws instead of a Government of violence and oppression?

8th. Are you in favor of maintaining the Constitutional rights of
the South?

9th. Are you in favor of the re-enfranchisement and emancipation of
the white men of the South, and the restitution of the Southern people to
all their rights, alike proprietary, civil, and political?

10th. Do you believe in the inalienable right of self-preservation of
the people against the exercise of arbitrary and unlicensed power?

The double-lynching of a Jew and a black, August 15, 1868

*S.A. Bierfeld, a young Russian Jew, operated a dry-goods store in the town of
Franklin, located in central Tennessee. He became one of the earliest white victims of the Ku Klux Klan.*

*Bierfeld was accused of encouraging blacks, and even supplying them
with ammunition, to murder a white man named Ezell who had participated in
the lynching of a black. That accusation was false, but Bierfeld was indeed
guilty of being a radical Republican who treated blacks as social equals. On the
night of August 15, 1868, Bierfeld and his black clerk, Lawrence Bowman, were
sharing a watermelon when the masked mob broke into the store. An official
investigation reported that Bierfeld was first tortured and then shot at such
close range that his clothes and skin were burned.*

At eleven or twelve o'clock on Saturday night, as great crowds of people were going to their homes after leaving Robinson's circus, a troop of

From *The Israelite*, Cincinnati, Ohio, August 28, 1868.

horsemen dashed into town, yelling frightfully, and telling the crowd which they passed to get into their houses as quickly as possible. In a few moments every one was indoors, and a dead silence reigned around, save when heavy sounds were borne on the night from the dry-goods store of one Bierfeld, an Israelite, who carried on a little business in that line, and had a Negro man employed selling goods for him. The horsemen were breaking in his house. They dragged the Israelite out. They were about to hang him when he escaped and ran some hundred yards away from his house and took refuge in a livery stable. His enemies were upon him immediately, pistol in hand. They shot four balls into him, from the effects of which he died almost instantly. The colored man remained in the store, where they found and shot him through the body. He died yesterday morning.

The cause of the intense enmity which could ripen into so fearful a crime is not definitely known. Our informants, Dr. Cliffe and N. J. Nichol, said it was thought that Bierfeld had something to do with the murder of young Ezell, some two or three weeks ago. . . . There is no apparent cause for the murder of the colored man. When the fiendish outrage had been committed, the squad of troopers rode furiously out of town, whooping and hallooing frightfully.

Since the above was in type, we have received the following statement from a gentleman from Franklin:

On Saturday night, the 15th, about eleven o'clock, Mr. Bierfeld, an Israelite, who was engaged in trading, fled from his store scared by men in disguise who had entered his place of business and attempted to conceal himself in Mr. Bostick's stable, but was pursued by the said disguised parties, and violently and forcibly dragged into the streets. While pleading for his life, and begging them to spare him for his mother's sake, he was shot four times in the breast. This happened in the streets of Franklin, near Mr. Briggs' store. If anyone offered to intercede for him, it is not known. The parties who say they know the reason why he was killed by the men in disguise, allege that he was in some way connected with the killing of Ezell, and that the foul deed was done in retaliation. Six or eight witnesses will testify that Mr. Bierfeld, on the night of the killing of Ezell, slept in the house of Mr. Colby. The good citizens condemn the atrocious act, while others attempt to justify the crime by saying that it was done in retaliation. Mr. Bierfeld was an active and prominent Republican, having considerable influence with the colored people.

Our informant says that was his only crime. A clerk of Mr. Bierfeld, whose name we cannot learn, was killed at the same time, and by the same parties. Mr. Bierfeld's body was brought to Nashville yesterday for interment.

The duty of black lawyers: from a commencement address at Howard University by Senator Charles Sumner, February 3, 1871

Of all radical Republican leaders, Senator Charles Sumner of Massachusetts was probably the most honest and most consistent advocate of equal rights for blacks. He was one of the earliest to insist that "equivalency" of education for blacks in separate facilities was not "equality": "He has equality only when he comes into your common-school and finds no exclusion there on account of his skin." Eighty years later the Supreme Court concurred.

The following are words of advice Sumner delivered to law graduates at Howard University in 1871.

There is one other remark which I hope you will allow me to make. Belonging to a race which for long generations has been oppressed and despoiled of rights, you must be the vigilant and sensitive defenders of all who suffer in any way from wrong. The good lawyer should always be on the side of Human Rights; and yet it is a melancholy fact in history that lawyers have too often lent learning and subtle tongue to sustain wrong. This you must scorn to do. In the sacred cause of Justice be faithful, constant, brave. No matter who is the offender—whether crime be attempted by political party, by Congress, or by President—wherever it shows itself, whether on the continent or on an island of the sea, you must be ready at all times to stand forth, careless of consequences, and vindicate the Right. So doing, you will uphold your own race in its unexampled trials.

Each of you is a unit of the mass. Therefore, sustaining the rights of all, you will sustain your own. Be not satisfied with anything less than the Rights of All. But while generously maintaining the rights of others, I venture to say that you will be entirely unworthy of the vantage-ground on which you now stand, if you do not insist at all times on those Equal Rights which are still denied to you. Here particularly is a duty. The poet has said that

Who would be free, themselves must strike the blow.

You are all free, God be praised! But you are still shut out from rights which are justly yours. Yourselves must strike the blow—not by violence, but in every mode known to the Constitution and Law. I do not doubt that every denial of Equal Rights, whether in the school-room, the jury box, the public hotel, the steamboat, or the public conveyance, by land or water, is contrary to the fundamental principles of Republican Government, and therefore to the Constitution itself, which should be corrected by the Courts, if not by Congress. See to it that this is done. The Constitution does

From *The Works of Charles Sumner* (Boston, 1883), Vol. XIV, pp. 148–50.

not contain the word "white"; who can insert it in the Law? Insist that the common-school, where the child is prepared for the duties of manhood, shall know no discrimination unknown to the Constitution. Insist, also, that the public conveyances and public hotels, owing their existence to Law, shall know no discrimination unknown to the Constitution, so that the Senator or the Representative in Congress, who is the peer of all at the National Capitol, shall not be insulted and degraded on the way to his public duties. Insist upon equal rights everywhere; make others insist upon them. Insist that our institutions shall be brought into perfect harmony with the promises of the Declaration of Independence, which is grand for its universality. I hold you to this allegiance—first, by the race from which you are sprung, and, secondly, by the profession you now espouse.

Violence in the coal mines: a partial list of "outrages" in Schuylkill and Shamokin regions, Pennsylvania, January–July 1875

Another type of post-Civil War violence was taking place in the North. There groups of miners, mainly Irish immigrants, employed the same techniques of intimidation and assassination they had used against English landlords at home. Organized as the "Molly Maguires," they sought to force an improvement in wages and working conditions. But the mine owners employed Pinkerton detectives who infiltrated the secret society and succeeded in destroying it. Twenty-four "Molly Maguires" were convicted, of whom ten were hanged.

January

Three tunnel contractors at Preston No. 2 colliery, John Finigan, Samuel Davies, William Williams, were notified to cease driving a tunnel, or submit a fine of fifty dollars each, imposed by the Miners' and Laborers' Benevolent Association.

February 14

About four o'clock in the morning, the shaft-frame at the West Norwegian shaft was destroyed by fire, the work of an incendiary.

March 19

J. Showerly, watchman at Ellsworth colliery, beaten and his revolver taken from him.

From F. P. Dewees, *The Molly Maguires: The Origin, Growth, and Character of the Organization* (Philadelphia, 1877), pp. 359–67.

March 20

Watchman at Mine Hill Gap colliery beaten and tied with a rope; watch stolen.

March 25

Train-employees of the Philadelphia and Reading Railroad Company quartered at Ashland were molested by parties of men. These persons endeavored by threats and persuasion to intimidate the men and induce them to leave the service of the company.

March 25

A train of one hundred loaded cars were started down the grade and run off the track on Excelsior branch. Eight of the cars were badly broken in consequence.

March 27

Train-hands on Philadelphia and Reading Railroad Company's train stoned at Locust Gap. A number of men sent from Reading were met on their arrival at Gordeon by a party of persons and persuaded not to go to work.

March 29

A large number of persons congregated at and near Locust Gap and stoned the crews of passing coal-trains.

March 30

Tool-house No. 5 broken open and tools stolen. Notice left there addressed to Daniel Yost, boss of section. New men were threatened, and left, saying they were afraid to work.

March 31

A party of men boarded a coal-train between Locust Gap and Alaska stations, drove off the engineer and crew, damaged the engine, and blocked the road with stones.

April 1

Threatening notice posted at Colket & Newkirk collieries: [Now men i have warented ye before and i willnt warind you no mor].

April 2

John Stephens, a brakeman, living at Mahanoy Plane, shot at and stoned for refusing to unite with the strikers.

April 7

A pistol notice was fastened to the black-smith shop at Newkirk colliery: [Notice is here given to you men the first and last Notice that you will get for no man to go Down this slope After to Night if yo Do you Can Bring your Coffon Along With you for By the internal Crist We mean What this Notice says . . . now men the Next Notice you Will get I Dont mean to Do it with my Pen I will Do it With that there Rolver I Don't Want no more Black legs at this Collary].

April 22

Special policeman Doolan, while in discharge of duty on train, attacked by five men, thrown from the train, and severely beaten.

April 23

Two railroad employees, Frank Backman and Owen Lawrence, having resigned their connection with their Union and agreed to go to work, their houses were visited by strikers, shots fired, and threatening language used to stop them from working.

April 28

House of Christian Galleary, miner, at Bast colliery, stoned, windows broken, and damage done to furniture.

April 29

Pistol notice posted at North Franklin collieries, where men were working at reduced wages: [Take notice Aney Black Leg that will Take Aney Eunnion man Plac will have A hard Road to travel].

May 2

The houses of men at Gordon, who had left the Miners' and Workingmen's Benevolent Association and gone to work, were visited at night by parties, threats made, and shots fired.

May 5

Heavy wire rope at Gordon Plane No. 1 cut. Loss about five hundred dollars. Telegraph-office at Locust Summit again destroyed by fire. Loss, two hundred and fifty dollars.

May 6

Attempt made to destroy the trestles at Locust Gap by boring holes in the timbers and charging them with dualin.

May 10

A mob of about two hundred and fifty armed men stopped the men who were about starting to work at Hickory Ridge colliery, maltreating the mine boss.

May 11

Assistant foreman Henry Lloyd, at Beechwood colliery, badly beaten by strange men.

May 19

Ticket-and telegraph-office at Excelsior station burned at about two A.M.

June 3

In the morning about seven o'clock, a large body of men, estimated to be from five hundred to one thousand in number, from Hazleton and vicinity, made their appearance in the neighborhood of Mahanoy City and stopped the men working the North Mahanoy, Primrose, Jones, Ward & Oliver's, Beaver Run, and Hartford collieries. About twelve o'clock a mob of men from Shenandoah and other localities in this region, numbering about twelve hundred, marched through Mahanoy City. Their first act was to demand the release from the lock-up of a man who had been arrested in the morning by the chief burgess; this they effected by paying the fine. At two o'clock several hundred of the mob gathered at the colliery worked by King, Tyler & Co., and compelled their men to quit work. Sheriff Werner ordered the rioters to disperse, and was reading the riot act, when he and his posse were fired upon by the rioters. Two policemen of the Mahanoy City force were slightly wounded. After this attack, the mob marched to St. Nicholas colliery and dispersed. Governor Hartranft, having been called upon, ordered companies of troops to Mahanoy City and Shenandoah to protect lives and property.

June 8

Some of the men going to work at the Locust Run colliery were driven back by a mob. The same day the party molested the platform men at Locust Run colliery and drove two men home.

June 12

At about half-past three o'clock P.M., Robert Gilgore and James O'Leary, contractors at the Oakdale colliery, left the mines to return to . . . their residence. . . . They were fired upon from the bushes by three men armed with shot-guns. O'Leary was shot in the arm in three places; Gilgore received a great number of shot in his arms, hands, and lower limbs.

June 28

About five o'clock in the morning, William Thomas was attacked in the stable of the Shoemaker colliery, near Mahanoy City, by seven strange men, firing at him several times, striking him in three places—in the neck, leg and about the front of the body.

July 6

About half past two o'clock in the morning, police officer Frank Yost, of the Tamaqua police, was shot by two men in Tamaqua. He lived until about ten o'clock that morning. Officer McCarron, who was standing across the street, fired at the men, but hit neither of them. At the time Yost was shot, he was on a ladder, at a lamp-post, turning off the gas. The night was very dark.

The American conception of politics in the Gilded Age: letters to Samuel J. Tilden, 1876

Walt Whitman wrote "with pride and joy" of America's technical achievements after the Civil War. But he lamented the "atmosphere of hypocrisy." Society, he noted, "is cankered, crude, superstitious, and rotten. Political or law-made society is, and private or voluntary society, is also." Americans assumed that all politicians were either corrupt or corruptible. Since Samuel J. Tilden was a

From John Bigelow, *The Life of Samuel J. Tilden* (New York, 1895), Vol. II, pp. 148–50, 153–55.

presidential candidate, and enormously wealthy, he was besieged with requests and even demands for funds to buy votes in his behalf.

From a hoosier

If you will send me some money ill help you along with a grate many more votes as there is a grate maney around here that will sell their votes fore anything.

From another hoosier

i have written you three letters and i think you election is very dootful in the Western States. i have traveled threw indiana illinois, masura, iway, cansas. peter cooper and hayes and you name is scarcely mentien and you haf to do something soon or you air beet. i can sell you twenty eighty hondred votse for eight hundred dolars.

From a Pennsylvanian "anxious to free our government from a mass of corruption"

[I am] foreman of a factory of 37 men of which 11 are Republicans. I am prepared to buy their votes at $5 each. If you can remit me the required amount my influence is at your command and the rights of our country.

From "a friend and a brother" of the black man

Sir: I wish you to send mez as much as $5. to Buye Whiskey to get all the colored votes I can for you.

From a Minnesota patriot

I feel very confident that with $10,000 I can get seven thousand votes.

From a Michigan lumberman

Sir, If you want to doo anney thing in the pine woods of Michigan you will have to send some money. This stump speeking dos for some folks but not for the Boys in the whoods. They whant a more excitement then that. I have no money and we air all poor but we have a vote just the same. I can do more on the day of election with some monney than all the stumping your great men can do in a year.

From a New Yorker

On this Campain we have used up all our money in working for you and we Have mad promises that we can't foolfil on this campain and hope that you Will Oblige us by sending us some money. We want to use some on Musick Band and also we have promised six cags of Bear after the closing of the Pols.

From a New York Republican, "but not a bigoted one"

If you think worth while to buy our votes we will go Democratic,—$50 apiece is the price. If you will send to my address before election $500 you will receive in return ten sound votes.

Collector of funds for the Tweed "Ring": the testimony of Elbert A. Woodward before the Board of Aldermen, 1869–78

Of the many examples of post-war public graft, locally or nationally, North or South, the most infamous and sophisticated system was devised by Boss Tweed in New York City. Fraudulent bills were submitted to and paid by corrupt administrators, after which hefty kickbacks were made to the politicians. Begun in 1869, the Tweed "Ring" reached the height of its power in 1871 before reformers, including Samuel J. Tilden, ended the swindling. Tweed died in jail in 1878. That year his collector, Elbert A. Woodward, explained how the system worked to an investigating committee. Woodward adamantly defended the "take": after all, he worked for it.

QUESTION: During the existence of what was called the Supervisors' "Ring," you had nothing to do with those percentages, either in demanding or receiving them, except in that case the particulars of which you have forgotten. When, then, did you begin to take an active part in collecting those percentages?

ANSWER: I think it was in 1869.

QUESTION: Tell me under what circumstances you first began to take an active part in that matter?

ANSWER: Watson [county auditor, New York], at that time, told the tradesmen who had bills against the city that I would manage the matter.

QUESTION: What matter did he tell them you were to manage?

From *Report of the Special Committee of the Board of Aldermen Appointed to Investigate the "Ring" Frauds, Together with the Testimony Elicited during the Investigation* (Board of Aldermen, New York City, January 4, 1878. Document No. 8, 1878) pp. 691, 697–700. I wish to thank my colleague, Dr. Alexander Callow, for bringing this selection to my attention.

ANSWER: That I would receive 65 percent of those bills and that I should pay 25 percent of that to William M. Tweed and the balance to him. I retained sometimes 2½ percent for myself, sometimes 5 percent, and sometimes nothing. . . .

QUESTION: The tradesmen who, from time to time, were engaged in these fraudulent practices, claimed that they had, at times, some basis for their bills; that part of their bills were for real work done and real materials furnished—now, was there ever any scrutiny into the facts concerning any bill?

ANSWER: I think not. But I always believed there was some foundation for every bill.

QUESTION: What foundation was there for your percentage?

ANSWER: I suppose there was as much foundation for that as for anything.

QUESTION: But what honest foundation was there for the 2½ percent you retained?

ANSWER: That might have been the honest part of the bill?

QUESTION: For all you know, the part you kept was the honest part of the bill?

ANSWER: I think so. I think it was the hardest earned.

QUESTION: So you don't think there was anything dishonest in your percentage?

ANSWER: No, sir, I don't.

QUESTION: And even now, don't you think there was anything wrong?

ANSWER: No, sir.

QUESTION: Were you at the time drawing a salary apart from these percentages?

ANSWER: Yes, sir.

QUESTION: What were the legitimate duties for which that salary was paid you, as near as you can make out?

ANSWER: To look after Mr. Tweed's interests. . . .

QUESTION: When you were paid a salary for looking after Mr. Tweed's interest do you think there was nothing necessarily wrong in your taking this percentage in addition to your salary?

ANSWER: No, sir.

QUESTION: And you still think so?

ANSWER: Yes, sir.

QUESTION: Do you think it was wrong for Tweed to take the 25 percent?

ANSWER: No, sir.

QUESTION: Or Connolly?

ANSWER: Yes, sir.

QUESTION: Was it wrong for Peter B. Sweeney?

ANSWER: Yes.

QUESTION: Was it wrong for Hall to take any?

ANSWER: Yes, sir.

QUESTION: Now will you explain why it was wrong for Hall, Sweeney, and Connolly to take percentages, and not wrong for you and Tweed?

ANSWER: Because those years there was a Republican Legislature, and that Republican Legislature had to be bought, and, as I understood it, Mr. Tweed had to pay the money, and I thought it right and proper for him to reimburse himself.

QUESTION: Do you think it right and proper to bribe a Legislature to procure legislation?

ANSWER: I had nothing to do with that.

QUESTION: But do you?

ANSWER: I think every legislature is bought more or less.

QUESTION: That is historical, not ethical. Do you think it is right?

ANSWER: I don't know whether it is right or wrong, I had nothing to do with it.

QUESTION: Well, letting the question of Tweed's moral responsibility pass, why was it right for you to take the money?

ANSWER: Well, I earned it.

QUESTION: How—in looking after the collection of this swag?

ANSWER: Call it what you please.

QUESTION: Well, percentages we will say instead of swag. You think you earned a share in getting it?

ANSWER: Yes, sir.

QUESTION: And you consider the city should have paid you for dividing this money among the members of the Ring?

ANSWER: Yes, sir.

QUESTION: What is your present occupation?

ANSWER: Farmer. . . .

Chief Sitting Bull describes "Custer's Last Stand" to a reporter, November 16, 1877

The battle of the Little Big Horn, in which the entire force of five companies of the Seventh Cavalry led by General George A. Custer was massacred on June 25, 1876, resulted from American cupidity and the commander's stupidity. The Sioux Indians had been exploited by agents on the Black Hills reservation, fed moldy wheat and spoiled beef, while the agents pocketed their annuities. Leaving the reservation to hunt the slopes of the Big Horn mountains, they were ordered to return to the reservation. Instead, the Indians declared war. Custer had been ordered to scout their position, but decided to ignore these orders and to attack. His recklessness cost the lives of all 265 soldiers.

From the *New York Tribune,* November 16, 1877.

"Well then," I inquired of Sitting Bull, "Did the cavalry, who came down and made the big fight, fight?"

Again Sitting Bull smiled.

"They fought. Many young men are missing from our lodges. But is there an American squaw who has her husband left? Were there any Americans left to tell the story of that day? No."

"How did they come on to the attack?"

"I have heard that there are trees which tremble."

"Do you mean the trees with trembling leaves?"

"Yes."

"They call them in some parts of the western country Quaking Asps; in the eastern part of the country they call them Silver Aspens."

"Hah! A great white chief, whom I met once, spoke these words 'Silver Aspens,' trees that shake; these were the Long Hair's [General Custer] soldiers."

"You do not mean that they trembled before your people because they were afraid?"

"They were brave men. They were tired. They were too tired."

"How did they act? How did they behave themselves?"

At this Sitting Bull again arose. I also arose from my seat, as did the other persons in the room, except the stenographer.

"Your people," said Sitting Bull, extending his right hand, "were killed. I tell no lies about deadmen. These men who came with the Long Hair were as good men as ever fought. When they rode up their horses were tired and they were tired. When they got off from their horses they could not stand firmly on their feet. They swayed to and fro—so my young men have told me—like the limbs of cypresses in a great wind. Some of them staggered under the weight of their guns. But they began to fight at once; but by this time, as I have said, our camps were aroused, and there were plenty of warriors to meet them. They fired with needle guns. We replied with magazine guns—repeating rifles. It was so (and here Sitting Bull illustrated by patting his palms together with the rapidity of a fusilade). Our young men rained lead across the river and drove the white braves back."

"And then?"

"And then, they rushed across themselves."

"And then?"

"And then they found that they had a good deal to do."

"Was there at that time some doubt about the issue of the battle, whether you would whip the Long Hair or not?"

"There was so much doubt about it that I started down there (here again pointing to the map) to tell the squaws to pack up the lodges and get ready to move away."

"You were on that expedition, then, after the big fight had fairly begun?"

"Yes."

"You did not personally witness the rest of the big fight? You were not engaged in it?"

"No. I have heard of it from the warriors."

"When the great crowds of your young men crossed the river in front of the Long Hair what did they do? Did they attempt to assault him directly in his front?"

"At first they did, but afterward they found it better to try and get around him. They formed themselves on all sides of him except just at his back."

"How long did it take them to put themselves around his flanks?"

"As long as it takes the sun to travel from here to here" (indicating some marks upon his arm with which apparently he is used to gauge the progress of the shadow of his lodge across his arm, and probably meaning half an hour. An Indian has no more definite way than this to express the lapse of time).

"The trouble was with the soldiers," he continued; "they were so exhausted and their horses bothered them so much that they could not take good aim. Some of their horses broke away from them and left them to stand and drop and die. When the Long Hair, the General, found that he was outnumbered and threatened on his flanks, he took the best course he could have taken. The bugle blew. It was an order to fall back. All the men fell back fighting and dropping. They could not fire fast enough, though. But from our side it was so," said Sitting Bull, and here he clapped his hands rapidly twice a second to express with what quickness and continuance the balls flew from the Henry and Winchester rifles wielded by the Indians. "They could not stand up under such a fire," he added.

"Were any military tactics shown? Did the Long Haired Chief make any disposition of his soldiers, or did it seem as though they retreated all together, helter skelter, fighting for their lives?"

"They kept in pretty good order. Some great chief must have commanded them all the while. They would fall back across a *coulee* and make a fresh stand beyond on higher ground. The map is pretty nearly right. It shows where the white men stopped and fought before they were all killed. I think that is right—down there to the left, just above the Little Big Horn. There was one part driven out there, away from the rest, and there a great many men were killed. The places marked on the map are pretty nearly the places where all were killed."

"Did the whole command keep on fighting until the last?"

"Every man, so far as my people could see. There were no cowards on either side."

The end of the open range: an account of the disastrous winter of 1886–87

By the early 1880's there were danger signs apparent to those perceptive enough to notice. The range was becoming overstocked, and all the efforts of the quickly formed cattle breeders' associations to limit the herds went for naught. The winter of 1886–87 nearly wiped out the cattlemen. Deep snow, numbing cold, and lack of freedom of movement killed tens of thousands of cattle. "We have had a perfect smashup all through the cattle industry," Theodore Roosevelt reported. The surviving cattle were dumped on the market in the spring, causing prices to plummet and forcing many cattlemen into bankruptcy. Thereafter the industry centered on the ranch rather than the range.

May was dry, June did not bring the usual rains, and by July 4th it looked so bad that we finally decided to do nothing. By August it was hot, dry, dusty and grass closely cropped. Every day made it apparent that even with the best of winters cattle would have a hard time and "through" cattle would only winter with a big percentage of loss. . . . [Nevertheless,] our neighbors kept piling cattle onto the bone dry range. The Continental Cattle Co. drove up 32,000 head of steers. The Worsham Cattle Co., with no former holdings turned loose 5,000 head or thereabouts. Major Smith, who had failed to sell 5,500 southern three-year-old steers, was forced to drive them to his range on Willow Creek near to Stoneville, now Alzada, Montana. The Dickey Cattle Co. had brought up 6,000 mixed cattle from the Cheyenne and Arapahoe country. . . . Thousands of other cattle were spread over the western and northwestern country in the most reckless way, no thought for the morrow. Even with the best of winters it would have been a case of suicide. As things turned out it was simple murder, at least for the Texas cattle. Winter came early and it stayed long. The owners were mostly absent and even those who remained could not move about or size up the situation.

It was not till the spring round-ups that the real truth was discovered and then it was only mentioned in a whisper. Bobby Robinson, acute judge of conditions, estimated the loss among through cattle at less than fifty percent. It turned out to be a total loss among this class of cattle and the wintered herds suffered from thirty to sixty percent. . . . It was simply appalling and the cowmen could not realize their position. From Southern Colorado to the Canadian line, from the 100th Meridian almost to the Pacific slope, it was a catastrophe which the cowmen of today who did not go through it can never understand. Three great streams of ill-luck, mismanagement, greed, met together. In other words, recklessness, want of foresight and the weather, which no man can control. The buffalo had probably gone through similar winters with enormous losses and thus

From John Clay, *My Life on the Range* (Chicago, 1924), pp. 177–79.

natural conditions were evened up in the countless years they had grazed the prairie, and in the survival of the fittest their constitutions had been built up to stand the rigors of winter and the drought of summer. . . .

The cowmen of the West and Northwest were flat broke. Many of them never recovered. They had not the heart to face another debacle such as they had gone through and consequently they disappeared from the scene. Most of the eastern men and the Britishers said "enough" and went away.

A labor "agitator" recalls the Haymarket Square bombing of May 4, 1886

One massive union, the Knights of Labor opened its ranks to blacks, to women, and to immigrants, but excluded doctors, lawyers, bankers, and politicians. After they organized several successful strikes against western railroads, their member-ship soared to 750,000. In 1886 a series of strikes had been called by local assemblies of the Knights of Labor in support of the eight-hour day. During a fracas at the McCormick Harvester plant a worker was killed, and a protest meeting was held on May 4, 1886, in Haymarket Square, Chicago. The events of that night, described below by a contemporary labor leader, shattered the popularity of the Knights. Although they had no connection with the bomb-throwers, the Knights became associated with radicalism and violence. Their membership fell off as quickly as it had climbed, and they were never again an effective force in American labor.

[In] May 1886 . . . the first extensive effort was made to inaugurate the eight-hour workday in the United States. A great many employers op-posed the demand for the shorter day, and strikes followed. There were serious conflicts between the strikers and their sympathizers on the one hand and the authorities on the other hand in several industrial centers, the disturbances at Chicago and Milwaukee being especially noteworthy. On the night of the 4th of May the tragedy of the Chicago Haymarket occurred. The events of that night have their place in the history of the country, and it is not incumbent upon the present writer to recount them here. It is enough if I recall to the reader's mind the connection between that meeting and the eight-hour movement of organized labor. In conse-quence of an eight-hour strike at the McCormick Reaper Works, in Chi-cago, there was a clash between the police and a crowd of workingmen— some of them being strikers—and several persons were seriously injured by the bullets and clubs of the policemen. A meeting was called for the following night, in the Haymarket Square, to "protest against the brutality of the police." The speakers at the meeting were all members of the An-archist groups, though some of them were also identified with the more

From Joseph R. Buchanan, *The Story of a Labor Agitator* (New York, 1903), pp. 294–97.

conservative branches of the labor movement. The speeches at this meeting were not nearly so violent in tone as had been numerous previous speeches, made by the same men, on the Lake Front and in other parts of Chicago. Carter Harrison the First was mayor of the city at the time. He was present at the meeting for nearly an hour—leaving for home a short time before the hour at which it was intended to close the meeting; and he declared, on the witness stand, that he heard nothing that presaged lawless acts. But within a few minutes after he had taken his departure several hundred policemen marched out of the Desplaines Street Station, half a block away, and headed for the crowd assembled around the truck, from which Sam Fielden was then making an address. The captain of the police ordered the meeting to disperse. Fielden said, "Captain, this is an orderly assemblage." The captain repeated his order, and some person—neither court proceedings nor any other record tells us who—threw a bomb into the midst of the policemen. Sixty-six policemen were prostrated by the explosion, seven never to rise again and an eighth to die soon after. It was reported that one man in the crowd was killed by the bullets of the policemen and several wounded, but there never was an authentic report of the casualties on that side made public. Many arrests were made of men charged with complicity in the bomb-throwing; eight were indicted. After a long trial, seven were found guilty of murder in the first degree and sentenced to be hanged, and one was sentenced to fifteen years in the state penitentiary for distributing the handbills announcing the Haymarket meeting.

Andrew Carnegie writes on "Wealth," 1889

The leading businessmen of the Gilded Age preached and practiced Darwin's biological theory of the survival of the fittest as applied to business. "The American Beauty rose," John D. Rockefeller explained in a Sunday school address, "can be produced in the splendor and fragrance which bring cheer to its beholder only by sacrificing the early buds which grow up around it. This is not an evil tendency in business. It is merely the working out of a law of nature and a law of God." James J. Hill, the railroad magnate, explained that " the fortunes of railroad companies are determined by the law of the survival of the fittest." Andrew Carnegie hailed this doctrine as an economic truth, "the highest results of human experience."

The Socialist or Anarchist who seeks to overturn present conditions is to be regarded as attacking the foundation upon which civilization itself rests, for civilization took its start from the day that the capable, industrious workman said to his incompetent and lazy fellow, "If thou dost not sow, thou shalt not reap," and thus ended primitive communism by separating

From Andrew Carnegie, "Wealth," in *North American Review,* Vol. CCCXCI, June 1889, pp. 656–57.

the drones from the bees. One who studies this subject will soon be brought face to face with the conclusion that upon the sacredness of property civilization itself depends—the right of the laborer to his hundred dollars in the savings bank, and equally the right of the millionaire to his millions. To those who propose to substitute communism for this intense individualism the answer, therefore is: The race has tried that. All progress from that barbarous day to the present time has resulted from its displacement. Not evil, but good, has come to the race from the accumulation of wealth by those who have the ability and energy that produce it. But even if we admit for a moment that it might be better for the race to discard its present foundation, individualism—that it is a nobler ideal that man should labor, not for himself alone, but in and for a brotherhood of his fellows, and share with them all in common—even admit all this, and a sufficient answer is, This is not evolution, but revolution. It necessitates the changing of human nature itself—a work of aeons, even if it were good to change it, which we cannot know. It is not practicable in our day or in our age. Even if desirable theoretically, it belongs to another and long-succeeding sociological stratum. Our duty is with what is practicable now: with the next step possible in our day and generation. It is criminal to waste our energies in endeavoring to uproot, when all we can profitably or possibly accomplish is to bend the universal tree of humanity a little in the direction most favorable to the production of good fruit under existing circumstances. We might as well urge the destruction of individualism, private property, the law of accumulation of wealth, and the law of competition; for these are the highest results of human experience, the soil in which society so far has produced the best fruit. Unequally or unjustly, perhaps, as these laws sometimes operate, and imperfect as they appear to the idealist, they are, nevertheless, like the highest type of man, the best and most valuable of all that humanity has yet accomplished.

Jacob Riis writes on "How the Other Half Lives," 1890

Jacob Riis had no particular sympathy for the economic underdog. He made no protest, as did many others, against a social system which rewarded the few with immense wealth and consigned the many to a life of poverty. Nor should it be thought that his account of slums and tenements was unique: the evils had long been recognized and discussed. But, from his years of experience as a police reporter in New York City, Riis had accumulated a storehouse of anecdotes about tenement existence which, with an uncommon ability for descriptive narrative, he incorporated in his book on How the Other Half Lives. *It constituted a warning to the middle classes to solve the evils bred in the slums lest they grow and infiltrate other areas.*

From Jacob A. Riis, *How the Other Half Lives* (New York, 1890), pp. 124–27.

With the first hot nights in June police despatches, that record the killing of men and women by rolling off roofs and window-sills while asleep, announce that the time of greatest suffering among the poor is at hand. It is in hot weather, when life indoors is well-nigh unbearable with cooking, sleeping, and working, all crowded into the small rooms together, that the tenement expands, reckless of all restraint. Then a strange and picturesque life moves upon the flat roofs. In the day and early evening mothers air their babies there, the boys fly their kites from the house-tops, undismayed by police regulations, and young men and girls court and pass the growler. In the stifling July nights, when the big barracks are like fiery furnaces, their very walls giving out absorbed heat, men and women lie in restless, sweltering rows, panting for air and sleep. Then every truck in the street, every crowded fire-escape, becomes a bedroom, infinitely preferable to any the house affords. A cooling shower on such a night is hailed as a heaven-sent blessing in a hundred thousand homes.

Life in the tenements in July and August spells death to an army of little ones whom the doctor's skill is powerless to save. When the white badge of mourning flutters from every second door, sleepless mothers walk the streets in the gray of the early dawn, trying to stir a cooling breeze to fan the brow of the sick baby. There is no sadder sight than this patient devotion striving against fearfully hopeless odds. Fifty "summer doctors," especially trained to this work, are then sent into the tenements by the Board of Health, with free advice and medicine for the poor. Devoted women follow in their track with care and nursing for the sick. Fresh-air excursions run daily out of New York on land and water; but despite all efforts the grave-diggers in Calvary work over-time, and little coffins are stacked mountains high on the deck of the Charity Commissioners' boat when it makes its semi-weekly trips to the city cemetery.

Under the most favorable circumstances, an epidemic, which the well-to-do can afford to make light of as a thing to be got over or avoided by reasonable care, is excessively fatal among the children of the poor, by reason of the practical impossibility of isolating the patient in a tenement. The measles, ordinarily a harmless disease, furnishes a familiar example. Tread it ever so lightly on the avenues, in the tenements it kills right and left. Such an epidemic ravaged three crowded blocks in Elizabeth Street on the heels of the grippe last winter, and, when it had spent its fury, the death-maps in the Bureau of Vital Statistics looked as if a black hand had been laid across those blocks. . . . The track of the epidemic through these teeming barracks was as clearly defined as the track of a tornado through a forest district. There were houses in which as many as eight little children had died in five months. The record showed that respiratory diseases, the common heritage of the grippe and the measles, had caused death in most cases, discovering the trouble to be, next to the inability to check the contagion in those crowds, in the poverty of the parents and the wretched home conditions that made proper care of the sick impossible. . . .

Every once in a while a case of downright starvation gets into the newspapers and makes a sensation. But this is the exception. Were the whole truth known, it would come home to the community with a shock that would rouse it to a more serious effort than the spasmodic undoing of its purse-strings. I am satisfied from my own observation that hundreds of men, women, and children are every day slowly starving to death in the tenements with . . . [the] complaint of "improper nourishment." Within a single week I have had this year three cases of insanity, provoked by poverty and want. One was that of a mother who in the middle of the night got up to murder her child, who was crying for food; another was the case of an Elizabeth Street truck-driver whom the newspapers never heard of. With a family to provide for, he had been unable to work for many months. There was neither food, nor a scrap of anything upon which money could be raised, left in the house; his mind gave way under the combined physical and mental suffering. In the third case I was just in time with the police to prevent the madman from murdering his whole family. He had the sharpened hatchet in his pocket when we seized him. He was an Irish laborer, and had been working in the sewers until the poisonous gases destroyed his health. Then he was laid off, and scarcely anything had been coming in all winter but the oldest child's earnings as cash-girl in a store, $2.50 a week. There were seven children to provide for, and the rent of the Mulberry Street attic in which the family lived was $10 a month. They had borrowed as long as anybody had a cent to lend. When at last the man got an odd job that would just buy the children bread, the week's wages only served to measure the depth of their misery. "It came in so on the tail-end of everything," said his wife in telling the story, with unconscious eloquence. The outlook worried him through sleepless nights until it destroyed his reason. In his madness he had only one conscious thought: that the town should not take the children. "Better that I take care of them myself," he repeated to himself as he ground the axe to an edge.

The Populist crusade: an address by the Governor of Kansas, July 26, 1894

The quest for justice ranged over the entire country—in the Northern urban slums, in the mill towns of New England and the coal districts of Pennsylvania, in the mining cities of Colorado, and in the rural regions of the South and West. But neither political party responded to these voices, and a crusade—the Populist movement—of farmers decided that political action was mandatory. Mary Lease advised them to "raise less corn and more hell." In 1892 their platform

From a speech of Lorenzo D. Lewelling, Governor of Kansas, at a Populist meeting at Huron Place, Kansas City, July 26, 1894, reprinted in George B. Tindall (ed.), *A Populist Reader* (New York: Harper and Row, Inc., 1966), pp. 149–58.

*proclaimed that "the fruits of the toil of millions are boldly stolen to build up
colossal fortunes for a few. . . . From the same prolific womb of governmental
injustice, we breed two great classes—tramps and millionaires." The following
excerpts are taken from a speech by the Populist governor of Kansas, made
in 1894.*

Now, there are 350,000 able-bodied men in Kansas, and their average
individual earnings last year and year before were $500 per man. That is
what they earned on an average, but I might imagine some of you people
here in this audience saying, "Well, I didn't get my share even of the $500,"
and I don't think you did. What has become of that $500 you were to get?
It has gone where the wang-a-doodle mourneth for its first born. It went
to pay excessive freight rates on commodities which we bought and sold,
and then it went to pay interest on your mortgages. Why, I might tell, and
I know something about it from experience, that the people of Kansas are
paying 6 percent, 8 percent, 10 percent and some as high as 12 and 15
percent per annum. Then, what is to become of us, my fellow citizens?
Where are we going to? Don't you see pretty clearly we are going into a
hole every year? . . .

I ask you now, what can the poor man do today that comes to you and
says, I have hands to work with, I have bodily strength, I am willing to
give all those for a morsel of bread—but you say, "I have no work to give
you." What is he to do then? Can he go and lie down on the street for rest?
No, because there [are] laws against vagabondage. Can he go and crawl
into a box car and take a nap there? No. Because he is trespassing upon the
rights and privileges of others. Can he go to the door and ask for something
to eat? No, because there [are] laws against begging. Can he go out into
the fields and cultivate the fields? No, because the field belongs to somebody else. Can he draw a drink of water out of the spring or well in the
field? No, because the spring or well belongs to the man who owns the field.
What in the name of goodness is he to do? Answer me that question in the
light of our present civilization and government. Don't you have some
sympathy for the men in this position? Senator [James] Ingalls, [Republi-
can senator from Kansas], told us some two years ago, there are over a
million men in the United States who are in that condition, and today that
number is swelled to three million. Oh, is it any wonder there are common-
wealers? Is it then a wonder there are anarchists? There is no greater crime
breeder in the world than poverty. Poverty is the mother of it all; and I
came here this evening asking you to join with me in the organization of
a great anti-poverty society. Will you do it? (Cheers, and cries of yes.)
. . . They say I am a "Calamity howler." If that is so, I want to continue to
howl until those conditions are improved. . . .

While I have talked to you about the condition of the laborer, the
condition of the farmer is about the same all over Kansas, and I am spe-
cially glad to know the farmers to be in hearty sympathy with the cause of

labor. Down in Arkansas City, they are bringing in supplies day by day to supply the men striking on the railroad. And I understand the same thing is done here. A friend of mine who is nominated for senator on the Populist ticket had the audacity, my friends, to contribute to the striking laborers of that town. Today he is arraigned by the United States Court and summoned to Topeka and placed on trial for aiding and abetting the strikers against the government of the United States. Think of it! . . .

Well, I set out to tell you and I got off my subject, what the condition of the farmer is and that is about the same as that of the laborer. His earnings are naught. Add several ciphers together and you will have the sum of his profits this year and last. Take his wheat, which is worth twenty-five cents a bushel, and cost forty cents to raise it. How is he going to come out this year? I will tell you something: did you know that forty-three percent of the homes of Kansas have already passed into the hands of landlords, who toil not neither do they spin? . . . I heard a man standing up in the pulpit with a black coat and a white necktie and discoursing loud and long over the evictions of the Irish tenants across the water, and I will tell you, we have got in the State of Kansas 10,000 people who are made homeless every year by the foreclosure of mortgages and this has been going on for several years. . . .

I say we have the Goulds and Vanderbilts and Rockefellers on the one side—why, Vanderbilt once deposited $50,000,000 of government bonds. How much money was that? The interest amounted to $5000. About $3.50 a minute, fifty cents every time the clock ticked. I simply say these men are arrayed on the one hand, and on the other, the industrial army, every man of which, like the Savior, has not where to lay his head. 30,000 tenants annually ejected in New York City. One tenth of all who die buried in the potter's field. 10,000 farmers made homeless in Kansas every year, and ten shelterless girls struggling in vain for every position of employment that is vacant in your cities for one who is successful in obtaining work. What becomes of the other nine? Those who fail—mark my words!—are driven to seek shelter with her whose ways take hold of hell, and lead to the chambers of death. Yet, these are the conditions which prevail in our civilization, and men are saying that this is the best government under the shining sun. It was in its original conception, and God forbid that it may go further astray than it has done at the present time. The great throbbing centers of civilization seem to me to be dead to the instincts of humanity and alike dead to the teachings of the man of Bethlehem. The night of despair seems to me to be upon us. Call me calamity howler if you will. I wish I had the voice and pen and reputation of Jeremiah that I might howl Calamity until the people all over this broad land should hear me. It seems to me that the night of despair is really at hand. And I ask you who is to be responsible for our civil government, if you please, by which we are turned into beasts by conditions that the government might and should prevent? The golden age of the 19th century!

Booker T. Washington's speech delivered at the opening of the Atlanta Cotton States and International Exposition, September 18, 1895

"I now come to that one of the incidents in my life," Booker T. Washington re-
called in his autobiography, "which seems to have excited the greatest amount of
interest." His "five-minute" speech at Atlanta on September 18, 1895, made
him a national figure. According to a newspaper reporter, "the fairest women of
Georgia stood up and cheered. . . . Governor Bullock rushed across the stage
and seized the orator's hand. Another shout greeted this demonstration, and
for a few minutes the two men stood facing each other, hand in hand." Grover
Cleveland wrote Washington that "your words cannot fail to delight and en-
courage all who wish well for your race." The editor of the Atlanta Constitution
noted that "the address was a revelation. The whole speech is a platform upon
which blacks and whites can stand with full justice to each other."

To those of the white race who look to the incoming of those of foreign birth and strange tongue and habits, for the prosperity of the South, were I permitted, I would repeat what I say to my own race—"Cast down your bucket where you are." Cast it down among the 8,000,000 Negroes whose habits you know, whose fidelity and love you have tested in days when to have proved treacherous meant the ruin of your firesides. Cast down your bucket among these people who have, without strikes and labor wars, tilled your fields, cleared your forests, builded your railroads and cities, and brought forth treasures from the bowels of the earth and helped make possible this magnificent representation of the progress of the South. Casting down your bucket among my people, helping and encouraging them as you are doing on these grounds, and to education of the head, hand and heart, you will find that they will buy your surplus land, make blossom the waste places in your fields and run your factories. While doing this, you can be sure in the future, as in the past, that you and your families will be surrounded by the most patient, faithful, law-abiding and unresentful people that the world has seen. As we have proved our loyalty to you in the past, in nursing your children, watching by the sick bed of your mothers and fathers and often following them with tear-dimmed eyes to their graves, so in the future in our humble way, we shall stand by you with a devotion that no foreigner can approach, ready to lay down our lives, if need be, in defense of yours, interlacing our industrial, commercial, civil and religious life with yours in a way that shall make the interests of both races one. In all things that are purely social we can be as separate as the fingers, yet one as the hand in all things essential to mutual progress.

There is no defence or security for any of us except in the highest

From Booker T. Washington, *Up From Slavery: An Autobiography* (New York, 1901), pp. 220–25.

intelligence and development of all. If anywhere there are efforts tending
to curtail the fullest growth of the Negro, let these efforts be turned into
stimulating, encouraging and making him the most useful and intelligent
citizen. Effort or means so invested will pay a thousand per cent interest.
These efforts will be twice blessed—"blessing him that gives and him
that takes. . . ."

Nearly sixteen millions of hands will aid you in pulling the load
upwards, or they will pull against you the load downwards. We shall constitute one-third and more of the ignorance and crime of the South, or one-
third its intelligence and progress; we shall contribute one-third to the
business and industrial prosperity of the South, or we shall prove a veritable
body of death, stagnating, depressing, retarding every effort to advance
the body politic.

Gentlemen of the Exposition, as we present to you our humble effort
at an exhibition of our progress, you must not expect over much. Starting
thirty years ago with ownership here and there in a few quilts, and pump-
kins and chickens (gathered from miscellaneous sources), remember the
path that has led from these to the inventions and production of agricultural
implements, buggies, steam engines, newspapers, books, statuary, carving,
paintings, the management of drug stores and banks. . . . While we take
pride in what we exhibit as a result of our independent efforts, we do not
for a moment forget that our part in this exhibition would fall far short of
your expectations but for the constant help that has come to our educational
life, not only from the Southern States, but especially from Northern phi-
lanthropists, who have made their gifts a constant stream of blessings
and encouragement.

The wisest among my race understand that the agitation of questions
of social equality is the extremest folly, and that progress in the enjoyment
of all the privileges that will come to us must be the result of severe and
constant struggle, rather than of artificial forcing. No race that has anything
to contribute to the markets of the world is long in any degree ostracized.
It is important and right that all privileges of the law be ours, but it is vastly
more important that we be prepared for the exercises of these privileges.
The opportunity to earn a dollar in a factory just now is worth infinitely
more than the opportunity to spend a dollar in an opera house.

In conclusion, may I repeat that nothing in thirty years has given us
more hope and encouragement, and drawn us so near to you of the white
race, as this opportunity offered by the Exposition; and, here bending, as it
were, over the altar that represents the results of the struggles of your race
and mine, both starting practically empty-handed three decades ago, I
pledge that in your effort to work out the great and intricate problem which
God has laid at the doors of the South, you shall have at all times the
patient, sympathetic help of my race; only let this be constantly in mind,
that while from representations in these buildings of the product of field,
of forest, of mine, of factory, letters and art, much good will come, yet far

above and beyond material benefits, will be that higher good, that let us pray God will come, in a blotting out of sectional differences and racial animosities and suspicions, in a determination to administer absolute justice, in a willing obedience among all classes to the mandates of the law. This, coupled with our material prosperity, will bring into our beloved South a new Heaven and a new earth.

The triumph of American conservatism: an interpretation of the election of 1896

In 1896 the Republicans stood strongly, if not unanimously, behind the gold standard. They nominated a party regular, the conservative William McKinley of Ohio, whose strongest asset was his campaign manager, Mark Hanna. The Democrats, yielding to Western pressures, selected William J. Bryan on a platform which promised the "free and unlimited coinage of silver at a ratio of 16:1." The Populists had no choice but to endorse Bryan. The great orator from Nebraska appealed not only to farmers, but to workers and other discontented Americans—his speeches often playing upon class animosities. When the results were in, Bryan had tallied over six million votes, yet McKinley was the decisive victor. According to one interpretation, that given below, the result proved that the masses of citizens were inherently conservative since they did not respond to Bryan's appeal. This may be so. But it is also true that the Republicans spent enormous sums in this campaign. Hanna "advertised McKinley," Theodore Roosevelt remarked, "as if he were a patent medicine."

Whatever else was demonstrated by the course of the campaign and the result of the election, there was shown beyond all question the essential conservatism and sagacity of the American people. The pessimists who have been pronouncing universal suffrage a failure, and popular self-government a disappointing experiment, can find no confirmation of their views in any fair interpretation of this last election.... A few years ago, nobody could have foretold with certainty which of the great parties would find itself at length committed to the policy of independent American bimetallism. Although a Democratic President [Cleveland] led the sharp reaction against the silver policy which, in 1893, secured the repeal of the compulsory silver purchase law of 1890, it happened that the silver men found the Republican party, by reason of its superior strength in the old commercial communities of the North and East, least willing to break away from the international measure of value; while the Democratic party, with its superior strength in the agricultural states of the South, where the silver sentiment had obtained a stronghold, proved unexpectedly easy of capture. The enthusiasm with which the Democratic party promulgated its free-

From *The Review of Reviews*, Vol. XIV, December 1896, pp. 643–44.

silver and antimonopoly platform, and enlisted under the banner of its ardent and self-confident young nominee [William J. Bryan], seemed for a time to be almost irresistible. Its appeal was made to farmers and working-men with passionate earnestness. Nearly all the prominent leaders of the anti-silver forces had at some time or other denounced the gold standard and demanded the restoration of silver in language which was now widely quoted against them with great effect. A large majority of the people of the country are farmers and wage earners. In view of the real difficulties under which agriculture has labored, and the dull times which have brought the wolf near the door of the average workingman, it would not have been a very conclusive proof of the failure of popular government if the free-silver cause had triumphed at the polls. The Senate of the United States had been absolutely controlled by the free-silver men for several years. If the states from which those Senators came had given large popular majorities in favor of the silver doctrine, at a time when restlessness and discontent due to industrial stagnation tempted the people to vote for some radical change, why should it have been thought very surprising? The thing that has made philosophers doubtful of the safety of popular self-government has been fear that changes would be demanded capriciously, and that civilization would suffer through the impatience and violence of great masses of men swayed by the spirit of radicalism. A severer test than that of this year is not likely to be made in our time; and the philosophers are answered. The American people, taken in the great mass, are shown to be funda-mentally conservative.

7
American Crusades

The rights of women: an optimistic report by Susan B. Anthony, 1897

William Allen White remembered the visits of Susan B. Anthony to his parental home in Kansas when he was a child. "I was scared of her," he recalled. "She seemed fierce and carnivorous—the kind that ate little boys alive." Zealous, courageous, indefatigable, and more impatient than the following selection reveals, Miss Anthony had devoted a lifetime of labor for various liberal reforms. It was she who coined the phrase "equal pay for equal work" for females, and helped organize a National Woman's Trade Union League to achieve this goal. It was she who insisted upon the right to vote by the Fourteenth Amendment, was indicted, and brought to trial. The court declared in United States v. Anthony *that the states would have to pass specific legislation to obtain female suffrage. By 1897, the year of this report, many states had yielded to suffragette pressures. But not until 1920, however, after her death, was the Nineteeenth Amendment—known as the Susan B. Anthony Amendment—approved, by which women were given national suffrage equal to men.*

Fifty years ago woman in the United States was without a recognized individuality in any department of life. No provision was made in public or private schools for her education in anything beyond the rudimentary branches. An educated woman was a rarity and was gazed upon with something akin to awe. . . . Such was the helpless, dependent, fettered condition of woman when the first Woman's Right Convention was called . . . by Elizabeth Cady Stanton and Lucretia Mott. While there had been individual demands, from time to time, the first organized body to formulate a declaration of the rights of women was the one which met at Seneca Falls, July 19–20, 1848, and adjourned to meet at Rochester two weeks later. In the Declaration of Sentiments and the Resolutions there framed, every point was covered that, down to the present day, has been contended for by the advocates of equal rights for women. . . .

Now, at the end of half a century, we find that with few exceptions, all of the demands formulated at this convention have been granted. The great exception is the yielding of political rights, and toward this one point are directed now all the batteries of scorn, of ridicule, of denunciation that formerly poured their fire all along the line. Although not one of the predicted calamities occurred upon the granting of the other demands, the world is asked to believe that all of them will happen if this last stronghold is surrendered. . . .

There is not one foot of advanced ground upon which women stand today that has not been obtained through the hard-fought battles of other women. The close of this 19th century finds every trade, vocation, and professsion open to women, and every opportunity at their command for preparing themselves to follow these occupations.

From *The Arena*, May 1897.

The girls as well as the boys of a family now fit themselves for such careers as their tastes and abilities permit. A vast amount of the household drudgery that once monopolized the whole time and strength of the mother and daughters has been taken outside and turned over to machinery in vast establishments. A money value is placed upon the labor of women. The ban of social ostracism has been largely removed from the woman wage earner. She who can make for herself a place of distinction in any line of work receives commendation instead of condemnation. Woman is no longer compelled to marry for support, but may herself make her own home and earn her own financial independence.

With but few exceptions, the highest institutions of learning in the land are as freely opened to girls as to boys, and they may receive their degrees at legal, medical, and theological colleges, and practise their professions without hindrance. In the world of literature and art, women divide the honors with men; and our civil service rules have secured for them many thousands of remunerative positions under the government. . . .

The department of politics has been slowest to give admission to women. Suffrage is the pivotal right, and if it could have been secured in the beginning, women would not have been half a century in gaining the privileges enumerated above, for privileges they must be called so long as others may either give or take them away. If women could make the laws or elect those who make them, they would be in the position of sovereigns instead of subjects. Were they the political peers of man, they could command instead of having to beg, petition, and pray. Can it be possible it is for this reason that men have been so determined in their opposition to grant to women political power?

But even this stronghold is beginning to yield to the long and steady pressure. In twenty-five states women possess suffrage in school matters; in four states they have a limited suffrage in local affairs; in one state they have municipal suffrage; in four states they have full suffrage, local, state, and national. Women are becoming more and more interested in political questions and public affairs. Every campaign sees greater numbers in attendance at the meetings, and able woman speakers are now found upon the platforms of all parties. Especial efforts are made by politicians to obtain the support of women, and during the last campaign one of the presidential candidates held special meetings for women in the large cities throughout the country. . . .

There is no more striking illustration of the progress that has been made by woman than that afforded by her changed position in the church. Under the old regime the Quakers were the only sect who recognized the equality of women. Other denominations enforced the command of St. Paul, that women should keep silence in the churches. A few allowed the women to lift up their voices in class and prayer meetings, but they had no vote in matters of church government. Even the missionary and charity work was in the hands of men. Now the Unitarians, Universalists, Congregationalists, Wesleyan and Protestant Methodists, Christians, Free-Will Baptists, and possibly a few others, ordain women as ministers, and many parishes, in all parts of the country, are presided over by women preachers. The charitable and missionary work of the churches is practically turned over to women, who raise and disburse immense sums of money. While many of the great denominations still refuse to ordain women, to allow them a seat in their councils, or a vote in matters of church government, yet women themselves are, in a large measure, responsible for this state of affairs. Forming, as they do, from two-thirds to three-fourths of the membership, raising the greater part of the funds, and carrying on the active work of the church, when they unite their forces and assert their rights, the small minority of men, who have usurped the authority, will be obliged to yield to their just demands. The creeds of the churches will recognize woman's equality before God as the codes of the states have acknowledged it before man and the law. . . .

From that little convention of Seneca Falls, with a following of a handful of women scattered through half-a-dozen different states, we have now the great National Association, with headquarters in New York City, and auxiliaries in almost every state in the Union. These state bodies are effecting a thorough system of county and local organizations for the purpose of securing legislation favorable to women, and especially to obtain amendments to their state constitutions. As evidence of the progress of public opinion, more than half of the legislatures in session during the past winter have discussed and voted upon bills for the enfranchisement of women, and in most of them they were adopted by one branch and lost by a very small majority in the other. The legislatures of Washington and South Dakota have submitted woman-suffrage amendments to their electors for 1898, and vigorous campaigns will be made in those states during the next two years. . . . While the efforts of each state are concentrated upon its own legislature, all of the states combined in the national organization are directing their energies toward securing a Sixteenth Amendment to the Constitution of the United States. The demands of this body have been received with respectful and encouraging attention from Congress. Hearings have been granted by the committees of both houses, resulting, in a number of instances, in favorable reports. Upon one occasion the question was brought to a discussion in the Senate and received the affirmative vote of one-third of the members.

Until woman has obtained "that right protective of all other rights—the ballot," this agitation must still go on, absorbing the time and the energy of our best and strongest women. Who can measure the advantages that would result if the magnificent abilities of these women could be devoted to the needs of government, society, home, instead of being consumed in the struggle to obtain their birthright of individual freedom? Until this be gained we can never know, we cannot even prophesy, the capacity and power of woman for the uplifting of humanity.

It may be delayed longer than we think; it may be here sooner than we expect; but the day will come when man will recognize woman as his peer, not only at the fireside, but in the councils of the nation. Then, and not until then, will there be the perfect comradeship, the ideal union between the sexes that shall result in the highest development of the race. What this shall be we may not attempt to define, but this we know, that only good can come to the individual or to the nation through the rendering of exact justice.

A correspondent's account of the American capture of Guam, 1898

To Secretary of State John Hay the Spanish-American conflict of 1898 was "a splendid little war." So it was, for Americans who sought to satisfy their martial spirit against the feeble Spanish forces. In the Philippines Commodore George Dewey destroyed the Spanish fleet at Manila Bay without losing a single man. In the Caribbean the United States suffered some 5,000 casualties, but these resulted in the main from spoiled food and disease rather than from enemy engagements. The capture of Guam provides a light comic-opera touch to the war. The Spanish garrison there did not know that war had been declared. They interpreted the firing from an American gunboat as a military salute, and apologized for being unable to return the courtesy. An American correspondent described the incident:

> "When we hit that good old town of Guam
> We will make the Spaniards cuss and damn.
> We'll introduce them to their Uncle Sam.
> There'll be a hot time in the old town that night."

The [American gunboat] *Charleston* was too far away for the reports of the guns to reach the transports, but for a few minutes the flashes and the puffs of smoke as the 3-pounders were fired filled the souls of the soldiers with glee and the cheering was tremendous. Then the firing stopped, the cheering died out and the action at Guam was all over. From first gun to last it was just four minutes and a half. It began at 3,000 yards and ended at 2,400. Seven shells were fired from the starboard 3-pounders and six from the port battery. It was 8:30 o'clock on the morning of Monday, June 20. Then there was a long wait that tried the patience of the eager spectators on the transports. The *Charleston* crawled along up the little peninsula for a few hundred yards and apparently stopped.

Two boats from shore got to the cruiser. In them were Lieutenant

From Oscar K. Davis, *Our Conquests in the Pacific* (New York, 1898), pp. 43, 51–54.

Garcia Gutierrez of the Spanish Navy, Captain of the Port of San Luis d'Apra, and Surgeon Romero of the Spanish Army, the health officer. They came up the gangway which had been rigged out on the starboard side of the *Charleston* and saluted the officer of the deck. They had with them Francis Portusac, a native of Guam who had been educated in the United States and who was naturalized in Chicago in 1888. He is a merchant in Agana and happened to be at the landing at Piti when the *Charleston* came along. He came with the officials to call on his "countrymen" on the *Charleston* and to act as interpreter for the Spaniards.

When they were seated Lieutenant Gutierrez, the port Captain, set the ball rolling with this soft observation:

"You will pardon our not immediately replying to your salute, Captain, but we are unaccustomed to receiving salutes here, and are not supplied with proper guns for returning them. However, we shall be glad to do our best to return your salute as soon as possible."

The port Captain spoke in Spanish. Captain Glass is sufficiently familiar with the language to need no interpretation of the Port Captain's speech. His reply was short and surprising to the Spanish officials.

"What salute?" he asked.

The Spaniards looked at each other with raised brows. It was odd that Captain Glass should ask such a question.

"The salute you fired," they responded together. "We should like to return it, and shall do so as soon as we can get a battery."

The puzzled look on the face of the American Captain faded into a suppressed smile as the meaning of the Spanish declaration dawned on him.

"Make no mistake, gentlemen," he said. "I fired no salute. We came here on a hostile errand. Our country is at war with yours. When I came in here I saw a fort and I fired a few small shells at it to unmask it and see if there was any response. When there was none I concluded it was unoccupied and ceased firing."

The Spaniards were astounded. This was their first intimation of the fact that war had been declared between the United States and Spain. They had not even known that the relations between the two countries were strained so as to approach the danger point. For a few moments the blunt announcement that war existed, and that this was a demonstration against them personally almost overcame them. They sat as if stupefied. When at length they recovered their composure they asked for more information. . . . Captain Glass quickly explained the cause of the delay of their mail boat. He told them of the battle in Manila Bay and the annihilation of the Spanish fleet by Dewey's squadron. It seemed as if it was impossible for the Spaniards to comprehend the magnitude of the disaster to their cause. They were very unhappy, but Portusac, the American citizen, had difficulty in keeping his politeness above his satisfaction and his amusement.

God instructs President McKinley to keep the Philippines, 1898

By the Teller Amendment of April 1898 the United States had pledged itself to acquire no Cuban territory from the conflict. This was to be a war of principle. But the treaty of peace signed in December 1898 gave Cuba—at least temporarily—as well as Puerto Rico and Guam to the United States. Moreover, for a consideration of $20,000,000, Spain also relinquished the Philippines. A war that Americans had precipitated and claimed to be fighting for the purest of motives, ended on an imperialistic note. President McKinley, speaking to a visiting group of Methodist clergymen, described how he prayed to God for guidance in the matter of the Philippines.

When next I realized that the Philippines had dropped into our laps I confess I did not know what to do with them. I sought counsel from all sides—Democrats as well as Republicans—but got little help. I thought first we would take only Manila; then Luzon; then other islands perhaps also.

I walked the floor of the White House night after night until midnight; and I am not ashamed to tell you, gentlemen, that I went down on my knees and prayed Almighty God for light and guidance more than one night. And one night late it came to me this way—I don't know how it was, but it came:

1. That we could not give them back to Spain—that would be cowardly and dishonorable;

2. That we could not turn them over to France or Germany—our commercial rivals in the Orient—that would be bad business and discreditable;

3. That we could not leave them to themselves—they were unfit for self-government—and they would soon have anarchy and misrule worse than Spain's *war;*

4. That there was nothing left for us to do but take them all, and to educate the Filipinos, and uplift and civilize and Christianize them as our fellow-men for whom Christ also died.

And then I went to bed and slept soundly, and the next morning I sent for the chief engineer of the War Department (our map-maker), and I told him to put the Philippines on the map of the United States (pointing to a large map on the wall of his office), and there they are, and there they will stay while I am President!

From Charles S. Olcott, *The Life of William McKinley* (Boston, 1916), Vol. II, pp. 110–11. Reprinted by permission of the publisher, Houghton Mifflin Co.

American military atrocities in the Philippines: testimony before a Senate committee, 1902

*A substantial number of Americans were opposed to the imperialistic route fol-
lowed by the United States government. Prominent men of both political parties
joined to form an Anti-Imperialist League which propagandized for "government by the consent of the governed." They particularly denounced the war
of subjugation in the Philippines. There Filipino insurgents, led by Emilio
Aguinaldo, fought as hard against their new American masters as they had
fought against the Spanish. The brutal methods practiced by the American
army were exposed by a Senate investigating committee.*

TESTIMONY OF BRIGADIER-GENERAL ROBERT P. HUGHES

SEN. RAWLINS: . . . [I]n burning towns, what would you do? Would
the entire town be destroyed by fire or would only offending portions of the
town be burned?

GEN. HUGHES: I do not know that we ever had a case of burning what
you would call a town in this country, but probably a barrio or a sitio;
probably half a dozen houses, native shacks, where the insurrectos would
go in and be concealed, and if they caught a detachment passing they would
kill some of them.

SEN. RAWLINS: What did I understand you to say would be the consequences of that?

GEN. HUGHES: They usually burned the village.

SEN. RAWLINS: All of the houses in the village?

GEN. HUGHES: Yes; every one of them.

SEN. RAWLINS: What would become of the inhabitants?

GEN. HUGHES: That was their lookout. . . .

SEN. RAWLINS: If these shacks were of no consequence what was the
utility of their destruction?

GEN. HUGHES: The destruction was as a punishment. They permitted
these people to come in there and conceal themselves and they gave no
sign. It is always—

SEN. RAWLINS: The punishment in that case would fall, not upon the
men, who could go elsewhere, but mainly upon the women and little
children.

GEN. HUGHES: The women and children are part of the family, and
where you wish to inflict a punishment you can punish the man probably
worse in that way than in any other.

SEN. RAWLINS: But is that within the ordinary rules of civilized war-

From Henry F. Graff (ed.), *American Imperialism and the Philippine Insurrection:
Testimony taken from Hearings on Affairs in the Philippine Islands before the Senate
Committee on the Philippines—1902* (Boston, Little, Brown and Co., 1969), pp.
64–65, 74–76. Reprinted by permission.

fare? Of course you could exterminate the family, which would be still worse punishment.

GEN. HUGHES: These people are not civilized.

TESTIMONY OF AN ENLISTED MAN, CHARLES S. RILEY

QUESTION: Did you pass up the stairway into the corridor above, that morning, and into the main hall?

ANSWER: Yes.

QUESTION: And as you passed up, you may state what you saw.

ANSWER: I saw the *presidente* standing in the—

QUESTION: Whom do you mean by the *presidente?*

ANSWER: The head official of the town.

QUESTION: The town of Igbaras?

ANSWER: Yes, sir.

QUESTION: A Filipino?

ANSWER: Yes, sir.

QUESTION: How old was he?

ANSWER: I should judge that he was a man of about forty or forty-five years.

QUESTION: When you saw him, what was his condition?

ANSWER: He was stripped to the waist; he had nothing on but a pair of white trousers, and his hands were tied behind him.

QUESTION: Do you remember who had charge of him?

ANSWER: Captain Glenn stood there beside him and one or two men were tying him.

QUESTION: You may state whether or not there was a water tank in the upper corridor.

ANSWER: Just at the head of the stairs on the right there was a large galvanized-iron tank, holding probably one hundred gallons, about two barrels. That was on a raised platform, about ten or twelve inches, I should think, and there was a faucet on the tank. It was the tank we used for catching rainwater for drinking purposes. . . .

QUESTION: What else did you observe being done with him?

ANSWER: He was then taken and placed under the tank, and the faucet was opened and a stream of water was forced down or allowed to run down his throat; his throat was held so he could not prevent swallowing water, so that he had to allow the water to run into his stomach.

QUESTION: What connection was there between the faucet and his mouth?

ANSWER: There was no connection; he was directly under the faucet.

QUESTION: Directly under the faucet?

ANSWER: Directly under the faucet and with his mouth held wide open.

QUESTION: Was anything done besides forcing his mouth open and allowing the water to run down?

ANSWER: When he was filled with water it was forced out of him by pressing a foot on his stomach or else with their hands. . . .

QUESTION: Did you observe whether the interpreter communicated with this *presidente?*

ANSWER: He did at different times. He practically kept talking to him all the time, kept saying some one word which I should judge means "confess" or "answer."

QUESTION: Could you understand what was said?

ANSWER: No, sir; I could not understand the native tongue at all.

QUESTION: At the conclusion, what then was done?

ANSWER: After he was willing to answer he was allowed to partly sit up, and kind of rolled on his side, and then he answered the questions put to him by the officer through the interpreter. . . .

QUESTION: Where did they take him?

ANSWER: They took him downstairs outside the building, and he stood in front of the building, waiting for his horse. He was to guide the expedition up into the mountains.

QUESTION: While standing on the sidewalk what took place?

ANSWER: More information was sought for; and as he refused to answer, a second treatment was ordered.

QUESTION: Where were you at that time?

ANSWER: I was in front of the building at the time, on the sidewalk.

QUESTION: In front?

ANSWER: Yes; on the stone walk. They started to take him inside the building and Captain Glenn said, "Don't take him inside. Right here is good enough." One of the men of the Eighteenth Infantry went to his saddle and took a syringe from the saddlebag, and another man was sent for a can of water, what we call a kerosene can, holding about five gallons. He brought this can of water down from upstairs, and then a syringe was inserted, one end in the water and the other end in his mouth. This time he was not bound, but he was held by four or five men and the water was forced into his mouth from the can, through the syringe.

SEN. BURROWS: Was this another party?

ANSWER: No; this was the same man. The syringe did not seem to have the desired effect, and the doctor ordered a second one. The man got a second syringe, and that was inserted in his nose. Then the doctor ordered some salt, and a handful of salt was procured and thrown into the water. Two syringes were then in operation. The interpreter stood over him in the meantime asking for this second information that was desired. Finally he gave in and gave the information that they sought, and then he was allowed to rise.

QUESTION: May I ask the name of the doctor?

ANSWER: Dr. Lyons, the contract surgeon.

QUESTION: An American?

ANSWER: Yes, sir.

W. E. Burghardt Du Bois answers Booker T.
Washington: from *The Souls of Black Folk*, 1903

W. E. B. Du Bois, who had earned a Doctorate in History from Harvard University, challenged Booker T. Washington's doctrine of accommodation and conciliation. Not for a moment, said Du Bois, should blacks surrender, even strategically, their insistence upon full equality. Washington had addressed his remarks primarily to whites; Du Bois spoke to blacks. The Souls of Black Folk, a Southern paper predicted, was "dangerous for the Negro to read, for it will only excite discontent and fill his imagination with things that do not exist, or things that should not bear upon his mind." Indeed it did. Du Bois's book became the bible of young black intellectuals long dissatisfied with Washington's philosophy.

Mr. Washington represents in Negro thought the old attitude of adjustment and submission; but adjustment at such a peculiar time as to make his programme unique. This is an age of unusual economic development, and Mr. Washington's programme naturally takes an economic cast, becoming a gospel of Work and Money to such an extent as apparently almost completely to overshadow the higher aims of life. Moreover, this is an age when the more advanced races are coming in closer contact with the less developed races, and the race-feeling is therefore intensified; and Mr. Washington's programme practically accepts the alleged inferiority of the Negro races. Again, in our own land, the reaction from the sentiment of war time has given impetus to race-prejudice against Negroes, and Mr. Washington withdraws many of the high demands of Negroes as men and American citizens. In other periods of intensified prejudice all the Negro's tendency to self-assertion has been called forth; at this period a policy of submission is advocated. In the history of nearly all other races and peoples the doctrine preached at such crises has been that manly self-respect is worth more than lands and houses, and that a people who voluntarily surrender such respect, or cease striving for it, are not worth civilizing.

In answer to this, it has been claimed that the Negro can survive only through submission. Mr. Washington distinctly asks that black people give up, at least for the present, three things:

First, political power,

Second, insistence on civil rights,

Third, higher education of Negro youth, and concentrate all their energies on industrial education, the accumulation of wealth, and the conciliation of the South. This policy has been courageously and insistently advocated for over fifteen years, and has been triumphant for perhaps ten years. . . .

From W. E. Burghardt Du Bois, *The Souls of Black Folk* (Chicago, 1903), pp. 50–51, 58–59.

His doctrine has tended to make the whites, North and South, shift the burden of the Negro problem to the Negro's shoulders and stand aside as critical and rather pessimistic spectators; when in fact the burden belongs to the nation, and the hands of none of us are clean if we bend not our energies to righting these great wrongs. The South ought to be led, by candid and honest criticism, to assert her better self and do her full duty to the race she has cruelly wronged and is still wronging. The North—her co-partner in guilt—cannot salve her conscience by plastering it with gold. We cannot settle this problem by diplomacy and suaveness, by "policy" alone. If worse come to worst, can the moral fibre of this country survive the slow throttling and murder of nine millions of men?

The black men of America have a duty to perform, a duty stern and delicate—a forward movement to oppose a part of the work of their greatest leader. So far as Mr. Washington preaches Thrift, Patience, and Individual Training for the masses, we must hold up his hands and strive with him, rejoicing in his honors and glorying in the strength of this Joshua called of God and of man to lead the headless host. But so far as Mr. Washington apologizes for injustice, North or South, does not rightly value the privilege and duty of voting, belittles the emasculating effects of caste distinctions, and opposes the higher training and ambition of our brighter minds—so far as he, the South, or the Nation, does this—we must unceasingly and firmly oppose them. By every civilized and peaceful method we must strive for the rights which the world accords to men, clinging unwaveringly to those great words which the sons of the Fathers would fain forget: "We hold these truths to be self-evident: That all men are created equal; that they are endowed by their Creator with certain unalienable rights; that among these are life, liberty, and the pursuit of happiness."

The philosophy of Theodore Roosevelt: from his letters of 1903–04

Many liberal Americans, according to a contemporary observer, "have been in a divided condition of minds towards Roosevelt. One day they love him and the next day they hate him." The same judgments of approval and dissent mark the writings of later scholars who have attempted to assess Roosevelt's role as President. In foreign affairs he practiced big-stick diplomacy, using whatever means were necessary to advance American interests. For those interests, he believed, benefited the whole world and were "in accord with the fundamental laws of righteousness." In domestic affairs, while his rhetoric frequently was radical, his actions were not. Roosevelt had a self-confessed "horror of extremes," preferring the middle way of compromise.

From Elting E. Morison (ed.), *The Letters of Theodore Roosevelt* (Cambridge, Mass.: Harvard University Press, 1951), Vol. III, pp. 662–63, 698–99, Vol. IV, p. 1023. Reprinted by permission.

ON PANAMA

To Otto Gresham   November 30, 1903

Panama revolted from Colombia because Colombia, for corrupt and evil purposes or else from complete governmental incompetency, declined to permit the building of the great work which meant everything to Panama. By every law, human and divine, Panama was right in her position. Now, how anyone can conceive that Colombia has the slightest right in the matter I do not understand. We have been more than just, have been generous to a fault, in our dealings with Colombia. It seems incredible to me that anyone could take the position which you speak of as being taken by some men, provided those men have either red blood or common sense in them. . . . On the score of morality it seems to me that nothing could be more wicked than to ask us to surrender the Panama people, who are our friends, to the Colombian people, who have shown themselves our foes; and this for no earthly reason save because we have, especially in New York City and parts of the Northeast, a small body of shrill eunuchs who consistently oppose the action of this government whenever that action is to its own interests, even though at the same time it may be immensely to the interest of the world, and in accord with the fundamental laws of righteousness—which is now a synonym for anemic weakness.

To Cecil Arthur Spring Rice   January 18, 1904

I have succeeded in accomplishing a certain amount which I think will stand. I believe I shall put through the Panama treaty (my worst foes being those in the Senate and not those outside the borders of the United States) and begin to dig the canal. It is always difficult for me to reason with those solemn creatures of imperfect aspirations after righteousness, who never take the trouble to go below names. These people scream about the injustices done Colombia when Panama was released from its domination, which is precisely like bemoaning the wrong done to Turkey when Herzegovina was handed over to Austria. It was a good thing for Egypt and the Sudan, and for the world, when England took Egypt and the Sudan. It is a good thing for India that England should control it. And so it is a good thing, a very good thing, for Cuba and for Panama, and for the world that the United States has acted as it has actually done during the last six years. The people of the United States and the people of the Isthmus and the rest of mankind will all be the better because we dig the Panama Canal and keep order in its neighborhood. And the politicians and revolutionists at Bogota are entitled to precisely the amount of sympathy we extend to other inefficient bandits.

ON LABOR AND CAPITAL

To Philander Chase Knox   **November 10, 1904**

More and more the labor movement in this country will become a factor of
vital importance, not merely in our social but in our political development.
If the attitude of the New York *Sun* toward labor, as toward the trusts,
becomes the attitude of the Republican party, we shall some day go down
before a radical and extreme democracy with a crash which will be disastrous to the Nation. We must not only do justice, but be able to show the
wageworkers that we are doing justice. We must make it evident that while
there is not any weakness in our attitude, while we unflinchingly demand
good conduct from them, yet we are equally resolute in the effort to secure
them all just and proper consideration. It would be a dreadful calamity if
we saw this country divided into two parties, one containing the bulk of
the property owners and conservative people, the other the bulk of the
wageworkers and the less prosperous people generally; each party insisting
upon demanding much that was wrong, and each party sullen and angered
by real and fancied grievances. The friends of property, of order, of law,
must never show weakness in the face of violence or wrong or injustice;
but on the other hand they must realize that the surest way to provoke an
explosion of wrong and injustice is to be shortsighted, narrow-minded,
greedy and arrogant, and to fail to show in actual work that here in this
republic it is peculiarly incumbent upon the man with whom things have
prospered to be in a certain sense the keeper of his brother with whom
life has gone hard.

The idea of conserving America's natural resources, 1909

*No one individual really "discovered" the idea of conservation, as Gifford Pinchot
claimed to have done in his autobiography,* Breaking New Ground, *published in
1947. Pinchot undoubtedly exaggerated his role in originating the conservation
movement; and yet no one did more than he to publicize it during the era of
Theodore Roosevelt. Until that time the abundance of natural resources had
been taken for granted. The wilderness was vast; waste appeared to be part of
the natural order of things; and exploitation of resources made little impact
upon the American mind. Gradually, however, through the work of men like
Pinchot, the public became aware of the need to preserve—as Pinchot wrote—
"for the benefit of the many, and not merely for the profit of a few."*

From a speech of Gifford Pinchot, Forester, United States Department of Agriculture,
Address and Proceedings of the First National Conservation Congress, 1909 (Washington, D.C., 1910), pp. 70–76.

The first thing to say about conservation [is that] it stands for development. There has been a fundamental misconception that conservation meant nothing but the husbanding of resources for future generations. There could be no more serious mistake. Conservation does mean provision for the future, but it means also and first of all the recognition of the right of the present generation to the fullest necessary use of all the resources that this country is so abundantly blessed with. It means the welfare of this generation and afterwards the welfare of the generation to follow.

The first principle of conservation is development, the use of the natural resources now existing on this continent for the benefit of the people who live here now. There may be just as much waste in neglecting the development and use of certain natural resources as there is in their destruction by waste. We have a limited supply of coal, and only a limited supply. Whether it is to last for a hundred or a hundred and fifty or a thousand years, the coal is limited in amount and except through geological changes which we can never see, there will never be any more of it than there is now. But coal is in a sense the vital essence of our civilization. If it can be preserved, if its life can be extended, if by preventing waste there can be more coal in this country when this generation is gone, after we have made every needed use of this source of power, then this country is just so much further ahead and the future so much the better off.

Conservation, then, stands emphatically for the use of substitutes for all the exhaustible natural resources, for the development and use of water power, and for the immediate development of water power as a substitute for coal. It stands for the immediate development of waterways under a broad and comprehensive plan as substitutes and assistants to the railroads. More coal and iron are required to move a ton of freight by rail than water, three to one. . . .

In the second place conservation stands for the prevention of waste. There has come gradually . . . in this country an understanding that waste is not a good thing and that the attack on waste is a necessary and possible attack. I recall very well indeed how, in the early days of forest fires, they were considered simply and solely as acts of God, against which any opposition was hopeless and any attempt to control them not merely hopeless but childish. It was assumed that they came in the natural order of things as inevitably as seasons or the rising and setting of the sun. Today we understand that forest fires are wholly within the control of human agency.

These conservation ideas cover a wider field than the field of natural resources alone. Conservation means the greatest good to the greatest number for the longest time. One of its great contributions is that it has added to the worn and well-known phrase, "the greatest good to the greatest number," the additional words, "for the longest time," thus recognizing that this nation of ours is to endure and shall endure in the best possible condition for all its people. Conservation advocates the use of foresight, prudence, thrift, and intelligence in dealing with public matters, for the same reasons and in the same way we use foresight, prudence, thrift, and intelligence in dealing with our own affairs. It proclaims the right and duty of the people to act for the benefit of the people. Conservation demands the application of common sense to the common problems for the common good.

The principles of conservation thus described have a general application which is growing wider and wider every day. The development of resources and the prevention of waste and loss, the protection of the public interests by foresight, prudence, and the ordinary business and home-making virtues, all these apply to other things as well as to the conservation resources. There is no interest of the people to which the principles of conservation do not apply.

The conservation point of view is valuable for education as well as in forestry; it applies to the body politic as well as to the earth and its minerals. A municipal franchise is as properly within its sphere as a franchise for water power. The same point of view governs in both. It applies as much to the subject of good roads as to waterways, and the training of our people in citizenship is as germane to it as to the productiveness of the earth. The application of common sense to any problem for the Nation's good, will lead directly to national efficiency wherever applied. In other words . . . we are coming to see that it is the logical and inevitable outcome, that these principles, which arose in forestry, and have their bloom in the conservation of natural resources, will have their fruit in the increase and promotion of national efficiency along other lines of national life.

The outcome of conservation, the inevitable outcome, is national efficiency. In the great commercial struggle between nations which is eventually to determine the welfare of all, national efficiency will be the deciding factor. So from every point of view conservation is a good thing for the American people. . . .

We are coming to be in a position more and more completely to say how much waste and destruction of natural resources is to be allowed to go on and where it is to stop. It is curious that the effort to stop waste, like the effort to stop forest fires, has often been considered as a matter controlled wholly by economic law. I think there could be no greater mistake. Forest fires were allowed to burn long after the people had means to stop them. The idea that men were helpless in the face of them held long after the time had passed when the means of control were fully within our reach. It was the old story that "as a man thinketh so is he"; we came to see that we could stop forest fires and we found the means at hand. When we came to see the control of logging in certain directions was profitable, we found it had long been possible. In all these matters of waste of natural resources, the education of the people to understand that they can stop these things comes before the actual stopping, and after the means of stopping them have long been ready at our hands.

There is a third principle about which I want to say a word. . . . It is this: the natural resources must be developed and preserved for the benefit of the many and not merely for the profit of a few. We are coming to understand in this country, as I have had occasion to say more than once, that public action for public benefit has a very much wider field and a much larger part to play than was the case when there were resources enough for everyone and before certain constitutional arrangements in this country of ours had given so tremendously strong a position to vested rights and property in general. . . . By reason of the fourteenth amendment to the Constitution, property rights in the United States occupy a stronger position than in any other country in the civilized world. . . . It becomes then a matter of multiplied importance, of a thousandfold importance, if you like, to see, when property rights once granted are so strongly entrenched, that they shall be granted only under such conditions as that the people shall get their fair share of the benefit which comes from the development of the country which belongs to us all. The time to do that is now. By so doing we shall avoid difficulties and conflicts which will surely arise if we allow vested rights to accrue outside the possibility of government and popular control.

The revolt of Republican progressives against the administration of William Howard Taft, 1910

William Howard Taft was not the complete bad-man progressive Republicans depicted. He did as much as Roosevelt in the field of conservation. In fact, he was the first to reserve federal lands upon which oil had been discovered. His administration was responsible for the Mann-Elkins Act which strengthened federal control of railroads. And under his direction the federal government instituted almost twice the number of proceedings against industrial trusts that Roosevelt had launched. Nevertheless, to progressive Republicans his administration was a catastrophe. Taft endorsed the conservative Speaker of the House, Joseph Cannon of Illinois, despite the protests of Republican reformers who favored George Norris of Nebraska. He signed the Payne-Aldrich tariff, contrary to his campaign promises, and audaciously called it "the best tariff the Republican party ever passed." And he further alienated the progressives by dismissing Gifford Pinchot—deservedly so—who had accused Secretary of the Interior Richard Ballinger of corruptly disposing of national lands to a Morgan-Guggenheim syndicate. The following article, by the brother of Gifford Pinchot, appeared in the muckraking journal McClure's Magazine.

No party ever began an administration with clearer principles and a greater public service to perform than the party of Taft. The whole country, Democrats and Republicans alike, was impatient to help some one to drive the trusts out of politics. No party since 1860 has had such an opportunity to combine service to the party with service to the country. No party in our political history has so completely failed to justify the hope of the people. Restoration of government by the majority, reduction of tariff, and a vigorous prosecution of the conservation program of the last administration were three things demanded by the country. If, after the election, the

From Amos Pinchot, "Two Revolts Against Oligarchy: The Insurgent Movements of the Fifties and Today," *McClure's Magazine*, Vol. XXXV, September 1910, pp. 588–90.

Regular party leaders had kept faith, if they had shown that they considered driving the trusts out of politics, tariff reduction, and conservation something more than mere catchwords of campaign oratory, there would have been no divided party today. If they had evinced a real purpose to reduce the tariff in spite of the special interests in the East and to save the people's domain in spite of the special interests in the West, and if they had made a real effort to drive the trusts and railroads out of politics both in the East and the West, there never would have arisen an insurgent element to vex the Republican reactionaries, just as the insurgent element fifty years ago vexed the reactionary Whigs.

But at the very beginning of the Taft administration a series of reactionary events took place which goaded the progressives into open revolt. First, the so-called Morgan-Guggenheim Syndicate—perhaps the most powerful combination of capital in the United States—needed a Secretary of the Interior indifferent to conservation and favorable to opening up the West, and especially Alaska coal deposits, to indiscriminate exploitation. Mr. Ballinger was appointed.

Second, the President chose a Cabinet of trust lawyers.

Third, the President publicly named as his adviser on tariff questions, and as the mentor of the administration, Senator Aldrich, the most powerful enemy of downward revision and the most conspicuous and effective ally of corporate wealth that has ever occupied a seat in the Senate of the United States.

Fourth, the administration endorsed the Payne-Aldrich Tariff Bill as a fit and proper redemption of campaign pledges, although it was practically an upward revision.

Fifth, the Republican leaders drew and presented to Congress a number of bills that were more favorable to the special interests than to the people. Among them was a railroad bill which, if passed as written, would virtually have repealed the Sherman Anti-Trust Law and discouraged competition by effectually preventing any new company from laying a mile of track in the United States. Conservation bills drawn by the Secretary of the Interior were presented which were, on the whole, vastly more favorable to exploitation than conservation.

Sixth, by the dismissal of public servants because they placed loyalty to the government and the people above loyalty to employers higher up, the administration promulgated the doctrine that where the interests of the government and the interests of an official superior clash, the subordinate must side with the latter.

Seventh, the administration has not realized that the people have a right to know how the government is conducted, and has tried to smother scandals in high places instead of investigating them.

Eighth, and last, but most important of all, the administration and its body-guard of reactionaries failed to read the signs of the times, and consistently refused to recognize the great progressive movement that sprang from the awakening of the public conscience.

By these effective means Mr. Taft and his advisers have aroused a deep-seated national anxiety, split the party, and established a progressive and aggressive wing known as the Insurgents. I speak with little fear of contradiction when I say that during the last year the Regulars of the administration and of Congress have dealt Republicanism the heaviest blows it has received since the days of its birth. They have set up false standards of party loyalty and official loyalty; they have persuaded the people that truth must be subordinated to party advantage; by concealment they have aroused the suspicion of the country; they have weakened the respect of the people for the government of the United States; they have reduced the Republican party to an organization whose only issue with the Democratic party is the question of which shall hold office; and they have done their best to check the advance of a great progressive movement.

The Insurgents are the true Republicans of today, for they represent the principles and ideals of the Republican party which the Regulars have repudiated. A political party or a public man is useful to his country in proportion to his success in fighting for better conditions of daily life for the whole people of the country. History proves that no cause other than the people's cause is worth fighting for. It is no exaggeration to say that, when the Republican leaders abandoned this cause, a spirit of confusion entered into them, and they ran down a steep place into the sea. From that day all hope in Republicanism as a power for good centered in the Insurgents. They became the real representatives of the progressive party, and the leaders of the progressive movement which Theodore Roosevelt initiated and led. . . . The most extraordinary hold which Theodore Roosevelt has upon the people of the United States has been due to their deep conviction that he is with them, heart and soul, in the great human task of social improvement. Mr. Roosevelt has neither piloted the country through a great crisis nor carried to the end a definite constructive program. His one impressive act of constructive statesmanship, the conservation policy, was hardly more than well begun before his administration ended. But, on the other hand, he has two great qualities—an instinctive faculty of understanding the needs and aspirations of the people, and the courage and spiritual intensity to fight for them.

Whom to support in 1912? The dilemma of a progressive, from the letters of Brand Whitlock, 1911–12

In 1912 the voters had four choices. Conservatives favored the Republican candidate, William Howard Taft, who had become more and more identified as a defender of American business interests. Radicals, dissatisfied with piecemeal reforms, favored the Socialist party candidate, Eugene V. Debs. This

From Allan Nevins (ed.), *The Letters of Brand Whitlock* (New York: Appleton-Century-Crofts, 1936), pp. 152–54, 156. Reprinted by permission.

left a vast number of liberal reformers and progressives to choose between Theodore Roosevelt, candidate of the Progressive "bull moose" party, and Woodrow Wilson, Democratic party nominee. Brand Whitlock, Mayor of Toledo at the time, wavered between the two. Many of his friends were climbing on the "bull moose" bandwagon, a movement "so young and so enthusiastic and so idealistic in all of its expressions that . . . it might afford congenial company." In the end, however, Whitlock supported Wilson, who received 6,300,000 votes compared to Roosevelt's 4,100,000. Taft ran a poor third, and Debs—with 900,000 votes—last.

To Major David Jewett Baker, Jr.   December 5, 1911

You would laugh if you were in this country now and were to see how the standpatters are trying to bring [Theodore Roosevelt] out as a candidate for President again, in order to head off La Follette, who is a very dangerous antagonist to Taft. Poor Taft! He has made so many blunders, the last of which is an interview in the *Outlook* in which he makes humiliating confessions of his own weaknesses and shortcomings, and of some of the failures of his Administration.

To Albert Jay Nock   August 17, 1912

I wish you would write me what you think about the Bull Moose party; so many of my friends are going into it because of its social program that I feel like doing so myself even if I did congratulate Governor Wilson and tell him I would vote for him. The whole thing is so young and so enthusiastic and so idealistic in all of its expressions that, notwithstanding the dubiety of some of the impressions concerning T.R., it might afford congenial company. Wilson seems to be piping a very low note; or trying to conciliate the reactionaries in his party, when he ought to know that you can conciliate privilege only by surrendering abjectly to it, and I am afraid that this course in that regard will weaken all of his influence for good.

To Marshall Sheppey   September 20, 1912

With the election seven weeks away, it seems that Wilson is certain of victory, with Taft a poor third. Roosevelt is exceedingly strong in the west, but not strong enough I think, to be elected. Of course, if the campaign warms up from now on, this prediction may be set entirely at naught. I think that old standpat Republican editor in Vermont expressed the situation pretty well when he said the other day: "Vote for Taft, pray for Roosevelt, and bet on Wilson." Of course, I agree with him only so far as his advice on the betting is concerned.

To Newton D. Baker   **September 28, 1912**

I was of course impressed by the enthusiasm with which the Progressive cause was launched, and I like the social program which it put forth; to that extent the movement gave expression to a beautiful sentiment in this land, which you and I have been trying to make concrete in our cities for many years. But that sentiment did not get itself fully, or adequately, expressed in the movement, and now it seems to have fallen back into the old partisan spirit, which is the very antithesis of that sentiment. If Governor Wilson had not been nominated at Baltimore, we should have had a new liberal party in this country, and the alignment at last would have been clear. But in his personality Governor Wilson himself wholly satisfies and sums up that democratic spirit which means everything to you and me, and it is personality that counts, that tells, more than creeds or platforms. Governor Wilson's ability, his services, his mastery of himself and of affairs, his imagination, his literary ability, his sense of humor, all those qualities combine to endow him with a rare culture, and his character is the best platform. And then, of course, I could not follow the Progressive party into the camp of protection; it seems absurd to launch a movement against privilege, and then propose a continuance of that very policy which is the parent of all privilege.

To Woodrow Wilson   **October 7, 1912**

I am leaving today for Europe, and I shall not be back until the election is over. . . . My one regret is that I shall not be here on election day to vote for you. . . . You are, of course, elected now. The whole sweep of sentiment is toward you, as well it might be for many reasons, not least among them, the dignified and sincere campaign you have made. Let me congratulate you now, as I shall do in November.

The Tampico incident: Woodrow Wilson's "moral" diplomacy in action, April 20, 1914

The reasoning behind Woodrow Wilson's new "moral" diplomacy was radically different from that of Theodore Roosevelt's "big-stick" or William Howard Taft's "dollar" diplomacy: but its application in Latin America had the same effect of leaving a festering legacy of distrust and bitterness. Wilson was anxious to spread American ideals of freedom and democracy south of the border; because of that anxiety he intervened on an unprecedented scale in the internal affairs of several Caribbean nations. His particular bête noire was the brutal General Victoriano Huerta, President of Mexico, an unscrupulous man who had

From Woodrow Wilson's address to Congress, April 20, 1914, *Foreign Relations of the United States, 1914* (Washington, D.C., 1922), pp. 474–76.

seized power after assassinating his predecessor. Wilson admired Huerta's "in-domitable, dogged determination," but he refused to accord American recog-nition to any government which had attained power by force and violence. Nonrecognition, of course, was a form of interference in Mexico's internal affairs, and a clear departure from the historic American practice of recognizing every legitimate government. However, when such methods proved insufficient to oust Huerta, Wilson employed a Rooseveltian tactic. Using the flimsy excuse of a minor insult to the flag in Tampico, Wilson asked Congress for authority to use military force on April 20, 1914.

On April 9, a Paymaster of the U.S.S. *Dolphin* landed at the Iturbide bridge-landing, at Tampico, with a whaleboat and boat's crew to take off certain supplies needed by his ship, and while engaged in loading the boat was arrested by an officer and squad of men of the army of General Huerta. Neither the Paymaster nor any of the crew was armed. Two of the men were in the boat when the arrest took place, and were obliged to leave it and submit to be taken into custody, notwithstanding that the boat carried, both at her bow and at her stern, the flag of the United States. The officer who made the arrest was proceeding up one of the streets of the town with his prisoners when met by an officer of higher authority, who ordered him to return to the landing and await orders, and within an hour and a half from the time of the arrest, orders were received from the commander of the Huertista forces at Tampico for the release of the Paymaster and his men. The release was followed by apologies from the commander and also by an expression of regret by General Huerta himself. General Huerta urged that martial law obtained at the time at Tampico, that orders had been issued that no one should be allowed to land at the Iturbide bridge, and that our sailors had no right to land there. Our naval commanders at the port had not been notified of any such prohibition, and, even if they had been, the only justifiable course open to the local authorities would have been to request the Paymaster and his crew to withdraw and to lodge a protest with the commanding officer of the fleet. Admiral Mayo regarded the arrest as so serious an affront that he was not satisfied with the apologies offered, but demanded that the flag of the United States be saluted with special ceremony by the military commander of the port.

The incident can not be regarded as a trivial one, especially as two of the men arrested were taken from the boat itself—that is to say from the territory of the United States; but had it stood by itself, it might have been attributed to the ignorance or arrogance of a single officer. Unfortunately, it was not an isolated case. A series of incidents have recently occurred which cannot but create the impression that the representatives of General Huerta were willing to go out of their way to show disregard for the dignity and rights of this Government, and felt perfectly safe in doing what they pleased, making free to show in many ways their irritation and contempt. . . . So far as I can learn, such wrongs and annoyances have been suffered to occur only against representatives of the United States. I have heard of no complaints from other governments of similar treatment. Subsequent explanations and formal apologies did not and could not alter the popular impression, which it is possible it had been the object of the Huertista authorities to create, that the Government of the United States was being singled out, and might be singled out with impunity, for slights and affronts in retaliation for its refusal to recognize the pretensions of General Huerta to be regarded as the Constitutional Provisional President of the Republic of Mexico. . . .

It was necessary that the apologies of General Huerta and his representatives should go much further, that they should be such as to attract the attention of the whole population to their significance, and such as to impress upon General Huerta himself the necessity of seeing to it that no further occasion for explanations and professed regrets should arise. I, therefore, felt it my duty to sustain Admiral Mayo in the whole of his demand and to insist that the flag of the United States should be saluted in such a way as to indicate a new spirit and attitude on the part of the Huertistas.

Such a salute General Huerta has refused, and I have come to ask your approval and support in the course I now purpose to pursue. This Government can, I earnestly hope, in no circumstances be forced into war with the people of Mexico. Mexico is torn by civil strife. If we are to accept the tests of its own Constitution, it has no government. General Huerta has set his power up in the City of Mexico, such as it is, without right and by methods for which there can be no justification. Only part of the country is under his control.

If armed conflict should unhappily come as a result of his attitude of personal resentment toward this Government, we should be fighting only General Huerta and those who adhere to him and give him their support, and our object would be only to restore to the people of the distracted republic the opportunity to set up again their own laws and their own government. But I earnestly hope that war is not now in question. I believe that I speak for the American people when I say that we do not desire to control in any degree the affairs of our sister republic. Our feeling for the people of Mexico is one of deep and genuine friendship, and everything that we have so far done or refrained from doing has proceeded from our desire to help them, not to hinder or embarrass them. We would not wish even to exercise the good offices of friendship without their welcome and consent. The people of Mexico are entitled to settle their own domestic affairs in their own way, and we sincerely desire to respect their right. The present situation need have none of the grave complications of interference if we deal with it promptly, firmly, and wisely. . . .

I therefore come to ask your approval that I should use the armed forces of the United States in ways and to such an extent as may be necessary to obtain from General Huerta and his adherents the fullest recognition of the rights and dignity of the United States, even amid the distressing conditions now unhappily obtaining in Mexico. There can in what we do be no thought of aggression or of selfish aggrandizement. We seek to maintain the dignity and authority of the United States only because we wish always to keep our great influence unimpaired for the uses of liberty, both in the United States and wherever else it may be employed for the benefit of mankind.

Senator George Norris of Nebraska opposes American entrance to World War I, April 4, 1917

The same moral fervor which marked Wilson's course in the Caribbean was apparent three years later when he asked Congress for a declaration of war upon Germany. "We desire no conquest, no dominion," he said on April 2, 1917. "We seek no indemnities for ourselves, no material compensation for the sacrifices we shall freely make. We are but one of the champions of the rights of mankind." Several congressmen delivered impassioned rebuttals. (Six senators and fifty representatives voted against the declaration of war). Senator George Norris's anti-war address was particularly notable.

I have no doubt but that in a great many instances, through what I believe to be a misunderstanding of the real condition, there are many honest, patriotic citizens who think we ought to engage in this war and who are behind the President in his demand that we should declare war against Germany. I think such people err in judgment and to a great extent have been misled as to the real history and the true facts by the almost unanimous demand of the great combination of wealth that has a direct financial interest in our participation in the war. We have loaned many hundreds of millions of dollars to the allies in this controversy. While such action was legal and countenanced by international law, there is no doubt in my mind but the enormous amount of money loaned to the allies in this country has been instrumental in bringing about a public sentiment in favor of our country taking a course that would make every bond worth a hundred cents on the dollar and making the payment of every debt certain and sure. Through this instrumentality and also through the instrumentality of others who have not only made millions out of the war in the manufacture of munitions, etc., and who would expect to make millions more if our country can be drawn into the catastrophe, a large number of the great newspapers and news agencies of the country have been controlled and enlisted in the greatest propaganda that the world has ever known, to manufacture sentiment in favor of war. It is now demanded that the American citizens shall be used as insurance policies to guarantee the safe delivery of munitions of war to belligerent nations. The enormous profits of munition

From a speech of Senator George Norris, April 4, 1917, *Congressional Record*, Sixty-fifth Congress, First Session, pp. 213–14.

manufacturers, stockbrokers, and bond dealers must be still further increased by our entrance into the war. This has brought us to the present moment, when Congress, urged by the President and backed by the artificial sentiment, is about to declare war and engulf our country in the greatest holocaust that the world has ever known. . . .

Their object in having war and in preparing for war is to make money. Human suffering and the sacrifice of human life are necessary, but Wall Street considers only the dollars and the cents. The men who do the fighting, the people who make the sacrifices, are the ones who will not be counted in the measure of this great prosperity that he depicts. The stock brokers would not, of course, go to war, because the very object they have in bringing on the war is profit, and therefore they must remain in their Wall Street offices in order to share in that great prosperity which they say war will bring. The volunteer officer, even the drafting officer will not find them. They will be concealed in their palatial offices on Wall Street, sitting behind mahogany desks, covered up with clipped coupons—coupons soiled with the sweat of honest toil, coupons stained with mothers' tears, coupons dyed in the lifeblood of their fellow men.

We are taking a step today that is fraught with untold danger. We are going into war upon the command of gold. We are going to run the risk of sacrificing millions of our countrymen's lives in order that other countrymen may coin their lifeblood into money. And even if we do not cross the Atlantic and go into the trenches, we are going to pile up a debt that the toiling masses that shall come many generations after us will have to pay. Unborn millions will bend their backs in toil in order to pay for the terrible step we are now about to take. We are about to do the bidding of wealth's terrible mandate. By our act we will make millions of our countrymen suffer, and the consequences of it may well be that millions of our brethren must shed their lifeblood, millions of broken-hearted women must weep, millions of children must suffer with cold, and millions of babes must die from hunger, and all because we want to preserve the commercial right of American citizens to deliver munitions of war to belligerent nations.

I know that I am powerless to stop it. I know that this war madness has taken possession of the financial and political powers of our country. I know that nothing I can say will stay the blow that is soon to fall. I feel that we are committing a sin against humanity and against our countrymen. I would like to say to this war god, You shall not coin into gold the lifeblood of my brethren. I would like to prevent this terrible catastrophe from falling upon my people. I would be willing to surrender my own life if I could cause this awful cup to pass. I charge no man here with a wrong motive, but it seems to me that this war craze has robbed us of our judgment. I wish we might delay our action until reason could again be enthroned in the brain of man. I feel that we are about to put the dollar sign upon the American flag.

The conscientious objector in World War I, 1917

Theodore Roosevelt's hatred for Woodrow Wilson bordered on the psycho-pathic. Nevertheless, he applauded Wilson's war message as "literally un-answerable," and begged for permission to lead a division of infantry—a request the government refused. Four of Roosevelt's children fought with the American forces, however, and one was killed in an aerial battle behind German lines. Roosevelt's tribute to his son was written with obvious pride and feeling: "Only those are fit to live who do not fear to die; and none are fit to die who have shrunk from the joy of life." Roosevelt was a "hawk," a simple straight-forward patriot who could not understand, let alone appreciate, the reasoning of those who refused to fight. The first selection is Roosevelt's attack on conscientious objectors; the second is a statement by Carl Haessler, a former Rhodes scholar and professor of philosophy, on why he could not participate in what he believed was a capitalist and a nationalist war.

THEODORE ROOSEVELT ON CONSCIENTIOUS OBJECTORS

It is certain that only a small fraction of the men who call themselves conscientious objectors . . . are actuated in any way by conscience. The bulk are slackers, pure and simple, or else traitorous pro-Germans. Some are actu-ated by lazy desire to avoid any duty that interferes with their ease and enjoyment, some by the evil desire to damage the United States and help Germany, some by sheer, simple, physical timidity. In the aggregate, the men of this type constitute the great majority of the men who claim to be conscientious objectors, and this fact must be remembered in endeavoring to deal with this class.

In some of our big cities, since the war began, men have formed vege-tarian societies, claiming to be exempt from service on the ground that they object to killing not merely men, but chickens. Others among the leading apostles of applied pacificism are not timid men; on the contrary they are brutal, violent men, who are perfectly willing to fight, but only for them-selves and not for the nation. These rough-neck pacifists have always been the potent allies of the parlor or milk-and-water pacifists; although they stand at the opposite end of the developmental scale. The parlor pacifist, the white-handed or sissy type of pacifist, represents decadence, represents the rotting out of the virile virtues among people who typify the unlovely senile side of civilization. The rough-neck pacifist, on the contrary, is a mere belated savage, who has not been educated to the virtues of national patriotism, and of willingness to fight for the national flag and the national ideal. . . . There remains the pacifist, the conscientious objector, who really does conscientiously object to war and who is sincere about it. As regards

From Theodore Roosevelt, *The Foes of Our Own Household* (New York, 1917), pp. 287–92. Reprinted by permission of the Theodore Roosevelt Association.

these men we must discriminate sharply between the men deeply opposed
to war so long as it is possible honorably to avoid it, who are ardent lovers
of peace, but who put righteousness above peace; and the other men who,
however sincerely, put peace above righteousness, and hereby serve the
Devil against the Lord.

The first attitude is that of great numbers of the Society of Friends
who in this war behave as so very many of the Friends did in the Civil War;
as that great English Quaker statesman, John Bright, lover of freedom and
righteousness, behaved in the Civil War. I wish all good American peace
lovers would read the recent address delivered by Professor Albert C.
Thatcher of Swarthmore, and signed by some scores of the Society of
Friends. He shows that in the Civil War it is probable that their branch of
the Society of Friends furnished more soldiers in proportion to their numbers than any other denomination. Liberty was part of their religion. They
not only fought, but they insisted that the war should go on, at whatever
cost, until it was crowned by complete victory. John Bright said, in speaking
of the pacifists who in the time of the Civil War wanted peace without victory: "I want no end of the war, and no compromise, and no re-union, 'till
the negro is made free beyond all chance of failure." He was for peace, but
he was not for peace at the price of slavery. In the same way now, the best
and most high-minded Friends, and lovers of peace in this country, are for
peace, but only as the result of the complete overthrow of the barbarous
Prussian militarism which now is Germany, and the existence of which is a
perpetual menace to our own country and to all mankind. The Friends and
peace lovers of this type are among the very best citizens of this country.
They abhor war; but there are things they abhor even more. Every good
citizen will support them in their opposition to wanton or unjust war, to any
war entered into save from the sternest sense of duty.

The peace people of the directly opposite type include the men who
conscientiously object to all participation in any war however brutal the
opponents, and however vital triumph may be to us and to mankind. These
persons are entitled to precisely the respect we give any other persons
whose conscience makes them do what is bad. We have had in this country
some conscientious polygamists. We now have some conscientious objectors
to taking part in this war. Where both are equally conscientious, the
former are, on the whole, not as bad citizens as the latter. Of course, if
these conscientious objectors are sincere they decline in private life to
oppose violence or brutality or to take advantage of the courage and
strength of those who do oppose violence and brutality. If these men are
sincere they will refuse to interfere (for moral suasion is not interference)
with a white-slaver who runs off with one of their daughters or a black-
hander who kidnaps and tortures a little child or a ruffian who slaps the
wife or mother of one of them in the face. They are utterly insincere unless
they decline to take advantage of police protection from burglary or highway robbery. Of course if such a man is really conscientious he cannot
profit or allow his family to profit in any way by the safety secured to him

and them by others, by soldiers in time of war, by judges and policemen in time of peace; for the receiver is as bad as the thief. I hold that such an attitude is infamous; and it is just as infamous to refuse to serve the country in arms during this war. If a man's conscience bids him so to act, then his conscience is a fit subject for the student of morbid pathology.

If a man does not wish to take life, but does wish to serve his country, let him serve on board a mine-sweeper or in some other position where the danger is to his own life and not to the life of any one else. But if he will take no useful and efficient part in helping in this war, in running his share of the common risk, and doing his part of the common duty, then treat him as having forfeited his right to vote. He has no right to help render at the polls any decision which in the long run can only be made good in the face of brutal and hostile men by the ability and willingness of good citizens to back right with might. The case has been admirably put by the Methodist Bishop, R. J. Cooke, of Helena, Montana. He points out that the vast majority of these conscientious objectors do not object to receiving the benefits from the suffering, hardships and deaths of other men; they only object to doing anything in return. Such a conscientious objector gives no service in return for the value he receives. He claims citizenship, but will not perform the duty of a citizen. Now, he has no moral right to take such a twofold position. "If any man will not work, neither shall he eat." If his conscience forbids him to work, do not violate his conscience, but refuse to feed him at the expense of somebody with a healthy conscience which does not forbid work. Service to the nation in war stands precisely on a footing with any other service. If a man will not perform it, let him lose all the benefits of war; and therefore let him lose the political rights which a free country can keep only if its free citizens are willing to fight for them. Respect the conscientious objector's opinions, but let him abide by the full consequences of his opinions. Universal suffrage can be justified only if it rests on universal service. We stand against all privilege not based on the full performance of duty; and there is no more contemptible form of privilege than the privilege of existing in smug, self-righteous, peaceful safety because other, braver, more self-sacrificing men give up safety and go to war to preserve the nation.

STATEMENT BY CARL HAESSLER

I, Carl Haessler, Recruit, Machine Gun Company, 46th Infantry, respectfully submit the following statement. . . . The willful disobedience of my Captain's and of my Lieutenant-Colonel's orders to report in military uniform arose from a conviction which I hesitate to express before my country's military officers but which I nevertheless am at present unable to shake off, namely, that America's participation in the World War was

Reprinted in Norman Thomas, *The Conscientious Objector in America* (New York, 1923), pp. 23–25.

unnecessary, of doubtful benefit (if any) to the country and to humanity, and accomplished largely, though not exclusively, through the pressure of the Allied and American commercial imperialists.

Holding this conviction, I conceived my part as a citizen to be opposition to the war before it was declared, active efforts for a peace without victory after the declaration, and a determination so far as possible to do nothing in aid of the war while its character seemed to remain what I thought it was. I hoped in this way to help bring the war to an earlier close and to help make similar future wars less probable in this country. I further believe that I shall be rendering the country a service by helping to set an example for other citizens to follow in the matter of fearlessly acting on unpopular convictions instead of forgetting them in time of stress. The crumbling of American radicalism under pressure in 1917 has only been equalled by that of the majority of German socialist leaders in August 1914.

Looking at my case from the point of view of the administration and of this court, I readily admit the necessity of exemplary punishment. I regret that I have been forced to make myself a nuisance and I grant that this war could not be carried on if objections like mine were recognized by those conducting the war. My respect for the administration has been greatly increased by the courteous and forbearing treatment accorded me since having been drafted, but my view of international politics and diplomacy, acquired during my three years of graduate study in England, has not altered since June 1917, when I formally declared that I could not accept service if drafted. Although officers have on three occasions offered me noncombatant service if I would put on the uniform, I have regretfully refused each time on the ground that "bomb-proof" service on my part would give the lie to my sincerity. . . . If I am to render any war services, I shall not ask for special privileges.

I wish to conclude this long statement by reiterating that I am not a pacifist or pro-German, not a religious or private objector, but regard myself as a patriotic political objector, acting largely from public and social grounds. I regret that, while my present view of this war continues, I cannot freely render any service in aid of the war. I shall not complain about the punishment that this court may see fit to mete out to me.

Woodrow Wilson's "Fourteen Points," January 8, 1918

If American military aid was necessary to win the war against Germanic despotism, Wilson believed, so American morality was necessary to fashion a just peace and create a stable world order. The "Fourteen Points" which he outlined to a joint session of Congress on January 8, 1918, became one of the major propaganda weapons of the war. Instead of a peace based on secret treaties, on economic privilege, on territorial expansion, and on vengeance, Wilson spoke of

From Woodrow Wilson's address to Congress, January 8, 1918, *Congressional Record*, Sixty-fifth Congress, Second Session, pp. 680–81.

a liberal and democratic settlement fashioned in a spirit of toleration and mag-
nanimity. Almost overnight, as news of his war aims spread, Wilson became a
hero to millions of war-weary Europeans. But European leaders remained skep-
tical. "President Wilson and his Fourteen Points bore me," said the French
leader, Clemenceau. "Even God Almighty has only ten."

We entered this war because violations of right had occurred which touched us to the quick and made the life of our own people impossible unless they were corrected and the world secured once for all against their recurrence. What we demand in this war, therefore, is nothing peculiar to ourselves. It is that the world be made fit and safe to live in; and particularly that it be made safe for every peace-loving nation which, like our own, wishes to live its own life, determine its own institutions, be assured of justice and fair dealing by the other peoples of the world as against force and selfish aggression. All the peoples of the world are in effect partners in this interest, and for our own part we see very clearly that unless justice be done to others it will not be done to us. The program of the world's peace, therefore, is our program; and that program, the only possible program, as we see it, is this:

I. Open covenants of peace, openly arrived at, after which there shall be no private international understandings of any kind, but diplomacy shall proceed always frankly and in the public view.

II. Absolute freedom of navigation upon the seas, outside territorial waters, alike in peace and in war, except as the seas may be closed in whole or in part by international action for the enforcement of international covenants.

III. The removal, so far as possible, of all economic barriers and the establishment of an equality of trade conditions among all the nations consenting to the peace and associating themselves for its maintenance.

IV. Adequate guarantees given and taken that national armaments will be reduced to the lowest point consistent with domestic safety.

V. A free, open-minded, and absolutely impartial adjustment of all colonial claims, based upon a strict observance of the principle that in determining all such questions of sovereignty the interests of the populations concerned must have equal weight with the equitable claims of the government whose title is to be determined.

VI. The evacuation of all Russian territory and such a settlement of all questions affecting Russia as will secure the best and freest cooperation of the other nations of the world in obtaining for her an unhampered and unembarrassed opportunity for the independent determination of her own political development and national policy and assure her of a sincere welcome into the society of free nations under institutions of her own choosing; and, more than a welcome, assistance also of every kind that she may need and may herself desire. The treatment accorded Russia by her sister nations in the months to come will be the acid test of their good will, of their comprehension of her needs as distinguished from their interests, and of their intelligent and unselfish sympathy.

VII. Belgium, the whole world will agree, must be evacuated and restored, without any attempt to limit the sovereignty which she enjoys in common with all other free nations. No other single act will serve as this will serve to restore confidence among the nations in the laws which they have themselves set and determined for the government of their relations with one another. Without this healing act the whole structure and validity of international law is forever impaired.

VIII. All French territory should be freed and the invaded portions restored, and the wrong done to France by Prussia in 1871 in the matter of Alsace-Lorraine, which has unsettled the peace of the world for nearly fifty years, should be righted, in order that peace may once more be made secure in the interest of all.

IX. A readjustment of the frontiers of Italy should be effected along clearly recognizable lines of nationality.

X. The peoples of Austria-Hungary, whose place among the nations we wish to see safeguarded and assured, should be accorded the freest opportunity of autonomous development.

XI. Rumania, Serbia, and Montenegro should be evacuated; occupied territories restored; Serbia accorded free and secure access to the sea; and the relations of the several Balkan states to one another determined by friendly counsel along historically established lines of allegiance and nationality; and international guarantees of the political and economic independence and territorial integrity of the several Balkan states should be entered into.

XII. The Turkish portions of the present Ottoman Empire should be assured a secure sovereignty, but the other nationalities which are now under Turkish rule should be assured an undoubted security of life and an absolutely unmolested opportunity of autonomous development, and the Dardanelles should be permanently opened as a free passage to the ships and commerce of all nations under international guarantees.

XIII. An independent Polish state should be erected which should include the territories inhabited by indisputably Polish populations, which should be assured a free and secure access to the sea, and whose political and economic independence and territorial integrity should be guaranteed by international covenant.

XIV. A general association of nations must be formed under specific covenants for the purpose of affording mutual guarantees of political independence and territorial integrity to great and small states alike.

In regard to these essential rectifications of wrong and assertions of right we feel ourselves to be intimate partners of all the governments and peoples associated together against the Imperialists. We cannot be separated in interest or divided in purpose. We stand together until the end.

Wilson at Versailles: some doubts about the peace settlement from the notebooks of Ray S. Baker, 1919

"It is incomprehensible," said the President of the German National Assembly, upon hearing the terms of the peace treaty, "that a man who had promised the world a peace of justice, upon which a society of nations would be founded, has been able to assist in framing this project dictated by hate." Faced with the demands of Lloyd George, Clemenceau, and Orlando, Wilson was forced to compromise his principles on a number of important issues. But he had obtained their consent to a League of Nations. The Covenant of the League was incorporated into the treaty, and Wilson hoped that one would overcome the other: that whatever inequities were contained in the settlement would be corrected by the League. But would it? Wilson's press secretary, Ray S. Baker, had some serious doubts.

I wonder if Wilson has not been recently thinking too much politically. He took hold of the living soul of the world while he was its prophet; how much has he lost by becoming its statesman? Every time he has made the gesture of defiance—as in the Italian matter—the masses of the world have loved him; every time he has yielded to compromise—as in the Chinese settlement—the world has been cold. It is a great question whether it would not have been better for him to have stood upon his "points" more sternly and gone home. He has wanted his League of Nations more than anything else; has he sacrificed too much for it? No one else has really sacrificed anything. He will get his League, but can it rest upon such a basis of greed and injustice?

It is noble in the prophet to assert that he has no selfish or material interests—it stirs the soul of man to its depths, starts an emotional tidal wave that may last for uncounted years—but when the prophet sits down with the poker players, each one of whom wants the jackpot, the aura fades. Every one of the leaders here except Wilson has been a pleader for some special interest or interests; and by agreement among themselves have been able sometimes to overwhelm him. Great Britain, especially, has quietly got all she really wants.

The President seems now to be losing the support he had among the liberal-minded people of the world, the idealists, the workers, the youth of

From Ray Stannard Baker, *American Chronicle* (New York: Charles Scribner's Sons, 1945), pp. 422–24. Copyright 1945 by Ray Stannard Baker. Reprinted by permission.

all nations—without gaining the support of the conservatives. The great liberal and labor papers—the *Manchester Guardian,* the *Labor Herald,* the Italian *Secolo,* the French *L'Humanite,* and others, are now critical. Yet his principles remain. They are true; he has stated them once and for all, but will he himself ever see the Promised Land?

Let me try to be clear in my own mind. As the responsible head of a great nation, the chief leader in a world torn with suffering and anarchy— could he pursue his own way unchanged and unchangeable? Has he a right to choose the path which, proving his own faithfulness to his principles, yet leaves the world in frightful disorder? Having agreed to co-operate with other nations in making a peace, can he enforce everything the Americans demand, yield nothing to anyone else? Is this the way humanity moves forward? How far must one work with the forces of his time, however passionate, ignorant, greedy? If he compromises, accepts the best he can get, he may not acquire the crown of prophecy, which is crucifixion, but he may win the laurels which posterity at length bestows upon the wise.

The alternative is not so simple as many facile critics here at Paris imagine; not between going home and staying here; it is between anarchy and organization.

Never was I more in doubt as to my own course. This Treaty seems to me, in many particulars, abominable. How can I go home and support it, support the League of Nations founded upon it, support Wilson? Yet I cannot commit the folly of mere empty criticism, harking back to what might have been done. I know too well the impossible atmosphere of greed, fear, hatred, he has had to work in. I have felt it myself, every day, every hour. I have wondered many a time how it was that he could have held on so grimly with almost everyone here against him—not only with direct attacks, but with the most insidious, underhanded, cruel indirect attacks. Has he not, considering the time and the place, considering the "slump in idealism" which followed the allied victory, got as much as any human being could get?

American enthusiasm for the League may be the element that finally carries it through. Many of us feel that this League when it comes into being will not long be dominated by the elements which have allowed it to be created. Time will reduce passion; when reason begins to prevail, new liberal governments will everywhere spring up and take charge of affairs; they will dominate the League and furnish a rallying place for settling world controversies without war. I think this is Wilson's firm conviction; all that reassures him when he looks steadily at the settlements.

Opposition to the treaty: from Senator Henry Cabot Lodge's speech, August 12, 1919

There is no doubt that Henry Cabot Lodge, the influential Republican chairman of the Senate Foreign Relations Committee, and Wilson's inveterate enemy, organized the campaign to defeat the Treaty of Versailles. Lodge was even contemptuous of its wording. "It might get by at Princeton," he sneered, "but certainly not at Harvard." But, as Harold Laski has noted, "it is equally important to realize that Lodge owed his victory, at least in part, to the lofty disdain with which the Senate was treated by President Wilson." Lodge's major criticism of the treaty was his contention that the covenant violated American sovereignty and was therefore unacceptable without significant amendments.

As it stands there is no doubt whatever in my mind that American troops and American ships may be ordered to any part of the world by nations other than the United States, and that is a proposition to which I for one can never assent. It must be made perfectly clear that no American soldiers, not even a corporal's guard, that no American sailors, not even the crew of a submarine, can ever be engaged in war or ordered anywhere except by the constitutional authorities of the United States. To Congress is granted by the Constitution the right to declare war, and nothing that would take the troops out of the country at the bidding or demand of other nations should ever be permitted except through congressional action. The lives of Americans must never be sacrificed except by the will of the American people expressed through their chosen Representatives in Congress. This is a point upon which no doubt can be permitted. American soldiers and American sailors have never failed the country when the country called upon them. They went in their hundreds of thousands into the war just closed. They went to die for the great cause of freedom and of civilization. They went at their service. We were late in entering the war. We made no preparation, as we ought to have done, for the ordeal which was clearly coming upon us; but we went and we turned the wavering scale. It was done by the American soldier, the American sailor, and the spirit and energy of the American people. They overrode all obstacles and all shortcomings on the part of the administration or of Congress and gave to their country a great place in the great victory. It was the first time we had been called upon to rescue the civilized world. Did we fail? On the contrary, we succeeded, succeeded largely and nobly, and we did it without any command from any league of nations. When the emergency came we met it, and we were able to meet it because we had built up on this continent the greatest and most powerful nation in the world, built it up under our own policies, in our own way, and one great element of our strength was the fact

From speech of Senator Henry Cabot Lodge, August 12, 1919, *Congressional Record*, Sixty-sixth Congress, First Session, pp. 3783–84.

that we had held aloof and had not thrust ourselves into European quarrels; that we had no selfish interest to serve. We made great sacrifices. We have done splendid work. I believe that we do not require to be told by foreign nations when we shall do work which freedom and civilization require. I think we can move to victory much better under our own command than under the command of others. Let us unite with the world to promote the peaceable settlement of all international disputes. Let us try to develop international law. Let us associate ourselves with the other nations for these purposes. But let us retain in our own hands and in our own control the lives of the youth of the land. Let no American be sent into battle except by the constituted authorities of his own country and by the will of the people of the United States. . . .

I have loved but one flag and I cannot share that devotion and give affection to the mongrel banner invented for a league. Internationalism, illustrated by the Bolshevik and by the men to whom all countries are alike, provided they can make money out of them, is to me repulsive. National I must remain, and in that way I, like all other Americans, can render the amplest service to the world. The United States is the world's best hope, but if you fetter her in the interests and quarrels of other nations, if you tangle her in the intrigues of Europe, you will destroy her power for good and endanger her very existence. Leave her to march freely through the centuries to come as in the years that have gone. Strong, generous, and confident, she has nobly served mankind. Beware how you trifle with your marvelous inheritance, this great land of ordered liberty, for if we stumble and fall, freedom and civilization everywhere will go down in ruin.

8
Prosperity and Disillusionment

American isolationism: from the letters and diary of Joseph C. Grew, 1922

"We have torn up Wilsonism by the roots," Henry Cabot Lodge gloated after the election of 1920. "I am not slow to take up my own share of vindication which I find in the majorities." The new President, Warren G. Harding, declared in his first message to Congress that the United States would have no connection whatsoever with the League of Nations. The vast majority of Americans agreed with Harding. Public opinion was so hostile to the League, that the diplomat Joseph C. Grew, was embarrassed when he ran into a correspondent for the Chicago Tribune—*a notoriously isolationist newspaper—while waiting for a friend in front of League headquarters in Geneva. Grew asked the correspondent not to report his presence at so incriminating a location.*

Letter to Arthur Bliss Lane   July 19, 1922

I had a long talk with the President and an equally long one with the Secretary [of State]. The attitude of the Department with regard to the League is to treat it with every courtesy and to answer every communication received. Hughes was under the impression that this had been done. There is however little hope at present of our joining any of the subsidiary bodies even unofficially, as the Department's hands are tied by the proviso in the Washington treaties to the effect that our government shall be represented on no international body without the consent of the Senate.

Letter to Leland Harrison, Assistant Secretary of State   August 10, 1922

After my talk with the Secretary I find that my attitude toward the League will have to be exactly the same as before, and that it will not be possible to establish any more open connections than formerly. I had hoped to be authorized to play the role of an unofficial observer, openly . . . but while the Secretary left the matter to my discretion, he emphasized the importance of avoiding publicity, and I cannot therefore run the risk of visiting the League's offices or of openly moving to Geneva during sessions of the Council or other bodies, although this would have enabled me to keep the Department more closely and fully informed.

Diary entry   September 11, 1922

On arriving at Geneva I took a taxi and stopped at the entrance of the League of Nations building to pick up Sweetser to motor out to Genthod

From Joseph C. Grew, *The Turbulent Era: A Diplomatic Record of Forty Years, 1904–1945* (Boston, 1953), Vol. I, pp. 459–61. Reprinted by permission of Houghton Mifflin Company.

together. We had arranged this by telephone as he was too busy to meet me elsewhere. I have always carefully avoided the League premises but it seemed safe enough merely to stop at the entrance to call for somebody. As luck, or ill-luck, would have it, the first person I ran into there was Henry Wales of the *Chicago Tribune*. . . . He said: "Hello, what are *you* doing here! Looking into the Arms Traffic Commission?" I replied that I was there in a purely personal capacity, was visiting friends in the country and had stopped to see Sweetser, an old friend. I asked him not to say anything about it as there was no news in it and it would embarrass me greatly. . . . When I saw Sweetser he thought the chances were decidedly in favor of Wales making a story of it. . . . I felt pretty uneasy during the next two days, but when the *Chicago Tribune* came from Paris two days later, there was not a word about my presence.

Harding and his friends: an interview with William A. White, 1923

No document better reveals the essential character of Warren G. Harding than the following interview reported by William A. White of the Emporia Gazette. *Lonely, troubled, bitter, and confused, he yearned to be back in Marion, Ohio, running the local newspaper, where the petty corruptions he and his friends practiced were understood and accepted. Those same practices of his friends— the "Ohio gang"—on a national scale turned Harding's administration into a personal catastrophe.*

I went into the Presidential office, where the President stepped forward cordially to greet me. He had been sick. There was a dark cast to his olive skin. He was dressed with exact sartorial propriety, with exactly the kind of boutonnière he should wear, with precisely the gray stripe in his trousers that the hour required, with a proper dark four-in-hand tied most carefully. For a moment or two, while he was offering cigars and moving festively out of the preliminaries of a formal conversation, he was socially and spiritually erect. But as we sat in the south sunshine flooding through the windows of his office, he warmed and melted and slouched a little. I had no idea why he had sent for me. I have precious little idea now, only a theory. I have a notion he was lonesome, and that he wanted to talk about the newspaper business. At least he talked of little else. He began by asking me what we were paying for print paper, where we got it, how many carloads we used a year, going into the terms of our contract which by some miracle I had in my mind. . . .

From *The Autobiography of William Allen White* (New York: The Macmillan Company, 1946), pp. 617–19. Copyright 1946 by The Macmillan Company. Reprinted with permission by The Macmillan Company.

He went on to ask about our profit-sharing plan, of which he had read something in the trade papers. He outlined his plan of distributing stock in the Marion Star to his employees, and explained that it worked well. He went into the matter of wages for reporters, linotype men, floor men, and the foreman, and we compared notes. While one of the White House servants was putting wood in the grate, we both watched him critically. Then the President walked over to the fire, stood with his hands behind him warming his back. One could see that he was physically subnormal. He had a powerful frame, strong, rather sloping shoulders, with just a hint of a stoop that tall men often need to get their eyes in focus with the common world a few inches below them. As he stood there by the glowing fire and mused a moment, he said:

"Well, when I first took this job, I had a lot of fun with it. I got a kick out of it every day for the first six months or so. But it has fallen into a routine, more or less."

He spoke slowly, dropping into a reminiscent mood, and went on: "You know every day at three-thirty, here in the midst of the affairs of state, I go to press on the Marion Star, I wonder what kind of a layout the boys have got on the first page. I wonder how much advertising there is; whether they are keeping up with this week last year. I would like to walk out in the composing room and look over the forms before they go to the stereo-typer. There never was a day in all the years that I ran the paper that I didn't get some thrill out of it."

He grinned and paused, and it wasn't for me to talk. I fancy he was getting out of me exactly what he wanted—an audience who would understand the touch of homesickness which had come to a man away from his life's work, a man who had been confined to his room and was a bit under himself physically. Suddenly he broke a minute's silence, left the fire, came over, sat down, crossed his legs, and asked abruptly:

"Say, how do you get the county printing?"

I told him that there was a gentleman's agreement between the Democratic paper and the Gazette that when the Democrats elected the county officers, whose business it was to let the county printing, we would not bid; or, if we did bid, we bid the full legal rate. So the Democrats let the printing to the Democratic paper. And when the county was Republican, the Democrats decently refrained from disturbing the legal rate by a cut-throat bid.

"That's fine, fine!" he answered, and a querulous strain rasped in his voice. "Do you know how we used to get it? Well, we all go in and bid and choose among ourselves the low bidder before we bid, and he adds enough to his bid to give us all a little slice of the profits above his low bid."

He paused a second and then turned toward me a troubled face, and he cried: "And that's the hell of it. Right now, at the moment, there is a bunch down at the Willard Hotel coming up here to see me this afternoon, good friends of mine from Ohio, decent fellows that I have worked with

thirty years. Some of them have supported me through thick and thin.
Well, there is an energetic district attorney down East here—maybe New
York, or Boston, or Philadelphia, it don't make any difference where—and
he has gone and indicted those fellows; is going to put them in jail for violating the antitrust law or some conspiracy law for doing exactly . . . what
I have done in printing for twenty years. *And*," he added, "they know all
about my method and they are going to ask me to dismiss the indictment.
I can't do that. The law is the law, and it is probably all right, a good law
and ought to be enforced. And yet I sit here in the White House and have
got to see those fellows this afternoon, and explain why I can't lift a hand
to keep them from going to jail. My God, this is a hell of a job! I have no
trouble with my enemies. I can take care of my enemies all right. But my
damn friends," he wailed, with sort of a serio-comic petulance, "my God-
damn friends, White, they're the ones that keep me walking the floor nights!"

Corruption in Washington: the diary of Senator Henry F. Ashurst, 1923–25

*Most of the scandals of the Harding administration were not made public until
after his death. His successor, Calvin Coolidge, projected such a solid image of
calm, stable, sober, incorruptibility, that the publicity about governmental corruption made less of an impact since there seemed to be little chance it would
be repeated. Besides, the American people had become a bit more cynical since
the war. The diary of an Arizona Senator, Henry Ashurst, recorded the more
important exposés from 1923 to 1925.*

October 22, 1923

General John F. O'Ryan, counsel for the Senate Committee to investigate
the Veterans' Bureau, was making charges of malversation of public funds
against Colonel Charles Forbes when a man with disheveled hair, loose
lips, troubled eyes, and trembling hands arose before the Committee and
shouted that he had come to defend himself. This agonized man was
Colonel Forbes, former Director of the Bureau.

In another room of the same building the Senate Committee on Public
Lands began investigating leasing of Teapot Oil Dome in Wyoming to Mr.
Harry Sinclair by Albert B. Fall, whilst Mr. Fall was Secretary of the Interior. Mr. Fall was present and had no troubled eye, no trembling hand, but
was belligerent and truculent.

From George F. Sparks (ed.), *A Many-Colored Toga: The Diary of Henry Fountain
Ashurst* (Tucson, Arizona: The University of Arizona Press, 1963), pp. 205–30. Reprinted by permission.

January 16, 1924

I wrote in this Diary on October 22 last, when the Senate Committee on Public Lands began to investigate leasing of Tea Pot Oil Dome to Harry Sinclair by Secretary of Interior Albert B. Fall, that *"Mr. Fall was present and had no troubled eye, no trembling hand, etc."* Alas, since I made that entry, evidence before the committee has been adduced carrying serious implications against Mr. Fall, who has sent a letter to the committee stating that he is too ill to "undergo the ordeal of an examination." Late in the year 1920 Mr. Fall was reported as arrear in his taxes. After leasing Tea Pot Oil Dome, he spent, so it is charged, nearly one hundred thousand dollars in acquiring additional lands in New Mexico; three thousand for Hereford bulls and eight thousand for back taxes. The ultimate facts are: the oil lands have been leased and Mr. Fall is unwilling or unable to explain his suddenly-acquired wealth.

January 24, 1924

Mr. Edward L. Doheny, oil magnate, appeared before the Senate Committee and testified that in November 1921, he loaned one hundred thousand dollars in cash to his old-time personal friend, Mr. Albert B. Fall. Mr. Doheny denied that the leases to himself of Naval Oil Reserve Number One, by Secretary Fall, was influenced by this loan.

Some weeks ago when Mr. Fall was before the committee he said: "I never approached E. L. Doheny or any one connected with him or any of his corporations, nor have I ever received from either of said parties (Doheny or Sinclair) one cent on account of any lease, or upon any other count whatsoever."

January 25, 1924

Mr. J. W. Zevely (attorney for Mr. Sinclair) testified before the committee that after Mr. Fall resigned as Secretary of the Interior, Mr. Sinclair loaned Mr. Fall about $25,000 and paid Fall's expenses to Russia where Mr. Fall and Sinclair's attorney went to explore oil possibilities. Alas! Alas! A tide of evidence surges against Albert B. Fall. Mr. Fall is broken in health and is abandoned by his fair weather friends.

January 28, 1924

Senator Walsh of Montana spoke three hours, urging President Coolidge to institute proceedings to cancel the oil leases to Doheny and Sinclair.

Ex-Secretary Fall is now ill and helpless. Every way he turns he is assailed by a new anguish. His career teaches us to walk humbly.

January 29, 1924

Galleries crowded all day. The exposé in the oil leases to Doheny and Sinclair overshadow all other questions before Congress. Secretary of the Navy, Denby, says the oil leases were unknown to him. He signed the leases and the Republican leaders are demanding that he defend them or resign.

January 30, 1924

Senator Norris of Nebraska laid responsibility for the oil leases at President Harding's door. Others spoke but all was anticlimax after the terrible speech of Senator Norris.

February 2, 1924

Ex-Secretary Fall appeared before Senate committee and declined to testify declaring that his answers might tend to incriminate him.

March 28, 1924

Attorney General Daugherty upon request of the President has resigned. Mr. Daugherty issued a statement implying that the President removed him because of "political expediency." Mr. Daugherty was confident that he could rely upon President Coolidge to sustain him, but is now disillusioned and has left Washington a gloomy man. He was born at Washington Court House, Ohio, was President Harding's close friend, and his efforts contributed not a little toward Mr. Harding's nomination.

April 1, 1924

Charges, denials, counter-charges, and denunciations fill the air. Suspicion and distrust pervade Washington.

April 8, 1924

Senator Burton K. Wheeler of Montana has been indicted by a federal grand jury in Montana, charged with accepting a fee for appearing before some department after his term as senator had commenced.

April 11, 1924

Sensations leap forth so swiftly that a brace of shorthand writers is required to record them. Last month the Senate authorized a special committee to investigate the Bureau of Internal Revenue. Secretary of the Treasury (Mellon) complained of this committee's special counsel and President Coolidge today sent to the Senate a message (one of the most censorious ever sent to the Senate by an executive) inveighing against this investigation.

May 23, 1924

The Senate adopted by fifty-six Yeas to five Nays the Borah Resolution exonerating Senator Wheeler. It was the opinion of some senators that the indictment of Wheeler had been secured to frustrate his investigation of the Department of Justice under Mr. Daugherty's regime.

May 29, 1924

"Detective" Gaston B. Means testified before Daugherty Investigation Committee. Mr. Means seems ubiquitous; he was here, he was there. He blows and swallows at one and the same time. He weighs three hundred pounds, rolls his huge head from side to side and thrusts out his beefy tongue before replying to questions. Senator Wheeler is assailed for calling such a witness to testify, and Wheeler retorts that Attorney General Daugherty appointed Means to be an "undercover" detective in the Department of Justice.

February 6, 1925

Healthy conservatism now characterizes the government. The Wilson struggle to elevate the "crowd" is absent. The Harding fraternizing is absent. Mr. Coolidge neither coddles politicians nor radiates camaraderie. He believes that if business prospers all else follows.

March 21, 1925

Are American politicians untrustworthy? Have idealism and noblesse oblige no place in our politics? Is politics the science of selfishness? Constituencies are not free from blame for the cynicism of their public men. Constituencies too often look upon magnanimity and moderation as flabbiness. The politician will practice the virtue of moderation only upon the demand of the constituency.

Fear of non-Anglo-Saxon immigrants: the quotas of the National Origins Act, 1924

At worst the immigrant was stereotyped as a bearded bomb-thrower. At best he was feared as a threat to Anglo-Saxon culture. So many southern and eastern Europeans had immigrated since the 1880's that in some cities foreigners outnumbered the native-born. Fewer entered during the war, but with peace the influx quickened once again. More than 800,000 arrived in 1921. Ellis Island in New York harbor became so jammed that the overflow had to be directed to Boston. Consuls in Europe reported that millions more were prepared to leave for the United States. These millions, wrote one author in the Saturday Evening Post, *would turn America into "a hybrid race of people as worthless and fertile as the good-for-nothing mongrels of Central America and Southeastern Europe." An emergency measure to stop this immigration was rushed through Congress in 1921; and in 1924 the National Origins Act was passed, which established the quotas—distinctly favorable to those from northern and western European countries—given below.*

Whereas it is provided in the act of Congress approved May 26, 1924, entitled "An act to limit the immigration of aliens into the United States, and for other purposes" that—

"The annual quota of any nationality shall be two per centum of the number of foreign-born individuals of such nationality resident in continental United States as determined by the United States census of 1890, but the minimum quota of any nationality shall be 100...."

Now, therefore, I, Calvin Coolidge, President of the United States of America acting under and by virtue of the power in me vested by the aforesaid act of Congress, do hereby proclaim and make known that on and after July 1, 1924, and throughout the fiscal year 1924–25, the quota of each nationality provided in said Act shall be as follows:

Country or Area of Birth

	Quota 1924–25		Quota 1924–25
Afghanistan	100	Bhutan	100
Albania	100	Bulgaria	100
Andorra	100	Cameroon (proposed British	
Arabian Peninsula	100	mandate)	100
Armenia	124	Cameroun (French mandate)	100
Australia, including Papua,		China	100
Tasmania, and all islands		Czechoslovakia	3,073
appertaining to Australia	121	Danzig, Free City of	228
Austria	785	Denmark	2,789
Belgium	512	Egypt	100

From the United States Bureau of Immigration, *Annual Report of the Commissioner-General of Immigration* (Washington, D.C., 1924), pp. 24–27.

	Quota 1924–25		Quota 1924–25
Esthonia	124	New Guinea, and other Pacific Islands under proposed Australian mandate	100
Ethiopia	100		
Finland	170		
France	3,954	Palestine, (with Trans-Jordan, proposed British Mandate)	100
Germany	51,227		
Great Britain and Northern Ireland	34,007	Persia	100
		Poland	5,982
Greece	100	Portugal	503
Hungary	473	Ruanda and Urandi (Belgium mandate)	100
Iceland	100		
India	100	Rumania	603
Iraq	100	Russia	2,248
Irish Free State	28,567	Samoa, Western (proposed mandate of New Zealand)	100
Italy, including Rhodes, Dodekanesia, and Castellorizzo	3,845	San Marino	100
		Siam	100
Japan	100	South Africa, Union of	100
Latvia	142	South West Africa (proposed mandate of Union of South Africa)	100
Liberia	100		
Liechtenstein	100		
Lithuania	344	Spain	131
Luxemburg	100	Sweden	9,561
Monaco	100	Switzerland	2,081
Morocco (French and Spanish Zones and Tangier)	100	Syria and The Lebanon (French mandate)	100
Muscat	100	Tanganyika (proposed British mandate)	100
Nauru (proposed British mandate)	100	Togoland (proposed British mandate)	100
Nepal	100	Togoland (French mandate)	100
Netherlands	1,648	Turkey	100
New Zealand (including appertaining islands)	100	Yap and other Pacific Islands (under Japanese mandate)	100
Norway	6,453	Yugoslavia	671

Black nationalism: the message of Marcus Garvey, 1920's

The Universal Negro Improvement Association, founded by a Jamaican, Marcus Garvey, had considerably more drawing power among blacks than the National Association for the Advancement of the Colored People, and a considerably different message. Not integration in America, but a return to Africa, was Garvey's cry. "The NAACP wants us all to become white by amalgamation," wrote Garvey, "but they are not honest enough to come out with the truth. To be a Negro is no disgrace, but an honor, and we of the UNIA do not want to become white." Garvey gave to millions of black men a sense of pride, of identification, of purpose, but his movement collapsed after he was convicted of using the mails to defraud. He was confined to Atlanta penitentiary, and later deported as an undesirable alien. Below are excerpts taken from his essays and speeches.

I believe that white men should be white, yellow men should be yellow, and black men should be black in the great panorama of races, until

From Amy J. Garvey (ed.), *Philosophy and Opinions of Marcus Garvey* (London, 1967), Vol. I, pp. 21–22, Vol. II, pp. 4, 56, 69, 102–03, 107, 213.

each and every race by its own initiative lifts itself up to the common standard of humanity, as to compel the respect and appreciation of all, and so make it possible for each one to stretch out the hand of welcome without being able to be prejudiced against the other because of any inferior and unfortunate condition.

The white man of America will not, to any organized extent, assimilate the Negro, because in so doing, he feels that he will be committing racial suicide. This he is not prepared to do. It is true he illegitimately carries on a system of assimilation; but such assimilation, as practiced, is one that he is not prepared to support because he becomes prejudiced against his own offspring, if that offspring is the product of black and white; hence, to the white man the question of racial differences is eternal. So long as Negroes occupy an inferior position among the races and nations of the world, just so long will others be prejudiced against them, because it will be profitable for them to keep up their system of superiority. But when the Negro by his own initiative lifts himself from his low state to the highest human standard he will be in a position to stop begging and praying, and demand a place that no individual, race or nation will be able to deny him.

In another one hundred years white America will have doubled its population; in another two hundred years it will have trebled itself. The keen student must realize that the centuries ahead will bring us an overcrowded country; opportunities, as the population grows larger, will be fewer; the competition for bread between the people of their own class will become keener, and so much more so will there be no room for two competitive races, the one strong, and the other weak. To imagine Negroes as district attorneys, judges, senators, congressmen, assemblymen, aldermen, government clerks and officials, artisans and laborers at work, while millions of white men starve, is to have before you the bloody picture of wholesale mob violence that I fear, and against which I am working.

Du Bois represents a group that hates the Negro blood in its veins, and has been working subtly to build up a caste aristocracy that would socially divide the race into two groups: One the superior because of color caste, and the other the inferior, hence the pretentious work of the National Association for the Advancement of "Colored" People. The program of deception was well arranged and under way for success when Marcus Garvey arrived in America, and he, after understudying the artful doctor and the group he represented, fired a "bomb" into the camp by organizing the Universal "Negro" Improvement Association to cut off the wicked attempt of race deception and distinction, and, in truth, to build up a race united in spirit and ideal, with the honest desire of adjusting itself to its own moral-social pride and national self-respect. When Garvey arrived in America and visited the office of the National Association for the Advancement of "Colored" People to interview Du Bois, who was regarded as a leader of the Negro people, and who had recently visited the West Indies, he was dumbfounded on approach to the office to find that but for Mr. Dill, Mr. Du Bois himself, and the office boy, he could not tell whether he was in a white office or that of the National Association for the Advancement of "Colored" People. The whole staff was either white or very near white, and thus Garvey got the first shock of the advancement hypocrisy. There was no representation of the race there that anyone could recognize. The advancement meant that you had to be as near white as possible, otherwise there was no place for you as stenographer, clerk or attendant in the office. . . .

What are you going to expect, that white men are going to build up America elsewhere and hand it over to us? If we are expecting that we are crazy, we have lost our reason. If you were white, you would see the rest in hell before you would deprive your children of bread to give it to others. You would give that which you did not want, but not that which is to be the sustenance of your family, and so the world thinks; yet a Du Bois and the National Association for the Advancement of Colored People will tell us by flattery that the day is coming when a white President of the United States of America will get out of the White House and give the position to a Negro, that the day is coming when a Mr. Hughes will desert the Secretaryship of State and give it to the Negro, James Weldon Johnson; that the time is just around the corner of constitutional rights when the next Ambassador to the Court of Saint James will be a black man from Mississippi or from North Carolina. Do you think that white men who have suffered, bled and died to make America and the world what it is, are going to hand over to a parcel of lazy Negroes the things that they prize most?

The danger of Communism to the Negro, in countries where he forms the minority of the population, is seen in the selfish and vicious attempts of that party or group to use the Negro's vote and physical numbers in helping to smash and overthrow, by revolution, a system that is injurious to them as the white underdogs, the success of which would put their majority group or race still in power, not only as communists, but as whitemen. To me there is no difference between two roses looking alike, and smelling alike, even if some one calls them by different names. Fundamentally what racial difference is there between a white Communist, Republican or Democrat?

Races and peoples are only safeguarded when they are strong enough to protect themselves, and that is why we appeal to the four hundred million Negroes of the world to come together for self-protection and self-preservation. We do not want what belongs to the great white race, or the yellow race. We want only those things that belong to the black race. Africa is ours. To win Africa we will give up America, we will give up our

claim in all other parts of the world; but we must have Africa. We will give
up the vain desire of having a seat in the White House in America, of having a seat in the House of Lords in England, of being President of France,
for the chance and opportunity of filling those positions in a country of
our own.

What are you going to do with this question of race? You may sit
quietly by, but it is going to be serious later on, and that is why the Universal Negro Improvement Association is endeavoring to assist you in solving
the Negro problem by helping the Negro become enterprising, independent
politically, and by having a country of his own. If you follow me down the
ages you will see within a hundred years you are going to have a terrible
race problem in America, when you will have increased and the country
will become over-populated. It will be a fight for existence between two
opposite races. The weak will have to go down in defeat before the strong.

The Scopes trial and Bryan's legacy, according to H. L. Mencken, 1925

*H. L. Mencken's acid wit and irreverent opinions delighted liberal students and
urban sophisticates, particularly when he dissected the bigotry and ignorance of
backwoods religious fundamentalists. In 1925 he covered the trial in Dayton,
Tennessee, which involved the prosecution of a biology teacher, John T. Scopes,
for violating the state law which forbid the teaching of "any theory that denies
the story of the Divine creation of man as taught in the Bible." To Scopes' defense came a battery of famous lawyers, including the renowned defense attorney, Clarence Darrow. To aid the prosecution came William J. Bryan, for three
decades the outstanding voice of rural, Midwestern America. Scopes lost, as
everyone had anticipated, but the sensational trial revealed Bryan's intellectual
shallowness when he was cross-examined by Darrow. A week after the trial
ended Bryan died. H. L. Mencken warned his readers that Bryan's death did
not end the fundamentalist threat.*

When I first encountered him, on the sidewalk in front of the office
of the rustic lawyers who were his associates in the Scopes case, the trial
was yet to begin, and so he was still expansive and amiable. I had printed
in the *Nation*, a week or so before, an article arguing that the Tennessee
anti-evolution law, whatever its wisdom, was at least constitutional—that
the rustics of the State had a clear right to have their progeny taught whatever they chose, and kept secure from whatever knowledge violated their
superstitions. The old boy professed to be delighted with the argument,

From *Prejudices: Fifth Series*, by H. L. Mencken, pp. 70–74. Copyright 1926 by
Alfred A. Knopf, Inc. and renewed 1954 by H. L. Mencken. Reprinted by permission
of the publisher.

and gave the gaping bystanders to understand that I was a publicist of parts. Not to be outdone, I admired the preposterous country shirt that he wore—sleeveless and with the neck cut very low. We parted in the manner of two ambassadors. But that was the last touch of amiability that I was destined to see in Bryan. The next day the battle joined and his face became hard. By the end of the week he was simply a walking fever. Hour by hour he grew more bitter. What the Christian Scientists call malicious animal magnetism seemed to radiate from him like a stove. From my place in the courtroom, standing upon a table, I looked directly down upon him, sweating horribly and pumping his palm-leaf fan. His eyes fascinated me; I watched them all day long. They were blazing points of hatred. They glittered like occult and sinister gems. Now and then they wandered to me, and I got my share, for my reports of the trial had come back to Dayton, and he had read them. It was like coming under fire.

Thus he fought his last fight, thirsting savagely for blood. All sense departed from him. He bit right and left, like a dog with rabies. He descended to demagogy so dreadful that his very associates at the trial table blushed. His one yearning was to keep his yokels heated up—to lead his forlorn mob of imbeciles against the foe. That foe, alas, refused to be alarmed. It insisted upon seeing the whole battle as a comedy. Even Darrow, who knew better, occasionally yielded to the prevailing spirit. One day he lured poor Bryan into . . . folly: his astounding argument against the notion that man is a mammal. I am glad I heard it, for otherwise I'd never believe it. There stood the man who had been thrice a candidate for the Presidency of the Republic—there he stood in the glare of the world, uttering stuff that a boy of eight would laugh at! The artful Darrow led him on: he repeated it, ranted for it, bellowed it in his cracked voice. So he was prepared for the final slaughter. He came into life a hero, a Galahad, in bright and shining armor. He was passing out a poor mountebank.

The chances are that history will put the peak of democracy in America in his time; it has been on the downward curve among us since the campaign of 1896. He will be remembered perhaps, as its supreme impostor, the *reductio ad absurdum* of its pretension. Bryan came very near being President. In 1896, it is possible, he was actually elected. He lived long enough to make patriots thank the inscrutable gods for Harding, even for Coolidge. Dullness has got into the White House, and the smell of cabbage boiling, but there is at least nothing to compare to the intolerable buffoonery that went on in Tennessee. The President of the United States may be an ass, but at least he doesn't believe the earth is square, and that witches should be put to death, and that Jonah swallowed the whale. The Golden Text is not painted weekly on the White House wall, and there is no need to keep ambassadors waiting while Pastor Simpson, of Smithville, prays for rain in the Blue Room. We have escaped something—by a narrow margin, but still we have escaped.

That is, so far. The Fundamentalists, once apparently sweeping

all before them, now face minorities prepared for battle even in the South
—here and there with some assurance of success. But it is too early, it seems
to me, to send the firemen home; the fire is still burning on many a far-flung
hill, and it may begin to roar again at any moment. The evil that men do
lives after them. Bryan, in his malice, started something that it will not be
easy to stop. In ten thousand country towns his old heelers, the evangelical
pastors, are propagating his gospel, and everywhere the yokels are ready
for it. When he disappeared from the big cities, the big cities made the
capital error of assuming that he was done for. If they heard of him at all,
it was only as a crimp for real-estate speculators—the heroic foe of the un-
earned increment hauling it in with both hands. He seemed preposterous,
and hence harmless. But all the while he was busy among his old lieges,
preparing for a *jacquerie* that should floor all his enemies at one blow. He
did his job competently. He had vast skill at such enterprises. Heave an
egg out of a Pullman window, and you will hit a Fundamentalist almost
everywhere in the United States today. They swarm in the country towns,
inflamed by their *shamans*, and with a saint, now, to venerate. They are
thick in the mean streets behind the gas-works. They are everywhere where
learning is too heavy a burden for mortal minds to carry, even the vague,
pathetic learning on tap in little red schoolhouses. They march with the
Klan, with the Christian Endeavor Society, with the Junior Order of United
American Mechanics, with the Epworth League, with all the rococo bands
that poor and unhappy folk organize to bring some light of purpose into
their lives. They have had a thrill, and they are ready for more.

Such is Bryan's legacy to his country. He couldn't be President, but he
could at least help magnificently in the solemn business of shutting off the
Presidency from every intelligent and self-respecting man. The storm, perhaps, won't last long, as times goes in history. It may help, indeed, to break
up the democratic delusion, now already showing weakness, and so hasten
its own end. But while it lasts it will blow off some roofs.

Christ and advertising: from the best-selling nonfiction book *The Man Nobody Knows*, 1925

*What Americans wanted, President Harding proclaimed, was "less government
in Business and more Business in government." President Coolidge put the matter even more succinctly: "The business of America is business." Many clerical
commentators insisted that the goals of American business and the precepts of
Christianity were identical. Bruce Barton, for example, referred to Christ as
"the founder of modern business," as "the most popular dinner guest in Jerusa-
lem," as a leader who "picked up twelve men from the bottom ranks of business
and forged them into an organization that conquered the world."*

From Bruce Barton, *The Man Nobody Knows* (Indianapolis, 1925), pp. 126–40. Copyright 1925 by the Bobbs-Merrill Company, Inc. R. 1952 by Bruce Barton. Reprinted
by permission of the publisher.

Let us begin by asking why he was so successful in mastering public attention and why, in contrast, his churches are less so? The answer is two-fold. In the first place he recognized the basic principle that all good advertising is news. He was never trite or commonplace; he had no routine. If there had been newspapers in those days, no city editor could have said, "No need to visit him to-day; he will be doing just what he did last Sunday." Reporters would have followed him every single hour, for it was impossible to predict what he would say or do; every action and word were news.

Take one single day as an example. . . . Let us look at his twenty-four hours' schedule; see how it bristles with front-page news. The activity begins at sunrise. Jesus was an early riser; he knew that the simplest way to live *more* than an average life is to add an hour to the fresh end of the day. At sunrise, therefore, we discover a little boat pushing out from the shore of the lake. It makes its steady way across and deposits Jesus and his disciples in Capernaum, his favorite city. He proceeds at once to the house of a friend, but not without being discovered. The report spreads instantly that he is in town, and before he can finish breakfast a crowd has collected outside the gate—a poor palsied chap among them. . . .

"Be of good cheer, my son," he cries, "your sins are all forgiven."

Sins forgiven! Indeed! The respectable members of the audience draw back with sharp disapproval. "What a blasphemous phrase," they exclaim. "Who authorized him to exercise the functions of God? What right has he to decide whose sins shall be forgiven? . . ."

"What's the objection?" he exclaimed, turning on the dissenters. "Why do you stand there and criticize? Is it easier to say, 'Thy sins be forgiven thee,' or to say, 'Arise, take up thy bed and walk?' The results are the same." Bending over the sick man again he said: "Arise, take up thy bed and go unto thine house." The man stirred and was amazed to find that his muscles responded. . . .

Can you imagine the next day's issue of the *Capernaum News,* if there had been one?

PALSIED MAN HEALED

JESUS OF NAZARETH CLAIMS RIGHT TO

FORGIVE SINS

PROMINENT SCRIBES OBJECT

"BLASPHEMOUS," SAYS LEADING CITIZEN.

"BUT ANYWAY I CAN WALK," HEALED MAN

RETORTS.

Front page story number one and the day is still young. One of those who had been attracted by the excitement was a tax-collector named Matthew. Being a man of business he could not stay through the argument, but slipped away early and was hard at work when Jesus passed by a few minutes before noon.

"Matthew, I want you," said Jesus. That was all. No argument; no offer of inducements; no promise of rewards. Merely, "I want you"; and the prosperous tax-collector closed his office, made a feast for the brilliant young teacher and forthwith announced himself a disciple.

PROMINENT TAX COLLECTOR JOINS
NAZARETH FORCES
MATTHEW ABANDONS BUSINESS TO PROMOTE
NEW CULT

GIVES LARGE LUNCHEON. . . .

A woman sick twelve years, and healed! A child whom the doctors had abandoned for dead, sits up and smiles! No wonder a thousand tongues were busy that night advertising his name and work. "The fame thereof went abroad into all that land," says the narrative. Nothing could keep it from going abroad. It was irresistible news!

He was advertised by his service, not by his sermons; this is the second noteworthy fact. Nowhere in the Gospel do you find it announced that:

JESUS OF NAZARETH WILL DENOUNCE
THE SCRIBES AND PHARISEES IN THE
CENTRAL SYNAGOGUE
TO-NIGHT AT EIGHT O'CLOCK
SPECIAL MUSIC. . . .

These are Jesus' works, done in Jesus' name. If he were to live again, in these modern days, he would find a way to make them known—to be advertised by his service, not merely by his sermons. One thing is certain: he would not neglect the market-place. Few of his sermons were delivered in synagogues. For the most part he was in the crowded places, the Temple Court, the city squares, the centers where goods were bought and sold. I emphasized this fact once to a group of preachers. "You mean that we ought to do street preaching," one of them exclaimed. . . .

No; the present day market-place is the newspaper and the magazine. Printed columns are the modern thoroughfares; published advertisements are the crossroads where the sellers and the buyers meet. Any issue of a national magazine is a world's fair, a bazaar filled with the products of the world's work. Clothes and clocks and candle-sticks; soup and soap and cigarettes; lingerie and limousines—the best of all of them are there, proclaimed by their makers in persuasive tones. That every other voice should be raised in such great market-places, and the voice of Jesus of Nazareth be still—this is a vital omission which he would find a way to correct. He would be a national advertiser today, I am sure, as he was the great advertiser of his own day.

The labor movement paralyzed: an analysis, 1926

One statistic tells the story: the total membership in American labor unions declined from 5,000,000 in 1920 to 3,440,000 in 1929. The radicalism of pre-war days all but vanished in an age which preached "normalcy" and worshipped "prosperity." "You can't lick this Prosperity thing," the comedian Will Rogers quipped, "even the fellow that hasn't got any is all excited over the idea." At a conference of the League for Industrial Democracy—a socialist organization which sought some form of workers' control over industry—the president of the Pennsylvania Federation of Labor, James H. Maurer, offered some acute comments to explain the impotence of the labor movement.

Some of us who have been pretty radical in our time are losing heart with the masses who don't seem to care to be radical. They would rather have it dished up to them in a sweet sort of no account form with which they can all agree and say it is all right. But if it is radical they get a little bit scared of it. . . .

A worker ordinarily asks the following questions about a labor union: What does it give me? What do I get out of it? And along comes the employer and decides that he is going to do more than the labor union can do. The labor union generally talks hours and wages. The employer comes along and says, I will pay you the wages and since we have the hours anyhow, I stand by the hours. Then he does what the union cannot do. He says, I will give you a policy for life insurance, health insurance, old age insurance. And he puts up community centers, golf links, lawn tennis, baseball, music, dancing, and all the things the unions cannot hope to give. And what is the result? The employers even go into the banking business, insisting that the workers save money and after they see a certain amount of deposits on hand, they then unload a little of their stock and take that away from them again. A very clever arrangement. But the effect it has is this: a man comes home and shows his wife what he has got, this security against sickness, compensation, protection against accident, death and old age. We might demonstrate that old age and other group insurances cannot hold out but the worker doesn't know that. He goes home and shows the policies to his wife. She feels secured. The family feels secured. The fear of sickness and death in the family, the fear of old age, is removed and

From Harry Laidler and Norman Thomas (eds.), *New Tactics in Social Conflict* (New York, 1926), pp. 20–22.

that man becomes a more subject slave to that employer than he ever would have been under any other condition. The young folks get their amusements—dancing, playing, singing, their golf and lawn tennis—and they commence to imitate and do the things that in the past only the rich or the employers could do. It changes their entire psychology.

There is another factor in the industrial situation. Skilled men and women are no longer required as they were in industry. There are some skilled trades still, but very few. The average among us are merely laborers, as it were. We go into a shop and get a job on a machine which pays just a little better than laboring. And if we learn to manipulate that machine by saving a minute here and a second there, and speeding up a little faster, we can finally work our wages up to perhaps double what we could earn as common laborers. Then we are slaves to that machine. We know full well that if we lose that position which we now consider skilled, we have to go back to the old unskilled trade. But it is not a question of skill, it is simply a case of adapting ourselves to the machine and, therefore, that again takes all the independence and fight out of the operator of such a machine. That is another angle of the whole subject.

Then we have the labor movement struggling for a hold to try to bring order out of this chaotic condition in industry. Some say then, well, let's own it. Mr. Soule has so aptly pointed out that the stockholders do not have any voice in the management, and perhaps it is just as well so. If they did they would know so little about the other end of it that they wouldn't be able to vote intelligently even though they had a vote. My experience has been that stockholders have little to do any more in management. It is being denied to them. But it is a fact that the big banking houses are the real owners today of modern industry. They are the men who dictate the policies, much more so than the managers. We know in the coal strike no matter what the coal operators think about settlement, they have no voice in it until the bankers tell them they can settle. Until that time, there is no settlement in the coal strike.

I can't see any other remedy to the present situation but the one I have believed in for these many years. I believe, that capitalism must run its course. Capitalism is not now beyond mending as we used to say twenty-five years ago, on the soap box. "It can't stand another patch!" You remember that talk. It used to go good. We were going to have the cooperative commonwealth some twenty years ago ushered in on a silver platter. We have found since then that capitalism will stand a good bit of patching and more patching. And don't misunderstand me, perhaps it is better so.

I don't believe that we are fit to take over industry until we can demonstrate that we will be able to do better with it than the ones who now control it have done. And until that time comes, we had better let that crowd have it. I would rather cuss that bunch than cuss my own bunch.

But I can see no other remedy but that we have to pave the way by educating ourselves, so that when the crash comes, and it is going to come, we will have the intelligence to take over the industry and operate it for use and not for profit.

Reinhold Niebuhr on American Society, 1927

The America which Reinhold Niebuhr viewed from his post at the Bethel Evangelical Church in Detroit, Michigan, was diametrically different from that of Bruce Barton. "What a civilization this is!" Niebuhr cried. Rich businessmen increasing their capital through stock manipulations, then playing the philanthropist; the myth of Henry Ford's mechanical genius contributing more to end poverty than any ideological doctrine; the desperation of blacks living in the motor city which gave only "incidental attention" to their human problems. The people of Detroit, he noted, "are spiritually isolated even though they are mechanically dependent upon one another. In such a situation it is difficult to create and preserve the moral and cultural traditions which each individual needs to save his life from anarchy."

Perhaps there is no better illustration of the ethical impotence of the modern church than its failure to deal with the evils and the ethical problems of stock manipulation. Millions in property values are created by pure legerdemain. Stock dividends, watered stock and excessive rise in stock values, due to the productivity of the modern machine, are accepted by the church without a murmur if only a slight return is made by the beneficiaries through church philanthropies.

Here is C——recapitalizing his business and adding six million dollars in stock. At least five of these millions will not be invested in physical expansion but pocketed by the owner. They simply represent capitalization of expected profits. Once this added burden has been placed upon the industry any demands of the workers for a larger share of the profits will be met by conclusive proof that the stock is earning only a small dividend and that further increase in wages would be "suicidal" to the business.

Meanwhile C——has become quite philanthropic. He gives fifty thousand dollars here and a hundred thousand there. Since the good man is a "Christian," religious organizations profit most by his benefactions. Every new donation is received with paeans of praise from church and press. What I wonder is whether the gentleman is deceiving himself and really imagines himself a Christian or whether he is really quite hard-boiled and harbors a secret contempt for the little men who buzz about his throne, singing their hallelujahs. One can never be sure how much we mortals are fooled by our own inadequate virtues and sanctified vices and how much we accept the world's convenient tribute without being convinced by it.

From Reinhold Niebuhr, *Leaves from the Notebook of a Tamed Cynic* (New York: Richard R. Smith, Inc., 1930), pp. 128–29, 134, 143, 154–55. Reprinted by permission.

Nor do I know which interpretation of the facts is to be preferred, not as a matter of truth, but as a matter of charity. What is worse—to be honest with yourself while you are dishonest to the world, or to be dishonest with the world because you have deceived yourself?

I fell in with a gentleman on the Pullman smoker today (Pullman smokers are perfect institutes for plumbing the depths and shallows of the American mind) who had make a killing on the stock exchange. His luck appeared like success from his perspective, and he was full of the confidence with which success endows mortals. He spoke oracularly on any and all subjects. He knew why the farmers were not making any money and why the Europeans were not as prosperous as we. Isn't it strange how gambler's luck gives men the assurance of wisdom for which philosophers search in vain? I pity this man's wife. But she probably regards a new fur coat as adequate compensation for the task of appearing convinced by his obiter dicta.

The situation which the colored people of the city [Detroit] face is really a desperate one, and no one who does not spend real time in gathering the facts can have any idea of the misery and pain which exists among these people recently migrated from the south and unadjusted to our industrial civilization. Hampered both by their own inadequacies and the hostility of a white world they have a desperate fight to keep body and soul together, to say nothing of developing those amenities which raise life above the brute level. I wish that some of our romanticists and sentimentalists could sit through a series of meetings where the real social problems of a city are discussed. They would be cured of their optimism. A city which is built around a productive process and which gives only casual thought and incidental attention to its human problems is really a kind of hell. Thousands in this town are really living in torment while the rest of us eat, drink, and make merry. What a civilization!

The new Ford car is out. The town is full of talk about it. Newspaper reports reveal that it is the topic of the day in all world centers. Crowds storm every exhibit to get the first glimpse of this new creation. Mr. Ford has given out an interview saying that the car has cost him about a hundred million dollars and that after finishing it he still has about a quarter of a billion dollars in the bank.

I have been doing a little arithmetic and have come to the conclusion that the car cost Ford workers at least fifty million in lost wages during the last year. No one knows how many hundreds lost their homes in the period of unemployment, and how many children were taken out of school to help fill the depleted family exchequer, and how many more children lived on short rations during this period. Mr. Ford refuses to concede that he made a mistake in bringing the car out so late. He has a way of impressing the public even with his mistakes. We are now asked to believe that the whole idea of waiting a year after the old car stopped selling, before bringing out a new one, was a great advertising scheme which reveals the perspicacity of this industrial genius. But no one asks about the toll in human lives.

What a civilization this is! Naive gentlemen with a genius for mechanics suddenly become the arbiters over the lives and fortunes of hundreds of thousands. Their moral pretensions are credulously accepted at full value. No one bothers to ask whether an industry which can maintain a cash reserve of a quarter of a billion ought not make some provision for its unemployed. It is enough that the new car is a good one. Here is a work of art in the only realm of art which we can understand. We will therefore refrain from making undue ethical demands upon the artists. Artists of all the ages have been notoriously unamenable to moral discipline. The cry of the hungry is drowned in the song, "Henry has made a lady out of Lizzy."

The final speeches of Sacco and Vanzetti to the court, April 9, 1927

Aliens and admitted anarchists, Nicola Sacco and Bartolomeo Vanzetti were convicted and sentenced to death in 1921 for payroll robbery and murder. Evidence presented at their trial was disputable. The judge, a pillar of Massachusetts society, was obviously biased. He was once overheard calling the defendants "those anarchist bastards." This perversion of justice outraged citizens more than any naked exercise of tyranny. For six years the execution was postponed while defenders in the United States and in Europe demanded that they be released or be given a fair trial. The protest did not help, and after every legal appeal was exhausted the two men died in the electric chair. After sentence was pronounced Vanzetti told a reporter: "If it had not been for these thing, I might have live out my life talking at street corners to scorning men. I might have die, unmarked, unknown, a failure. Now we are not a failure. This is our career and our triumph. Never in our full life could we hope to do such work for tolerance, for joostice, for man's onderstanding of man as now we do by accident. Our words—our lives—our pains—nothing! The taking of our lives—lives of a good shoemaker and a fish-peddler—all! That last moment belong to us—that agony is our triumph."

CLERK: *Nicola Sacco,* have you anything to say why sentence of death should not be passed upon you?

NICOLA SACCO: Yes, sir. I am no orator. It is not very familiar with me the English language, and as I know, as my friend has told me, my

From Marion D. Frankfurter and Gardner Jackson (eds.), *The Letters of Sacco and Vanzetti* (New York), pp. 361–77. Copyright 1928, renewed 1956 by The Viking Press, Inc. Reprinted by permission of The Viking Press, Inc.

comrade Vanzetti will speak more long, so I thought to give him the chance.

I never knew, never heard, even read in history anything so cruel as this Court. After seven years prosecuting they still consider us guilty. And these gentle people here are arrayed with us in this court today. I know the sentence will be between two classes, the oppressed class and the rich class, and there will be always collision between one and the other. We fraternize the people with the books, with the literature. You persecute the people, tyrannize them and kill them. We try the education of people always. You try to put a path between us and some other nationality that hates each other. That is why I am here today on this bench, for having been of the oppressed class. Well, you are the oppressor.

You know it, Judge Thayer—you know all my life, you know why I have been here, and after seven years that you have been persecuting me and my poor wife, and you still today sentence us to death. I would like to tell all my life, but what is the use? You know all about what I say before, that is, my comrade, will be talking, because he is more familiar with the language, and I will give him a chance. My comrade, the kind man to all the children, you sentenced him two times, in the Bridgewater case and the Dedham case, connected with me, and you know he is innocent.

You forget all this population that has been with us for seven years, to sympathize and give us all their energy and all their kindness. You do not care for them. Among that peoples and the comrades and the working class there is a big legion of intellectual people which have been with us for seven years, to not commit the iniquitous sentence, but still the Court goes ahead. And I want to thank you all, you peoples, my comrades who have been with me for seven years, with the Sacco-Vanzetti case, and I will give my friend a chance.

I forget one thing which my comrade remember me. As I said before, Judge Thayer know all my life, and he know that I am never guilty, never —not yesterday, nor today, nor forever.

CLERK: *Bartolomeo Vanzetti,* have you anything to say why sentence of death should not be passed upon you?

BARTOLOMEO VANZETTI: Yes. What I say is that I am innocent, not only of the Braintree crime, but also of the Bridgewater crime. That I am not only innocent of these two crimes, but in all my life I have never stolen and I have never killed and I have never spilled blood. That is what I want to say. And it is not all. Not only am I innocent of these two crimes, not only in all my life I have never stolen, never killed, never spilled blood, but I have struggled all my life, since I began to reason, to eliminate crime from the earth. . . .

It is seven years that we are in jail. What we have suffered during these seven years no human tongue can say, and yet you see me before you, not trembling, you see me looking you in your eyes straight, not blushing, not changing color, not ashamed or in fear. Eugene Debs said that not even a dog—something like that—not even a dog that kill the chickens would have been found guilty by an American jury with the evidence that the Commonwealth have produced against us. I say that not even a leprous dog would have had his appeals refused two times by the Supreme Court of Massachusetts—not even a leprous dog. . . .

We know that you have spoken yourself, and have spoke your hostility against us, and your despisement against us, with friends of yours on the train, at the University Club of Boston, at the Golf Club of Worcester. I am sure that if the people who know all what you say against us have the civil courage to take the stand, maybe your Honor—I am sorry to say this because you are an old man, and I have an old father—but maybe you would be beside us in good justice at this time. . . .

We were tried during a time whose character has now passed into history. I mean by that, a time when there was a hysteria of resentment and hate against the people of our principles, against the foreigner, against slackers, and it seems to me—rather, I am positive of it, that both you and Mr. Katzmann [prosecuting attorney] have done all what it were in your power in order to work out, in order to agitate still more the passion of the juror, the prejudice of the juror, against us. . . . The jury were hating us because we were against the war, and the jury don't know that it makes any difference between a man that is against the war because he believes that the war is unjust, because he hate no country, because he is a cosmopolitan, and a man that is against the war because he is in favor of the other country that fights against the country in which he is, and therefore a spy, an enemy, and he commits any crime in the country in which he is in behalf of the other country in order to serve the other country. We are not men of that kind. Nobody can say that we are German spies or spies of any kind. Katzmann knows very well that. Katzmann knows that we were against the war because we did not believe in the purpose for which they say that the war was fought. We believed that the war is wrong, and we believe this more now after ten years. . . .

From the day that I went in Charlestown, the misfortunate, the population of Charlestown, has doubled in number. Where is the moral good that war has given to the world? Where is the spiritual progress that we have achieved from the war? Where are the security of life, the security of the things that we possess for our necessity? Where are the respect for human life? Where are the respect and the admiration for the good characteristics and the good of the human nature? Never before the war as now have there been so many crimes, so much corruption, so much degeneration as there is now. . . .

This is what I say: I would not wish to a dog or to a snake, to the most low and misfortunate creature of the earth—I would not wish to any of them what I have had to suffer for things that I am not guilty of. I am suffering because I am a radical and indeed I am a radical; I have suffered because I was an Italian, and indeed I am an Italian; I have suffered more for my family and for my beloved than for myself; but I am so convinced to be right that you can only kill me once but if you could execute me two times, and if I could be reborn two other times, I would live again to do what I have done already.

I have finished. Thank you.

The beginning of the "good neighbor" policy: Dwight Morrow in Mexico, as reported by Will Rogers, December 3, 1927

In Latin America the United States practiced the opposite of what it preached for Europe. Instead of seeking isolation, Republican administrations continued the long tradition of involvement. By 1924 the United States was directing the financial affairs of no less than ten Latin American countries. To be sure, Harding withdrew American troops from the Dominican Republic, and Coolidge recalled the marines from Nicaragua—only to order them back once again in 1927. The conscience of Americans, always uneasy at such examples of bald-faced imperialism, now appeared outraged. Coolidge was severely criticized, even by members of his own party. The time was ripe for a policy aimed at winning friends rather than creating enemies.

A first step in this direction was taken when Coolidge appointed Dwight Morrow as ambassador to Mexico. "I do not know what I can do in Mexico," Morrow wrote, "but I can like the Mexicans." A fast friendship developed between Morrow and the Mexican president, Elías Calles. Mexican fears of American armed intervention were dissipated; thorny issues involving oil holdings, land distribution, and anticlericalism, were resolved. In a sense Morrow started what the next President, Herbert Hoover, called the Good Neighbor Policy. In an open letter to Coolidge, the comedian Will Rogers comments on the wisdom of the new policy.

My dear Calvin: Well, I just got down here as you suggested me doing. You said I ought to go somewhere, so I figured it was Mexico. I kinder kept waiting for my transportation and expense money, but as it dident come I figured that with Congress there watching you, and you talking so much Economy, that it would naturally look kinder bad for you to be raiding the Treasury just to send another Ambassador where we already had one. I took a receipt for the fare and will put in a claim, and by the time it goes through all the various departments it will mean a nice little nest egg for my grandchildren.

We've started in to pay some attention to our neighbors on the south. Up to now our calling card to Mexico or Central America has been a gunboat or a bunch of Violets shaped like Marines. We could never understand why Mexico wasent just crazy about us; for we had always had their good-

From Donald Day (ed.), *The Autobiography of Will Rogers* (Boston: Houghton Mifflin Co., 1949), pp. 165–67. Reprinted by permission.

will, and Oil and coffee and minerals, at heart. Of course, as you know up there, Mr. President, some were just for going down and taking Mexico over. Where did this country down here, with no great chains of Commercial Clubs, and Chambers of Commerce and Junior and Freshman Chamber of Commerces, and Rotary and Kiwanis and Lions and Tigers Clubs, and No golf pants, and no advertising Radio programs—where did a Nation like that come in to have Oil anyhow? It was a kind of an imposition on their part to even have to go to the trouble of going down and taking their country over.

But our wiser heads got to thinking, "Well, we picked up the Phillipines and now we got no place to lay it down." Then some that had studied History says, "Look at England! They took everything that wasent nailed down and look at 'em." Then somebody got to figuring out: "We better find some other way."

Now I don't know if it was you, Calvin, or not. I kinder give you credit for doping it out. Well, asking a man to go to Mexico at that time in the interests of the United States was just like saying "Your tumbler of Carbolic acid is ready, Sir. Would you like water with it?" You just said, "I wonder if we tried using kindness and common sense would it do any good, or would it be such a novelty that Mexico would think we were kidding 'em?"

That's when I think your thoughts hit on Morrow. Well, I am not kidding you when I tell you you was inspired. You hit on him when nobody else was thinking about him, and here there was a couple of hundred so-called Diplomats laying off that would have even been willing to go to Haiti. Well, if you remember, when you appointed him he gave up his job with Morgan. That made a hit with everybody, for it showed that he didn't have the least inkling of a Politician in him. For it's not necessary or even customary to give up a side line when taking on any kind of Government work. . . .

You know, this Morrow does a lot of things that I imagine are not in the book that tells what Diplomats should do. You know, he kinder figures out that if Calles is the man he was sent there to deal with, that Calles is the man that he should know and understand. Diplomats, when they get to a Country, they figure they must first meet the rich people of their own Country who are living there, and then the rich ones who belong in the Country. But as far as the Government officials are concerned, why, they will perhaps know them at some time through the exchange of official visits.

You know, the other night on the train, I was late for dinner, and when I come into the diner, the President had the interpreter say to me very sternly and with much gravity:

"Mr. Rogers, you are late for dinner. I don't know if you know it or not, but that is a very grave breach of etiquette. In fact, it is an insult to the President for you not to be here to sit down with him when he arrives. What have you to say?"

"Well, I just want to tell the President that I am sorry. I was up in the front cars with some of the soldiers. I have only been in Mexico one week, but you tell him I have learned that it's better to stand in with the Soldiers of Mexico than with the President."

Well, he got quite a kick out of that, and to show you he was there with a Nifty, he said, "You tell Mr. Rogers that that was very smart of him to find that out, but that I found it out years before he did—that's why I am President."

The election of 1928: Al Smith's speech against religious bigotry, September 1928

Having lost in 1924 with John W. Davis as their candidate, the Democrats in 1928 nominated Governor Alfred E. Smith of New York—who was handicapped by his Tammany Hall background, his Catholicism, his open opposition to prohibition, even by his distinct New York accent. It is difficult to assess how significant the religious issue was in Smith's defeat, but its presence was obvious. A Republican committeewoman from Virginia published a letter saying: "We must save the United States from being Romanized and rum-ridden." Such remarks were typical in many parts of America. Smith's Catholicism was an "underground issue," until he brought it out into the open in a fiery speech in Oklahoma City, before a hostile Protestant audience.

Now there is another lie, or series of lies, being carefully put out around the country, and it is surprising to find the number of people who seem to believe it. I would have refrained from talking about this if it were not for the avalanche of letters that have poured into the National Committee, and have poured into my own office in the Executive Department at Albany, asking for the facts. And that is the lie that has been spread around that since I have been Governor of the State of New York nobody has ever been appointed to office but Catholics.

The cabinet of the Governorship is made up of fourteen men. Three of them are Catholics, ten of them are Protestants, and one of them is a Jew. Outside of the cabinet members, the Governor appoints two boards and commissions under the cabinet, twenty-six people. Twelve of them are Protestants. Aside from that, various other State officials, making up boards and commissions, were appointed by the Governor, making a total of 157 appointments, of which 35 were Catholics, 106 were Protestants, 12 were Jewish, and four we were unable to find out about. . . .

Now just another word and I am going to finish. Here is [a circular], the meanest thing that I have seen in the whole campaign. It is the product of the lowest and most cunning mind that could train itself to do something

From *The New York Times,* September 21, 1928.

mean or dirty. This was sent to me by a member of the Masonic Order, a personal friend of mine. It purports to be a circular sent out under Catholic auspices to Catholic voters, and tells how "we have control in New York; stick together and we'll get control of the country." And designedly, it said to the roster of the Masonic Order in my State, because so many members of that order are friends of mine and have been voting for me for the last ten years, "Stand together."

Now I disown that circular; the Democratic Party disowns it; and I have no right to talk for the Catholic Church, but I'll take a chance and say that nobody inside the Catholic Church has been stupid enough to do a thing like that.

Let me make myself perfectly clear. I do not want any Catholic in the United States of America to vote for me on the 6th of November because I am a Catholic. If any Catholic in this country believes that the welfare, the well-being, the prosperity, the growth, and the expansion of the United States is best conserved and best promoted by the election of Hoover, I want him to vote for Hoover and not for me. But, on the other hand, I have the right to say that any citizen of this country that believes I can promote its welfare, that I am capable of steering the ship of State safely through the next four years, and then votes against me because of my religion, he is not a real, pure, genuine American.

Epitaph for the 1920's: by James T. Adams, 1931

"Given a chance to go forward with the policies of the last eight years," declared Herbert Hoover in 1928, "we shall soon with the help of God be in sight of the day when poverty will be banished from this nation." The stock market crash and national depression shattered such wild-eyed utopian visions and exposed the fragile base upon which prosperity had rested. For a decade Americans had listened to the gospel of wealth and prosperity, and had followed the creed. Disillusioned by World War I, they had sacrificed idealism for materialism, only to discover that the new gods were false. In 1931 the historian James T. Adams reviewed the meaning of the 1920's in an uncommonly perspicacious part of a larger study of American history.

In the government of Harding, likable but weak, scandals piled up. ... But no one cared. We wanted "normalcy" and money. When Harding died in office, Coolidge succeeded to the Presidency, and the steady work of paying off the national debt and of manufacturing prosperity continued. We asked for nothing better than higher and higher prices in the stock mar-

From James T. Adams, *The Epic of America* (Boston: Atlantic-Little, Brown and Co., 1931), pp. 397–400. Copyright 1931, 1933, copyright renewed 1959 by James Truslow Adams. Reprinted by permission.

ket. We initiated conferences for reducing armaments, the last two of which accomplished little or nothing. Some of the Great Powers adhered to our so-called Kellogg Pact to "outlaw war," though it is somewhat difficult to discern just what may have been gained by that idealistic gesture. In international affairs our participation remained much that of the "darling daughter" who was allowed to go swimming providing she "hung her clothes on a hickory limb and did not go near the water." No influential statesman dared urge our joining the League with which we had saddled Europe, and suggestions that we should adhere to the World Court for the settlement of international disputes, though we had formerly been forward in such movements, fell on deaf ears. Public opinion, at the first real touch of international responsibility, appeared to have shut up like a "sensitive plant," the leaves of which close together tightly at the touch of the human hand.

We had accepted the great corporations, partly because we were making money in the rise in their stocks and partly because we realized that the needs of modern business on a world scale somehow called for their existence. Our mass production was insisting on world markets, and our greatest industries, such as motor-car manufacture and moving pictures, rested in part on certain essentials which could only be procured in foreign countries. We were trying to force our goods on every nation. Our great business enterprises, such as the International Harvester, Standard Oil, Ford Motor, and others, were building plants and investing tens of millions of dollars in France and England and Germany and other countries. Our banks were opening branches in London, Paris, Buenos Aires, everywhere. But we still were trying to live in the frontier stage of thought and believed we could live to ourselves by saying we would. To a great extent, we had given up counting on our State Commissions of many sorts, and had come to realize that under modern conditions only Federal regulation would serve. We still insisted, however, upon dividing the world into water-tight compartments in spite of every evidence that it had become a unified organism in which each part depended upon free circulation with all other parts. Under President Hoover, who had been considered to be the great engineering mind applied to the problems of modern business and government, we enacted a tariff that almost staggered ourselves with the prohibitive height to which duties were raised, in spite of the fact that we insisted upon collection from other nations of over $11,000,000,000 in loans even the interest on which could only be paid by selling goods to us.

The battle cries of Roosevelt and Wilson in the struggle to realize the American dream had been changed into the small-town Chamber of Commerce shouts for "Coolidge Prosperity." We were told by our leaders that a new era had dawned in which we were forever to lift ourselves by our own bootstraps and everyone could buy whatever he chose as long as his credit held out with bank or salesman. The wild speculation in the stock market, which sucked in not only the old semi-gambling elements but stenographers, elevator boys, barbers, every type of individual—even hitherto cautious men and women who were beginning to be unable to make both ends meet under the insistent demands of our "high standard of living"—rose to more and more fantastic heights. When sane voices were raised in protest, the President or his Secretary of the Treasury would make a statement assuring the public that all was well. The latter, Mellon, with his wealth that was popularly estimated at several hundred millions, carried great weight, owing to his public position and presumed private shrewdness. When Coolidge, at the end of his second term, declined to run again, Hoover was elected on his promises of a still greater "prosperity" which was to be put on a scientific basis and to last forever. Poverty was to be abolished, and we were to live in an economic paradise. In spite of religious and other issues injected into the "whispering" campaign against his opponent "Al" Smith—an able executive but son of an immigrant, a "Wet," and a Roman Catholic—the real issue was the continuance of the wild speculation and of that business "prosperity" which in fact had begun to crack before Hoover was elected, in spite of the denials of the highest officials in the government.

At length, after a few months more, the inevitable crash which had long been foreseen by sane business men came. Hoover struggled against both adversity and truth, and Mellon soon wrapped himself in silence and his millions. The people paid, and the wake of ruin was as broad as the land. The situation was not merely American. It was world-wide. We had hung our clothes on the hickory limb, but it had done us no good. We had tried not to go near the water, and the water had rushed over us. It was the surge of that world panic and depression which was as inevitable after the great destruction of capital in the World War as severe weakness would be in a man after amputation of both legs. This had been predicted for months in print by the ablest bankers in Europe and America while the American government had encouraged the college professors and stenographers and bootblacks to pay their way by carrying stocks on margin. . . .

We had got tired of idealism and had been urged to place our destinies in the hands of the safe realists, hard-headed business men who would stand no nonsense about "moral issues," of which we were told we had had enough, and would be practical. Our most conspicuously successful manufacturer, Mr. Ford, announced . . . that "we now know that anything which is economically right is also morally right. There can be no conflict between good economics and good morals." As the successful business man would consider himself the best interpreter of good economics, he thus set himself up as the best judge of national morals. Long ago we noted the beginning of the confusion in the American mind between business and virtue. That confusion by 1930 had gone full circle. By then it had become complete. If what was economically right was also morally right, we could surrender our souls to professors of economics and captains of industry.

But, having surrendered idealism for the sake of prosperity, the "prac-

tical men" bankrupted us on both of them. We had forgotten, though no
post-war leader dared to remind us of the fact, that it is impractical to be
only "practical." Without a vision the people perish. The waste of war is
always spiritual as well as material, and post-war decades are ever periods
in which the fires of noble aims flicker but feebly. By 1930 our post-war
decade and our post-war prosperity were over. Let us hope that our post-
war materialism may also pass. We have yet to see what shall come, but the
task clearly lies before us to

> Rebuild in beauty on the burnt-out coals,
> Not to the heart's desire, but the soul's.

"Racketeering" in America: a report by an anonymous author, 1932

*From the beginning prohibition failed to operate as the reformers had intended.
Criminals, such as "Scarface" Al Capone, built underworld empires based on
smuggling, manufacturing, and distributing alcohol, and then extended their
interests into prostitution, gambling, drugs, and other rackets. Gang-wars and
gang-murders were common, as were the bribing of police, judges, and politicians. So powerful were these racketeers that in 1931 the author of the following
essay decided that it was wiser to remain anonymous. It was included in a book
of short essays by various authors describing America for European readers.*

It is difficult to think of crime in the United States without thinking
also of Prohibition, for it is Prohibition which lies at the root of the organized crime with which the country is disturbed—the gang-crime which
goes by the typically American name of "racketeering. . . ." Prohibition was
not two years old before it became apparent that there were enormous
profits to be gained from the illegal distribution of alcoholic beverages. The
first illicit salesmen—or bootleggers, as they are termed—were casual individuals who fell more by chance than by plan into the sale and delivery
of forbidden liquors. But as the country at large began to react from the
sudden passage of the law, and to have a normal, human desire for a drink
of whiskey or wine or beer, shrewder fellows undertook seriously to supply
the demand. A dozen gangs, or rings, or illegal companies sprang up in the
populous metropolitan centers and undertook the importation of whiskey
from Canada, Cuba, and Europe—the manufacture of synthetic liquor from
industrial alcohol—the clandestine manufacture of beer—and, just as
important, the efficient distribution of this product.

From Fred J. Ringel (ed.), *America as Americans See It* (New York), pp. 171–175.
Copyright 1932 by Harcourt Brace Jovanovich, Inc. Copyright 1960 by Fred J. Ringel.
Reprinted by permission of the publishers.

The most impressive growth among these gangs was in the City of Chicago, rather than in New York, and the most typical as well as the most successful of the Chicago gangs was that headed by the notorious Al Capone. To understand the workings and the behavior of Al Capone's gang is to understand organized crime in the United States—the only sort of crime which is the least bit different from the crime which is familiar in every European country. By his energy and his cunning and his strength, the Italian immigrant Al Capone built up his powerful organization. He is the sole dictator, and his authority includes the giving of life and death to his subordinates. The gang gives employment to hundreds of men and a considerable number of women, and of all these it demands an unswerving loyalty. Any momentary lapse from this loyalty is punishable by death, and the punishment is invariably carried out without qualms.

The basic enterprise of the Capone gang has always been "bootlegging" or the concentration and distribution of illicit liquors. This enterprise is complex in the extreme, and requires systematic business methods which might well be adopted by many more respectable organizations. Huge and steady convoys of whiskey and beer and wine are brought by motor across international borders. Millions of gallons of industrial alcohol are diverted from their usual channels by falsification of records and bribery of government inspectors. Salesmen and delivery trucks operate on regular schedules. The whiskey and beer business of the Capone gang was, in 1929, a fifty million dollar enterprise. The gross receipts were approximately that amount. It is obvious that such a considerable business must be protected from interference, and that there are two obstacles that lie in its path: the forces of law, and the activities of competing gangs. It is equally obvious that there are two ways to deal with each of these obstacles: the use of armed forces, and the use of money in liberal amounts. In the case of the competitors, the former method has been adopted. In the case of the law, it has been deemed simpler to buy immunity from interference.

The entire law enforcement agency of the United States has been affected by the growth of the gangs—and the tremendous sums of money which the gangs are willing to pay constables, detectives, prosecuting attorneys, judges, and jurors. It has been estimated that of the fifty million dollars taken in by the Capone gang in 1929, at least ten million dollars was paid out for government protection: paid to government servants of the municipality, the state, and the federal system. The result was what might be expected. Neither policemen, detectives, sheriffs, nor prosecuting attorneys made any serious efforts to impede the business of the gang. Prohibition agents earning two thousand dollars a year have grown mysteriously rich. Judges have been discovered to be the tools of the bootleggers. In New York City, not long ago, two scows owned by the city and commonly used for hauling garbage out to be dumped into the ocean, were discovered loaded with contraband whiskey.

It is not surprising that the corruption of law enforcement agencies, brought about by Prohibition, should affect the entire national viewpoint toward law and order. With the newspapers carrying daily stories of dishonor in high places, the high respect for the laws has collapsed alarmingly. As a result of this, the percentage of those crimes that we call ordinary—robbery and swindling and murders of passion—have naturally increased to a considerable extent.

In dealing with their competitors, the gangs have adopted the frontier law of the bullet. Three to four hundred gangsters are murdered in the streets or in saloons or in secret apartments every year. They are murdered by rival gangsters, and nobody is ever punished. The code of these bands—never reveal anything to the police—holds good without fail, even on the deathbed, and such a thing as a formal accusation against an assailant is utterly unknown. The dying gangster depends upon his friends to provide revenge for him.

The gangs discovered, four or five years ago, that with their excellent organization, their control by bribery over the police, and the terrifying strength of their revolvers and machine guns and bombs, that there were other sources of profit in addition to "bootlegging." They began to prey upon merchants and manufacturers of nearly every class. As an example: A gang will take out a license as the Milk Dealers' Protective Association. Representatives of the gang will call upon all the dairymen of a city, and offer membership in their association for a monthly payment of one hundred dollars. They will say that certain unscrupulous men wish to damage milk dealers, and that the Association will provide protection against these marauders—who are, of course, the very gangsters of the association. If the dairyman pays his hundred dollars monthly, he is unmolested. If he refuses, his buildings are burned, his drivers beaten, or tablets put in his milk to sour it beyond use. That is the typical "racket" which preys upon every division of industry, except, of course, the great manufacturing corporations which are too powerful to be intimidated.

Robbers and thieves—criminals who once made their living by burglary or picking pockets or safe-cracking—have taken a leaf from the forthright methods of the gangs. House-breaking and such similar crimes have almost disappeared in the great American cities. In their stead we have the hold-up: the simple, blunt robbery at the point of a pistol, usually in the street or in a shop. It is simpler to procure a pistol, walk into a shop, and demand the contents of the cash drawer on pain of death, than to carry out an elaborate and dangerous campaign of entering that same shop by night, silently rifling the drawer, and sneaking off through the empty streets. . . .

Thus we arrive at the discovery that crime in America is not, in modern times, a thing of cunning, of hidden plans and hidden performances in the dark, of sinister fellows who creep about the underworld and suddenly prey upon citizens who have their backs turned, or who are asleep. It is the outright use of force, and of money for bribing officers.

There are no secrets about it. And the very criminals who are making millions out of American citizens walk openly through the streets, or drive through the streets in their magnificent automobiles. It is impossible to get the evidence that will convict them—because the police are bribed or rendered helpless by the protective silence that meets them when they go searching for evidence.

On the other hand, I might say that the ordinary, peaceful citizen is in no danger to speak of—that he is rarely thrown into contact with the criminals, and that when he is, his life is in no grave peril. They use their weapons chiefly upon each other. Furthermore, it is to these same criminals that the citizen is indebted for his quiet glass of beer, his cocktail, or his whiskey when he is in a mood for revelry.

The depression in America: three accounts, 1932

Millions were out of work. Factories were closed down. Homeless men wandered the city streets, or drifted aimlessly from town to town. Many families made the long trek to California in search of a livelihood. Starvation was not uncommon, although the statistics called it malnutrition. Riots erupted in hundreds of communities for food, for jobs, for a living wage. Thousands of veterans marched on Washington demanding payment of a bonus that was not due until 1945, and were driven out by force. Brutality was widespread. The following three accounts capture the feeling of hopelessness and desperation which pervaded the land.

THE DEPRESSION IN NEW YORK

After vainly trying to get a stay of dispossession until Jan. 15 from his apartment at 46 Hancock Street, in Brooklyn, yesterday, Peter J. Cornell, 48 years old, a former roofing contractor out of work and penniless, fell dead in the arms of his wife.

A doctor gave the cause of his death as heart disease, and the police said it had at least partly been caused by the bitter disappointment of a long day's fruitless attempt to prevent himself and his family being put out on the street.

Just before he died Cornell had carried a bag of coal he had just received from the police upstairs.

Cornell owed $5 in rent in arrears and $39 for January which his landlord required in advance. Failure to produce the money resulted in a dispossess order being served on the family yesterday and to take effect at the end of the week.

From *The New York Times*, January 16, 1932.

After vainly seeking assistance elsewhere, he was told during the day by the Home Relief Bureau that it would have no funds with which to help him until Jan. 15.

THE DEPRESSION IN WISCONSIN

Machine-guns were used by a sheriff's posse in evicting a farm family from their home in Wisconsin. Fortunately, no one was injured, although hundreds of shots were fired on both sides. Throughout the middle west the tension between the farmers and authorities has been growing ... as a result of tax and foreclosure sales. In many cases evictions have been prevented only by mass action on the part of the farmers. However, until the Cichon homestead near Elkhorn, Wisconsin, was besieged on December 6 by a host of deputy sheriffs armed with machine-guns, rifles, shotguns, and tear-gas bombs, there had been no actual violence. Max Cichon's property was auctioned off at a foreclosure sale last August, but he refused to allow either the buyer or the authorities to approach his home. He built a barbed-wire entanglement around the buildings and held off unwelcome visitors with a shotgun. The sheriff called upon Cichon to submit peacefully. When he refused to do so, the sheriff ordered deputies to lay down a barrage of machine-gun and rifle fire. The battle lasted twenty minutes. Cichon is now in jail in Elkhorn, and his wife and two children, who were with him in the house, are being cared for in the county hospital. Cichon is not a trouble-maker. He enjoys the confidence and respect of his neighbors, who only recently elected him justice of the peace of the town of Sugar Creek. That a man of his standing and disposition should go to such lengths in defying the authorities is a clear warning that we may expect further trouble in the agricultural districts unless the farmers are soon helped.

From *The Nation*, December 21, 1932, p. 600. Reprinted by permission.

THE DEPRESSION IN THE WEST

In the state of Washington I was told that the forest fires raging in that region all summer and fall were caused by unemployed timber workers and bankrupt farmers in an endeavor to earn a few honest dollars as fire-fighters. The last thing I saw on the night I left Seattle was numbers of women searching for scraps of food in the refuse piles of the principal market of that city. A number of Montana citizens told me of thousands of bushels of wheat left in the fields uncut on account of its low price that hardly paid for the harvesting. In Oregon I saw thousands of bushels of

From *Unemployment in the United States. Hearings before a Subcommittee of the Committee on Labor, Seventy-second Congress, First Session* (Washington, D.C., 1932), pp. 98–99.

apples rotting in the orchards. Only absolute[ly] flawless apples were still salable, at from 40 to 50 cents a box containing 200 apples. At the same time, there are millions of children who, on account of the poverty of their parents, will not eat one apple this winter.

While I was in Oregon the Portland *Oregonian* bemoaned the fact that thousands of ewes were killed by the sheep raisers because they did not bring enough in the market to pay the freight on them. And while Oregon sheep raisers fed mutton to the buzzards, I saw men picking for meat scraps in the garbage cans in the cities of New York and Chicago. I talked to one man in a restaurant in Chicago. He told me of his experience in raising sheep. He said that he had killed 3,000 sheep this fall and thrown them down the canyon, because it cost $1.10 to ship a sheep, and then he would get less than a dollar for it. He said he could not afford to feed the sheep, and he would not let them starve, so he just cut their throats and threw them down the canyon.

The roads of the West and Southwest teem with hungry hitchhikers. The campfires of the homeless are seen along every railroad track. I saw men, women, and children walking over the hard roads. Most of them were tenant farmers who had lost their all in the late slump in wheat and cotton. Between Clarksville and Russellville, Arkansas, I picked up a family. The woman was hugging a dead chicken under a ragged coat. When I asked her where she had procured the fowl, first she told me she had found it dead in the road, and then added in grim humor, "They promised me a chicken in the pot, and now I got mine."

9
The Era
of
Franklin D.
Roosevelt

The philosophy of Herbert Hoover: from a campaign speech, October 31, 1932

During the depression Hoover appeared to be obsessed with the idea of a balanced budget. "Prosperity," he once said, "cannot be restored by raids on the public Treasury." Hoover was not heartless or indifferent to public suffering. He was concerned about the homeless, the jobless, and the indigent, but he was committed to the principle that federal funds would wreck individual initiative. "If we start appropriations of this character," he announced, "we have not only impaired something infinitely valuable in the life of the American people but have struck at the roots of self-government." In the 1932 campaign Franklin D. Roosevelt never defined with any precision what he meant by a "new deal," but Hoover suspected that it posed a threat to the tradition of American individualism which was the cornerstone of his philosophy.

This campaign is more than a contest between two men. It is more than a contest between two parties. It is a contest between two philosophies of government. We are told by the opposition that we must have a change, that we must have a new deal. It is not the change that comes from normal development of national life to which I object, but the proposal to alter the whole foundations of our national life which have been builded through generations of testing and struggle, and of the principles upon which we have builded the Nation. The expressions our opponents use must refer to important changes in our economic and social system and our system of Government, otherwise they are nothing but vacuous words. And I realize that in this time of distress many of our people are asking whether our social and economic system is incapable of that great primary function of providing security and comfort of life to all of the firesides of our 25,000,000 homes in America, whether our social system provides for fundamental development and progress of our people, whether our form of government is capable of originating and sustaining that security and progress.

This question is the basis upon which our opponents are appealing to the people in their fears and distress. They are proposing changes and so called new deals which would destroy the very foundations of our American system. Our people should consider the primary facts before they come to the judgment—not merely through political agitation, the glitter of promise, and the discouragement of temporary hardships—whether they will support changes which radically affect the whole system which has been builded up by 150 years of the toil of our fathers. They should not approach the question in the despair with which our opponents would clothe it. . . .

We have heard a great deal in this campaign about reactionaries, con-

From Herbert Hoover, *Campaign Speeches of 1932* (New York, 1933), pp. 167–68, 191–92.

servatives, progressives, liberals, and radicals. I have not yet heard an attempt by any one of the orators who mouth these phrases to define the principles upon which they base these classifications. There is one thing I can say without any question of doubt—that is, the spirit of liberalism is to create free men; it is not the regimentation of men. It is not the extension of bureaucracy. I have said . . . before that you cannot extend the mastery of government over the daily life of a people without somewhere making it master of people's souls and thoughts. Expansion of government in business means that the Government, in order to protect itself from the political consequences of its errors, is driven irresistibly to greater and greater control of the Nation's press and platform. Free speech does not live many hours after free industry and free commerce die. It is a false liberalism that interprets itself into Government operation of business. Every step in that direction poisons the very roots of liberalism. It poisons political equality, free speech, free press, and equality of opportunity. It is the road not to liberty but to less liberty. True liberalism is found not in striving to spread bureaucracy, but in striving to set bounds to it. True liberalism seeks all legitimate freedom first in the confident belief that without such freedom the pursuit of other blessings is in vain. Liberalism is a force truly of the spirit proceeding from the deep realization that economic freedom cannot be sacrificed if political freedom is to be preserved.

The philosophy of Franklin D. Roosevelt: from the memoirs of Frances Perkins, 1930's

Despite the warnings and laments and prophecies of disaster made by laissez-faire Republicans, Roosevelt was hardly a revolutionary. Harold Laski has noted that Roosevelt "had very great qualities, imagination, a sense of humor (a supreme need in a democratic statesman), an inner self-confidence born, no doubt, of his own triumph over physical difficulty, the gift of magnanimity, the power of direct approach, the great art of working in cooperation with others, and creating in them, by his own inner generosity, the sense of high adventure. . . . But he was never convinced that the foundations of the Americanism he inherited were really inadequate to the demands made upon its institutional expression. A large part of his approach to the problems of his time was conditioned by his belief that the pathology of American life, especially of its economic life, was occasioned by the malpractices of evil men; and from this he drew the inference that it is in the power of legislation within the existing legal framework, to correct those malpractices. . . . It was always his assumption that restoration, and not innovation, was his major task." Roosevelt has thus been seen as the savior of capitalism and its destroyer—depending upon the per-

From Frances Perkins, *The Roosevelt I Knew* (New York: The Viking Press, Inc., 1946), pp. 329–30. Reprinted by permission.

spective of the critic. Frances Perkins' account of Roosevelt's beliefs include the
humorous story of a reporter frustrated in his attempt to classify Roosevelt's
thought into some rigid philosophic niche.

Roosevelt was entirely willing to try experiments. He had no theoreti-
cal or ideological objections to public ownership when that was necessary,
but it was his belief that it would greatly complicate the administrative
system if we had too much. He recognized, however, that certain enterprises could best be carried on under public control. He recognized that we
probably would never have enough cheap electric power to supply the
needs of the people if the Government did not undertake vast programs in
the Tennessee and Missouri valleys, and he believed that plenty of power
at low rates was necessary for the development of a high standard of living
and for business progress. Just as the need for production in wartime is so
great that the government must take a hand in it, so he was able to accept
the idea that in peacetime too the Government must sometimes carry on
enterprises because of the enormous amount of capital expenditure required
or the preponderance of the experimental element. He was willing to concede that there were some fields in which such Government participation
might be required permanently. But he always resisted the frequent suggestion of the Government's taking over railroads, mines, etc., on the
grounds that it was unnecessary and would be a clumsy way to get the
service needed.

A superficial reporter once said to Roosevelt in my presence, "Mr.
President, are you a Communist?"

"No."

"Are you a capitalist?"

"No."

"Are you a Socialist?"

"No," he said, with a look of surprise as if he were wondering what he
was being cross examined about.

The young man said, "Well, what is your philosophy then?"

"Philosophy?" asked the President, puzzled. "Philosophy? I am a
Christian and a Democrat—that's all."

Those two words expressed, I think, just about what he was. They
expressed the extent of his political and economic radicalism. He was willing to do experimentally whatever was necessary to promote the Golden
Rule and other ideals he considered to be Christian, and whatever could be
done under the Constitution of the United States and under the principles
which have guided the Democratic party.

Having fun with Mordecai Ezekiel: Congress debates the Agricultural Adjustment Act, April 10, 1933

The American experience seemed to reverse the history of mankind. While people elsewhere starved because of scarcity, in the United States starvation occurred in the midst of abundance. Too many hogs, too much wheat and corn and milk and cotton, resulted in rockbottom market prices. Obviously, legislation was needed to bring into balance the production and consumption of farm products.

Farm leaders, meeting with Secretary of Agriculture Henry Wallace and his advisers, worked out a program which Congress debated for nearly two months—the Agricultural Adjustment Act. The floor manager of the act in the upper House was Senator Ellison D. Smith, familiarly known as "Cotton Ed" since he raised that product on his South Carolina plantation, and was unusually sympathetic to the interests of cotton planters. The major arguments for the act were tended by Senator Joseph T. Robinson of Arkansas, referred to by the sharecroppers of his state as "Greasy Joe." These two could not do much when Republican Senators, abetted by Huey Long, the Louisiana Kingfish, read obscure and complicated statistical explanations from the writings of a Department of Agriculture economist, Mordecai Ezekiel. Long charged that the bill was a "half-baked scheme" fashioned by Ezekiel.

[ARTHUR H.] VANDENBURG: Senator [Smith] seems to be having some trouble with the price-fixing factors of the bill. . . . I have in my hand a pamphlet issued by the Department of Agriculture under the authorship of Mr. Mordecai Ezekiel, who, I understand, will be one of the high administrators of the new system.

[ELLISON D.] SMITH: What is the name?

VANDENBURG: Mr. Mordecai Ezekiel.

SMITH: Yes, sir.

VANDENBURG: In dealing with the price factors affecting hogs, Mr. Ezekiel makes the whole thing very plain, and I want to read Senator Smith these sentences.

SMITH: In reference to what?

VANDENBURG: The price of hogs, which are affected by this bill. . . .

The price for each month may be conceived as represented by a small black ball, suspended above the line for its own date, at the height of the average price for that month, and as far over from right to left as indicated by the supply for that month. There would necessarily be only one ball for each month. These balls, however, would all be very close to the demand surface, a little above it for those months when the actual price was higher than the price as shown by

From the *Congressional Record,* Seventy-third Congress, First Session, pp. 1446–47.

the correlation formula and a little lower for the months when the actual price was a little below the estimated price. In general, however, it would be seen that the demand surface approximated the position that these prices occupy, as they were thus suspended through space and time.

I want to know if that does not clear it up. [Laughter]

SMITH: I should like to have the Senator explain that explanation. . . .

[M. M.] LOGAN: I should like to know the name of the authority.

VANDENBURG: The authority is Mr. Mordecai Ezekiel, who is to be one of the high administrators of the new farm relief bill.

LOGAN: He would not be supposed to know anything about hogs, would he, with that name? [Laughter] . . .

[HUEY P.] LONG: It is hardly fair to the Department which has issued the bulletin to which attention has been called to have excerpts read . . . without the accompanying descriptive matter. . . . I ask that the portion on page 34 may be read by the clerk.

THE PRESIDING OFFICER: The clerk will read.

The legislative clerk read as follows:

Factors X_1, X_2, and X_3, were included as different measures of the influence of supply; factors X_4, X_5, X_6, X_7, and X_8 as factors influencing demand; X_9 to allow for any trend in price apart from that accounted for by the factors stated; and X_{10} to adjust for the effect of changes in the value of money upon hog prices. Since practically all of the factors were thought to have a relative rather than an additive relation to price, all of the factors except X_9, time, were stated as logarithms. Correlating the factors thus stated, a multiple correlation of hog prices with the 10 other factors of $R = 0.936$ was obtained. Correlating this to take account of the fact that 10 constants were determined with only 90 observations, the true multiple correlation is reduced to 0.928.

The regression equation is as follows: $\log X_{11} = -0.09443 \log X_1 + 0.15888 \log X_2 - 0.21986 \log X_3 - 0.23675 \log X_4 - 0.07250 \log X_5 + 2.23777 \log X_6 + 0.04759 \log X_7 + 0.22659 \log X_8 - 0.03036 \log X_9 + 1.63099 \log X_{10} - K.$ [Laughter]

[BURTON K.] WHEELER: Mr. President, are they still talking about hogs? [Laughter] . . .

[JOSEPH T.] ROBINSON: Mr. President, it is perfectly manifest that higher mathematics has not much recognition in this body.

Propaganda for the National Recovery Administration: The Blue Eagle Drive, August 1933

General Hugh Johnson, the tough and colorful ex-cavalry officer who was chosen to administer the National Industrial Recovery Act, predicted that it will be "red fire at first and dead cats afterwards." Johnson made the Blue Eagle the symbol of the NRA and, by pageantry and persuasion, attempted to arouse popular allegiance. His technique is evident in the following instructions to volunteer NRA workers preparing for a week-long drive to launch the program. The Blue Eagle was seen everywhere—on billboards and fences, on trees, in store windows, pasted on cars, printed on newspaper mastheads. A quarter of a million people marched down New York's Fifth Avenue in a Blue Eagle parade. But Johnson's prediction was correct. The NRA proved to be one of the most serious blunders of the New Deal. The Blue Eagle signs faded; their torn and dusty remnants became a mocking reminder that prosperity could not be gained by faith and ballyhoo.

THE BLUE EAGLE DRIVE

MILLION AND A HALF VOLUNTEERS TO TAKE THE FIELD AUGUST 28
OBJECTIVE: EVERY EMPLOYER ON THE DOTTED LINE

Almost every city, hamlet, and village in the United States has been organized by its leading citizens, and an army of a million and a half volunteer workers is either now in the field or ready to take the field to insure the success of the President's reemployment campaign.

Activities of every nature have been under way for several weeks in many communities. These activities should be continued without slackening.

To insure that every employer in your community will sign the President's reemployment agreement, it has been decided that an intensive campaign shall be made in every community in America during the week beginning August 28.

TO RECEIVE MARCHING ORDERS

On Sunday, August 27, every NRA volunteer organization in America will receive its marching orders for this intensive Blue Eagle drive. Practically all other programs on the air will be suspended for a period of one hour—9:45 P.M. to 10:45 P.M., eastern standard time—during which time there will be broadcast from Washington and other points in the United States a program of unsurpassed excellence, introducing prominent person-

From the National Recovery Administration, Speakers' Division, *Pointed Paragraphs for Speakers: The Blue Eagle Drive* (Washington, D.C., 1933), reprinted in E. David Cronon (ed.), *Twentieth Century America* (Homewood, Illinois: The Dorsey Press, 1966), Vol. II, 89–92.

alities from the Pacific to the Atlantic. Appearing in this hour's broadcast will be—

Gen. Hugh S. Johnson	United States Marine Band
Will Rogers	Howard Barlow Orchestra
John Charles Thomas	Freddie Rich Orchestra
Army Band	Frank Black Orchestra
Navy Band	Walter Damrosch Orchestra
Jessica Dragonette	Al Jolson
Eddie Cantor	Jack Pearl
Burns & Allen	Bing Crosby
Kate Smith	Mino Martini
Mme. Ernestine Schumann-Heink	Ruth Etting

As the closing feature of this great broadcast, Gen. Hugh S. Johnson, the field marshall for the Blue Eagle drive, will give his final marching orders to the army of 1,500,000 volunteers in all parts of America.

YOUR SPEAKING CAMPAIGN

During the week of August 28 an intensive speaking campaign should be carried out. To organize this campaign you should begin immediately. To assist, we are sending this pamphlet with additional material that will be helpful in the Blue Eagle drive. Every meeting in your community should be addressed by your best local speakers or others that you may secure elsewhere. One of the plans in the Blue Eagle drive is a house-to-house and business-to-business canvass by the "shock-troops" of this huge volunteer army. To stimulate their efforts, to spur them on, and to create a public sentiment that will make their work the more effective, this intensive speaking campaign should be carried out. . . .

SPEECH SUGGESTION FOR OPENING DRIVE

(The following general outline can be easily adapted, elaborated, and localized by speakers opening the Blue Eagle Drive.)

The hour is here! From the highest command has come the order to move forward. THE BLUE EAGLE DRIVE IS ON!

A million and a half patriotic citizens have enlisted in the ranks—the shock troops in the greatest peace-time drive in American history. A million and a half volunteers—mobilized almost overnight, as it were, with a burst of patriotic fervor unprecedented in peace time. A vast army of men and women—standing shoulder to shoulder in a common cause—heading the marching orders as they reverberate down through the ranks and into every community in America. The final word has been given, and now, as our President so clearly prophesied a few short weeks ago, "we shall move forward as a great team."

THE BLUE EAGLE DRIVE IS ON! The objective has been set. America is to sign up on the dotted line and *do it now!* From midnight

August 27 to midnight September 3 this determined army of volunteer workers will push forward in a Nation-wide campaign to have 5,000,000 unemployed men and women back to work by Labor Day.

And what a glorious Labor Day it promises to be! An epochal date that should be written in big letters on history's pages. Labor Day, 1933, ushering in at last the long awaited era of better times and happier days; a Labor Day unforgettably marked by the return of millions of our people to their jobs—and better still, to their self-respect. A Labor Day that presages definitely the dawn of the New Deal.

Let me tell you, I am thrilled with the immensity of this gigantic program, and I am honored to be asked to play a modest part in carrying it out. You may be interested in another modern miracle—30,000 speakers, representing every section of the country, have also been enlisted in this cause to explain the President's program to the American people and to point out to them the necessity for a united front in this crucial hour.

We'll do this job, President Roosevelt! You are doing your part—and more. Your patience, your frankness, your tireless devotion to this great cause, your constant demand for action—and still more action—has fired the imagination and the hopes of our people and, keyed to a wartime pitch, Mr. President, we stand solidly behind you.

So let's get to work, America. Let's do this job. Let's pull the country out of the depression. Officially the big program for this week is called THE BLUE EAGLE DRIVE. I would go further and call it an American crusade, for there is something about it all that rekindles our patriotism and stirs our hearts to the very depths.

America is watching the President's reemployment program. The whole civilized world is watching it—anxiously and hopefully—praying that out of it all will come something—anything—that will bring solace to a sick, weary, and badly disordered world.

Fail? Why, we cannot fail. *We dare not fail.* This is a great age; we must dare greatly. There can be no turning back, no evasion of duty. There's no room here for the shirkers or the slackers. Every person in this country—has a definite task to perform in this drive. If you are a merchant or industrialist, sign your codes and live up to them. If you are a housewife, buy and buy generously—and be sure you follow the trail of the Blue Eagles when you make your purchases. Help those who are taking the initiative in getting this big program underway. The merchant and the manufacturer hold the throttle. It is for them to start the reemployment machinery. You see you have a part, no matter what may be your calling. This program is first of all for your direct benefit, and for mine. It is a highly personalized program, to be carried out, not only by the energetic and highly capable forces at Washington but also by all of us, acting individually and as a united people. It is purely a copartnership between our country and ourselves.

So, I say to you that, with the Blue Eagle soaring ever higher in the skies; with our marching orders laid out before us; with public opinion—that highly important, yes, almost omnipotent, ally of all human progress—behind us; and with the inspiration of that great calm leadership of Franklin D. Roosevelt, we shall go forward to victory.

Yes, Mr. President; at last we are on our way. At last AMERICA MOVES!

Roosevelt defends the Tennessee Valley Authority: a press conference, October 1934

The Tennessee Valley Authority, created by Congress in May 1933, was a public agency in the form of a corporation. Empowered to construct dams to generate hydroelectric power and to control floods, it was designed to bring about the comprehensive development of the Tennessee River and Valley. Thus the TVA was authorized to market its power, to manufacture fertilizer, to encourage soil conservation, even to build recreational facilities.

In 1931 Hoover had vetoed a similar bill with these words: "This bill raises one of the most important issues confronting our people. That is squarely the issue of Federal Government ownership and operation of power utilities upon a basis of competition instead of by the proper government function of regulation. . . . I hesitate to contemplate the future of our institutions, of our country, if the preoccupation of its officials is to be no longer the promotion of justice and equal opportunity but is to be devoted to barter in the markets. That is not liberalism, it is degeneration. . . . The real development of the resources and the industries of the Tennessee Valley can only be accomplished by the people in that valley themselves."

Roosevelt's view was diametrically opposed to Hoover's as indicated by his answers in the following press conference.

QUESTION: Do you mind telling us what your ideas are regarding private power companies?

THE PRESIDENT: . . . I can put it this way: Power is really a secondary matter. What we are doing there [at Muscle Shoals] is taking a watershed with about three and a half million people in it, almost all of them rural, and we are trying to make a different type of citizen out of them from what they would be under their present conditions. Now, that applies not only to the mountaineers—we all know about them—but it applies to the people around Muscle Shoals. Do you remember that drive over to Wheeler Dam the other day? You went through a county of Alabama where the standards of education are lower than almost any other county in the

From *The New York Times*, October 1, 1934.

United States, and yet that is within twenty miles of the Muscle Shoals Dam. They have never had a chance. All you had to do was to look at the houses in which they lived. Heavens, this section around here is 1,000 percent compared with that section we went through. The homes through here are infinitely better.

So T.V.A. is primarily intended to change and to improve the standards of living of the people of that valley. Power is, as I said, a secondary consideration. Of course it is an important one because if you can get cheap power to those people, you hasten the process of raising the standard of living. The T.V.A. has been going ahead with power, yes, but it has been going ahead with probably a great many other things besides power and dam building. For instance, take fertilizer, you talk about a "yard-stick of power."

Dr. H. A. Morgan is running the fertilizer end of it and at Muscle Shoals he is turning out, not a nitrate—the plant was originally built for a nitrate plant—but he is turning out a phosphate. He is conducting a very fine experiment with phosphate of lime. They believe that for this whole area around here, and that would include this kind of soil around here, phosphate of lime is the best thing you can put on land in addition to being the cheapest. Now at once, the fertilizer companies, the National Fertilizer Association . . . say, "Are you going into the fertilizer business?" The answer is a very simple one. The plant is primarily an experimental plant. That is the primary purpose. Therefore, they are going to take this year a thousand acres of Government land, worn-out land typical of the locality, and they are going to use this phosphate of lime on these thousand acres and show what can be done with the land. They are going to give a definite demonstration. They will compare it with the other fertilizers, putting them in parallel strips, and they will see which works out best and at the lowest cost. Having the large plant, they will be able to figure out what is a fair price for the best type of fertilizer.

Having done that and having figured out the fair price, it becomes a process of education. If the farmers all through that area can be taught that that type of fertilizer at x number of dollars a ton is the best thing for them to use, then it is up to the National Fertilizer Association and its affiliated companies to meet that price. Now, that is the real answer, and we hope that they will meet that price, adding to the cost of manufacture a reasonable profit. We shall know what the cost of manufacture is, and it is very easy to say what a reasonable profit is. Now, if those gentlemen fail to avail themselves of this magnificent opportunity to conduct a sound business and make a profit, well, it is just too bad. Then somebody will get up in Congress and say, "These fellows are not meeting their opportunities and the farmers will have to have the fertilizer and of course we shall have to provide it." But I, for one, hope that that day will never come. Now, that is not holding a big stick over them at all. It is saying to them, "Here is your opportunity. We go down on our knees to you, asking you to take it."

QUESTION: Just a little guiding light.

THE PRESIDENT: In other words, what we are trying to do is something constructive to enable business ...

MRS. ROOSEVELT: An intimation. (laughter)

THE PRESIDENT: No, it is not even an intimation. No, it is a generous offer.

The study of ancient safety pins: Harry Hopkins interviewed on federal relief projects, April 4, 1935

As the chief administrator of federal relief programs, Harry Hopkins was subjected to enormous abuse by the anti-New Deal press. His own attitude towards relief was succinctly expressed when an idea was suggested to him which required some time but would "work out in the long run." Hopkins snapped back: "People don't eat in the long run—they eat every day." Under his supervision federal funds were expended on the building of schools, airports, playgrounds, roads, the laying of sewer pipe, as well as for artists, writers, and scholars. "Hell! They've got to eat just like other people," Hopkins once told a critic of the Federal Arts Project. Some of these relief projects seemed a bit fantastic, such as the study of ancient safety pins, which Hopkins defended in the following press interview.

QUESTION: Are you contemplating any Federal investigation of any kind of the general situation in New York City?

ANSWER: No. You mean apropos of this stuff in the paper a day or two ago?

QUESTION: Apropos of the project for safety pins.

ANSWER: Sure, I have something to say about that.

QUESTION: I asked first, have you contemplated making an investigation?

ANSWER: Why should I? There is nothing the matter with that. They are damn good projects—excellent projects. That goes for all the projects up there. You know some people make fun of people who speak a foreign language, and dumb people criticize something they do not understand, and that is what is going on up there—God damn it! Here are a lot of people broke and we are putting them to work making researches of one kind or another, running big recreational projects where the whole material costs 3 percent, and practically all the money goes for relief. As soon as you begin doing anything for white collar people, there is a certain group of people who begin to throw bricks. I have no apologies to make. As a matter of fact, we have not done enough. The plain fact of the matter is that there

From Robert E. Sherwood, *Roosevelt and Hopkins: An Intimate History* (New York: Harper & Row, 1948), pp. 59–61. Reprinted by permission.

are people writing and talking about these things in New York who know nothing about research projects. They haven't taken the trouble to really look into it. I have a pile of letters from businessmen, if that is important, saying that these projects are damn good projects. These fellows can make fun and shoot at white collar people, if they want to. I notice somebody says facetiously, "repair all streets." That is all they think about—money to repair streets. I think there are things in life besides that. We have projects up there to make Jewish dictionaries. There are rabbis who are broke and on the relief rolls. One hundred and fifty projects up there deal with pure science. What of it? I think those things are good in life. They are important in life. We are not backing down on any of those projects. They can make fun of these white collar and professional people if they want to. I am not going to do it. They can say, let them use a pick and shovel to repair streets, when the city ought to be doing that. I believe every one of these research projects are good projects. We don't need any apologies!

QUESTION: In that connection, I am not trying to argue with you.

ANSWER: I am not really mad. . . .

QUESTION: About this white collar—there are 300 million dollars for white collar relief. Would it be your idea in administering 300 million, that you might just as well continue?

ANSWER: The best of them will be continued, sure. Those are research projects they are jumping on.

QUESTION: As a matter of fact, don't you think there are a lot of research projects that would be more valuable to mankind in general than the classic example of ancient safety pins?

ANSWER: That is a matter of opinion. You may be interested in washing machines—somebody else in safety pins. Every one of those projects are worked out by technical people. In the field of medical science, we have doctors; in the physical, we have physicists; in the social, social research people. You can make fun of anything; that is easy to do. A lot of people are opposed to the whole business. Let these white collar professional fellows sit home and get a basket of groceries, that is what a lot of people want.

QUESTION: You say that people don't want to work?

ANSWER: No, these fellows want to work, but there are a lot of people who don't believe in the work program and want people to go back to direct relief. These people who want direct relief will always kick about these technical projects. Anything that from their point of view isn't utilitarian.

The Louisiana Kingfish, Huey Long, attacks the New Deal: at Des Moines, Iowa, April 27, 1935

In 1935 Roosevelt continued to preach class harmony and a team alliance of banking, agriculture, industry, labor, and capital—with himself as quarterback. But by that time the NRA was disparagingly referred to as the "National Run-Around," the New Deal was stalled, the economy listless, and other leaders began to attract audiences of respectable size. Three men in particular became nationally prominent, powerful enough to challenge Roosevelt's political hegemony: Dr. Francis E. Townsend, Father Charles Coughlin, and Senator Huey Long. Townsend's pension plan for the aged was so appealing that nearly five million fanatic supporters joined his movement. Ultimately, as a result of corruption within their movement and some congressional hostility, the power of the Townsend movement waned and finally vanished from the American scene. Charles Coughlin was known as the "radio priest," with more listeners and fan mail than the President. But as his lectures became more violent and fascistic in tone, his audience dwindled. The main challenge and most ominous threat to Roosevelt was made by Huey Long. A poll estimated that Long could carry 3 to 4 million votes in 1936 and that, if the depression continued, he could conceivably win the presidential nomination by 1940. Long's "Share the Wealth" plan which promised to tax the rich and distribute the proceeds so that every family would have a radio, a car, and a home, together with the folksy anti-aristocratic image he carefully cultivated, was immensely appealing to middle-America. An example of Long's method, a meeting at Des Moines, Iowa, on April 27, 1935, is reported below. Four months later Long was assassinated at the State House in Baton Rouge, Louisiana.

Senator Huey P. Long of Louisiana poured out a torrent of criticism late today on the national Democratic administration's agricultural program for burning up "the surplus when it found people starving in the midst of too much food." As a remedy for "this depressing situation," he offered his "share the wealth" program to give every family a homestead worth $5,000 and an annual income of from $2,000 to $2,500.

"The Lord has called America to a barbecue," he exhorted. "And 50 million people are starving."

A farmer's holiday convention crowd, estimated at 10,000 persons by L. M. Peet, convention director, raucously clapped hands and stomped feet, interrupting the "share-the-wealth" address numberless times. Hundreds milled around in the paddock below the speakers' platform. The self-styled Louisiana Kingfish called for a vote of approval as he finished his address and thousands extended their hands into the cold wind which swept the state fair grounds.

"You newspapermen take that vote and record it," the senator directed as he stepped away from the table of microphones.

From the *Kansas City Star*, April 28, 1935.

Long denied his intention of criticizing either of the major political parties at the start of his explanation of his program but inserted into his speech denunciations of every administration since Woodrow Wilson. He handed to President Roosevelt the title of "Prince Franklin, knight of the Nourmahal" and repeated his designations of Secretary [Henry] Wallace as "Lord Destroyer" or "Lord Corn Wallace" and Secretary [Harold] Ickes as "Lord High Chamberlain, the chinchbug of Chicago."

Long followed Milo Reno, national holiday president, in a calumny heaped upon the administration for what he said were broken promises. Reno introduced the visiting senator as "a man qualified to meet the situation, a man who has guts."

Laughter swept the grandstand when the senator told the crowd, "I don't intend to oppose either one of the political parties. I'm like a sinner in a church: I've been converted by both preachers so many times. I'm still in good standing in the Democratic party—at this time."

Roosevelt and Hoover have agreed in the purpose of decreasing extreme wealth, "cutting down the big men and building up the small men," Long told the audience, "and they said the same words for which I have been called a radical." "The only difference," Senator Long said, "is it's all right to say it but be damned sure you don't intend to do it."

In 1930, the speaker said, one percent owned 60 percent of the wealth, and "today in 1935, probably one-half of 1 percent own 60 to 70 percent of the wealth." "Seventy-five percent of the people don't own enough to pay their debts," he said urging the audience to reduce their thinking to a matter of simple arithmetic.

"The Lord called America to a barbecue," he shouted. "There was too much of everything and so 22 million are on a dole and 22 million more are trying to get on a dole." "This is the only country anytime, anywhere," Long thundered, "where 50 million people are starving while they have too much."

"Hoover proposed to plow up every fourth row of cotton," he said, "Roosevelt went him one better and plowed up every third row." "They burned up the surplus and eased the pain (for people who didn't have enough) by putting it out of sight."

Long charged into the fairgrounds under escort of his two "secretaries" and a police convoy. The officers were forced to halt as he stopped to buy a bag of peanuts.

The senator's entrance interrupted a musical program on the speaking stage as the crowd rose to its feet in a huge display of applause. As the "Little German Band" swept into the senator's own composition, "When Every Man's a King," Long marched straight to the microphone and sang the chorus.

Little Ethel Grimes of Des Moines, in a stiff, red, silk dress presented him a poem and he kissed her on the forehead. The crowd remained standing and hundreds pushed their way to the iron stairs leading to the platform. Senator Long autographed a number of match books, envelopes and papers shoved into his hands by the holders of platform seats.

A national poll predicts Roosevelt's defeat in the election of 1936

In the campaign of 1936 Roosevelt no longer spoke of "team harmony" with himself as "quarterback." Instead, he lacerated the "economic royalists" and selfish forces of "organized money." He reminded audiences of the "better, happier America" created by the New Deal, recited the list of administration reforms, and promised more. His political sagacity was confirmed by the results. Socialist and Communist party candidates received far less than 1 percent; the "Union" party supported by Dr. Townsend and Father Coughlin received less than 2 percent; the Republican candidate, Alf Landon of Kansas, received less than 40 percent. In fact, Roosevelt won by the greatest landslide in American history to that date: 27.5 million votes for Roosevelt to 16.7 million for Landon.

One of the famous pre-election polls conducted by The Literary Digest *had assured its readers that Landon would be a sure victor. Their error was partly responsible for the demise of the* Digest.

Well, the great battle of the ballots in the poll of 10 million voters, scattered throughout the forty-eight states of the Union, is now finished, and in the table below we record the figures received up to the hour of going to press. These figures are exactly as received from more than one in every five voters polled in our country—they are neither weighted, adjusted, nor interpreted.

Never before in an experience covering more than a quarter of a century in taking polls have we received so many different varieties of criticism—praise from many; condemnation from many others—and yet it has been just of the same type that has come to us every time a Poll has been taken in all these years. A telegram from a newspaper in California asks: "Is it true that Mr. Hearst has purchased *The Literary Digest*?" A telephone message only the day before these lines were written: "Has the Republican National Committee purchased *The Literary Digest*?" And all types and varieties, including: "Have the Jews purchased *The Literary Digest*?" "Is the Pope of Rome a stockholder of *The Literary Digest*?" And so it goes—all equally absurd and amusing. . . .

Now, are the figures in this Poll correct? In answer to this question we will simply refer to a telegram we sent to a young man in Massachusetts the other day in answer to his challenge to us to wager $100,000 on the accuracy of our Poll. We wired him as follows:

From *The Literary Digest,* October 31, 1936, pp. 5–6.

For nearly a quarter century, we have been taking Polls of the voters in the forty-eight States, and especially in Presidential years, and we have always merely mailed the ballots, counted and recorded those returned and let the people of the Nation draw their conclusions as to our accuracy. So far, we have been right in every Poll. Will we be right in the current Poll? That, as Mrs. Roosevelt said concerning the President's reelection, is in the "lap of the gods."

We never make any claims before election but we respectfully refer you to the opinion of one of the most quoted citizens today, the Hon. James A. Farley, Chairman of the Democratic National Committee. This is what Mr. Farley said October 14, 1932:

> "Any sane person cannot escape the implication of such a gigantic sampling of popular opinion as is embraced in *The Literary Digest* straw vote. I consider this conclusive evidence as to the desire of the people of this country for a change in the National Government. *The Literary Digest* Poll is an achievement of no little magnitude. It is a Poll fairly and correctly conducted."

... The Poll represents the most extensive straw ballot in the field—the most experienced in view of its twenty-five years of perfecting—the most unbiased in view of its prestige—a Poll that has always previously been correct. Even its critics admit its value as an index of popular sentiment. As one of these critics, *The Nation*, observes: "Because it indicates both the 1932 and 1936 vote, it offers the raw material for as careful a prognostication as it is possible to make at this time."

	Electoral Vote	Landon 1936 Total Vote for State	Roosevelt 1936 Total Vote for State
Ala.	11	3,060	10,082
Ariz.	3	2,337	1,975
Ark.	9	2,724	7,608
Calif.	22	89,516	77,245
Colo.	6	15,949	10,025
Conn.	8	28,809	13,413
Del.	3	2,918	2,048
Fla.	7	6,087	8,620
Ga.	12	3,948	12,915
Idaho	4	3,653	2,611
Ill.	29	123,297	79,035
Ind.	14	42,805	26,663
Iowa	11	31,871	18,614
Kans.	9	35,408	20,254
Ky.	11	13,365	16,592
La.	10	3,686	7,902
Maine	5	11,742	5,337
Md.	8	17,463	18,341
Mass.	17	87,449	25,965

	Electoral Vote	Landon 1936 Total Vote for State	Roosevelt 1936 Total Vote for State
Mich.	19	51,478	25,686
Minn.	11	30,762	20,733
Miss.	9	848	6,080
Mo.	15	50,022	38,267
Mont.	4	4,490	3,562
Nebr.	7	18,280	11,770
Nev.	3	1,003	955
N.H.	4	9,207	2,737
N.J.	16	58,677	27,631
N.M.	3	1,625	1,662
N.Y.	47	162,260	139,277
N.C.	13	6,113	16,324
N.Dak.	4	4,250	3,666
Ohio	26	77,896	50,778
Okla.	11	14,442	15,075
Ore.	5	11,747	10,951
Pa.	36	119,086	81,114
R.I.	4	10,401	3,489
S.C.	8	1,247	7,105
S.Dak.	4	8,483	4,507
Tenn.	11	9,883	19,829
Texas	23	15,341	37,501
Utah	4	4,067	5,318
Vt.	3	7,241	2,458
Va.	11	10,223	16,783
Wash.	8	21,370	15,300
W.Va.	8	13,660	10,235
Wis.	12	33,796	20,781
Wyo.	3	2,526	1,533
State Unknown		7,158	6,545
Total	531	1,293,669	972,897

Two opinions of Roosevelt's "court-packing" plan, 1937

Roosevelt had ample precedent for an attack upon the Supreme Court. After all, America's strongest presidents—Jefferson, Jackson, Lincoln, and Theodore Roosevelt—had either quarreled with or bitterly resented the powers exercised by the nation's highest judicial authority. The Supreme Court had struck down the NRA, the AAA, and other New Deal laws concerning railroad workers' pensions, farm mortgages, bankruptcy, and the bituminous coal industry. Roosevelt feared that the Social Security Act and the Wagner Act would suffer a similar fate of being declared unconstitutional.

His plan was considerably less radical than other proposals which were suggested: in essence, it stated that for every federal judge who refused to retire at age 70, Roosevelt would be permitted to appoint another, to a maximum of six new judges on the Supreme Court and forty-four in the lower courts. According to this strategy, either the reactionary justices would be frightened into resigning or the new appointees would out-vote them. But the court-packing plan proved a political blunder. The issue consumed 168 days of acrimonious congressional controversy before Roosevelt reluctantly conceded defeat. Given below are two different appraisals of the plan, from a conservative newspaper and a liberal journal.

A VOICE OF OPPOSITION

In this one hundred and sixty-first year of the independence of the United States, President Roosevelt has brought forward a proposal which, if enacted into law, would end the American State as it has existed throughout the long years of its life. The plan is put forward with all the artistry of the President's political mind. He speaks in the name of "youth," always a popular and appealing note. He dangles before the House and Senate fifty new and important jobs, always ripe and luscious bait for the Congressional mind. He ingeniously conveys the impression that all he seeks is a routine and moderate effort to speed up justice and improve the whole Federal bench. Yet, beneath this veneer of politeness, the brutal fact is that President Roosevelt would pack the Supreme Court with six new justices of his own choosing.

No President of the United States ever before made the least gesture toward attempting to gain such a vast grant of power. Mr. Roosevelt demands it, calmly, artfully. By one legislative act, availing himself of the one loophole in the Constitution—the failure to specify the number of members in the Supreme Court—he would strike at the roots of that equality of the three branches of government upon which the nation is founded, and centralize in himself the control of judicial, as well as executive functions.

It was a French King, Louis XIV, who said, "L'etat, c'est moi"— "I am the State." The paper shell of American constitutionalism would continue if President Roosevelt secured the passage of the law he now demands. But it would be only a shell.

From *The New York Herald Tribune*, February 6, 1937.

A VOICE OF SUPPORT

That the President's indictment of the Court, at last made with such vigor and frankness, is a just one, seems to us beyond dispute. . . . The members of the majority have demonstrated time and time again that when there is a conflict between human rights and those of property it is to the latter

From "The President Faces the Court," *The New Republic*, March 17, 1937.

that their allegiance is given. They have created, as Mr. Roosevelt pointed out last week ... a no man's land in which neither federal nor state government is able to control. They refuse to admit the necessities of a changing world, no matter how great may be the cost of their refusal in the frustration and suffering of millions of their fellow Americans.

It is quite true that the President's proposal does not completely solve the problem presented by the fact that the Court in recent decades has arrogated to itself vast powers never contemplated by the authors of the Constitution. Indeed, his suggestion is only a first step. Everyone recognized that the future course of action of additional Justices appointed by Mr. Roosevelt or any of his successors is unpredictable. There is no magic in a Court of any given size and no guarantee that a new personnel would invariably pursue a course in the best interest of all the American people. We have repeatedly pointed out in recent weeks that the President's suggestion is but a necessary first step, a breaking of the immediate deadlock by the only device, so far as we are aware, that anyone has suggested that is both constitutional and capable of being put into effect within a reasonably brief period of time. Additional action is also needed and undoubtedly this additional action includes a constitutional amendment. It will in all probability take many years to deflate the Court and restore it to its proper relationship to other government branches.

It is now clear, in our opinion, that neither the President nor anyone else has any marked enthusiasm for the device now under consideration. But no one has any enthusiasm, either, for the situation into which the conservative majority of the Court has brought us by a series of political decisions, politically inspired. Those who are now protesting with hysterical vehemence against a "presidential dictatorship" were silent over many years about a far more serious Court dictatorship, one that carried a deeper threat to American institutions than anything President Roosevelt has done or tried to do. The chief valid criticism of Mr. Roosevelt is not that he is now seeking to mitigate that dictatorship but that for so long a period of time he should have passively accepted its consequences.

The New Deal reviewed, 1940

There have been many assessments of the New Deal, by contemporaries and by later scholars. It has been condemned as a catastrophe which never unlocked the depression enigma, which saddled America with a vast bureaucracy and constantly augmented indebtedness, and which either corrupted or destroyed the character of the people. And it has been defended for preserving democracy in a time of depression when other countries were turning to fascism or commu-

From "The New Deal in Review—1936–1940," *The New Republic*, May 20, 1940, pp. 707–08.

*nism, for giving people hope during this period of despair, and for fashioning
significant social reforms which virtually all Americans have accepted and both
political parties now endorse.*

*The following is a thoughtful and sympathetic appraisal of the New Deal,
particularly of its second phase.*

One need only recall what conditions were in 1932 to realize the amaz-
ing change in our national thinking that has taken place in eight years.
While there is still complaint about paternalism and centralized government
(from the Republicans who were the great exponents of these ideas,
applied under special circumstances, for the first seventy-five years of their
party's life) it is obvious that even the critics are only halfhearted in what
they say. As a nation we have agreed, once and forever, that the individual
must not bear the sole responsibility for his failure to cope with economic
problems of unemployment or old age which are, quite obviously, beyond
his powers, and that society as a whole must take over a substantial part of
the burden. We have at last learned that laissez-faire has been dead for
years; that the unguided lust of the business man for profit does not infal-
libly produce Utopia. And finally, we have reaffirmed in these past eight
years an early American doctrine that had been all but forgotten in preceding decades: that the country exists for the welfare and happiness of all its
inhabitants; and that when this condition is not met, reformation is in order
no matter how drastic it may be or how much it may be disliked by existing
privileged minorities.

The New Deal, even in its second term, has clearly done far more for
the general welfare of the country and its citizens than any administration
in the previous history of the nation. Its relief for underprivileged producers
in city and country, though inadequate to the need, has been indispensable.
Without this relief an appalling amount of misery would have resulted, and
a dangerous political upheaval might have occurred. Since the expenditure
of money for relief—even the insufficient amounts recently appropriated—
has been the principal target of the administration's conservative enemies,
this accomplishment alone would be sufficient reason for support of the
New Deal. This assertion of the reactionaries that if the federal budget were
balanced by cutting expenses, business would revive sharply enough to
absorb the unemployed and make relief expenditure unnecessary, is incapable of proof and seems highly improbable.

In addition, the New Deal in this second period has accomplished
much of permanent benefit to the nation. Perhaps its most important
achievement was the National Labor Relations Act, the result of which was
to inhibit employers' opposition to union organization and true collective
bargaining, so that trade-union membership was more than doubled. This
was not a mere act of justice; it was the laying of a solid foundation for our
society in the future. Without a strong, alert and independent labor move-

ment a modern industrial nation is in constant danger from the enemies of political and social democracy. Second only to the strengthening of unions is the establishment of minimum labor standards. The fury with which reactionaries have attacked these two labor measures is an index of their importance.

Other permanent improvements are the impetus given to conservation of soil and forests, the many-sided TVA, a great road-building program, flood control, a good beginning at slum clearance and adequate housing for those not provided for by private construction, great hydro-electric projects, extension of electricity at reasonable rates through the Rural Electrification Administration, and the inauguration of insurance against unemployment and the other forms of social security.

The government as an instrument of democratic action in the future has also been strengthened and renovated. This is not merely a matter of the addition of many new agencies, but of the more efficient organization of the whole executive department—including a planning board under the President which so far has been relatively unimportant but is capable of future development. The Courts, too, have been revivified, partly by legislation, but principally by excellent new appointments, so that we now have a Supreme Court which is abreast of the times. It is improbable that these permanent changes will be or even can be destroyed by any new administration.

All these extraordinary accomplishments must be remembered when we speak of the points at which the New Deal has been disappointing in its second phase. The most important of these is of course its failure to discover or apply a genuine remedy for the stagnation of our economy, and for unemployment. These years have seen no return to the conditions of 1932 or 1933, to be sure, but on the other hand no great or permanent improvement in national income, production or employment above the level already achieved in 1936. Nor have they seen the adoption of any important new means of bringing about such improvement. The President has apparently been hoping continually that business and investment would gain momentum of their own accord, while business spokesmen have been blaming what they called the hostile attitude of the New Deal for the lack of confidence which they charged with responsibility for retarding advance. It is doubtful, however, whether they are right about this, in the view of economists who have studied the problem intensively. On two occasions during the past few years the President has heeded business advice, at least in part, by trying to cut recovery expenditures in the hope that a permanent improvement in business was in prospect—once in 1937 and again in 1939. On both occasions a sharp slump followed. The upswing which was occurring when the cuts were made turned out to have been due to an accumulation of inventories by business, which overshot the demand from consumers, and reaction under such circumstances was inevitable.

The reason for the failure of our economy to come back to really prosperous levels is not known with certainty, but there is no such mystery about it as many believe. . . . One assigned reason is the failure of construction fully to revive. Closely associated with this is the high price of steel, other capital goods, and high building costs themselves. Such progress as has been made is largely due to government efforts to reduce the price of and access to capital for home-owners through the FHA, and the valuable but insufficient work of the USHA in organizing and financing large low-cost housing projects. The anti-trust prosecutions of the Department of Justice may help in the future. Another assigned reason is high prices of industrial products in general. Too few privately controlled industries follow the policy of low prices leading to enlarged sales. Anti-trust action may remedy this in the relatively few cases in which illegal monopoly exists, but that is hardly enough. The third important reason is the lack of old or rapidly expanding new industries in which capital investment may take place. The government might remedy this situation by a drastic railroad-reorganization program, or by a carefully planned scheme of large-scale public investment. It has not moved in either direction.

The President's failure to make more progress in tackling the central problem of our economy is probably due mainly to two things—the strengthening of conservative opposition, especially since the 1938 election, and concentration on the European situation. The country is weaker, whether for war or for peace, because of this slackening of pace in the New Deal. If our foreign policy can avoid involvement in the war, we shall be fortunate. But in any case we should not rely on war, whether we are in it or not, to do for us the domestic job that remains. If the New Deal is to deserve our support in the future, it must not rest on what it has already done, great as that is, but tell us how it is going to finish the task.

The significance of Roosevelt's victory in the election of 1940

Class cleavages over political issues were sharpening all through the 1930's. The division was not so apparent in 1936, since Roosevelt received a surprising number of votes from the more prosperous part of the community. But by 1940 the class bias was obvious. Wendell Willkie, the Republican candidate, ran well in the farms and country towns of the Midwest. But in the major cities, particularly in working-class sections, Roosevelt ran up huge majorities. By 1940 the Republican party embraced many New Deal measures. But the poor, the blacks, the workers, remained loyal to Roosevelt. "Win with Willkie," Republicans proclaimed. "To Hell with Willkie," factory workers in industrial centers replied.

From Samuel Lubell, "Postmortem: Who Elected Roosevelt?" *Saturday Evening Post*, Vol. CCXIII, January 25, 1941, pp. 9–10, 96. Reprinted by permission of *Saturday Evening Post*, copyright 1941, The Curtis Publishing Co.

Much more than the third-term tradition was shattered when President Roosevelt took the oath of office again on Monday. Who elected him? As in all elections, there are many cross-currents, but the 1940 answer is simple and inescapable. The little fellow elected him, because there are more of the little fellow and because he believed Mr. Roosevelt to be his friend and protector. Roosevelt won by the vote of Labor, unorganized as well as organized, plus that of the foreign born and their first and second generation descendants. And the Negro.

It was a class-conscious vote for the first time in American history, and the implications are portentous. The New Deal appears to have accomplished what the Socialists, the I.W.W. and the Communists would never approach. It has drawn a class line across the face of American politics. That line seems to be there to stay. While thousands of wage earners, even voters on relief, voted for Willkie, we are talking here about groups as wholes.

Mr. Roosevelt is the first President to owe his election in such great measure to the teeming cities. On the farms and in the towns Mr. Willkie more than held his own. It was in the industrial centers that the Republican hopes were blacked out in factory smoke. The Republican campaign had virtually no effect on this vote, the evidence argues. I doubt that anything Willkie might have done would have affected it. The election was not decided on the issues he debated, but on forces long at work—economic status, nationalities, birth rates. The rise of Government as an employer on a scale rivaling the biggest business is a fourth. And the indications are that this vote might have gone to Roosevelt for a fourth or fifth term as readily as for a third.

The Republicans do not know what hit them; and the Democrats, certainly as distinguished from the New Dealers, do not know what they hit the Republicans with. The New Deal has aimed at a bloodless revolution. In 1940 it went a long way toward accomplishing it.

In numbers it was no great victory. Roosevelt won by the smallest plurality and the smallest percentage of the total vote since the neck-and-neck election of 1916. If his strength should diminish between now and 1944 at the same rate it did between 1936 and 1940, he would be beaten in 1944. The opposition is taking comfort in these figures, but the 1940 vote upset the fundamentals of our old two-party system, and when the fundamentals are overturned, past-performance figures are worthless. In considerable measure the vote was personal for Mr. Roosevelt. No one may say how far, if he does not run for a fourth term, he might be able to deliver this vote in 1944 to an heir.

What is clear is that, once Roosevelt is out of the picture, this vote will not slip back automatically into its former slots. The political wars henceforth will be fought with new tactics and new weapons to unpredictable results. . . .

In 1932 Roosevelt became President in a popular recoil against the depression. His third-term victory, however, is the result of an upsurging of the urban masses. In the New Deal they have found their leveling philosophy; under it they have been given recognition through patronage, benefits and new opportunities; they have been awakened to the consciousness of the power of their numbers.

From the GOP viewpoint, the harshest fact this post-mortem reveals is that the Republicans are on the wrong side of the birth rate, not so much the current rate as the birth rates of 1890, 1900, 1910 and 1920, which are beyond their rectifying. Grade-school enrollments have begun to fall, but not high-school enrollments as yet. For another two or three presidential elections the elements which re-elected Roosevelt will continue to grow in voting strength, actually and relatively.

Thus far, these elements are united behind Roosevelt personally. Can the Democratic Party hold them, apart from Roosevelt? If it can, then it may become the normal majority party, with the Republicans occupying the unenviable position of the Democrats after the Civil War.

American isolationism in a world at war: pro and con, 1940–41

Isolationists were furious with what they considered Franklin D. Roosevelt's duplicity in foreign affairs. Under the guise of promising to keep America out of European wars, and against the expressed wishes of most citizens, so they charged, Roosevelt's every action led to deeper involvement. Many isolationists believed that Germany was invincible and the United States could "do business" with Hitler. They feared that America was unprepared, and that to ally with Britain was to court certain defeat. Some isolationists, such as Colonel Charles Lindbergh, spokesman for the America First Committee, injected anti-Semitism into their arguments, accusing "the British, the Jewish, and the Roosevelt administration" as the "three most important groups which have been pressing the country toward war." Others, such as Robert A. Taft of Ohio, presented a more rational plea for the United States to remain strictly neutral.

Internationalists argued that neutrality was no longer feasible in the mid-twentieth century when distances had vanished, strategy was global, and freedom everywhere could be endangered. "It is not the water that bars the way," Secretary of State Cordell Hull warned. "It is the resolute determination of British arms. Were the control of the seas by Britain lost, the Atlantic would no longer be an obstacle—rather, it would become a broad highway for a conqueror moving westward."

THE ISOLATIONIST POSITION: SPEECH OF SENATOR ROBERT A. TAFT, MARCH 2, 1940

War is so horrible today that the reasons against it, unless forced by direct national interest, are obvious to all. The glamour and romance of an

From *Vital Speeches of the Day,* March 1940, pp. 345–48.

earlier day, always largely imaginary, have been completely destroyed by the modern methods developed in the [first] World War and since. No man wants to spend months or years himself in the trenches. Every parent dreads the day his or her sons might sail away to war. But it is said that we cannot stay out, and maybe people still seem to feel that because we chose to participate in the World War we must inevitably be drawn into this war. Certainly we can stay out if we are determined and remain determined to do so. We have stayed out of many European wars. If we admit that we cannot stay out, we will be perpetually involved in war, for Europe's quarrels are everlasting. There is a welter of races there so confused that boundaries cannot be drawn without leaving minorities which are a perpetual source of friction. National animosities are traditional and bitter. Only in this country have they been laid aside and have different races learned how to live together in peace. . . .

When I see the freedom of independent nations like Czechoslovakia, Poland and Finland destroyed, my deepest sympathies are aroused in their behalf. It is contrary to human nature to have no sympathies between contesting European nations, but because we sympathize with one side is no reason why we should run onto the field and try to play in the game. Of course we can stay out if we wish to do so. Holland and Switzerland stayed out of the World War, although they were in the very midst of it. We have an isolated position, and it is still isolated in spite of all the improvements on sea and in the air. In fact, developments in this war seem to show that effective aerial attack cannot be made over any considerable distance. I find that many people who say that we cannot stay out, at the bottom of their hearts do not wish to stay out. Certainly this argument presents no reason for not trying to stay out.

It has been widely argued that we should enter the war to defend the democracies against dictatorships. The President's own expressions even this year have indicated a leaning to this belief. No one can sympathize more than I do with the success of democratic governments against dictatorships. No one desires more strongly than I the end of Communism and Nazism, but I question whether war is the effective method of destroying them. Our experience in the World War did not indicate that we could interfere in European quarrels and work out any permanent or satisfactory solution. The World War did not even save democracy, but resulted in the creation of more dictatorships than the world has seen for many years. Nothing is so destructive of forms of government, particularly forms of democratic government, as war.

Our going to war would be more likely to destroy American democracy than to destroy German dictatorship. There are pending in Congress measures designed to have the government take over all business and property, fix prices and wages, and regulate every detail of private employment and commercial life. The President already has statutory power to take over the railroads and manufacturing plants in case of threatened war. I have little doubt that he would exercise most of these powers. . . . I believe we will do the cause of democracy much more good if we maintain our neutrality, and show that a great nation can get through a crisis of this kind without abandoning democratic principles. There is only one way to spread democracy throughout the world—that is by showing the people that under democratic government they are more likely to have peace and happiness than under any other form. Democracy spread through the world in the nineteenth century from our example, and it can do so again.

THE INTERNATIONALIST POSITION: FROM THE NEW YORK TIMES, APRIL 30, 1941

. . . There is no isolation. There are only lines of defense. Distance is vanishing. Strategy is everything. And strategy in this year of grace has become the art and science of survival: survival in the personal sense, survival of ideas, survival of culture and tradition, survival of a way of life. Those who tell us now that the sea is still our certain bulwark, and that the tremendous forces sweeping the Old World threaten no danger to the New, give the lie to their own words in the precautions they would have us take.

To a man they favor an enormous strengthening of our defenses. Why? Against what danger would they have us arm if none exists? To what purpose would they have us spend these almost incredible billions upon billions for ships and planes, for tanks and guns, if there is no immediate threat to the security of the United States? Why are we training the youth of the country to bear arms? Under pressure of what fear are we racing against time to double and quadruple our industrial production? No man in his senses will say that we are arming against Canada or our Latin-American neighbors to the south, against Britain or the captive states of Europe. We are arming solely for one reason. We are arming against Hitler's Germany—a great predatory Power in alliance with Japan.

It has been said, times without number, that if Hitler cannot cross the English Channel he cannot cross three thousand miles of sea. But there is only one reason why he has not crossed the English Channel. That is because forty-five million determined Britons in a heroic resistance have converted their island into an armed base from which proceeds a steady stream of sea and air power. As Secretary [of State Cordell] Hull has said: "It is not the water that bars the way. It is the resolute determination of British arms. Were the control of the seas by Britain lost, the Atlantic would no longer be an obstacle—rather, it would become a broad highway for a conqueror moving westward." That conqueror does not need to attempt at once an invasion of continental United States in order to place this country in deadly danger. We shall be in deadly danger the moment British sea

From "Let Us Face the Truth," *The New York Times*, April 30, 1941. © 1941 by The New York Times Company. Reprinted by permission.

power fails; the moment the eastern gates of the Atlantic are open to the aggressor; the moment we are compelled to divide our one-ocean Navy between two oceans simultaneously.

The combined Axis fleets outmatch our own: they are superior in numbers to our fleet in every category of vessel, from warships and aircraft-carriers to destroyers and submarines. The combined Axis air strength will be much greater than our own if Hitler strikes in time—and when has he failed to strike in time? The master of Europe will have at his command shipways that can outbuild us, the resources of twenty conquered nations to furnish his materials, the oil of the Middle East to stoke his engines, the slave labor of a continent—bound by no union rules, and not working on a forty-hour week—to turn out his production.

Grant Hitler the gigantic prestige of a victory over Britain, and who can doubt that the first result, on our side of the ocean, would be the prompt appearance of imitation Nazi regimes in a half-dozen Latin-American nations, forced to be on the winning side, begging favors, clamoring for admissions to the Axis? What shall we do then? Make war upon these neighbors; send armies to fight in the jungles of Central and South America; run the risk of outraging native sentiment and turning the whole continent against us? Or shall we sit tight while the area of Nazi influence draws ever closer to the Panama Canal and a spreading checkerboard of Nazi air-fields provides ports of call for German planes that may choose to bomb our citizens? . . .

Prejudice against Japanese-Americans, 1941–42

With one glaring exception, there was no official vindictiveness toward any minority group during World War II, as there had been during World War I. That exception was the treatment of Americans of Japanese descent. Few, painfully few voices of protest were raised to protest this serious breach of civil liberty, when over 100,000 Japanese-Americans were removed from their West Coast residences and placed in detention centers. The following eight excerpts give some idea of the frenzied hostility, the accusations of treason and sabotage —charges which were wholly unfounded. But liberals like Walter Lippmann and conservatives like Westbrook Pegler were caught up in the atmosphere of hatred and emotional distrust. General John DeWitt, of the Western Defense Command, advised the Secretary of War that "the Japanese race is an enemy race." Because of this military pressure and public alarm, Roosevelt signed the order for their removal. The Supreme Court in 1944 decided that removal on grounds of race was justified (Korematsu v. United States), though Justice Frank Murphy wrote a blistering dissent.

From Jacobus Tenbroek, Edward N. Barnhard, and Floyd W. Matson, *Prejudice, War and the Constitution* (Berkeley, 1954), pp. 75, 77, 80, 86–87, 110, 350. Originally published by the University of California Press; reprinted by permission of The Regents of the University of California.

Congressman John Rankin of Mississippi   December 15, 1941

[I am] for catching every Japanese in America, Alaska, and Hawaii now and putting them in concentration camps and shipping them back to Asia as soon as possible. . . . This is a race war, as far as the Pacific side of this conflict is concerned. . . . The white man's civilization has come into conflict with Japanese barbarism. . . . One of them must be destroyed. . . . I say it is of vital importance that we get rid of every Japanese whether in Hawaii or on the mainland. They violate every sacred promise, every canon of honor and decency. . . . These Japs who had been [in Hawaii] for generations were making signs, if you please, guiding the Japanese planes to the objects of their iniquity in order that they might destroy our naval vessels, murder our soldiers and sailors, and blow to pieces the helpless women and children of Hawaii.

　　Damn them! Let's get rid of them now!

Leo Carillo, movie star   January 6, 1942

Why wait until [the Japanese] pull something before we act? . . . Let's get them off the coast into the interior. . . . May I urge you in behalf of the safety of the people of California to start action at once.

Henry McLemore, ex-sports writer   January 29, 1942

The only Japanese apprehended have been the ones the FBI actually had something on. The rest of them, so help me, are free as birds. There isn't an airport in California that isn't flanked by Japanese farms. There is hardly an air field where the same situation doesn't exist. . . . I know this is the melting pot of the world and all men are created equal and there must be no such thing as race or creed hatred, but do those things go when a country is fighting for its life? Not in my book. No country has ever won a war because of courtesy and I trust and pray we won't be the first because of the lovely, gracious spirit. . . . I am for immediate removal of every Japanese on the West Coast to a point deep in the interior. I don't mean a nice part of the interior either. Herd 'em up, pack 'em off and give 'em the inside room in the badlands. Let 'em be pinched, hurt, hungry and dead up against it. . . .

　　Personally, I hate the Japanese. And that goes for all of them.

General John DeWitt
Commanding Officer, Pacific Coast   January 1942

In the war in which we are now engaged racial affinities are not severed by migration. The Japanese race is an enemy race and while many second and third generation Japanese born on United States soil, possessed of United States citizenship, have become "Americanized," the racial strains are un-diluted. . . . It therefore follows that along the vital Pacific Coast over 112,000 potential enemies of Japanese extraction are at large today.

Walter Lippmann, columnist   **February 12, 1942**

The Pacific Coast is officially a combat zone: some part of it may at any moment be a battlefield. Nobody's constitutional rights include the right to reside and do business on a battlefield. . . . There is plenty of room elsewhere for him to exercise his rights.

Westbrook Pegler, columnist   **February 16, 1942**

Do you get what [Lippmann] says? . . . The enemy has been scouting our coast. . . . The Japs ashore are communicating with the enemy offshore . . . and on the basis of "what is known to be taking place" there are signs that a well-organized blow is being withheld only until it can do the most damage. . . . We are so dumb and considerate of the minute constitutional rights and even of the political feelings and influence of people whom we have every reason to anticipate with preventive action!

Senator Tom Stewart of Tennessee   **February 26, 1942**

A Jap born on our soil is a subject of Japan under Japanese law; therefore, he owes allegiance to Japan. . . . The Japanese are among our worst enemies. They are cowardly and immoral. They are different from Americans in every conceivable way, and no Japanese . . . should have a right to claim American citizenship. A Jap is a Jap anywhere you find him, and his taking the oath of allegiance to this country would not help, even if he should be permitted to do so. They do not believe in God and have no respect for an oath. They have been plotting for years against the Americas and their democracies.

Managing Secretary of
Grower-Shipper Vegetable Association   **May–June 1942**

We're charged with wanting to get rid of the Japs for selfish reasons. We might as well be honest. We do. It's a question of whether the white man lives on the Pacific Coast or the brown man. They came into this valley to work, and they stayed to take over. . . . If all the Japs were removed tomor-row, we'd never miss them in two weeks, because the white farmers can take over and produce everything the Jap grows. And we don't want them back when the war ends, either.

What are we fighting for? By the historian
Carl Becker, 1944

Morale during World War II, Robert Sherwood has noted, "was never partic-ularly good nor alarmingly bad. There was a minimum of flag-waving and parades. It was the first war in American history in which the general disillusion-ment preceded the firing of the first shot." Unlike 1917, there were few demon-strations of super-patriotic zeal, but there was a steady determination to defeat the Axis powers. Americans knew their cause was just. The moral issues were clear. "When we resort to force, as now we must," said Roosevelt, "we are deter-mined that this force shall be directed toward ultimate good as well as against immediate evil. We Americans are not destroyers—we are builders." The historian Carl Becker wrote the following thoughtful analysis of why Americans were fighting.

What are we fighting for? In general terms we may answer the ques-tion as follows. We, the people of the United Nations, are fighting (those who are fighting—a good number are not fighting at all) for a common purpose—for the preservation or recovery of national independence, and for the cause of human freedom, against the Nazi barbarism, whether of the German or the Japanese variety. The people of those countries that have been devastated and despoiled by Nazi barbarism certainly know better than the others what they are fighting *against,* and for that reason they perhaps know somewhat better what they are fighting *for.* But at all events, they are all fighting primarily for the preservation of something they have or the recovery of something they have lost—their native soil, their national independence, their familiar institutions and way of life. In this sense they are all fighting for the cause of human freedom. But it is not for human freedom in the abstract, or for some imagined but non-existent ideal freedom, that they are fighting. On the contrary, each country is fight-ing for the particular sort of freedom—the particular set of political and social institutions—with which it is familiar and to which it is attached. They are all fighting, in short, for the preservation of what they had before the war began.

I was on the point of saying that they are all fighting for the preserva-tion or the restoration of the status quo ante; but "status quo" is a fighting term. Better not use it without smiling, or at least without explaining what one means by it. . . . I have much admiration, and some sympathy, for the author writing in *The New York Times,* who stuck his neck out in defense of the status quo. He made no bones about it.

> What is this America that we are now fighting to defend? For more than a year after the collapse of France, England alone held the gate against Hitler. Without the English stand America would have had no time to become the arsenal of democracy. But without the good hope of American aid England might have been unequal to the mighty task. We are the hope of the world today in the sense that we have the final say. We have the casting vote for victory, and we have cast it for humanity and civilization.
>
> That is the kind of America people are asked to defend—the hope, the old record. When our young people a few years ago envied the flaming faith in the hearts of Hitler's and Mussolini's young men, did they happen to note the identity of the country to which the victims of Hitler's and Mussolini's crusading faith were fleeing for refuge? The refugees came to America, as the refugees have been coming to America for more than 300 years. The victims of the Hitler terror did not stipulate for a better America before they consented to seek refuge here. Our old American Status Quo was plenty good enough for them. Our old American Status Quo gave them life, liberty and livelihood.
>
> What, then, do we seriously mean that America of the 12,000,000 unemployed ten years ago is the hope of the world? Yes.
>
> America of the Economic Royalists and utility pirates the hope of the world? Yes.
>
> America of the Ku Klux fanatics, of the Negro lynchings, of the Dillingers and the corrupt politicans—this America the hope of the world? Yes.
>
> One need not take America's word for it. Ask the people of Britain, Russia, China and the conquered and martyred nations of Europe what they think of the American record.

This writer does not, I suppose, wish to preserve the status quo in all respects. I suppose he wishes as much as anyone to get rid of unemployment, utility pirates, Ku Klux Klan fanatics, Negro lynchings, corrupt politicians, and all the rest of it. But he has the sense to see these things in perspective, as undesirable aspects of the status quo which certainly no one wishes to preserve, in their proper relation to the fundamental aspects of the status quo which most of us certainly do wish to preserve. In talking about the new and better world, and still more in trying to make one, it is highly important not to lose sight of, or fail to take into account, the status quo as a whole, its fundamental virtues as well as its superficial defects.

The primary purpose of this war, unless I am completely mistaken, is to preserve the status quo in its fundamentals, even if that involves preserving its superficial defects. We are certainly (everyone says so) fighting to preserve our American way of life. And what are the fundamentals of our way of life? They are what they have always been since 1789—the sovereign political independence of the United States; the system of representative government as defined in the Constitution; free economic enterprise tempered by such social regulation as from time to time seems to be essential; and the constitutional guarantees of the right of the individual to freedom from arbitrary arrest and imprisonment, freedom to choose one's occupation and to be secure in it, freedom of religion, of speech and the press, and of learning and teaching. Imperfectly realized these freedoms are, certainly; and certainly the system of government is capable of improvement. But this system of government and these freedoms, such as they are, are what we have. They are the fundamentals of the status quo. And they are what we are fighting to preserve.

The decision to drop the atomic bomb, 1945

President Harry Truman learned of the new instrument of destruction scientists had fashioned the day after Roosevelt died—April 13, 1945. Three months later the first atomic explosion was set off on the desert flats of Alamogordo, New Mexico. Japan was warned to surrender or to suffer "prompt and utter destruction," but the bomb was not mentioned. The warning went unheeded, and on August 6, over Hiroshima, the bomb was dropped. About 75,000 persons were killed, 100,000 injured, and nearly 96 percent of the buildings destroyed. The Japanese hesitated, and three days later a second atomic bomb was dropped on Nagasaki. Whether the decision to use the bomb in this fashion was necessary, or wise, or moral, remains a subject of fierce controversy.

Admiral William D. Leahy

Once it had been tested, President Truman faced the decision as to whether to use it. He did not like the idea, but was persuaded that it would shorten the war against Japan and save American lives. It is my opinion that the use of this barbarous weapon at Hiroshima and Nagasaki was of no material assistance in our war against Japan. The Japanese were already defeated and ready to surrender because of the effective sea blockade and the successful bombing with conventional weapons. It was my reaction that the scientists and others wanted to make this test because of the vast sums that had been spent on the project. Truman knew that, and so did the other

From William D. Leahy, *I Was There* (New York: Whittlesey House, McGraw-Hill, 1950), pp. 441–42, reprinted by permission; Leslie R. Groves, *Now It Can Be Told* (New York: Harper & Row, 1961), pp. 266–67, reprinted by permission; Winston Churchill, *Triumph and Tragedy* (Boston: Houghton Mifflin Co., 1953), p. 639, reprinted by permission; Henry L. Stimson and McGeorge Bundy, *On Active Service in Peace and War* (New York: Harper & Row, 1947), pp. 630–31, reprinted by permission; Dwight D. Eisenhower, *Mandate for Change* (New York: Doubleday & Co., Inc., 1963), pp. 312–13. Copyright © 1968 by Dwight D. Eisenhower, reprinted by permission of Doubleday & Co., Inc.

people involved. However, the Chief Executive made a decision to use the bomb on two cities in Japan.

General Leslie R. Groves

A debate arose about how the bomb should be employed. Should we conduct a demonstration of its power for all the world to see, and then deliver an ultimatum to Japan, or should we use it without warning? It was always difficult for me to understand how anyone could ignore the importance of the effect on the Japanese people and their government of the overwhelming surprise of the bomb. To achieve surprise was one of the reasons we had tried so hard to maintain our security.

President Truman knew of these diverse and conflicting opinions. He must have engaged in some real soul-searching before reaching his final decision. In my opinion, his resolve to continue with the original plan will always stand as an act of unsurpassed courage and wisdom—courage because, for the first time in the history of the United States, the President personally determined the course of a major military strategical and tactical operation for which he could be considered directly responsible; and wisdom because history, if any thought is given to the value of American lives, has conclusively proven that his decision was correct.

Winston Churchill

[At Potsdam] there never was a moment's discussion as to whether the atomic bomb should be used or not. To avert a vast, indefinite butchery, to bring the war to an end, to give peace to the world, to lay healing hands upon its tortured peoples by a manifestation of overwhelming power at the cost of a few explosions, seemed, after all our toils and perils, a miracle of deliverance. . . . The historic fact remains, and must be judged in the after-time, that the decision whether or not to use the atomic bomb to compel the surrender of Japan was never an issue. There was unanimous, automatic, unquestioned agreement around our table; nor did I ever hear the slightest suggestion that we should do otherwise.

Henry L. Stimson

In March 1945 our Air Force had launched its first great incendiary raid on the Tokyo area. In this raid more damage was done and more casualties were inflicted than was the case at Hiroshima. Hundreds of bombers took part and hundreds of tons of incendiaries were dropped. Similar successive raids burned out a great part of the urban area of Japan, but the Japanese fought on. On August 6 one B-29 dropped a single atomic bomb on Hiroshima. Three days later a second bomb was dropped on Nagasaki and the war was over. So far as the Japanese could know, our ability to execute atomic attacks, if necessary by many planes at one time, was unlimited. As Dr. Karl Compton has said, "It was not one atomic bomb, or two, which brought surrender; it was the experience of what an atomic bomb will actually do to a community, *plus the dread of many more,* that was effective."

Dwight D. Eisenhower

During [Stimson's] recitation of the relevant facts, I had been conscious of a feeling of depression and so I voiced to him my grave misgivings, first on the basis of my belief that Japan was already defeated and that dropping the bomb was completely unnecessary, and secondly because I thought that our country should avoid shocking world opinion by the use of a weapon whose employment was, I thought, no longer mandatory as a measure to save American lives. It was my belief that Japan was, at that very moment, seeking some way to surrender with a minimum loss of "face." The Secretary was deeply disturbed by my attitude, almost angrily refuting the reasons I gave for my quick conclusions.

10
America Searches for Peace

The Cold War: the Marshall Plan and Russian reaction, 1947

Franklin D. Roosevelt died before the atomic bombs exploded over Hiroshima and Nagasaki; nor did he live to attend the meeting at San Francisco to establish the United Nations. But even as he was mourned, at the moment of allied victory, American and British distrust of Russia was mounting. Without a common enemy, relations between the allies began to chill. The Cold War started to jell. In March 1946, at Fulton, Missouri, Winston Churchill delivered his famous "Iron Curtain" speech, in which he spoke of the "expansionist tendencies" of Russia and of "an iron curtain which has descended across the continent." That same month President Truman went before a joint session of Congress and requested $400 million for military and economic aid to the governments of Greece and Turkey to resist Communist encroachment in those countries. "I believe," he said, "that it must be the policy of the United States to support free people who are resisting attempted subjugation by armed minorities or by outside pressures."

The Truman Doctrine was an expression of the defensive, military side of American policy. To give form to the non-military, Secretary of State George C. Marshall in a speech at Harvard University, announced the administration's plan for a program of economic aid to all European nations, Russia included. The word "communism" did not appear in his speech. The enemy was poverty, and the unrest it engendered. The "Marshall Plan" called for a sum of $20 billion, to be administered by Europeans, for their own economic reconstruction. The American Congress, alarmed by the Communist seizure of Czechoslovakia, and relieved that a suspicious U.S.S.R. and her satellites refused to participate in the program, passed the Marshall Plan in 1948 and eventually appropriated $12 billion.

SECRETARY OF STATE GEORGE C. MARSHALL'S ADDRESS AT HARVARD UNIVERSITY JUNE 5, 1947

In considering the requirements for the rehabilitation of Europe, the physical loss of life, the visible destruction of cities, factories, mines, and railroads was correctly estimated, but it has become obvious during recent months that this visible destruction was probably less serious than the dislocation of the entire fabric of European economy. For the past ten years conditions have been highly abnormal. The feverish preparation for war and the more feverish maintenance of the war effort engulfed all aspects of national economies. Machinery has fallen into disrepair or is entirely obsolete. Under the arbitrary and destructive Nazi rule, virtually every possible enterprise was geared into the German war machine. Long-standing commercial ties, private institutions, banks, insurance companies, and shipping companies dis-

From "European Initiative Essential to Economic Recovery," *Department of State Bulletin*, Vol. XVI, June 15, 1947, pp. 1159–60.

appeared, through loss of capital, absorption through nationalization, or by simple destruction. In many countries, confidence in the local currency has been severely shaken. The breakdown of the business structure of Europe during the war was complete. Recovery has been seriously retarded by the fact that two years after the close of hostilities a peace settlement with Germany and Austria has not been agreed upon. But even given a more prompt solution of these difficult problems, the rehabilitation of the economic structure of Europe quite evidently will require a much longer time and greater effort than had been foreseen.

There is a phase of this matter which is both interesting and serious. The farmer has always produced the foodstuffs to exchange with the city dweller for other necessities of life. This division of labor is the basis of modern civilization. At the present time it is threatened with breakdown. The town and city industries are not producing adequate goods to exchange with the food-producing farmer. Raw materials and fuel are in short supply. Machinery is lacking or worn out. The farmer or the peasant cannot find the goods for sale which he desires to purchase. So the sale of his farm produce for money which he cannot use seems to him an unprofitable transaction. He, therefore, has withdrawn many fields from crop cultivation and is using them for grazing. He feeds more grain to stock and finds for himself and his family an ample supply of food, however short he may be on clothing and the other ordinary gadgets of civilization. Meanwhile people in the cities are short of food and fuel. So the governments are forced to use their foreign money and credits to procure these necessities abroad. This process exhausts funds which are urgently needed for reconstruction. Thus a very serious situation is rapidly developing which bodes no good for the world. The modern system of the division of labor upon which the exchange of products is based is in danger of breaking down.

The truth of the matter is that Europe's requirements for the next three or four years of foreign food and other essential products—principally from America—are so much greater than her present ability to pay that she must have substantial additional help or face economic, social, and political deterioration of a very grave character. The remedy lies in breaking the vicious circle and restoring the confidence of the European people in the economic future of their own countries and of Europe as a whole. The manufacturer and the farmer throughout wide areas must be able and willing to exchange their products for currencies the continuing value of which is not open to question.

Aside from the demoralizing effect on the world at large and the possibilities of disturbances arising as a result of the desperation of the people concerned, the consequences to the economy of the United States should be apparent to all. It is logical that the United States should do whatever it is able to do to assist in the return of normal economic health in the world, without which there can be no political stability and no assured peace. Our policy is directed not against any country or doctrine but against hunger, poverty, desperation, and chaos. Its purpose should be the revival of a working economy in the world so as to permit the emergence of political and social conditions in which free institutions can exist. Such assistance, I am convinced, must not be on a piecemeal basis as various crises develop. Any assistance that this Government may render in the future should provide a cure rather than a mere palliative. Any government that is willing to assist in the task of recovery will find full cooperation, I am sure, on the part of the United States Government. Any government which maneuvers to block the recovery of other countries cannot expect help from us. Furthermore, governments, political parties, or groups which seek to perpetuate human misery in order to profit therefrom politically or otherwise will encounter the opposition of the United States.

It is already evident that, before the United States Government can proceed much further in its efforts to alleviate the situation and help start the European world on its way to recovery, there must be some agreement among the countries of Europe as to the requirements of the situation and the part those countries themselves will take in order to give proper effect to whatever action might be undertaken by this Government. It would be neither fitting nor efficacious for this Government to undertake to draw up unilaterally a program designed to place Europe on its feet economically. This is the business of the Europeans. The initiative, I think, must come from Europe. The role of this country should consist of friendly aid in the drafting of a European program and of later support of such a program so far as it may be practical for us to do so. The program should be a joint one, agreed to by a number, if not all, European nations. . . . With foresight, and a willingness on the part of our people to face up to the vast responsibility which history has clearly placed upon our country, the difficulties I have outlined can and will be overcome.

E. VISHNEV OF THE SOVIET UNION ANALYZES THE MARSHALL PLAN

Marshall is the Secretary of State of the United States of America (in this country he is called Minister of Foreign Affairs). Last summer Marshall made a speech in which he declared that in European countries there prevails at present economic chaos and that the United States are ready to help these lands restore their economies. Marshall proposed to the European lands first of all to consult among themselves how they could help one another. "Just let these countries," said Marshall, "calculate what resources they have themselves and what are their needs. Then America will decide

From Walter Bedell Smith, *My Three Years in Moscow* (Philadelphia: J. B. Lippincott Company, 1950), pp. 198–200. Copyright 1949 by Walter Bedell Smith. Reprinted by permission of J. B. Lippincott Company.

how it can help them." The American papers immediately raised a great noise about this plan. In different terms, they emphasized the "magnanimity" of America which had decided to help war-stricken Europe.

However, actually, this cunning plan pursued entirely different aims. The American capitalists want to use the help of the Marshall Plan to overwhelm Europe and bring it into subjection to themselves. The government of the Soviet Union at once recognized the real meaning of the Marshall Plan and definitely refused to take part in setting it up.

But sixteen European states adopted the Marshall Plan against the wishes of their people. . . . Representatives of these sixteen European states met together and calculated that they had to receive from the U.S.A. 29 billion dollars to restore their economies. The Americans answered that this sum was too high and asked for its reduction to 20-22 billion dollars. The Americans, moreover, attached the following condition: they themselves will dictate to each European country what branch of economy it must develop and what it must curtail. For example, they say to Britain: "You Britishers, build fewer ships for yourselves; you will buy ships from us in America." They propose to the French a reduction in the production of automobiles— American factories can make automobiles for France.

It goes without saying that this was very useful for American capitalists. In America everybody is fearfully awaiting "the economic crisis," i.e., the time when many factories and industries suddenly close and millions of people are left without work. At that time it will be difficult for manufacturers to get rid of their out-put. A man out of work has nothing with which to buy them. So the American capitalists are greatly concerned how to sell profitably their output in Europe. Further, the European countries inevitably will become dependent on America: once they make a few machines, tools and automobiles, it means that willy-nilly they must defer to the Americans. . . .

Belgium has a colony, the Congo, in Africa. Rich deposits of uranium ore exist there. This ore is needed for the production of atom bombs. In the French colony of [New] Caledonia are deposits of nickel. Nickel is a metal which is very important for the making of armaments. The Americans are demanding that Belgium and France hand over the uranium ore and nickel to America.

But this isn't all. The American capitalists have still another dastardly aim. After using the Marshall Plan to reduce the European countries, they want to unite them in a military alliance for a future war against the democratic states. The Marshall Plan is highly profitable to the United States. For the European countries it brings only poverty. Any land which wants to receive "aid" by means of this plan will be entirely dependent on America. Its economy will not be assisted: on the contrary, it will fall into greater ruin because the country will have to close many of its industries and plants and hundreds of thousands of people will be out of work. This is why both in America itself and in all other lands progressive people are opposing the Marshall Plan with all their strength.

The hot war: *Truman* v. *MacArthur,* 1951

The Cold War verged on becoming a hot war in several places during the administration of Harry Truman. But the president neither succumbed to Communist pressures, nor yielded to those American hawks who wanted a major war against Russia. At Berlin, for example, in 1949, when the Russians shut off all land traffic to that isolated city, Truman ordered an "airlift" of supplies, bringing in over 2.5 million tons of food in nine months. Eventually the Russians ended the blockade.

Similarly, in Korea, when North Koreans attacked southward across the 38th parallel on June 25, 1950, Truman acted decisively. He ordered American troops to the defense of South Korea—his intention, however, was not to achieve total victory by any and all means, but to deny the spoils to an aggressor. After Chinese troops entered the battle in overwhelming numbers, Truman refused to sanction the use of nuclear weapons or bombing north of the Yalu River— though General Douglas MacArthur openly demanded such action. MacArthur's virtual insubordination forced Truman to remove him from command. The American public gave MacArthur a spectacular reception. But the Joint Chiefs of Staff supported the president, agreeing with General Omar Bradley that an enlarged war with China would be "the wrong war, in the wrong place, at the wrong time."

GENERAL DOUGLAS MACARTHUR TO REPRESENTATIVE JOSEPH MARTIN, READ BEFORE CONGRESS, APRIL 5, 1951

My views and recommendations with respect to the situation created by Red China's entry into war against us in Korea have been submitted to Washington in most complete detail. Generally these views are well known and clearly understood, as they follow the conventional pattern of meeting force with maximum counter-force as we have never failed to do in the past. . . .

It seems strangely difficult for some to realize that here in Asia is where the Communist conspirators have elected to make their play for global conquest, and that we have joined the issue thus raised on the battlefield; that here we fight Europe's war with arms while the diplomats there still fight it with words; that if we lost the war to communism in Asia the fall of Europe is inevitable, win it and Europe most probably would avoid war and yet

From *The Military Situation in the Far East: Hearings before the Committee on Armed Services and the Committee on Foreign Relations,* Eighty-second Congress, First Session, pp. 323–26, 3543–44, 3550–58.

preserve freedom. As you pointed out, we must win. There is no substitute for victory.

HARRY S. TRUMAN'S ADDRESS TO THE NATION, APRIL 11, 1951

We do not want to see the conflict in Korea extended. We are trying to prevent a world war—not to start one. The best way to do that is to make it plain that we and the other free countries will continue to resist the attack. But you may ask why can't we take other steps to punish the aggressor. Why don't we bomb Manchuria and China itself? Why don't we assist Chinese Nationalist troops to land on the mainland of China? If we were to do these things we would be running a very grave risk of starting a general war. If that were to happen, we would have brought about the exact situation we are trying to prevent. If we were to do these things, we would become entangled in a vast conflict on the continent of Asia and our task would become immeasurably more difficult all over the world. What would suit the ambitions of the Kremlin better than for our military forces to be committed to a full scale war with Red China?

It may well be that, in spite of our best efforts, the Communists may spread the war. But it would be wrong—tragically wrong—for us to take the initiative in extending the war. The dangers are great. Make no mistake about it. Behind the North Koreans and Chinese Communists in the front lines stand additional millions of Chinese soldiers. And behind the Chinese stand the tanks, the planes, the submarines, the soldiers, and the scheming rulers of the Soviet Union.

Our aim is to avoid the spread of the conflict.

The course we have been following is the one best calculated to avoid an all-out war. It is the course consistent with our obligation to do all we can to maintain international peace and security. Our experience in Greece and Berlin shows that it is the most effective course of action we can follow.

First of all, it is clear that our efforts in Korea can blunt the will of the Chinese Communists to continue the struggle. The United Nations forces have put up a tremendous fight in Korea and have inflicted very heavy casualties on the enemy. Our forces are stronger than they have been before. These are plain facts which may discourage the Chinese Communists from continuing their attack.

Second, the free world as a whole is growing in military strength every day. In the United States, in western Europe, and throughout the world, free men are alert to the Soviet threat and are building their defenses. This may discourage the Communist rulers from continuing the war in Korea— and from undertaking new acts of aggression elsewhere.

If the Communist authorities realize that they cannot defeat us in Korea, if they realize it would be foolhardy to widen the hostilities beyond Korea, then they may recognize the folly of continuing their aggression. A peaceful settlement may then be possible. The door is always open. . . .

GENERAL DOUGLAS MACARTHUR'S ADDRESS
TO CONGRESS

There are some who for varying reasons would appease Red China. They are blind to history's clear lesson. For history teaches with unmistakable emphasis that appeasement but begets new and bloodier war. It points to no single instance where the end has justified that means—where appeasement has led to more than a sham peace. Like blackmail, it lays the basis for new and successively greater demands, until, as in blackmail, violence becomes the only other alternative. Why, my soldiers asked of me, surrender military advantages to an enemy in the field? I could not answer. Some may say to avoid the spread of the conflict into an all-out war with China; others, to avoid Soviet intervention. Neither explanation seems valid. For China is already engaging with the maximum power it can commit and the Soviet will not necessarily mesh its actions with our moves. Like a cobra, any new enemy will more likely strike whenever it feels that the relativity in military or other potential is in its favor on a world-wide basis. . . .

I have just left your fighting sons in Korea. They have met all the tests there and I can report to you without reservation they are splendid in every way. It was my constant effort to preserve them and end this savage conflict honorably and with the least loss of time and a minimum sacrifice of life. Its growing bloodshed has caused me the deepest anguish and anxiety. Those gallant men will remain often in my thoughts and in my prayers always.

I am closing my fifty-two years of military service. When I joined the Army even before the turn of the century, it was the fulfillment of all my boyish hopes and dreams. The world has turned over many times since I took the oath on the plain at West Point, and the hopes and dreams have long since vanished. But I still remember the refrain of one of the most popular barracks ballads of that day which proclaimed most profoundly that—

Old soldiers never die; they just fade away.

And like the old soldier of that ballad, I now close my military career and just fade away—an old soldier who tried to do his duty as God gave him the light to see that duty.

SECRETARY OF DEFENSE GEORGE C. MARSHALL'S
TESTIMONY BEFORE CONGRESS, MAY, 7, 1951

General MacArthur . . . would have us, on our own initiative, carry the conflict beyond Korea against the mainland of Communist China, both from the sea and from the air. He would have us accept the risk of involvement not only in an extension of the war with Red China, but in an all-out war with the Soviet Union. He would have us do this even at the expense of losing our allies and wrecking the coalition of free people throughout the world. He would have us do this even though the effect of such action might expose Western Europe to attack by the millions of Soviet troops poised in Middle and Eastern Europe.

This fundamental divergence is one of judgment as to the proper course of action to be followed by the United States. This divergence arises from the inherent difference between the position of a field commander, whose mission is limited to a particular area and a particular antagonist, and the position of the Joint Chiefs of Staff, the Secretary of Defense, and the President, who are responsible for the total security of the United States, and who, to achieve and maintain this security must weigh our interests and objectives in one part of the globe with those in other areas of the world so as to attain the best over-all balance. . . .

It became apparent that General MacArthur had grown so far out of sympathy with the established policies of the United States that there was grave doubt as to whether he could any longer be permitted to exercise the authority in making decisions that normal common functions would assign to a theater commander. In this situation, there was no other course but to relieve him.

The technique of Senator Joseph McCarthy: from the Army-McCarthy hearings, April 22, 1954

The era of Joseph McCarthy, the junior Republican Senator from Wisconsin, extended from 1950 to 1954. He first claimed national attention by announcing that he had in his possession the names of fifty-seven Communists and fellow travelers who were responsible for shaping policy in the State Department. The charge was fraudulent, but many Americans chose to believe that it was true. After all, Alger Hiss, the darling of American liberals, was found guilty of perjury. Some respectable scientists, like Klaus Fuchs, were working for the Soviet Union. Where there was smoke, McCarthyites were convinced, there was Red fire. Thus, in the next four years his reckless accusations created a national hysteria. Hundreds of civil servants, clergymen, and college teachers were dismissed for alleged disloyalty.

Finally, in 1954, McCarthy attacked the American army itself, accusing Secretary of the Army Robert T. Stevens of being a Communist "dupe," and of attempting to blackmail his Senate committee. The resulting Army-McCarthy hearings were nationally televised, and a high point was the cross examination of Roy M. Cohn (special counsel to McCarthy's committee) by Joseph Welch (chief counsel for the army). McCarthy broke into the testimony to accuse a

From the *Special Senate Committee on Charges and Countercharges involving Secretary of the Army Robert T. Stevens,* Eighty-third Congress, Second Session, pp. 2424–30.

young lawyer on Welch's staff of membership in a Communist organization. Welch, an urbane, witty, gentle man, rebuffed this attempt at character assassination: "Have you no sense of decency, sir, at long last? Have you left no sense of decency?" The American audience saw plainly that he did not. Soon thereafter, McCarthy's power was broken. Censured by the Senate, he continued periodically to issue wild statements, but the country no longer listened.

MR. WELCH: To come back, Mr. Cohn, to the item that we were talking about this morning. I gathered, to sum it up a little, that as early as the spring, which must mean March or April, you knew about this situation of possible subversives and security risks, and even spies at Fort Monmouth, is that right?

MR. COHN: Yes, sir.

MR. WELCH: And I think you have used the word "disturbing," that you found it a disturbing situation? . . .

MR. COHN: Well, sir, it was certainly serious enough for me to want to check into it and see how many facts we could check out and—

MR. WELCH: And stop it as soon as possible?

MR. COHN: Well, it was a question of developing the—

MR. WELCH: But the thing that we have to do is stop it, isn't it?

MR. COHN: Stop what, sir?

MR. WELCH: Stop the risk?

MR. COHN: Stop the risk, sir?

MR. WELCH: Yes.

MR. COHN: Yes, what we had to do was stop the risk and—

MR. WELCH: That is right, get the people suspended or get them on trial or fire them or do something, that is right, isn't it?

MR. COHN: Partly, sir.

MR. WELCH: Sir?

MR. COHN: Partly sir.

MR. WELCH: But it is primarily the thing, isn't it?

MR. COHN: Well, the thing came up—

MR. WELCH: Mr. Cohn, if I told you now that we had a bad situation at Monmouth, you would want to cure it by sundown, if you could, wouldn't you?

MR. COHN: I am sure I couldn't, sir.

MR. WELCH: But you would like to, if you could?

MR. COHN: Sir—

MR. WELCH: Isn't that right?

MR. COHN: No, what I want—

MR. WELCH: Answer me. That must be right. It has to be right.

MR. COHN: What I would like to do and what can be done are two different things.

MR. WELCH: Well, if you could be God and do anything you wished, you would cure it by sundown, wouldn't you?

MR. COHN: Yes, sir. . . .

MR. WELCH: When did you first meet Secretary Stevens?

MR. COHN: I first met Secretary Stevens September 7 I believe it was. . . .

MR. WELCH: And you knew that he was the new Secretary of the Army?

MR. COHN: Yes; I did know he was the Secretary of the Army.

MR. WELCH: And you must have had high hopes about him, didn't you?

MR. COHN: I don't think I gave it too much thought, sir.

MR. WELCH: Anybody wants the Secretary of the Army to do well, no matter what party he is from, do we not?

MR. COHN: Surely, sir.

MR. WELCH: And on September 7, when you met him, you had in your bosom this alarming situation about Monmouth, is that right?

MR. COHN: Yes; I knew about Monmouth, then. Yes, sir.

MR. WELCH: And you didn't tug at his lapel and say, "Mr. Secretary, I know something about Monmouth that won't let me sleep nights?" You didn't do it, did you?

MR. COHN: I don't—as I testified, Mr. Welch, I don't know whether I talked to Mr. Stevens about it then or not. I know that on the 16th I did. Whether I talked to him on the 7th or not, is something I don't know.

MR. WELCH: Don't you know that if you had really told him what your fears were, and substantiated them to any extent, he could have jumped in the next day with suspensions?

MR. COHN: No, sir.

MR. WELCH: Did you then have any reason to doubt his fidelity?

MR. COHN: No, sir.

MR. WELCH: Or his honor?

MR. COHN: No.

MR. WELCH: Or his patriotism?

MR. COHN: No.

MR. WELCH: And, yet, Mr. Cohn, you didn't tell him what you knew?

MR. COHN: I don't know whether I did or not. I told him some of the things I knew, sir. I don't think I told him everything I knew on the first occasion. After the first two or three occasions, I think he had a pretty good idea of what we were working on.

MR. WELCH: Mr. Cohn, tell me once more: Every time you learn of a Communist or a spy anywhere, is it your policy to get them out as fast as possible?

MR. COHN: Surely, we want them out as fast as possible, sir.

MR. WELCH: And whenever you learn of one from now on, Mr. Cohn, I beg of you, will you tell somebody about them quick?

MR. COHN: Mr. Welch, with great respect, I work for the committee here. They know how we go about handling situations of Communist infiltration. If they are displeased with the speed with which I and the group of men who work with me proceed, if they are displeased with the order in which we move, I am sure they will give me appropriate instructions along those lines, and I will follow any which they give me.

MR. WELCH: May I add my small voice, sir, and say whenever you know about a subversive or a Communist or a spy, please hurry. Will you remember those words? . . .

SENATOR MCCARTHY: Mr. Chairman, in view of that question—

SENATOR MUNDT: Have you a point of order?

SENATOR MCCARTHY: Not exactly, Mr. Chairman, but in view of Mr. Welch's request that the information be given once we know of anyone who might be performing any work for the Communist Party, I think we should tell him that he has in his law firm a young man named Fisher whom he recommended, incidentally, to do work on this committee, who has been for a number of years a member of an organization which was named, oh, years and years ago, as the legal bulwark of the Communist Party, an organization which always swings to the defense of . . . [any] Communists. I certainly assume that Mr. Welch did not know of this young man at the time he recommended him as the assistant counsel for this committee, but he has such terror and such a great desire to know where anyone is located who may be serving the Communist cause, Mr. Welch, that I thought we should just call to your attention the fact that your Mr. Fisher, who is still in your law firm today,whom you asked to have down here looking over the secret and classified material, is a member of an organization, not named by me but named by various committees, named by the Attorney General, as I recall, and I think I quote this verbatim, as "the legal bulwark of the Communist Party." He belonged to that for a sizeable number of years, according to his own admission, and he belonged to it long after it had been exposed as the legal arm of the Communist Party.

Knowing that, Mr. Welch, I just felt that I had a duty to respond to your urgent request that before sundown, when we know of anyone serving the Communist cause, we let the agency know. We are now letting you know that your man did belong to this organization for either three or four years, belong to it long after he was out of law school. . . . I have hesitated bringing that up, but I have been rather bored with your phony requests to Mr. Cohn here that he personally get every Communist out of government before sundown. Therefore, we will give you information about the young man in your own organization.

I am not asking you at this time to explain why you tried to foist him on this committee. Whether you knew he was a member of that Communist organization or not, I don't know. I assume you did not, Mr. Welch, because I get the impression that, while you are quite an actor, you play for a laugh. I don't think you have any conception of the danger of the Communist Party. I don't think you yourself would ever knowingly aid the Communist cause. I think you are unknowingly aiding it when you try to burlesque this hearing in which we are attempting to bring out the facts, however. . .

MR. WELCH: Mr. Chairman, under these circumstances I must have something approaching a personal privilege.

SENATOR MUNDT: You may have it, sir. It will not be taken out of your time.

MR. WELCH: Senator McCarthy, I did not know—Senator, sometimes you say "May I have your attention?"

SENATOR MCCARTHY: I am listening to you. I can listen with one ear.

MR. WELCH: This time I want you to listen with both.

SENATOR MCCARTHY: Yes.

MR. WELCH: Senator McCarthy, I think until this moment—

SENATOR MCCARTHY: Jim, will you get the news story to the effect that this man belonged to this Communist-front organization? Will you get the citations showing that this was the legal arm of the Communist Party, and the length of time that he belonged, and the fact that he was recommended by Mr. Welch? I think that should be in the record.

MR. WELCH: You won't need anything in the record when I have finished telling you this.

Until this moment, Senator, I think I never really gaged your cruelty or your recklessness. Fred Fisher is a young man who went to the Harvard Law School and came into my firm and is starting what looks to be a brilliant career with us.

When I decided to work for this committee I asked Jim St. Clair, who sits on my right, to be my first assistant. I said to Jim, "Pick somebody in the firm who works under you that you would like." He chose Fred Fisher and they came down on an afternoon plane. That night, when he had taken a little stab at trying to see what the case was about, Fred Fisher and Jim St. Clair and I went to dinner together. I then said to these two young men, "Boys, I don't know anything about you except I have always liked you, but if there is anything funny in the life of either one of you that would hurt anybody in this case you speak up quick."

Fred Fisher said, "Mr. Welch, when I was in law school and for a period of months after, I belonged to the Lawyers Guild," as you have suggested, Senator. He went on to say, "I am secretary of the Young Republicans League in Newton with the son of Massachusetts' Governor, and I have the respect and admiration of my community and I am sure I have the respect and admiration of the twenty-five lawyers or so in Hale & Dorr."

I said, "Fred, I just don't think I am going to ask you to work on the case. If I do, one of these days that will come out and go over national television and it will just hurt like the dickens."

So, Senator, I asked him to go back to Boston.

Little did I dream you could be so reckless and so cruel as to do injury to that lad. It is true he is still with Hale & Dorr. It is, I regret to say, equally true that I fear he shall always bear a scar needlessly inflicted by you. If it were in my power to forgive you for your reckless cruelty, I will do so. I like to think I am a gentleman, but your forgiveness will have to come from someone other than me.

SENATOR McCARTHY: Mr. Chairman.

SENATOR MUNDT: Senator McCarthy?

SENATOR McCARTHY: May I say that Mr. Welch talks about this being cruel and reckless. He was just baiting; he has been baiting Mr. Cohn here for hours, requesting that Mr. Cohn, before sundown, get out of any department of Government anyone who is serving the Communist cause. I just give this man's record, and I want to say, Mr. Welch, that it has been labeled long before he became a member, as early as 1944—

MR. WELCH: Senator, may we not drop this? We know he belonged to the Lawyers Guild, and Mr. Cohn nods his head at me. I did you, I think, no personal injury, Mr. Cohn.

MR. COHN: No, sir.

MR. WELCH: I meant to do you no personal injury, and if I did, I beg your pardon.

Let us not assassinate this lad further, Senator. You have done enough. Have you no sense of decency, sir, at long last? Have you left no sense of decency?

Brown et al. v. *The Board of Education of Topeka et al.,* May 17, 1954

By a unanimous decision, the Supreme Court in Brown v. *Board of Education declared that racial segregation in the public schools was unconstitutional. The old legal doctrine which permitted "separate" facilities for blacks, so long as they were "equal" to that for whites, was specifically overturned. The finding was immensely significant, since it affected millions of school children, both in the North and in the South.*

But the Supreme Court does not have its own police or army. It merely interprets; and the federal administration has the responsibility of enforcing the decisions of the court. That responsibility has not been fulfilled. Although the Court, in 1955, ordered that desegregation be achieved with "deliberate speed," the phrase was ambiguous, in fact meaningless. Local officials violated its intent; federal officials enforced the decision, at best, sporadically and ineffectively.

CHIEF JUSTICE WARREN: These cases come to us from the States of Kansas, South Carolina, Virginia, and Delaware. They are premised on

From *Brown* v. *Board of Education,* 247 U.S. pp. 483–95.

different facts and different local conditions, but a common legal question justifies their consideration together in this consolidated opinion.

In each of the cases, minors of the Negro race, through their legal representatives, seek the aid of the courts in obtaining admission to the public schools of their community on a nonsegregated basis. In each instance, they had been denied admission to schools attended by white children under laws requiring or permitting segregation according to race. This segregation was alleged to deprive the plaintiffs of the equal protection of the laws under the Fourteenth Amendment. In each of the cases other than the Delaware case, a three-judge federal district court denied relief to the plaintiffs on the so-called "separate but equal" doctrine announced by this Court in *Plessy* v. *Ferguson*. Under that doctrine equality of treatment is accorded when the races are provided substantially equal facilities, even though these facilities be separate. . . .

Today, education is perhaps the most important function of state and local governments. Compulsory school attendance laws and the great expenditures for education both demonstrate our recognition of the importance of education to our democratic society. It is required in the performance of our most basic public responsibilities, even service in the armed forces. It is the very foundation of good citizenship. Today it is a principal instrument in awakening the child to cultural values, in preparing him for later professional training, and in helping him to adjust normally to his environment. In these days, it is doubtful that any child may reasonably be expected to succeed in life if he is denied the opportunity of an education. Such an opportunity, where the state has undertaken to provide it, is a right which must be made available to all on equal terms.

We come then to the question presented: Does segregation of children in public schools solely on the basis of race, even though the physical facilities and other "tangible" factors may be equal, deprive the children of the minority group of equal educational opportunities? We believe that it does.

In *Sweatt* v. *Painter,* in finding that a segregated law school for Negroes could not provide them equal educational opportunities, this Court relied in large part on "those qualities which are incapable of objective measurement but which make for greatness in a law school." In *McLaurin* v. *Oklahoma State Regents* the Court, in requiring that a Negro admitted to a white graduate school be treated like all other students, again resorted to intangible considerations: ". . . his ability to study, to engage in discussions and exchange views with other students, and, in general, to learn his profession." Such considerations apply with added force to children in grade and high schools. To separate them from others of similar age and qualifications solely because of their race generates a feeling of inferiority as to their status in the community that may affect their hearts and minds in a way unlikely ever to be undone. The effect of this separation in their educational opportunities was well stated by a finding in the Kansas case by a court which nevertheless felt compelled to rule against the Negro plaintiffs:

Segregation of white and colored children in public schools has a detrimental effect upon the colored children. The impact is greater when it has the sanction of the law; for the policy of separating the races is usually interpreted as denoting the inferiority of the negro group. A sense of inferiority affects the motivation of a child to learn. Segregation with the sanction of law, therefore, has a tendency to [retard] the educational and mental development of the negro children and to deprive them of some of the benefits they would receive in a racial[ly] integrated school system.

Whatever may have been the extent of psychological knowledge at the time of *Plessy* v. *Ferguson*, this finding is amply supported by modern authority. Any language in *Plessy* v. *Ferguson* contrary to this finding is rejected.

We conclude that in the field of public education the doctrine of "separate but equal" has no place. Separate educational facilities are inherently unequal. Therefore, we hold that the plaintiffs and others similarly situated for whom the actions have been brought are, by reason of the segregation complained of, deprived of the equal protection of the laws guaranteed by the Fourteenth Amendment.

The failure of Eisenhower: a review of his Presidency, 1953–60

The nation seemed to rest on dead-center during the Eisenhower administration. These years of relative calm and absence of politically induced change, either forward or backward, may have been psychologically necessary to a nation whose exertions in the 1930's and 1940's had been enormous. "Perhaps the time was ripe," Sidney Hyman commented, "for a Presidency that would devote itself to consolidating gains. . . . Perhaps we all needed a breather. . . ." But Hyman concluded that Eisenhower must be judged a failure. Dynamic forces were at work reshaping the American landscape, creating a host of problems which Eisenhower either postponed or ignored. Those problems, Hyman predicted, "will burst upon the [next] president in the 1960's."

The heart of the trouble with the Eisenhower Presidency . . . has been its failure to accept the reality of the shift in executive-legislative relations that has occurred within the Constitution. It has not firmly grasped the responsibility of Presidential leadership from above, yet it has refused to allow Congress to improvise a substitute leadership from below to fill the vacuum. It has not marched at the head of affairs to force events into being of a kind favorable to America and the Grand Alliance. It has bent the weight of its energies to the end of stopping things which have been put into motion elsewhere. What it has done throughout is to seek the best of

From Sidney Hyman, "The Failure of the Eisenhower Presidency," *The Progressive*, May 1960, pp. 12–13. Reprinted by permission.

both worlds: to claim all the credit for the sunshine and to blame everyone else for the rain; to allow no voice but its own to be heard, yet to make Congress assume a large measure of the responsibility for all miscarriages of Administration policy.

The full proof of these charges would require a day-to-day listing of the actions of the Eisenhower Administration since it came to power in 1953. But a few representative instances, chosen without reference to any time sequence, will make an adequate case.

Item. In the last session of Congress, the President exercised his veto power 150 times, yet lent his approval to the Republican policy of calling the Democratic-controlled 86th Congress a "do-nothing Congress." How could it do anything when the veto power is equal to two-thirds the combined strength of the entire Congress, and a majority of that size is rarely on the same side of legislation? How could Congress attend, for example, to the needs of education, housing, and urban redevelopment when measures of this kind were beaten down by Executive veto—all in the name of a balanced budget?

Item. The Senate Preparedness Subcommittee on Armed Services sat day after day, week after week, heard hundreds of witnesses, took testimony from dozens of men, and unanimously made seventeen recommendations urging this nation to accelerate its defense program. Few of the recommendations have been carried out by the President. Moreover, at least one billion dollars of defense money the Congress has appropriated has been impounded, sunk, or hidden by the President while Congress is virtually powerless to make him do what it wants done.

Item. The President repeatedly talked of how important it was to provide long-term economic assistance to the underdeveloped countries. In the last session, the Foreign Relations Committee, which was of the same mind, labored long and hard and issued a nearly unanimous report which would have enabled the Development Loan Fund to plan its operations on a long-term basis. Yet, when there was a crucial vote on the floor of the Senate, the White House, swayed by the Treasury Department and the Bureau of the Budget (over the opposition of the State Department) sent word to party lieutenants to cut down the Development Loan Proposal. And it was cut down.

Item. When Charles E. Wilson was Secretary of Defense, Congress appropriated about $175 million for basic research. When asked why he had not spent the money, Wilson was quoted as saying that in his mind basic research was what you were doing when you did not know what to do. There was no word of correction from the White House. When asked about the lagging space program, Wilson said he had enough troubles on earth. There was no word of correction from the White House.

Item. After the Suez war, to whose onset the Administration contributed through its own blunders, the Eisenhower Doctrine was proclaimed as the nostrum which would set everything right in the Middle

East. Congress was not consulted in the period while that Doctrine was being formulated within the Executive. The terms were first leaked to the press, and once they were in public print, the Administration invoked the holy name of bipartisanship to insure its adoption by Congress, just as it had previously done in the case of the Formosa Resolution.

In both cases, Congress was informed that it had to support the position of the Administration because otherwise the Russians and the rest of the world would think we were sorely divided. That support was forthcoming because the leaders of Congress were convinced of the wisdom of the Administration's course. They were not at all convinced of the wisdom of the Administration's policy. They were convinced that the course was either dangerous or meaningless. Yet in Lebanon, just as in Quemoy and Matsu, Congress suddenly discovered that the Eisenhower Doctrine was *its* doctrine, and, the Formosa Resolution was *its* resolution.

Item. The Administration repeatedly emphasized the imperative necessity of maintaining "fiscal solvency." To be sure, at one point, it developed a deficit of $12.5 billion. At that same point, the Democratic members of Congress observed that something like $4 billion in dividend income in this country goes unreported; if there was a dividend withholding tax, as in the case of many other sources of income, the government would collect at least a billion dollars of the dividend-based revenues that were due it. This Democratic proposal was killed by the Administration, as was the case with another proposal that there be a tightening up of the tax-free expense allowances. Yet, for all its own negligence in enforcing existing tax laws, the Administration at every turn blasted the Democrats for being "reckless spenders."

Item. The President has spoken eloquently about the virtues of democracy. He would most certainly agree that free and open discussion is a leading factor in the actual workings of democracy. Yet his general tendency has been to shut off all debate by asserting that he knows more than "almost anyone" about military matters. Those who disagree with his judgements are, to him, "noisy extremists." They are, he says, unpatriotic because they have "the tendency to disparage our country" with their "spurious" assertions. The earnest men who are worried about our country's security are told by him that they are "political morticians exhibiting a breast-beating pessimism."

There is a case to be made for Mr. Eisenhower, albeit a small one. After twenty years of innovation under the Presidencies of Franklin D. Roosevelt and Harry S. Truman in meeting the social, political, and military revolutions of the day, perhaps the time was ripe for a Presidency that would devote itself to consolidating the gains made. Perhaps we all needed a breather in which to look around and reappraise where we stood as individuals in relationship to our own government, and where our government stood in relation to other nations. In such an interval of pause, existing programs could have been refined, the fast setting mold of habit could have been breached to allow for an entry of fresh air, the whole administrative machinery of government could have been renovated. Moreover, at any time, there is a place for a veto, for a disengagement from dangerous points of exposure, and for a political dialectic in which the negative arm is stronger than the affirmative arm.

If President Eisenhower had in fact been a consolidator in some such manner; if he had in fact used his negative arm to stop dangerous tendencies or to withdraw from them, his Presidency would have had a material relevance to the hour at which we stand in our history. Yet his has been the period of a falling apart, of a loss of élan and dash, of a veto for the sake of saying no, of a widening breach between power and responsibility. The legacy he leaves his successor in the White House, whoever he may be, is unenviable. Demands long postponed or ignored will burst upon the President in the 1960's. If President Eisenhower's successor rises to meet them, as he must if we are to continue to be a major power, it seems fairly certain that he will be damned for somehow violating the Constitution because he might insist on acting not like Mr. Eisenhower but like a President. It seems fairly certain that he will be damned for being a divisive influence, a source of acrimonious dispute, and worse. Yet one must hope that the next President will have the courage and the magnanimity to make his office respond to the needs of the time; to reunite power and responsibility in it; and to revive our sagging constitutional morality by restoring discussion itself to the governmental process.

A chronology of brutality and intimidation in Mississippi: August-October 1961

In the final years of the Eisenhower administration the country entered a new era in race relations. Black protest, formerly conducted by an elite of NAACP lawyers whose arena was the courts, began to transform itself into a mass movement which exerted direct pressure in public places. The spontaneous drugstore lunch counter sit-ins by black college students in Greensboro, North Carolina, in 1960 demonstrated the extent to which a new spirit of direct action had permeated the younger generation of blacks. Under the leadership of the Reverend Martin Luther King, Jr., the new tactics of mass protest were conducted in a spirit of Christian-Gandhian nonviolence. The Student Nonviolent Coordinating Committee (SNCC), formed in 1960 to coordinate sit-in activities, turned to the problem of helping blacks register as voters in 1961. White Mississippians responded with acts of violence and intimidation, as the following chronology indicates.

From the Committee for the Distribution of the Mississippi Story, *Mississippi Violence vs. Human Rights*, reprinted in Staughton Lynd (ed.), *Nonviolence in America: A Documentary History* (Indianapolis: Bobbs-Merrill Co., 1966), pp. 434–36. Reprinted by permission.

Amite County, August 15

Robert Moses, Student Non-Violent Coordinating Committee (SNCC) registration worker, and three Negroes who had tried unsuccessfully to register in Liberty, were driving toward McComb when a county officer stopped them. He asked if Moses was the man ". . . who's been trying to register our niggers." All were taken to court and Moses was arrested for "impeding an officer in the discharge of his duties," fined $50 and spent two days in jail.

Amite County, August 22

Robert Moses went to Liberty with three Negroes, who made an unsuccessful attempt to register. A block from the courthouse, Moses was attacked and beaten by Billy Jack Caston, the sheriff's first cousin. Eight stitches were required to close a wound in Moses' head. Caston was acquitted of assault charges by an all-white jury before a justice of the peace.

McComb, Pike County, August 26

Hollis Watkins, 20, and Elmer Hayes, 20, SNCC workers, were arrested while staging a sit-in at the F. W. Woolworth store and charged with breach of the peace. They spent 36 days in jail.

McComb, Pike County, August 27 and 29

Five Negro students from a local high school were convicted of breach of the peace following a sit-in at a variety store and bus terminal. They were sentenced to a $400 fine each and eight months in jail. One of these students, a girl of 15, was turned over to juvenile authorities, released, subsequently arrested, and sentenced to 12 months in a state school for delinquents.

McComb, Pike County, August 29

Two Negro leaders were arrested in McComb as an aftermath of the sit-in protest march on city hall, charged with contributing to the delinquency of minors. They were Curtis C. Bryant of McComb, an official of the NAACP, and Cordelle Reagan, of SNCC. Each arrest was made on an affidavit signed by Police Chief George Guy, who said he had information that the two ". . . were behind some of this racial trouble."

McComb, Pike County, August 30

SNCC workers Brenda Travis, 16, Robert Talbert, 19, and Isaac Lewis, 20, staged a sit-in in the McComb terminal of the Greyhound bus lines. They were arrested on charges of breach of the peace and failure to obey a police-man's order to move on. They spent 30 days in jail.

Liberty, Amite County, September 5

Travis Britt, SNCC registration worker, was attacked and beaten by whites on the courthouse lawn. Britt was accompanied at the time by Robert Moses. Britt said one man hit him more than 20 times. The attackers drove away in a truck.

Tylerton, Walthall County, September 7

John Hardy, SNCC registration worker, took two Negroes to the county courthouse to register. The registrar told them he "... wasn't registering voters" that day. When the three turned to leave, Registrar John Q. Wood took a pistol from his desk and struck Hardy over the head from behind. Hardy was arrested and charged with disturbing the peace.

Jackson, Hinds County, September 13

Fifteen Episcopal ministers (among them three Negroes) were arrested for asking to be served at the lunch counter of the Greyhound bus terminal. They were charged with inviting a breach of the peace. They were found not guilty of the charge on May 21, 1962, by County Judge Russell Moore.

Liberty, Amite County, September 25

Herbert Lee, a Negro who had been active in voter registration, was shot and killed by white state representative E. H. Hurst in downtown Liberty. No prosecution was undertaken, the authorities explaining that the repre-sentative had shot in self-defense.

McComb, Pike County, October 4

The five students who were arrested as a result of the August 29 sit-in in McComb returned to school, but were refused admittance. At that, 116 stu-dents walked out and paraded downtown to the city hall in protest. Police arrested the entire crowd, but later released all but 19, all of whom were 18 years old or older. They were charged with breach of the peace and con-tributing to the delinquency of minors and allowed to go free on bail total-ling $3,700. At the trial on October 31, Judge Brumfield, finding the students guilty, said "Some of you are local residents, some of you are outsiders. Those of you who are local residents are like sheep being led to the slaughter. If you continue to follow the advice of outside agitators, you will be like sheep and be slaughtered."

The death of John F. Kennedy: a memorial poem by Molly Kazan, 1963

Measured by accomplishment, John F. Kennedy was not a great President. In foreign affairs he blundered by permitting an American-supported Cuban force to invade Cuba in 1961. The landing was crushed by the Communist government of Fidel Castro. In domestic affairs he left America pretty much where he found it, with decaying cities, too many poor, a worsening race situation, and an economy producing much less than it might. But he brought to the Presidency a freshness and vigor, a passionate concern for the national welfare, a courage and humor America had not known since the time of Abraham Lincoln. Dedicated followers came to Washington to participate in Kennedy's New Frontier, to help fashion the reforms vital in an age of war and revolution. Whether he could have, in time, accomplished some of his goals, is hypothetical. Thirty-four months after his inauguration, in Dallas, Texas, he was assassinated.

Millions of people around the world grieved. The following poem by Molly Kazan caught the style and spirit of the President, and the sense of bereavement at his loss.

I think that what he gave us most was pride.
It felt good to have a President like that:
bright, brave and funny and goodlooking.

I saw him once drive down East Seventy-Second Street
in an open car, in the autumn sun
(as he drove yesterday in Dallas).
His thatch of brown hair looked as though it had grown extra
    thick
the way our wood animals in Connecticut
grow extra fur for winter.
And he looked as though it was fun to be alive,
to be a politician,
to be President,
to be a Kennedy,
to be a man.

He revived our pride.
It felt good to have a President
who read his mail,
who read the papers,
who read books and played touch football.
It was a pleasure and a cause of pride
to watch him take the quizzing of the press

From *Memorial and Addresses in the Congress of the United States and Tributes in Eulogy of John Fitzgerald Kennedy, Late a President of the United States* (Washington, D.C., 1964), pp. 658–59.

with cameras grinding—
take it in his stride,
with zest.
He'd parry, thrust, answer or duck,
and fire a verbal shot on target,
hitting with the same answer, the segregationists in a Louisiana
    hamlet and a government in South East Asia.
He made you feel that he knew what was going on
in both places.
He would come out of a quiz with an "A" in Economics, Military
    Science, Constitutional Law, Farm Problems and the
    moonshot program
and still take time to appreciate Miss May Craig.

We were privileged to see him on the worst day
(till yesterday),
The Bay of Pigs day,
and we marveled at his coolth and style
and were amazed at an air (that plainly was habitual)
of modesty
and even diffidence.
It felt good to have a President
who said, It was my fault.
And went on from there.

It felt good to have a President
who looked well in Vienna, Paris, Rome, Berlin
and at the podium of the United Nations
—and who would go to Dublin,
put a wreath where it did the most good
and leave unspoken
the satisfaction of an Irishman
en route to 10 Downing Street
as head of the U.S. government.

What was spoken
was spoken well.
What was unspoken
needed to be unspoken.
It was none of our business if his back hurt.

He revived our pride.
He gave grist to our pride.
He was respectful of intellect;
he was respectful of excellence;
he was respectful of accomplishment and skill;
he was respectful of the clear and subtle uses of our language;

he was respectful of courage.
And all these things he cultivated in himself.

He was respectful of our heritage.
He is now part of it.

He affirmed our future.
Our future is more hopeful
because of his work
but our future is not safe nor sure.
He kept telling us that.
This is a very dangerous and uncertain world.
I quote. He said that yesterday.

He respected facts.
And we must live with the fact of his murder.

Our children cried when the news came. They phoned and we
    phoned
and we cried and we were not ashamed of crying but we were
    ashamed of what had happened.
The youngest could not remember any other President, not
    clearly.
She felt as if the world had stopped.

We said, It is a shame, a very deep shame.
But this country will go on
more proudly
and with a clearer sense of who we are
and what we have it in us to become
because we had a President like that.
He revived our pride.
We are lucky that we had him for three years.

How the United States became involved in Vietnam: by Senator J. William Fulbright, 1966

As the war in Vietnam claimed more and more of the American budget, costing roughly $24 billion in 1966 alone, it became the center of a great controversy. The administration of Lyndon B. Johnson argued that Communist subversion must not be allowed to topple the South Vietnamese government lest all Southeast Asia fall—as a previous President, Dwight Eisenhower, had said—like dominoes. But as Johnson escalated the war—by committing more combat troops, and by ordering the bombing of North as well as South Vietnam—and as the costs *and the casualties mounted, criticism reached a level unknown in any other previous American military engagement in the twentieth century. Protests were heard in the Senate, the universities, the press, and the pulpit. Critics marched, staged "teach-ins," and organized peace tickets at every political level. One of the best summaries of how the United States became involved in Vietnam, by a critic of American policy, was written by Senator J. William Fulbright.*

How did it happen that America, the foremost advocate of colonial liberation after World War II, who set an example by liberating its own Philippine colony in 1946, allowed itself to be drawn into a colonial war and then a civil war in Indochina?

President Roosevelt's attitude toward Indochina during the war years was one of traditional American anti-colonialism. In a memorandum sent to Cordell Hull in January 1944, Roosevelt wrote: "France has had the country—thirty million inhabitants—for nearly one hundred years, and the people are worse off than they were at the beginning. . . . France has milked it for one hundred years. The people of Indochina are entitled to something better than that."

In the postwar years American enthusiasm for Vietnamese nationalism declined as rapidly as American concern with communism grew, which is to say very rapidly indeed. To an indeterminate but undoubtedly significant degree, the initial American involvement in Vietnam was influenced by two extraneous factors: Korea and [Senator] McCarthy. After North Korea invaded South Korea in a direct and unambiguous act of aggression, the United States, understandably but inaccurately, came to regard the French war in Indochina as analogous to the war in Korea, overlooking extremely important considerations of nationalism and anti-colonialism. This view of the Indochinese was reinforced by the McCarthy hysteria at home, which fostered undiscriminating attitudes of fear and hostility toward communism in all its forms. Not only were Americans disinclined in the late forties and early fifties to make distinctions among communist movements (with the notable exception of Yugoslavia), but at that time the communist world looked very much more like a monolith than it did a few years later. It was under these circumstances that the United States began indirect military assistance to the French in Indochina at the end of 1950. In September 1951 the United States signed an agreement for direct economic assistance to Vietnam and in October 1952 the two hundredth American ship carrying military aid arrived in Saigon.

The Eisenhower Administration went to the brink in 1954 but then decided against United States military intervention. The decision against intervention was taken largely on the advice of General Matthew Ridgway, then Army Chief of Staff. In his memoirs published in 1956 General Ridgway relates how he concluded, on the basis of a report by a team of Army experts, that it would be disastrous for the United States to intervene with ground forces in Indochina. General Ridgway wrote: "We could have fought in Indochina. We could have won, if we had been willing to pay the tremendous cost in men and money that such intervention would have required—a cost that in my opinion would have eventually been as great as, or greater than . . . we paid in Korea. In Korea, we had learned that air and naval power alone cannot win a war and that inadequate ground forces cannot win one either. It was incredible to me that we had forgotten that bitter lesson so soon—that we were on the verge of making the same tragic error. That error, thank God, was not repeated."

The Geneva Agreements were signed in July 1954. They explicitly prohibited the introduction into Vietnam of additional military forces and explicitly provided that general elections would be held in Vietnam by July 1956. They also explicitly stated that the demarcation line between North and South Vietnam at the 17th parallel was "provisional and should not in any way be interpreted as constituting a political or territorial boundary," a fact which is overlooked by those who maintain that North Vietnam is engaged in aggression against a *foreign* country rather than supporting a domestic insurrection. In its unilateral statement of July 21, 1954, the United States indicated, with respect to the Accords, that it would "refrain from the threat or use of force to disturb them," and further stated that the United States would "continue to seek to achieve unity through free elections, supervised by the U.N. to insure that they are conducted fairly."

It is not useful to try to assign degrees of guilt to each side for violations of the Geneva Accords. It suffices to note that there have been violations by all concerned, including the United States, which, in violation of its commitment of 1954, supported President Ngo Dinh Diem in his refusal to hold the elections provided for in the Geneva Accords, presumably because he feared that the communists would win. Whatever short-term advantages the many violations of the Geneva Agreements by both sides have brought their perpetrators, their cumulative effect has been the destruction of each side's trust in the word of each other, greatly complicating present prospects for a new agreement. Hanoi's stubborn and puzzling refusal to negotiate may therefore reflect neither a preference for war nor confidence in victory but simply an unwillingness to believe that a negotiated settlement would be honored.

Through a series of small steps, none extremely important or irrevocable in itself, the United States gradually took over the French commitment in South Vietnam after the French withdrawal. The United States Military Assistance Advisory Group took over the training of the South Vietnamese Army in 1955 and thereafter the United States became increasingly committed to the Diem regime by means of economic and military support and public statements. In 1960 President Eisenhower increased the number of American military advisers from 327 to 686. Further increase followed and by February 1962 the number of United States military personnel in South

Vietnam had reached four thousand. Step by step, as it became increasingly clear that the South Vietnamese Army was being defeated, the American commitment increased. The result has been that through a series of limited escalations, each one of which has been more or less compatible with the view that the war was not our war and would have to be won or lost by the South Vietnamese themselves, the war has indeed become our war. Gradually, almost imperceptibly, the commitment to support the South Vietnamese in a war which it was said *they* must either win or lose was supplanted by a commitment, as Secretary [of Defense] McNamara has put it, "to take all necessary measures within our capability to prevent a Communist victory."

The United States is now involved in a sizable and "open-ended" war against communism in the only country in the world which won freedom from colonial rule under communist leadership. In South Vietnam as in North Vietnam, the communists remain today the only solidly organized political force. That fact is both the measure of our failure and the key to its possible redemption.

So-called "wars of national liberation" are political wars, whose outcome depends on a combination of political and military factors. The communist guerrillas in Malaya could not have been beaten without hard fighting, but neither, in all probability, could they have been beaten had Malaya not been given its independence. The Hukbalahaps were defeated in the Philippines primarily because of the political isolation imposed on them by the reforms of President Ramon Magsaysay. The major reason for the success of the Viet Cong in South Vietnam has not been aid from the North but the absence of a cohesive alternative nationalist movement in the South. Both the success of the communists in South Vietnam and their failure in India, Burma, Malaya, Indonesia, and the Philippines strongly suggest that "wars of national liberation" depend for their success more on the weakness of the regime under attack than on the strength of support from outside.

Our search for a solution to the Vietnamese war must begin with the general fact that nationalism is the strongest single political force in the world today and the specific fact, arising from the history to which I have referred, that in Vietnam the most effective nationalist movement is communist-controlled. We are compelled, therefore, once again to choose between opposition to communism and support of nationalism. I strongly recommend that for once we give priority to the latter. The dilemma is a cruel one, and one which we must hope to avoid in the future by timely and unstinting support of non-communist nationalist movements, but it is too late for that in Vietnam. I strongly recommend, therefore, that we seek to come to terms with both Hanoi and the Viet Cong, not, to be sure, by "turning tail and running," as the saying goes, but by conceding the Viet Cong a part in the government of South Vietnam.

Lyndon Johnson announces that he will not be a candidate, 1968

Lyndon B. Johnson, suddenly thrust into the presidental office in November, 1963, was a typical product of the American political tradition: a master politician, he believed in consensus government and progress through compromise. "Sometimes I have been called a seeker of consensus," Johnson admitted, "more often in criticism than in praise. And I have never denied it. Because to heal and to build in support of something worthy is, I believe, a noble task." Congress had stymied Kennedy's program. But the assassination seemed to create a national mood favorable to decisive action, and Johnson moved with rare political skill to exploit this mood and to guide into law a broad range of federal programs which embodied all that Kennedy had asked for and more. It was a rare achievement. But one issue—Vietnam—could not be settled by compromise.

As Johnson continued to prosecute the war, and continued to promise victory in Southeast Asia, the public lost confidence in the administration. His popularity ratings began to dip. Senator Eugene McCarthy, an early opponent of the war, defeated Johnson in the New Hampshire primaries; Robert Kennedy of New York also entered the race as an outspoken critic of the President's foreign policies. Facing a divided nation, President Johnson on March 31, 1968, announced a bombing halt north of the 38th parallel, and then stunned the country by adding that he would not be a candidate for another term of office.

Television broadcast   **March 31, 1968**

Fifty-two months and ten days ago, in a moment of tragedy and trauma, the duties of this office fell upon me. I asked then for your help and God's, that we might continue America on its course, binding up our wounds, healing our history, moving forward in new unity, to clear the American agenda and to keep the American commitment for all of our people.

United we have kept that commitment. United we have enlarged that commitment. Through all time to come, I think America will be a stronger nation, a more just society, and a land of greater opportunity and fulfillment because of what we have all done together in these years of unparalleled achievement. Our reward will come in the life of freedom, peace, and hope that our children will enjoy through ages ahead.

What we won when all of our people united must not now be lost in suspicion, distrust, selfishness, and politics among any of our people.

Believing this as I do, I have concluded that I should not permit the Presidency to become involved in the partisan divisions that are developing in this political year.

With America's sons in the fields far away, with America's future under challenge right here at home, with our hopes and the world's hopes for peace in the balance every day, I do not believe that I should devote

Included in James M. Burns (ed.), *To Heal and to Build: The Programs of President Lyndon B. Johnson* (New York, 1968), pp. 464–66.

an hour or a day of my time to any personal partisan causes or to any duties other than the awesome duties of this office—the Presidency of your country.

Accordingly, I shall not seek, and I will not accept, the nomination of my party for another term as your President.

But let men everywhere know, however, that a strong, a confident, and a vigilant America stands ready tonight to seek an honorable peace—and stands ready tonight to defend an honored cause—whatever the price, whatever the burden, whatever the sacrifice that duty may require.

Speech to the National Association of Broadcasters   April 1, 1968

As I said last evening there are very deep and very emotional divisions in this land that we love today, domestic divisions, divisions over the war in Vietnam. With all of my heart I just wish this weren't so. My entire career in public life—some 37 years of it—has been devoted to the art of finding an area of agreement because generally speaking I have observed that there are so many more things to unite us Americans than there are to divide us.

But somehow or other we have a faculty sometimes of emphasizing the divisions and the things that divide us instead of discussing the things that unite us.

Sometimes I have been called a seeker of "consensus"—more often in criticism than in praise. And I have never denied it. Because to heal and to build in support of something worthy is, I believe, a noble task. In the region of the country where I have spent my life, where brother was once divided against brother, this lesson has been burned deep into my memory. Yet along the way I learned somewhere that no leader can pursue public tranquility as his first and only goal.

Because for a President to buy public popularity at the sacrifice of his better judgment is too dear a price to pay.

This nation cannot afford such a price and this nation cannot long afford such a leader. So the things that divide our country this morning will be discussed throughout the land and I'm certain that the very great majority of informed Americans will act as they have always acted to do what is best for their country and what serves the national interest. . . .

Huey Newton, a black militant, speaks from prison, 1968

The civil rights movement, at the time of Martin Luther King, Jr., had been optimistic, reasonably patient, and dedicated to the integration of blacks into the white world. But deep frustrations were tearing apart the old civil rights movement in the mid-1960's, and a new black-national movement came to the fore. Urban blacks in significant numbers joined the Nation of Islam, rejecting white culture, and taking on with their Moslem names a new demeanor of pride

From Huey Newton, "Huey Newton Speaks from Jail," *motive*, Vol. XXIX, October 1968. Reprinted by permission of *motive*, P.O. Box 871, Nashville, Tennessee, 37202.

and militancy. Malcolm X spoke of the need for racial pride and solidarity, criticized integration, and seemed strongly antiwhite. When Stokely Carmichael became chairman of SNCC, he began to reject the assistance of the whites who had helped register black voters in Mississippi. Carmichael espoused "black power," defining it as follows: "This country does not function by morality, love, and non-violence, but by power. Thus we [blacks] are determined to win political power, with the idea of moving on from there into activity that would have economic effect."

Younger blacks in particular adopted the styles of black nationalism: African dress, fierce racial pride, a suspicion that all whites were either conscious or unconscious racists, and demands for better but separate schools and living conditions. They turned to more radical leaders, such as Eldridge Cleaver, the articulate West Coast black whose book Soul on Ice *expressed the prevailing mood of bitter militancy. Another leader, the Black Panther spokesman Huey Newton concluded that the American system, as constituted, was incapable of solving the problems blacks faced in this country. In 1968 he answered the following questions while in prison.*

QUESTION: Other black groups seem to feel that from past experience it is impossible for them to work with whites and impossible for them to form alliances. What do you see as the reasons for this and do you think that the history of the Black Panther makes this less of a problem?

HUEY: There was a somewhat unhealthy relationship in the past with the white liberals supporting the black people who were trying to gain their freedom. I think that a good example of this would be the relationship that SNCC had with its white liberals. I call them white liberals because they differ strictly from the white radicals. The relationship was that the whites controlled SNCC for a very long time. From the very start of SNCC until recently, whites were the mind of SNCC. They controlled the program of SNCC with money and they controlled the ideology, or the stand SNCC would take. The blacks in SNCC were completely controlled program-wise; they couldn't do any more than the white liberals wanted them to do, which wasn't very much. So the white liberals were not working for self-determination for the black community. They were interested in a few concessions from the power structure. They undermined SNCC's program.

Stokely Carmichael came along, and realizing this, started Malcolm X's program of Black Power. Whites were afraid when Stokely said that black people have a mind of their own and that SNCC would seek self-determination for the black community. The white liberals withdrew their support, leaving the organization financially bankrupt. The blacks who were in the organization, Stokely and H. Rap Brown, were left angry and bewildered with the white liberals who had been aiding them under the guise of being sincere.

As a result, the leadership of SNCC turned away from the white liberal, which was good. I don't think they distinguished between the white liberal and the white revolutionary; because the revolutionary is white also, and they are very much afraid to have any contact with white people—even to the point of denying that the white revolutionaries could help. . . . The Black Panther Party has NEVER been controlled by white people. We have always had an integration of mind and body. We have never been controlled by whites and therefore we can't fear the white mother country radicals. Our alliance is one of organized black groups with organized white groups. As soon as the organized white groups do not do the things that would benefit us in our struggle for liberation, that will be the point of our departure. So we don't suffer in the hang-up of a skin color. We don't hate white people; we hate the oppressor.

QUESTION: You indicate that there is a psychological process that has historically existed in white-black relations in the U. S. that must change in the course of revolutionary struggle. Would you like to comment on this?

HUEY: Yes. The historical relationship between black and white here in America has been the relationship between the slave and the master; the master being the mind and the slave the body. The slave would carry out the orders that the mind demanded him to carry out. By doing this, the master took the manhood from the slave because he stripped him of a mind. In the process, the slave-master stripped himself of a body. As Eldridge Cleaver puts it, the slave-master became the omnipotent administrator and the slave became the super-masculine menial. This puts the omnipotent administrator into the controlling position or the front office and the super-masculine menial into the field.

The whole relationship developed so that the omnipotent administrator and the super-masculine menial became opposites. The slave being a very strong body doing all the practical things, all of the work becomes very masculine. The omnipotent administrator in the process of removing himself from all body functions realized later that he has emasculated himself. And this is very disturbing to him. So the slave lost his mind and the slave-master his body.

This caused the slave-master to become very envious of the slave because he pictured the slave as being more of a man, being superior sexually, because the penis is part of the body. The omnipotent administrator laid down a decree when he realized that in his plan to enslave the black man, he had emasculated himself. He attempted to bind the penis of the slave. He attempted to show that his penis could reach further than the super-masculine menial's penis. He said, "I, the omnipotent administrator, can have access to the black woman." The super-masculine menial then had a psychological attraction to the white female (the ultra-feminine freak) for the simple reason that it was forbidden fruit. The omnipotent administrator decreed that this kind of contact would be punished by death. At the same time, in order to reinforce his sexual desire, to confirm, to assert his manhood, he would go into the slave quarters and have sexual relations with the black women (the self-reliant Amazon), not to be satisfied but simply to confirm his manhood. If he could only satisfy the self-reliant Amazon then he would be sure that he was a man. Because he didn't have a body, he didn't have a penis, but psychologically wanted to castrate the black man. The slave was constantly seeking unity within himself: a mind and a body. He always wanted to be able to decide, to gain respect from his women, because women want one who can control.

I give this outline to fit into a framework of what is happening now. The white power structure today in America defines itself as the mind. They want to control the world. They go off and plunder the world. They are the policemen of the world exercising control especially over people of color.

The white man cannot gain his manhood, cannot unite with the body, because the body is black. The body is symbolic of slavery and strength. It's a biological thing as he views it. The slave is in a much better situation because his not being a full man has always been viewed psychologically. And it's always easier to make a psychological transition than a biological one. If he can only recapture his mind, then he will lose all fear and will be free to determine his own destiny. This is what is happening today with the rebellion of the world's oppressed people against the controller. They are regaining their mind and they're saying that we have a mind of our own. They're saying that we want freedom to determine the destiny of our people, thereby uniting the mind with their bodies. They are taking the mind back from the omnipotent administrator, the controller, the exploiter. . . .

Statements for and against a guaranteed annual income, 1968

Pollution and poverty became the two most important domestic issues in the 1960's. Both had existed for some time, but their "discovery" shocked Americans. Mass poverty persisted despite the relative affluence of the American economy, and despite substantial welfare and relief expenditures on the state and federal levels. Studies of the "subculture of the poor" showed that poverty tended to cost society enormous sums, not only in welfare payments, but in idleness and undeveloped talents, and in enlarged police services. By the early 1970's shock had given way to despair, and a sense of anger, as the tax burden of Middle America continued to mount, and the poverty cycle remained unbroken. One solution, suggested by both liberal and conservative economists, was for a guaranteed minimum annual income, which would replace a variety of other welfare programs. But critics opposed the measure as one which would destroy individual initiative, an argument Herbert Hoover had used in attacking the New Deal policies of the 1930's.

From the testimony before the Joint Economic Committee, subcommittee on fiscal policy, *Hearings on Income Maintenance Programs,* Ninetieth Congress, Second Session (Washington, D.C., 1968), pp. 302–05.

PRO: STATEMENT BY JOHN K. GALBRAITH,
PAUL A. SAMUELSON, AND OTHERS,
ENDORSED BY OVER 200 ECONOMISTS

The Poor People's Campaign in Washington is demanding a guaranteed minimum income for all Americans. The Kerner Commission . . . called for a national system of income supplements. A group of business leaders recently advocated a "negative income tax." These proposals are all similar in design and purpose.

Like all civilized nations in the twentieth century, this country has long recognized a public responsibility for the living standards of its citizens. Yet our present programs of public assistance and social insurance exclude millions who are in need, and meet inadequately the needs of millions more. All too often these programs unnecessarily penalize work and thrift and discourage the building of stable families.

The country will not have met its responsibility until everyone in the nation is assured an income no less than the officially recognized definition of poverty. A workable and equitable plan of income guarantees and supplements must have the following features: (1) Need, as objectively measured by income and family size, should be the sole basis of determining payment to which an individual and/or family is entitled. (2) To provide incentive to work, save and train for better jobs, payments to families who earn income should be reduced by only a fraction of their earnings.

Practical and detailed proposals meeting these requirements have been suggested by individual sponsors of this statement and by others. The costs of such plans are substantial but well within the nation's economic and fiscal capacity.

CON: STATEMENT OF HENRY HAZLITT BEFORE THE
CONGRESSIONAL COMMITTEE

The first thing to be said about this scheme economically is that if it were put into effect it would not only be enormously expensive to the taxpayers who are forced to support it, but that it would destroy the incentive to work and production on an unparalleled scale. As one commentator has put it: "Those who believe that men will want to work whether they have to or not seem to have lived sheltered lives. . . ."

Both the straight guaranteed income and its tapered-off form known as the negative income tax are attempts to escape the allegedly humiliating and administratively troublesome means test. But if the Government wishes to protect itself from massive chiseling and swindling, under any giveaway program, it cannot avoid a conscientious investigation case by case, and applicant by applicant. The guaranteed income and negative income tax proposals do not solve the administrative problem; they simply shut their eyes to it.

The guaranteed income and negative income tax are proposed by some of their sponsors as a complete substitute for all existing forms of relief and welfare. But does anyone seriously believe the present beneficiaries of social security benefits, or unemployment benefits, or medicare, or veterans' benefits, or training programs, or educational grants, or farm subsidies, are going to give up what they have already gained? The new handouts would simply be piled on top of everything else.

The welfare bill is already staggering. Federal aid to the poor, under that official label, has risen from $9.5 billion in 1960 to $27.7 billion in the fiscal year 1969. But if we add up all the welfare payments in the 1969 budget—farm subsidies, housing and community development, health, labor, and welfare, education, and veterans benefits, we get an annual total in excess of $68 billion. Even this is not all. We must add a social welfare burden on the States and localities of more than $41 billion, making a grand total of $110 billion. This load has already brought not only very burdensome taxation, but chronic deficits and inflation that are undermining the value and integrity of the dollar and bringing social insecurity for all of us.

I have talked here only of what should not be done, and have left myself no time to discuss what should be done. But if I may take the liberty of stating, as I see it, the problem that faces your distinguished committee— I should put it this way: how can the Government mitigate the penalties of failure and misfortune without undermining the incentives to effort and success? I do not wish to underrate the importance of the first half of this problem, but it seems to me that the second half deserves much more earnest attention than it has recently received.

Senator Barry Goldwater defends the military-industrial complex, April 1969

In his farewell address of January 17, 1961, President Eisenhower attempted to alert the public to the existence of a military-industrial complex in America whose "total influence—economic, political, even spiritual—is felt in every city, every state house, every office of the Federal Government." Eisenhower was warning the nation that this unprecedented concentrated power constituted a prime danger to "our liberties or democratic processes." It was an impressive and surprising farewell message from a President noted for his bland mediocrity.

His advice went unheeded, and in the following years the military-industrial complex continued its rapid growth. By the close of the 1960's many voices of warning were heard: protests against the interlocking directorate of generals and capitalists, the unconscionable profits each derived from their association, the threat to Constitutional freedoms which it posed. But others defended the complex as a bulwark of freedom for all Americans, an inevitable necessity for a nation in a life and death struggle with international communism. Such was

From the *Congressional Record,* Ninety-first Congress, First Session, pp. 3719–21.

the logic of Senator Barry Goldwater in the following speech delivered on April 15, 1969.

I believe it is long past the time when questions relating fundamentally to the defense of this nation should be placed in their proper perspective. Let us take the military-industrial complex and examine it closely. What it amounts to is that we have a big Military Establishment, and we have a big industrial plant which helps to supply that establishment. This apparently constitutes a complex. If so, I certainly can find nothing to criticize but much to be thankful for in its existence.

Ask yourselves, for example, why we have a large, expensive Military Establishment and why we have a large and capable defense industry. The answer is simply this: We have huge worldwide responsibilities. We face tremendous challenges. In short, we urgently require both a big defense establishment and a big industrial capacity. Both are essential to our safety and to the preservation of freedom in a world fraught with totalitarian aggression. Merely because our huge responsibilities necessitate the existence of a military-industrial complex does not automatically make that complex something we must fear or feel ashamed of. You might consider where we would be in any negotiations which might be entered into with the Soviet Union if we did not have a big military backed by a big industrial complex to support our arguments. . . .

What would the critics of the military-industrial complex have us do? Would they have us ignore the fact that progress occurs in the field of national defense as well as in the field of social sciences? Do they want us to turn back the clock, disband our Military Establishment, and do away with our defense-related industrial capacity? Mr. President, do these critics of what they term a military-industrial complex really want to default on our worldwide responsibilities, turn our back on aggression and slavery, and develop a national policy of selfish isolation?

Rather than deploring the existence of a military-industrial complex, I say we should thank heaven for it. That complex gives us our protective shield. It is the bubble under which our nation thrives and prospers. It is the armor which is unfortunately required in a world divided. For all those who complain about the military-industrial complex, I ask this question: "What would you replace it with? Would you have the Government do it?" Well, our Government has tried it in the past, and failed—dismally so.

What is more, I believe it is fair to inquire whether the name presently applied is inclusive enough. Consider the large number of scientists who contributed all of the fundamental research necessary to develop and build nuclear weapons and other products of today's defense industries. Viewing this, should not we call it the "scientific-military-industrial complex?" By the same token, do not forget the amount of research that has gone on in our colleges and universities in support of our defense-related projects.

Maybe we should call it an "educational-scientific-military-industrial com-plex." Then, of course, the vast financing that goes into this effort certainly makes the economic community an integral part of any such complex. Now we have a name that runs like this: "An economic-educational-scientific-military-industrial complex. . . ."

Many of the problems that are being encountered in the area of national defense today stem not so much from a military-industrial complex as they do from the mistakes and miscalculations of a "civilian complex" or perhaps I should say a "civilian-computer-complex." My reference here, of course, is to the Pentagon hierarchy of young civilians—often referred to as the "whiz kids"—which was erected during the McNamara era in the questionable name of "cost effectiveness." And this complex, Mr. President, was built in some measure to shut out the military voice in a large area of defense policy decision making.

I suggest that the military-industrial complex is not the all-powerful structure that our liberal friends would have us believe. Certainly nobody can deny that this combination took a drubbing at the hands of Mr. McNamara and his civilian cadres during the last 8 years. . . . If the military-industrial complex had been the irresistible giant its critics describe, we would certainly today be better equipped. We would undoubtedly have a nuclear-powered Navy adequate to the challenge presented by the Soviet naval might. We would certainly have in the air—and not just on a drawing board—a manned, carry-on bomber. We would never have encountered the kind of shortages which cropped up in every area of the military as a result of the demands from Vietnam. There would have been no shortage of mili-tary helicopters. There would have been no shortage of trained helicopter pilots. There would have been no need to use outdated and faulty equip-ment. No concern ever would have arisen over whether our supply of bombs was sufficient to the task in Southeast Asia.

In conclusion, Mr. President, I want to point out that a very strong case can be made for the need for a more powerful military-industrial com-plex than we have had during the past eight years. At the very least, I wish to say that the employment practices of industries doing business with the Pentagon—practices which lead them to hire the most knowledgeable men to do their work—are no cause for shock. Nor are these practices dangerous to the American people.

I have great faith in the civilian leaders of our Government and of our military services. I have no desire to see the voice of the military become all-powerful or even dominant in our national affairs. But I do believe that the military viewpoint must always be heard in the highest councils of our Government in all matters directly affecting the protection and security of our nation.

Bruno Bettelheim on the psychological causes of student discontent, 1969

Not Vietnam, or the hydrogen bomb, or any other specific political or economic grievance was at the root of campus unrest in America, Bruno Bettelheim reasoned before a congressional investigating committee. The cause was much deeper. America had changed drastically in the past fifty years—today's youth, even young married couples, take their parental support for granted well into post-adolescence. Bettelheim sees this long period of dependence as unnatural, unfulfilling, even emasculating. His argument is both cogent and stimulating, but nevertheless debatable. For he believes that student rebellion occurs "where affluence exists, only in the modern, industrial state," while the evidence is that the disruptions have been worldwide.

It is my conviction that Vietnam and the bomb serve youth as a screen for what really ails them: their feeling that youth has no future because modern technology has made them obsolete—socially irrelevant, and, as persons, insignificant. Youth feels its future is bleak not with the prospect of nuclear war ... but because of their feeling that nobody needs them, that society can do nicely without them. This is the even bleaker anxiety behind their feeling that youth has no future. Because, if a young man does not feel it is he who will be building the future, is sorely needed to bring it about, then the feeling is that he has none. That is why, in hopes of denying such an anxious conviction, students insist that their mission is to build a wholly new and different future. Their anxiety is not—as they claim— about a future atomic war. It is not that society has no future. Their existential anxiety is that they have no future in a society that does not need them to go on existing. . . .

It is education that prepares us for our place in the work of society, and if education today prepares us only to be replaceable items in the production machine, to program its computers, then it seems to prepare us not for a chance to emerge in importance as persons, but only to serve the machine better.

Behind all this lie more fundamental reasons why adolescent malaise grows so widespread. These begin to emerge when we look in quite another direction—when we recognize that adolescent revolt is not a stage of development that follows automatically from our natural makeup, because what makes for adolescent revolt is the fact that society keeps the next generation too long dependent in terms of mature responsibility and a striving for independence. This I believe, is the common denominator wherever student rebellion occurs. And the fact that it occurs where affluence exists, only in

From the testimony before the Senate Committee on Government Operations, subcommittee on investigations, Ninety-first Congress, First Session, *Hearings on Riots, Civil and Criminal Disorders* (Washington, D.C., 1969), pp. 3069–79.

the modern, industrial state, is merely the same common denominator as seen from the outside.

Years ago, when schooling ended for the vast majority at 14 or 15, and therefore one became self-supporting, got married and had children, there was no need for adolescent revolt. Because while puberty is a biological fact, adolescence as we know it with its identity crises is not. All children grow up and become pubertal. By no means do they all become adolescents. To be adolescent means that one has reached and even passed the age of puberty, is at the very height of one's physical development—healthier, stronger, even handsomer than one has been, or will be, for the rest of one's life—but must nevertheless postpone full adulthood till long beyond what any other period in history has considered reasonable.

With no more open frontiers left, our society has no special place for adolescents today, with the single exception of our colleges and universities. Moreover, we push our young people toward maturity nowadays even while overextending the years of their dependence. We start them sooner and sooner in school and make a farce of graduations—even from kindergarten now—until school becomes a rat race with never a home stretch in sight. And, so, by the time they get to college, they have had it. I doubt whether life was ever less of a rat race than today. But it only became a senseless rat race when more and more people got to feeling they were racing after goals that were not really worthwhile or urgent, because survival seems assured by the affluent state.

At the same time, the educational experience today, whether in the home or the school, prepares only a small minority of youth well for such a prolonged waiting, for controlling their angry impatience. Here we should not overlook the symbolic meaning of the student's invading the office of the president or dean, violently, or through sit-ins. Big in size and age, those who sit-in feel like little boys with a need to play big by sitting in papa's big chair. They want to sit in the driver's seat, want to have a say in how things are run, not because they feel competent to do so, but because they cannot bear to feel incompetent a moment longer.

I think it is unnatural to keep a young person in dependence for some twenty years attending school. This may be a way of life for that small elite which would always have chosen it in the past. There were always those who could go to school for twenty years, but they were never more than a small percentage of the population—even of the university population which included those attending as a matter of caste. Now the tremendous push on everyone to go to college has brought incredibly large numbers to the university who do not find their self-realization through study or the intellectual adventure—or not at that point in their lives. What they still want urgently, however, is to find their manhood.

To make matters worse, our institutions of higher learning have expanded too fast. Under public pressure for more education for all, they have steadily increased enrollment without the means to make parallel adjustments in the learning situation. One result is far too large classes. Another is the anonymity, the impersonal nature of student-faculty contacts that students rightly complain of.

But essentially it is the waiting for things—for the real life to come—that creates a climate in which a sizable segment of the students are chronically seduced into following the lead of a small group of militants. In the words of Jerry Rubin, yippie organizer, "Who the hell wants to 'make it' in America any more? The American economy no longer needs young whites and blacks. We are waste material. We fulfill our destiny in life by rejecting a system which rejects us."

Campus rebellion seems to offer youth a chance to shortcut the empty waiting and prove themselves real adults. This can be seen from the fact that most rebellious students, here and abroad, are either undergraduates or those studying the social sciences and humanities. There are precious few militants among students of medicine, chemistry, engineering, the natural sciences. Student power has no meaning in the laboratory; there no one doubts the need for leadership by the most experienced of the less experienced. Moreover, while the social science student can easily convince himself that he knows precisely what is wrong with society, particularly if his friends all agree, it is impossible for the medical student to fool himself that he knows what went wrong in the cancerous cell. Nor can such a student believe that what he is doing, or the discipline it demands, is irrelevant.

Those who cannot find themselves in their studies or their work are hence the most vocal in finding the university irrelevant. Typically, the militant finds his largest following among the newcomers, those with least time or chance as yet to find a place for themselves at the university. This place some try to find quickly by plunging into active, even violent, battle against the existing order. Except that if they should win they would be changing the university into an institution that no longer serves inquiry and study, but a belligerent reshaping of society.

I maintain that, despite the high-sounding moral charges against the sins of our society, those sins—in the hearts and minds of youth—are not the destruction of youth in Vietnam but of neglecting youth on the home front, of finding them "waste material" so that they must "reject a system that rejects us." This is the socio-psychological situation which permits the extremist leaders to find a mass following without which their efforts at disruption would soon collapse or could readily be contained.

Violence in America: Report of the National Commission on the Causes and Prevention of Violence, 1969

The assassinations, the bombings, the riots, all appeared somewhat confusing and paradoxical to many Americans who witnessed the successful growth of their country from the depression days of the 1930's to the prosperous conditions of the 1960's and 70's. But certain types of violence are an old part of American history. In the following essay the authors place this violence in historical perspective. In the past, they note, "The dominant groups in American society . . . moved over enough to give the immigrant, the worker, the suffragette, better—not the best—seats at the American feast of freedom and plenty. Many . . . think the feast is bounteous enough for the dissatisfied students, the poor, the Indians, the blacks." But is it? Or is it too late? Some who have turned to violence, completely alienated, believe the feast is rotten, and they will not come to the table.

Only a decade ago America's historians were celebrating the emergence of a unique society, sustained by a burgeoning prosperity and solidly grounded on a broad political consensus. We were told—and the implications were reassuring—that our uniqueness was derived from at least half a dozen historical sources which, mutually reinforcing one another, had joined to propel us toward a manifestly benevolent destiny. We were a nation of immigrants, culturally enriched by the variety of mankind. Sons of the frontier, our national character has grown to reflect the democratic individualism and pragmatic ingenuity that had conquered the wilderness. Our new nation was born in anticolonial revolution and in its crucible was forged a democratic republic of unparalleled vitality and longevity. Lacking a feudal past, our political spectrum was so truncated about the consensual liberal center that, unlike Europe, divisive radicalism of the left or right had found no sizable constituency. Finally, we had both created and survived the great transformations from agrarian frontier to industrial metropolis, to become the richest nation of all time.

It was a justly proud legacy, one which seemed to make sense in the relatively tranquil 1950's. But with the 1960's came shock and frustration. It was a decade against itself: the students of affluence were marching in the streets; middle-class matrons were besieging the Pentagon; and Negro Americans were responding to victories in civil rights and to their collectively unprecedented prosperity with a paradoxical venting of outrage. In a fundamental sense, history—the ancient human encounter with poverty, defeat, and guilt as well as with affluence, victory, and innocence—had

From Hugh D. Graham and Ted R. Gurr, *Violence in America: Historical and Comparative Perspectives. A Report of the National Commission on the Causes and Prevention of Violence* (Washington, D.C., 1969), Vol. II, pp. 624–27.

finally caught up with America. Or at least it had caught up with white America.

Historical analysis of our national experience and character would suggest that the seeds of our contemporary discontent were to a large extent deeply embedded in those same ostensibly benevolent forces which contributed to our uniqueness. *First*, we are a nation of immigrants, but one in which the original dominant immigrant group, the so-called Anglo-Saxons, effectively preempted the crucial levers of economic and political power in government, commerce, and the professions. This elite group has tenaciously resisted the upward strivings of successive "ethnic" immigrant waves. The resultant competitive hierarchy of immigrants has always been highly conducive to violence, but this violence has taken different forms. The Anglo-Americans have used their access to the levers of power to maintain their dominance, using legal force surrounded by an aura of legitimacy for such ends as economic exploitation; the restriction of immigration by a national-origin quota system which clearly branded later immigrants as culturally undesirable; the confinement of the original Indian immigrants largely to barren reservations; and the restriction of blacks to a degraded caste. But the system was also conducive to violence among the latter groups themselves—when, for instance, Irish-Americans rioted against Afro-American "scabs." Given America's unprecedented ethnic pluralism, simply being born American conferred no automatic and equal citizenship in the eyes of the larger society. In the face of such reservations, ethnic minorities had constantly to affirm their Americanism through a kind of patriotic ritual which intensified the ethnic competition for status. As a fragment culture based on bourgeois-liberal values, . . . yet one populated by an unprecedented variety of immigrant stock, America's tightened consensus on what properly constituted "Americanism" prompted status rivalries among the ethnic minorities which, when combined with economic rivalries, invited severe and abiding conflict. . . .

The *second* major formative historical experience was America's uniquely prolonged encounter with the frontier. While the frontier experience indubitably strengthened the mettle of the American character, it witnessed the brutal and brutalizing ousting of the Indians and the forceful incorporation of Mexican and other original inhabitants . . . Further, it concomitantly created an environment in which, owing to the paucity of law enforcement agencies, a tradition of vigilante "justice" was legitimized. The longevity of the Ku Klux Klan and the vitality both of contemporary urban rioting and of the stiffening resistance to it owe much to this tradition. . . . Vigilantism has persisted as a socially malleable instrument long after the disappearance of the frontier environment that gave it birth, and it has proved quite congenial to an urban setting.

Similarly, the revolutionary doctrine that our Declaration of Independence proudly proclaims stands as a tempting model of legitimate violence to be emulated by contemporary groups, such as militant Negroes and

radical students who confront a system of both public and private government that they regard as contemptuous of their consent. Entranced by the
resurgence of revolution in the underdeveloped world and of international
university unrest, radical students and blacks naturally seize upon our historically sacrosanct doctrine of the inherent right of revolution and self-
determination to justify their rebellion. That their analogies are fatefully
problematical in no way dilutes the majesty of our own proud Declaration.

The *fourth* historic legacy, our consensual political philosophy of
Lockean-Jeffersonian liberalism, was premised upon a pervasive fear of governmental power and has reinforced the tendency to define freedom nega-
tively as freedom *from*. As a consequence, conservatives have been able
paradoxically to invoke the doctrines of Jefferson in resistance to legislative
reforms, and the Sumnerian imperative that "stateways cannot change folk-
ways" has historically enjoyed a wide and not altogether unjustified allegiance in the public eye (witness the debacle of the first Reconstruction,
and the dilemma of our contemporary second attempt). Its implicit corol-
lary has been that forceful and, if necessary, violent local and state
resistance to unpopular federal stateways is a legitimate response; both Calhoun and Wallace could confidently repair to a strict construction of the
same document invoked by Lincoln and the Warren court.

A *fifth* historic source both of our modern society and our current
plight is our industrial revolution and the great internal migration from the
countryside to the city. Yet the process occurred with such astonishing
rapidity that it produced widespread socio-economic dislocation in an
environment in which the internal controls of the American social structure
were loose and the external controls were weak. . . .

The *final* distinctive characteristic—in many ways perhaps our most
distinctive—has been our unmatched prosperity; we have been, in the
words of David Potter, most characteristically a "people of plenty." Ranked
celestially with life and liberty in the sacrosanct Lockean trilogy, property
has generated a quest and prompted a devotion in the American character
that has matched our devotion to equality and, in a fundamental sense, has
transformed it from the radical leveling of the European democratic tradition into a typically American insistence upon equality of opportunity. In an
acquisitive society of individuals with unequal talents and groups with
unequal advantages, this had resulted in an unequal distribution of the
rapid accumulation of abundance that, especially since World War II, has
promised widespread participation in the affluent society to a degree unprecedented in history.

Violence in Vietnam: testimony at the trial of Lieutenant William Calley for the My Lai massacre, 1971

There are enough historical examples of brutality by the American army in wartime—against civilians and prisoners—to fill several volumes. But those examples have been taken as exceptions. The tradition has been that the American army was different from others—we believed in fair play in war, as in games; we maintained no double standard of morality for war and for peace; we were a civilian army fighting not for plunder or domination, but always for democracy. Thus, the 1968 My Lai massacre seared the conscience of the nation. Lieutenant William Calley was charged with murdering at least one hundred "oriental human beings,"—men, women, and children who had been rounded up by his platoon and herded into two groups to two main execution sites. On March 29, 1971, a court-martial jury found him guilty of premeditated murder. Calley, reduced to tears, stated: "I had to value the lives of my troops, and I feel that's the only crime I ever committed." An enormous number of Americans agreed with him, and President Nixon ordered the Lieutenant confined to quarters—rather than in prison—while his case was reviewed.

TESTIMONY OF PAUL MEADLO

QUESTION: Did you get instruction about following orders?

ANSWER: Yes. We were taught that in a combat situation, if you disobey an order you're liable to get shot right on the spot, or else go before a court-martial. In basic training, if they thought you were slow in carrying out an order, they'd come up and hit you on the head. If you weren't quick enough with your mask, they'd slap it against your face, and a bunch of other rinky-dink. You are supposed to obey orders. If you're told to go out in the middle of the highway and stand on your head, you're supposed to do it.

QUESTION: Lieutenant Calley ordered you to fire into groups of villagers?

ANSWER: Yes.

QUESTION: Why did you comply?

ANSWER: I got emotionally upset, but I continued to carry out my orders. In the briefing the day before we went into My Lai we were told everybody in the village would be Viet Cong or VC sympathizers. I still believe they were all VC or VC sympathizers.

QUESTION: You killed men, women and children?

ANSWER: Yes.

QUESTION: You were ordered to do so?

ANSWER: Yes. . . .

Reconstructed from accounts in the *New York Times,* the *Saint Louis Post-Dispatch,* the *Los Angeles Times,* the *Santa Barbara News-Press,* the *New Orleans Times-Picayune,* and other newspapers, January 12–14, 1971.

QUESTION: What were the babies doing?

ANSWER: They were in their mothers' arms.

QUESTION: Were you afraid the babies might attack you?

ANSWER: Yes. Any baby might have been loaded with grenades that the mother could have throwed.

QUESTION: Were they making any move to attack?

ANSWER: Not at that time, no ...

QUESTION: What were the mothers doing?

ANSWER: Squatting down.

QUESTION: Did Lieutenant Calley say anything?

ANSWER: He said, 'We've got another job to do Meadlo.' Lieutenant Calley started shoving them and shooting into the ravine. He ordered me to help kill the Viet Cong.

QUESTION: What did you do?

ANSWER: I started shoving them and shooting.

QUESTION: How long did you fire?

ANSWER: I don't know.

QUESTION: Did you change magazines?

ANSWER: Yes.

QUESTION: Did Lieutenant Calley change magazines?

ANSWER: Yes.

QUESTION: Do you recall how many times Lieutenant Calley changed magazines?

ANSWER: Ten to fifteen times.

QUESTION: Were all the people killed?

ANSWER: I couldn't tell if they were mortally wounded. I didn't check them out.

ANSWER: Calley returned and asked: 'How come they're not dead?' I said I didn't know we were supposed to kill them. He said: 'I want them dead.' He backed off about 20 or 30 feet and started shooting, automatic, into the people, the Viet Cong. He was beside me. He told me to help him shoot. I helped him shoot.

QUESTION: [Were you crying as you fired?]

ANSWER: I imagine I was. I can't recall.

QUESTION: [Your impression of Calley?]

ANSWER: I thought Lieutenant Calley was doing his duty and doing his job.

QUESTION: Did you get the impression that he was violent, raving mad?

ANSWER: No.

ANSWER: I took my orders from Lieutenant Calley but I thought everything was OK because Captain Medina was there ... I seen him ...

All the bodies were laying around . . . Why didn't he put a stop to all the killing?

ANSWER: [Captain Medina instructed the company] to destroy everything in My Lai, and that included women, children, and livestock . . . Captain Medina saw us shooting a group of civilians in a clearing, and he did not try to stop us.

TESTIMONY OF CHARLES W. HALE

ANSWER: Conti told me he had attempted to have sex with one of the village women and had threatened one of her children with a weapon. He said Calley had stopped him and made him go down the trail. Conti went on to say that after he left Calley had wasted [killed] the people anyway.